AFTER
COLLAPSE

The End of America and
the Rebirth of Her Ideals

MAX BORDERS

**SOCIAL
EVOLUTION**

SOCIAL
EVOLUTION

Social Evolution
hello@social-evolution.com

To
Sid,
Felix,
and Sophia
because they carry the fire.

Praise for
The Social Singularity

"One of the books I recommend the most, and secretly wish the whole world would read."
- Brian Robertson, creator of Holacracy

"Max has become a master of persuasion and an intellectual force of nature. This book is going to totally reframe the way people think about societal change."
- Jessica Arman, CEO Magic Mud

"If you're interested in 'what comes next' in the human collective experience, it's well worth the read."
- Matt Kreinheder, author of *Awakening the Mystics*

"Social Singularity is the greatest and most profound book of the decade."
- Stephen Drake

CONTENTS

FOREWORD

What is it, Papa?
Nothing. We're okay. Go to sleep.
We're going to be okay, aren't we Papa?
Yes. We are.
And nothing bad is going to happen to us.
That's right.
Because we're carrying the fire.
Yes. Because we're carrying the fire.
        Cormac McCarthy, from *The Road*

Sophia was in utero when it hit us.
    I'd begun to read stories of people falling to a respiratory virus in China. One theory said that someone with exotic tastes had eaten an infected pangolin bought in a wet market. Another, that scientists had pulled horseshoe bats from a cave with a hook, and runnels of infected blood had fallen upon exposed skin. In yet another, guano samples were collected and stored in 2013 and then taken out again in 2019. Bizarrely, one of the scientists from the Wuhan Institute of Virology had disappeared.

    Were they just careless? Was it a bioweapon? Chinese officials gave an official story, but the Communist Party had lost credibility. Either way, someone had blood on their hands. Either way, all of these different variations read like synopses of Dean Koontz novels.

    Soon, we learned of hospitals overwhelmed in Italy. Closer to home, cruise liners sat in port as our leaders fiddled. People started to have opinions about everything:

"What about the flu?" some said. "Flatten the curve," others parroted. These eventually became partisan bumper stickers as a cascade of uncertainty, fear, and competing models kept the rest of us confused and obedient. The United States hadn't seen anything like this since 1918. There had been viruses, but always somebody else's viruses. This felt more like we were standing at the base of a snowy mountain. Hearing the rumble. Looking up. And knowing there was nowhere to run.

What about Sophia?

I gorged on information sent from faraway places, words and images mediated by screens, transmitted as bits and signals. None of it made much sense. Except for the goddamn house and our dystopian grocery store, screens and signals had become my entire world. I was like that poor guy in *A Clockwork Orange*, only there was no need to pry open my eyes.

Most people I knew seemed to be in denial until the mayor, the governor, and the president put everyone on lockdown. Only "essential" businesses would be allowed to function, which were coincidentally also the biggest companies. I braced myself and watched things die even before any cases in my area could be confirmed. The SXSW festival canceled. Future Frontiers, an annual conference I co-founded, had no future.

People close to me began to lose their jobs. One friend, a restaurant manager, was asked to lay off her entire staff only a week before she was shown the door herself. My dearest friends, a husband and wife team who had pioneered charcoal oral care products, saw retail's biggest names cancel purchase orders.

My partner Jenny, a yoga instructor, found that her classes dwindled until all of the *chaturangas* were, finally, relegated to Zoom rooms. Then those dwindled, too, as her yogis ran out of money. Though she continued to teach and practice, the pandemic had taken her livelihood. In some ways, it suspended her identity. Now and then, I would find her sneaking off to cry as we "sheltered in place." This bright, independent feminist from Hyde Park, Chicago was going to have to protect Sophia, depend on me, and somehow still keep her dignity.

Here it is. Another liminal event.

What about Sophia? And what about Sid and Felix, my two boys, already thirteen and four?

Like everybody else, I wanted answers. But under this strange form of house arrest, I couldn't bear to read another article about how "the world would never be the same." Breathless prognosticators were already imagining a world of VR workplaces, the state tracking your vitals, and autarky — the fancy word for a closed economy. *Could we afford to trade with people in other countries? They eat bats, and also make too many of our medicines. Something bad might happen. Globalization is dangerous. We need a Universal Basic Income.*

The more banal predictions were grist for the mill, while others were plausible enough to be dangerous. Many of the commentariat who, only months before, had been admonishing us to practice daily mindfulness and take screen time sabbaticals, were now drafting blueprints for a world that looked like a cross between *Snow Crash* and *Walden*, only controlled by a powerful surveillance state. I didn't want my family living in a simulation, or a cabin in the woods. I didn't want their vitals monitored by the NSA.

Fear-based thinking starts in the reptile brain and ends up with the proposition: *Ban all risk by whatever means.* Lurking behind this is the idea that if I'm not in control, somebody else damn well better be. It's a submission reflex. We become so governed by our anxiety that we'd let anyone govern us in any manner they choose, so long as they promised to make us feel safe again. We had forgotten just how unsafe this proposition had made us throughout history.

The biggest stimulus package in history went through in an instant. *Now back to our regularly scheduled death count.*

To be fair, when everyone is sitting at home waiting for a crisis to end, they either pass the hours like kidney stones or thrust the fear-industrial complex into overdrive. The trouble is, fear tends to drown wisdom. And counting on that submission reflex are people in the world who want nothing but for us to submit. If we let the politically powerful construct our world for us under such conditions, there may be no turning back. Instead, we have to find courage. We have to turn to each other. We have to do things ourselves. And we have to create systems for doing things *together*, as starlings in murmuration.

My thoughts turned again to Sophia, waiting to be born. *Into what world?* I fell into a fitful sleep and dreamed of the plague doctor, his black bird-mask descending as she slept next to me, inside of her mother. Jenny is a Jew, which means Sophia is, too. Maybe they would be spared from this, just as their ancestors had been from the frogs and flies and boils. *Pass them over. Just take me.*

But not just yet.

The next morning I realized my dreams were evidence that this parallel virus — a pandemic of fear — was infecting me, too. Sure, any one of us could catch this novel coronavirus and die. But amid the chaos and confusion, other themes were starting to reveal themselves.

INTRODUCTION

He who promises runs in debt.

The Talmud

24,221,670,739,204.

That was U.S. debt in dollars somewhere near the middle of my writing this, well before these words will reach your eyes. To most people, this is just a great big number, almost meaningless. The difference between a billion and a trillion and a jillion is like numerology. Someone will ascribe some significance to it, but it's too abstract to have any real meaning.

To put it in perspective, though, we can divide this very long number by 325 million, approximately the U.S. population. Now the result seems a little more concrete: $75,000. That is the bill the federal government will hand Sophia when she is born — unless her children end up with it. It's an amount she might have used to pay too much for college.

Of course, this is not just Sophia's bill. It will be the bill for every man, woman, and child in America. I don't know about you, but I don't have that kind of money. Every year after 2020, you can add a trillion dollars (or more — up to $24.2 trillion) like a ticking clock. And remember that this figure came quietly from the Government Accountability Office, with a note attached:

"Long-term fiscal projections by GAO, CBO, and in

the 2019 Financial Report show that absent policy changes, the federal government continues to face an unsustainable long-term fiscal path."

Although each of these long-term projections uses somewhat different assumptions, their conclusions are the same: Over the long term, the imbalance between spending and revenue built into current policy will lead to (1) deficits exceeding $1 trillion each year beginning in fiscal-year 2020 and (2) both the annual deficit and cumulative total debt held by the public growing as shares of GDP.

Never before had the American public been in so much debt. And yet the grand narrative was that it was somehow inhumane to even think about the economy as people were *dying*. Maybe these moralists were right. I couldn't help but think that the economy was critical to life, especially to living. The whole thing seemed like one titanic trolley problem. Keep the trolley straight, and a million people might die. Pull the lever and destroy the lives and businesses of 60 million people for months, maybe years. Sitting on the horns of this enormous dilemma were not you and me, but authorities. It meant that all the paths they never took yielded outcomes we'd never know.

The Idea

Although it's part of the story, I should let you know that this book is not really about the collapse of the financial system — only Michael Lewis could pull that off. This is one of those books that strikes fear in the heart of an editor because it's not about just one thing. Instead, it's a way to understand the forces that can either animate or destroy us.

Robert Oppenheimer famously, ominously, said, "Now I am become Death, the destroyer of worlds," quoting the *Bhagavad Gita*. He was talking about us. And we had better listen.

Our unifying theme, as Americans, is collapse. We will

explore the ways in which Americans have become less resilient, and their associated systems more fragile. We will refer to these phenomena as breakdowns. As we'll see, some of these breakdowns are a consequence of a denial that has spanned decades, a blind habit of shoring up a system of convenience and comfort that may no longer be sustainable. I will argue that we have made far too many bargains with the devil along far too many dimensions of life. This has created a single point of failure in the nexus which connects the federal government, the central bank, and us. That failure will cascade throughout the rest of society, for the rest of our lives.

And we are not prepared.

The Debt

When a government fails to pay back its debts, it's called a sovereign default. That government may start to pay smaller amounts, or cease payment altogether. In this condition, the jig is up. Officials have no way to fund programs, employees, welfare entitlements, or war-making capabilities. The government must prioritize things, for perhaps the first time. Make no mistake: that prioritization would be national triage.

To avoid a default, most governments and central bankers will inflate their currencies. But that, of course, also means devaluing their currencies. Whether that devaluation occurs through quantitative easing, money printing, or banning conversion into precious metals or competing currencies, prices go up for everyone. Purchasing power goes down. If lenders get wise, they'll raise their interest rates to compensate for the risk. And when interest rates rise dramatically due to this fear, it's called a sovereign debt crisis.

The Devil's Fork has two tines: default or inflation. Each tine means hardship, short and devastating or protracted and seemingly endless. The precise magnitude of the hardship is difficult to predict, but the American people will not have seen such a severe contraction since 1933. It could resemble the zombie apocalypse, hordes roaming the streets, some being shot from rooftops. We could endure a multi-decadal malaise, similar to life under President Jimmy Carter. High inflation. Stagnation. Urban decay. A hard life for 30 to 60 million people. Maybe you call that collapse. Maybe you call it slow-motion suicide. Whatever you call it, it requires changes to our systems.

Some experts claim that debt spending will never be a real problem due to the United States' military and economic power or, more fancifully, to theories like modern monetary theory (MMT). I take the former more seriously, but either view is terrible to get wrong.

Global strategist Peter Zeihan, who specializes in global finance, argues that crises tend to pull the world to the dollar; that it's already the world's reserve currency, but it is still more attractive than any of its competitors. "Capital flight to the United States – already at record levels pre-coronavirus – has only accelerated,"[1] Zeihan explained. "As one might expect, when the Americans finalized their plans for $2.2 trillion in deficit spending, the U.S. dollar dipped for the first time in the crisis. Never before has the 'exorbitant privilege' of being the world's reserve currency felt more exorbitant or more like a privilege."[2]

Zeihan goes on to argue that the centralization of global wealth into U.S. dollar assets, pulling us in like some black hole, would cause a cascade of other effects throughout the global financial system that would impact "everything." And yet he's mum about what he thinks would be the nature of that impact. Zeihan is also referring to a record stimulus package passed during the sudden arrest of virtually all economic life in the United States. The rescue package itself had used "more ammo than was put to use in the last three recessions combined," and Zeihan noted at the time that we were only two weeks into the new crisis. He was not only correct that the *relative* position of the U.S. dollar was still good, but that the rest of the world's nations were also drowning in debt.

We are now entering a new era. Many of the events unfolding as I write are unprecedented. Can such global profligacy go on forever? Empires fall, some quickly, others quietly. Even though the bailouts of 2007-2009 did not come with the kind of inflation many feared they would, other seeds were sown. Officials set the precedent of socializing the losses of financial institutions. Our debt load would weigh down recovery. And failures to fundamentally reform the system would cause greater distortion, moral hazard, and poor investment in the future. The debt monster would be left to gorge itself on the future — thus leading to the world's greatest financial bubble.

The only lesson authorities took away from the whole sordid affair was that it seems possible to paper over problems and go back to business as usual. There's nothing anyone can do about it. An imperial government, a financial elite, and a dependent electorate have been locked in an unholy triune since 1913.

That year had already seen the creation of a national tax on personal income. On December 23, though, President Woodrow Wilson had planted the seeds of today's collapse when his signature encoded the Federal Reserve Act, conjuring into being what would become the most powerful central bank on earth. Imagine for a moment if the government had contracted with a private company to manage the money supply, protect the currency's value, and promote employment. If that company went on to produce a Great Depression, a series of recessions, volatile swings in employment, and a dollar that would end up with less than a dime's worth its former purchasing power, Congress would have fired that company long ago. Yet this creature, slinking at the bottom of an ocean of red ink, cannot be fired.

Peter Zeihan might be right. It might be difficult to unseat the dollar as the world's reserve currency. But it's not impossible. Even Zeihan admits that the "centralization of global wealth into U.S. dollar assets will trigger cascade effects," though he might not see this statement as an admission. He might not see that those cascade effects, far from shoring up American power in the twenty-first century, will bring it down. Eventually, *centralization is the problem*.

Up to this point, it has been worth it for governments to accept the dollar's hegemony. What if it became clear that this state of affairs could no longer stand? All it would take is a bloc of countries to say "enough is enough,' collude, declare a sovereign debt jubilee, and walk away from the dollar, returning to a gold standard. Horror of horrors, these colluding nations would no longer be able to spend beyond their means. But the dollar would be moribund.

We have only seen the first decade or so of cryptocurrencies evolving to become increasingly secure, utile, and adaptive. Pick whatever property you like, and it can probably be programmed. Some currencies share the properties of gold; others can have gold backing. Some seek stability. Still, as more and more users adopt them, they will stabilize. To the central banks, these innovations might look like dangerous viruses; their adoption a potential pandemic. Nevertheless, we can imagine a currency that uses a tokenized index fund. The fund might be composed of a basket of cryptocurrencies, or assets, or pretty much anything you please. Such a currency would be useful, stable, and retain its value. If those currencies became a secure destination for capital flight, more people would migrate to them. Like other centralized systems, the dollar regime could turn out to be fragile.

Maybe the debt hawks are wrong. If they are, then authorities can avert a sovereign debt crisis and the greatest of all depressions. The money printer can go brrrr, and we can live in a matrix of the dollar's privilege throughout our lifetimes. But if the debt hawks are right, then the United States will collapse onto itself like a neutron star, pulling most of the world's satellite economies down with it.

THE COLLAPSE

Most Americans are already swimming in four trillion dollars in consumer debt, including credit cards, student loans, auto loans, and mortgages. And millions will stop paying when the crisis arrives. No interest payment. No minimum payment. Nothing. The banks will start to scramble, too.

One of the first things likely to happen is panic by the savvier elites. Investors will begin to withdraw funds from money market accounts, where many businesses keep resources to operate. Too many sudden withdrawals, and business will grind to a stop. This won't be a shelter in place order, but rather organizations, like living organisms, bleeding to death. Bank runs might be stemmed temporarily by modern measures, but desperate people will try to pull out cash that is already rapidly diminishing in value. As treasury notes turn into monopoly money, the issue of what had been "guaranteed" by the FDIC will become irrelevant — at least to the degree that the Fed prints money or buys government debt.

Eventually, the U.S. government will get to a point where it can no longer step in to control this process as they have in the past. Put simply: we will reach the point at which they can no longer throw money at the problem. The wizards will only be able to watch it happen, as if in slow motion. The goliath central banks will be tapped, their principals having long ago left the building, dumping their dollars weeks before. Welfare lines will turn into riotous mobs. Checks, if they come at all, will be like photos of deceased family members, symbols of a better time.

When the accounts dry up, the trucks will stop rolling. Communications networks will be spotty. Supermarkets will run out of food. People will get desperate. Crime will go up. Energy grids will experience blackouts as utility companies scramble to keep power flowing as fewer, weaker dollars trickle in. Armies of unemployed workers will roam the cities. A new class of beggars will carry small children to gain pity, but like dried beans or fresh fruit, pity will be harder to come by.

Where once there were credit cards, there will be guns. Preppers in the countryside will hunker down behind fences with signs that read: *Trespassers will be shot on sight.* And we will suddenly admire them for their foresight.

Out of options, people will scramble to be near their families, idling for hours along clogged interstates. Eventually, they will arrive to find their loved ones no better off, wondering where to turn and what to do. Most have forgotten how to plant. Most have forgotten how to husband animals. And those who haven't will be defending their flocks and hen houses from you and me, as we lurk in the woods, considering a rather unseemly career change.

THE COMPETITION

All this talk of collapse might seem sensational. If it bleeds it leads, they say: Tweak the reader's amygdala in just the right way, and you've got a sale. Whether one is fascinated by fear, or they just genuinely want to know what's coming, a reader is as likely to pick this book up out of anxiety as out of curiosity. *You're playing on people's emotions*, the chorus might say. And they're not entirely wrong. But there are two main reasons to use such a charged word as "collapse."

First, I'm in an attention arms race. Other sensational titles are out, and The End could be its own genre. The publishing world engages in meme wars, too, and one has to compete with doomsayers who've shown real potency selling catastrophic visions. In a fitness landscape like the book market, we have to find a way to cut through the noise. It's a perverse paradox: To lead readers to bitter truths, you have to risk making them suspicious of your motives. But this ain't chicken soup for the soul. Look at what we're up against.

"If you're younger than sixty, you have a good chance of witnessing the radical destabilization of life on earth," writes author Jonathan Franzen in *The New Yorker*. Such catastrophe includes "massive crop failures, apocalyptic fires, imploding economies, epic flooding, hundreds of millions of refugees fleeing regions made uninhabitable by extreme heat or permanent drought. If you're under thirty, you're all but guaranteed to witness it."[3]

Well, now. How can anyone compete with that?

My second reason for warning of collapse is more straightforward: I am warranted. What you're about to read is how I justify my concerns about what is likely to transpire in the next twenty years, give or take. As I mentioned, my justification will be imperfect, and mediated by imperfect people. But I will do my best to marshall a mix of theory and data to support the idea that a significant transition is coming. Whether people choose to act on this information, either before or after the event, is not up to me. I can only shout into the oncoming storm and hope that somebody hears me.

HALL OF MIRRORS

Our means of making sense of the world are failing us; we are drowning in a sea of dubious science, fake news, and questionable data. But floating around in that sea are grains of truth. The skeptical philosopher knows one thing: he cannot step outside of his perceptions to verify, once and for all, the existence of tables and chairs. It's worse for prognosticators and pundits. It's nigh impossible to go beyond our device screens to check the truth of some claim. The low-cost proposition is to appeal to sources that confirm our biases. Until we can figure out a way to put more skin in the game, for there to be a cost for being wrong or misleading, we're all in a sense-making labyrinth — a hall of mirrors.

I'm sure that Jonathan Franzen is dead serious about his version of the end. Whether he or anyone else is telling noble lies or is locked in an arms race of heartfelt warnings, it doesn't change the fact that catastrophe sells. Memetic warfare extends to images, books, movies, articles, and the nightly news. If tracking truth is a game, almost all of the information we consume is mediated by someone with skin in a different game.

The incentives to propagate false information or bad ideas can be strong, and not all incentives are financial. Some are ideological. Some are even personal. We can be motivated by a desire to signal status or goodness or membership in an in-group. We are human. That means that publishers with biases have to offer books with biases to people with biases written by authors with biases. There is no escape. Writers have to make tradeoffs. We have to put a lot of faith in someone else's research, statistics, and sense-making apparatuses.

But even as some compete for mindshare by selling hysteria, Eric Weinstein, founding member of the Intellectual Dark Web (IDW), thinks that there currently exists a perverse system that *suppresses* information likely to be true. Why? Because truth challenges core institutions. He calls the suppression system the distributed information suppression complex, or DISC.

> The most important ideas are likely to be the ideas that are the most disruptive. What if the entire food pyramid, for example, was wildly off? What if fats were not the great danger we thought they were, and those waving fields of wheat that are fabled in an American song, in fact, give rise to carbs, which

> are very dangerous to us all? So if everything were
> inverted, let's say, we're in a world where instead
> of banishing volatility during the so-called great
> moderation before 2008, we were actually building
> the tinder for the world's largest financial forest fire.
> What if in fact we had all sorts of things exactly
> backwards and completely wrong?[4]

Note that Weinstein is not pointing to a conscious, central conspiracy of suppression, but rather an emergent system organized to protect the "gated institutional narrative." The gated institution goes by many names. The Blue Church. The Cathedral. The Tower. The Matrix.

What you'll find in this book is the opposite. It's an effort to spray neon graffiti on the Washington Monument, shout at *The New York Times* with a 100,000 decibel megaphone, and scribble a warning onto the institution gate with a pocket knife. Those gatekeepers will ignore me. Their supplicants might well hurl invectives at me, as gibbons with feces. When it comes to the pursuit of truth, I don't mind pulling the crazy card. Those who don't like what I have written should refer to my old friend H.L. Mencken, who wrote: "The liberation of the human mind has been best furthered by gay fellows who heaved dead cats into sanctuaries and then went roistering down the highways of the world, proving to all men that doubt, after all, was safe – that the god in the sanctuary was a fraud."

If your god is social justice, expert opinion, or power politics, this book is your dead cat.

EXISTENTIAL RISKS

Before we turn to the most salient conditions of collapse, we should not fail to comment on the general category of existential risks. Some existential risks are based on models of technological advances, where the innovations have inherent risks. We need to take these risks very seriously, perhaps much more than others.

Existential risks can include big, planetary events such as a giant asteroid hitting the earth. But there's not much we can do about that, so we should focus on dangers presented by exponential technologies of our own making, but that have only been around for a blink in geological time. In other words, channeling futurist Stewart Brand, we are getting to be as gods, only we're not yet very good at it yet. What might happen given the rapid advance of artificial intelligence? Could some malevolent scientist create a lab-grown pandemic? What about a cyberterrorism attack that takes down critical infrastructure? When it comes to these sorts of risks, the logic goes something like this: The more we learn and share what we know, the easier it is for somebody, somewhere, to do a lot of damage.

Think of it like this: The atomic bomb was invented more than eighty years ago. It took the finest minds on earth with multi-million dollar laboratories and remote desert test sites to make it a reality. There was no internet, only libraries. Today, all it takes is an evil genius with WiFi to make an entire seaboard go dark. All it takes is an angry young man with a cotton swab in an insecure biotech lab to wipe out millions with a virus. Nano-manufacturing machines of the future could self-replicate, infest the world, and turn everything into grey goo. So if governments can't stop men with box cutters from flying into skyscrapers, or prevent a lone Kiwi with a semi-automatic rifle from shooting up a mosque, how is *anyone* going to stop the exponential terrorist when his moment arrives? How will we stop the dirty bomb? The nanobots? The infected mosquitos?

I don't have a clue. But neither, really, does anyone else. Once people appreciate the real possibility of these scenarios coming to pass, they fall into two camps: *pessimists* and *optimists*.

"If you're scaling towards the power of gods, then you have to have the wisdom and the love of gods, or you'll self-destruct,"[5] writes Daniel Schachtenberger. He argues that we need to rethink how we live and organize ourselves, or the human race is bound to terminate itself. But if you believe optimists like Steven Pinker, you might agree that "apocalyptic thinking has serious downsides. One is that false alarms to catastrophic risks can themselves be catastrophic."[6]

Is it possible there is wisdom in each perspective?

Maybe we have to settle on hanging out somewhere in between, a kind of Schrödinger's apocalypse. But if we stand with one foot in order and one foot in chaos, we need to keep our eyes wide open, focus on the knowledge we have, and stand humble before all that we don't yet know. We should be just as concerned about cocking up our human systems as we are about a network of garage-bound Prometheans. Yet it's not implausible to think that someone could open Pandora's Box.

"We have not evolved mechanisms, either biologically or culturally, for managing such risks,"[7] writes philosopher Nick Bostrom. We're used to the adapted responses to threats like volcanic eruptions, smallpox, and automobile accidents. "But tragic as such events are to the people immediately affected, in the big picture of things – from the perspective of humankind as a whole – even the worst of these catastrophes are mere ripples on the surface of the great sea of life."[8]

And it is with all humility we have to reckon with all the possibilities and perils of being human, to get better at being gods, all while realizing that there are no angels among us. Gene editing technologies are quickly proliferating, as the costs have gone down enough for an amateur to adapt humanity's source code in his garage. Machine learning techniques are accelerating at a pace that suggests a technological singularity lies on the not-too-distant horizon. As we start to understand that so much of life is code, we must acknowledge that the geeks have already inherited the earth. What percentage of these coders will act out of hubris instead of reflection, precaution, or wisdom? Whether all of this power is ultimately an existential threat or a profound opportunity, the pace of change could accelerate beyond our ability to cope with it.

Some unintended effects will flood out into the world. We must learn to surf or we will drown.

Happily, some brilliant people are starting to look more deeply into the questions of existential risk. Thinkers like Nick Bostrom, Jordan Hall, and Daniel Schmachtenberger have become explorers, asking how we can evolve our institutions and ourselves to guard against these risks. It's a work in progress. And though they have different perspectives, they are part of a small-but-growing movement committed to some sort of conscientious transition. One can't help but be influenced by them. So in the finest tradition of intellectual shamanism, their voices and those of others will figure in as guides, even as we stake out our own territory.

WHAT THIS BOOK IS NOT ABOUT

To talk about human systems collapse, we have to separate the kinds of collapse scenarios we're not as concerned with. That's risky, to be sure. People have their pet causes, so I write with gritted teeth. This book is not about climate change, resource depletion, or existential threats. It is about the collapse of human systems. I write at a time in which fears about those other matters are taking on eschatological proportions. There are plenty of other writers selling those narratives, and you should read them as critically as you read this.

Although we are not giving other types of collapse a full treatment, I offer a series of sketches to explain why I think these competing collapse scenarios are less likely. I'm under no illusions about blowback. To worry about the collapse of human systems could be perceived as a means to distract people from more pressing concerns. Some will think that I am irresponsible. Others will say I am evil. But we should remember that, just because one narrative grabs headlines, doesn't mean that other concerns are less important. In the current state of discourse, points like these get lost in *cause celebre* meme wars. Critical thinking suffers.

Is it possible to engage in good discourse even if we don't share priorities? I hope so. Though we'll discuss some of those competing collapse narratives, I hope I am not alone in thinking we'll be better able to deal with global problems if we adapt our human systems.

GAME MECHANICS

Which brings us to Game A and Game B, terms coined by Jim Rutt and Brett Weinstein in various ongoing discussions circa 2014, and have been picked up in earnest by Jordan Hall and Daniel Schmactenberger.

Games A and B are shorthand for what we might think of as how human beings organize themselves, what we have called human systems. The "game" trope is not accidental. Game theoretical constructs, including different rules, incentives, actions, and agents, certainly apply. In attempting to articulate these types of games, one risks getting it wrong in someone else's eyes, especially as articulating these systems is yet a work in progress. I'll do my best to sketch them here.

Game A is a human organization system that tends to rely on large mediating institutions, such as corporations or governments. These hierarchies are set up to achieve social control and coherence. In many respects, they were a form that evolved after human populations, and their interactions, began to scale beyond Dunbar's number. But this type of system cannot scale indefinitely. According to Schmachtenberger, Game A brings with it destructive win-lose dynamics that make it unsustainable. Such dynamics include resource extraction and taking advantage of others. Game A systems are also limited in their ability to manage complexity. In some sense, then, a transition is upon us, one that functions less on consumption rivalry, advantage taking, and environmental extraction. Game A, to the extent that it builds in zero-sum or negative-sum dynamics — accelerated by exponential technologies — will eventually self-terminate. Or so the story goes.

Game B, tentatively, is a hypothetical system of human organization that seeks to preserve civilization by introducing new rules, tools, and paths to wisdom. These approaches will give rise to more collaboration and less competition. In Game B, people will self-organize, perhaps in lighter-touch collaboration networks. We'll have to bring these systems online with upgrades to our own culture and cognition, too. All of this will allow humanity to flourish, thanks to omni-win dynamics. In Game B, you benefit when everyone else does. There is room for experimentation, but failures are localized, which allows us to learn quickly from error. In other words: Failures will be proximate and temporary, as opposed to deep and system-wide. Perverse multipolar traps fade away. More trust is built. The game is to cooperate, as it were, rather than to sacrifice people or planet to maintain some competitive advantage. Game B systems, to the extent that they tolerate hierarchies at all, will include the emergent, vascular systems that accommodate currents of flow and change. In addition to being win-win-win, Game B will live in the sweet spot between order and chaos.

In talking of games, one might nod to classic game theory models, such as the Prisoner's Dilemma. That's because the general idea here is that we'd all be relatively better off if people didn't defect from cooperative agreements and trust arrangements. Incentives push them to defect. Game A competition can force people into perverse arms races. They have no choice: compete or lose out.

Imagine two powerful countries engaged in a trade war, which then turns into a cold war. Each country is organized so that elites run the show. The elites see themselves as competing on a massive global chessboard against other elites for land, resources, and market share. Each country's officials sit atop a hierarchy designed for self-preservation and social control. When the elites think their hierarchy will falter due to the other's strategy, they turn away from the win-win dynamics of global trade and enter a trade war. This tack fuels a perverse competition that comes mostly at the expense of their peoples. Each nation projects military and economic power such that it maintains access to resources. Weaker neighboring states fall into line. Tit-for-tat tariffs bring harm to both domestic and foreign markets until goods and services stop crossing borders. As trade slows, tensions ratchet up.

Now, each country's officials waste more resources on missiles capable of destroying the world many times over. But each side reasons: *If the other has more missiles, they could gain the advantage. We can't let that happen.* That brings about a fragile, costly peace. If they cooperated fully in trust, each would benefit, and neither would have to engage in expensive trade wars or fill nuclear weapon silos. Sound familiar?

The only way to win is to play a different game.

That's the idea, anyway. Depending on how one defines Games A and B more specifically, there is much to agree with. And yet, under some definitions of Game A, there might be aspects we wouldn't want to throw out with the bathwater. For example, suppose Game A is framed entirely as a system of competitive dynamics. In that case, competition *always* forces people to shift costs, mistreat people, and despoil the earth. Under this dreary view, we might overlook a lot of social upside to entrepreneurial markets.

But we also know that competition among firms frequently gives rise to higher quality, lower prices, and greater variety, not to mention better treatment of those

firms' employees. Lose talent, lose market share. Competition for conscientious customers means that firms have
to operate in broader stakeholder networks, as those
stakeholders now have the time, money, and motivation
to demand that executives behave ethically. Competition
among jurisdictions means chances for people to exit a
given jurisdiction if it has become insufferable due to
corruption, poverty, or crime. In short, competition and
collaboration are the twin forces of human endeavor.

What about "capitalist" competition? Doesn't it create
exploitive races to the bottom? Competition among
ocean fisheries, for example, risked tragedies of the ocean
commons — until aquaculture and catch shares took on
a growing share of the fish market. Ocean-caught fish,
therefore, peaked in the 1990s. Markets found a way, and
competition was part and parcel to the market process. So
if a move to Game B ends up defined as a move away from
private property, honest enterprise, and open markets, that
might *not* give us the desired outcome. Those disposed to
the tradeoff mindset always ask: *As compared to what?* If the
answer is *I don't know yet,* then all the proto-games could turn
out to be abortive experiments. But if something like Game
B is realized, it might well embrace some aspects of Game
A, even as it transcends it.

Now, if you asked twenty different people familiar with
the trope to define Games A and B, you'd get twenty different definitions. In this way, the whole exercise can degener-
ate into people reading an ideological inkblot. But perhaps
we can all agree about this: Game A collapse is likely to
follow what Schmachtenberger refers to as "differential
advantage seeking... by damaging others." As cognitive
psychologist Steven Pinker puts it: "We'd be wiser to nego-
tiate a social contract that puts us in a positive-sum game:
neither gets to harm the other, and both are encouraged to
help the other."[9]

The kinds of alternative human systems you are likely

to see set out in this book, far from being handed down as the Ten Commandments, might retain some of the better aspects of Game A. Still, we leave room for experimental discovery processes that could take us to a more idealized form. My hope in sketching Games A and B here is to continue a conversation. Because one thing seems clear: Game A brings with it the seeds of collapse.

What This Book is About

Those seeds of collapse have been planted. The whole "thing" — i.e. America as we know it — could come down at any time. Our fragile human system, after all, is controlled in great measure by elites. In this case, "fragile" refers to a system that is the opposite of what Nicolas Nassim Taleb talks about in his famous 2012 book *Antifragile:* "Some things benefit from shocks. They thrive and grow when exposed to volatility, randomness, disorder, and stressors and love adventure, risk, and uncertainty."

America, like many other nation-state systems, has always been a mix of fragile and antifragile elements. The trouble is, the mixture has been changing. America is fast becoming maladaptive and top-heavy, too many big decisions being made on behalf of too many by too few. Along critical dimensions, we could be more resilient, even antifragile. But America is breaking down.

I have insisted up to this point that this book is about the collapse of human systems. But what *is* a human system?

A human system can be brought into existence by accident, by agreement, or by force. It is a socially constructed reality with invisible rules. But amid all these rules are humans, *real flesh and blood people* who think and feel and act. For better or worse, these systems are channels for how things *flow*. Because our human systems are almost always invisible, we take them for granted, although they are fundamental to who we are. Our human story has undoubtedly been about how we have played our parts within different rules of different games. But it has also been about great transitions *between games*. Nomadic clan. Feudal hierarchy. Wealthy city-state. Colonial settlement. Modern empire.

Through it all, there has been money.

One day, a hairless ape admired someone else's seashell. Someone else still admired his smooth stone. They grunted, they pointed, and eventually, they exchanged. They soon figured out that to give up one trinket for another was better than having your skull bashed in. Over time, their respective tribes used these trinkets as mediums of exchange. *If everybody's happier, maybe it's better to trade than to raid*, they thought. This simple human system could help them satisfy their wants and needs while avoiding bloodshed.

We still use that system today. Maybe in your pocket there is a rectangular piece of paper. It's elaborately designed but otherwise useless, except that you can turn it into a meal. How odd, that. It must be something to do with the runes, symbols, and esoterica on the note. If you take a dollar in your hand, its markings signify a portal which leads to a group of wizards with enormous power. They live in marble palaces with byzantine halls.

You're now in possession of their talisman, which affords you a tiny fraction of their power. Give this talisman to a stranger, and they produce hot food for you. These talismans circulate, like blood, through other human systems, such as firms, cities, and global networks. Eventually, within vast ecosystems of production and trade. It's magnificent.

But what if the wizards' power failed one day?

Currently, all of our human systems are connected, one way or another, to the U.S. government. This point cannot be understated. And though no liminal event has a single cause, that great pyramidal structure depicted on the dollar is not as stable as it looks. Any collapse waiting in our future is a consequence of a million decisions extending into the past. Those decisions' loci lie in two power centers: New York City and Washington, D.C.

With the way sufficiently paved, it's time to go on our journey together. From this point on, two themes divide the book into two corresponding parts:

In Part One, I'll explain how seemingly disparate phenomena have all helped create the conditions for collapse.

In Part Two, I'll turn to ideas about how we can ward off collapse or rebuild, after collapse, to create a society of happiness, harmony, and resilience.

Before we turn to the conditions of collapse, remember that I offer hope in these pages, too, though the lede is somewhat buried. Much of the book is about a new way of seeing the world that might just help us save it. I want to persuade you not only that we can avoid collapse, but that we can recover and become stronger even if we do. It won't be easy, but we'll get through it. And when we do, life will be better — for everyone.

PART
I

BEFORE
COLLAPSE

1

THE BREAKDOWN OF OUR METAPHORS AND MODELS

The despot is not a man. It is the Plan. The
correct, realistic, exact plan, the one that
will provide your solution once the problem
has been posited clearly, in its entirety, in its
indispensable harmony.

Le Corbusier

In the Amazon, far below the rainforest canopy, a network of roots stabilizes a thick tree trunk. Mirroring the branches and twigs among the leaves above, the roots below split into smaller roots, which split into yet smaller roots, extending outward to absorb water. All of that water gets stored in the tree's cells.

A few miles away, a mighty river rushes. That river carries watercraft and fish, a few large and many small, inexorably toward a delta. What feeds the great river are smaller rivers, Apurimac and Mantaro, then tributaries, which are fed by streams, which are fed by brooks, which are fed by sources high in the Peruvian Andes.

Navigating the river early in the morning, an old woman goes fishing. Her body contains a system of veins and arteries that carry blood, enriched or depleted, to nourish every cell in her body. Likewise, her brain and limbs are animated by information signals within a network of nerves. These signals have to be processed by an organ of fractal complexity, or the old woman would be unable to navigate, much less fish.

Everywhere in the world, we see these sorts of living systems. They display the property researchers Adrian Bejan and Sylvie Lorente refer to as "few large, many small."[10] This stunning vascularization of *everything* means that even inorganic systems can have a kind of life, where life is defined as accommodating currents of flow and change. Living systems are thus *flow systems*. And if a system is no longer able to deal with currents of flow and change, it dies.

We can say the same of human systems. To the extent that a human system can accommodate flow is the extent to which it will persist in time — that is, to live. In some fundamental sense, this idea, strange and wonderful, is the guiding idea of this work.

This framing, of living systems as flow systems, has everything to do with collapse and renewal. But let me not get ahead of myself.

MODELS AND METAPHORS

The language we use creates our models of reality. In *Metaphors We Live By* (1980), cognitive linguists George Lakoff and Mark Johnson argue that figurative language is more than literary decoration: It is a fundamental aspect of human thought and language. Metaphors help us navigate the world with a degree of efficiency that literal language can't offer. They can even change our perceptions of reality.

Words on this very page can evoke physical sensations in our minds. One brain study showed that participants reading the sentence "he had a rough day" activated the part of the brain associated with texture.[11] Likewise, when I write about human systems as *flow* systems, I'm hoping to evoke the concept of a liquid, even though I might be talking about an economy.

So far, so good. But therein lies a paradox: Less accurate or even less truthful statements can be more *persuasive* than true statements. So if we are truthful, we might be sacrificing persuasive power. Likewise, persuasively powerful messages can lack truth content.

How far can we take these insights?

Armed with a view of figurative language as frames, George Lakoff has become one of the most celebrated messaging consultants in politics. He's written books that urge partisans not only to use metaphor more consciously but to "reframe" ordinary concepts like freedom in ways that make illiberal ideas more palatable. Even if that's a good strategy for one's political party, it might not be that good for the goal of tracking truth.

Cognitive scientist Steven Pinker thinks that Lakoff is off the deep end with his framing. In response to Lakoff's *Whose Freedom? The Battle over America's Most Important Idea* (2007), Pinker accuses Lakoff of "cognitive relativism," a view that reduces "mathematics, science, and philosophy [to] beauty contests between rival frames rather than attempts to characterize the nature of reality."[12]

Who's right? Is reality to be rewritten, or should metaphors track the truth? One of the biggest problems we face as a civilization is that too many people, especially experts, speak and see falsely through metaphor, meaning that some of our metaphors are misleading us. The very language we use to understand ourselves and our society is breaking down.

MISSION CONTROL

The Apollo missions are by now a part of our collective unconscious. Very smart people from the U.S. government's most celebrated agency sat in a big room in Houston.

The room had giant display screens and machines. The machines had toggles, switches, and rheostats. The astronauts had instrument panels in space. All of those complicated machines were spread out before the team to help them do one job: *get a spacecraft of astronauts to the moon and back.* Complicated calculations for a simple objective. They called it "mission control." Men controlling machines made it all happen.

Machines have parts — gears, pumps, valves, wires, dials, and buttons — that make up a whole. These parts fit together in a certain way, a way that can be known. Indeed, if these are things that can be known, they can also be designed and manipulated. The whole machine can be broken down into parts, which are themselves static. The relationships among the parts are cause-and-effect. So, if you're smart enough, you know how one thing effects another. When everything is working correctly, machines run well. If something breaks down, it has to be fixed. Ultimately, machines work better due to good engineering: the product of a mind or group of minds tasked with designing or operating a complicated system.

The trouble with this kind of thinking is that people think it extends to society, too.

Society is Not a Machine

The idea that you can order society is a kind of fallacy.[13] *If we can design and build a nuclear submarine, we can design and build a society.* We can compare society's administrative ordering to the piecing together of a machine with its transistors, cogs, and pumps. Proponents, struck by the progress made by useful machine inventors, came to think of nature and society as machines, too.

And it's no wonder: In the first half of the twentieth century, technocrats witnessed the introduction of the automobile, electricity, and, eventually, nuclear power.

If geniuses could be hustled together to build a weapon capable of razing whole cities in an instant, surely social engineers could be gathered to make great civilizations. But that would take more than largesse.

When we moved into the second half of the twentieth century, we saw the development of even more sophisticated machines. Computing devices could solve seemingly intractable math problems. Experts could use computers to predict the weather, design buildings, or simulate the development of cities. With each advance, it seemed like humans could design anything at all.

HIGH MINDS AND HIGH MODERNISM

"I believe that many of the most tragic episodes of state development in the late nineteenth and twentieth centuries originate in a particularly pernicious combination of three elements," writes political scientist James C. Scott. "The first is the aspiration to the administrative ordering of nature and society.... 'High modernism' seems an appropriate term for this aspiration."[14]

Folks across ideologies began to share this aspiration to order nature and society. Its exponents were planners, technocrats, administrators, architects, scientists, and outright utopians. Call these faithful High Minds. They are fond of scientism, which is the notion that science can and should be applied to domains once belonging to philosophy. Frequently, one appeals to science *methods*, which get used to justify those attempts by a single mind (or small group of minds) to order society along some dimension. The trouble with scientism is that science is ill-equipped to answer the question of whether societies *ought* to be administratively ordered, much less whether they *can* be. Behind appeals to science and its methods is almost always the urge to control.

There are Low Minds, too, who play handmaidens to High Minds. Low Minds gather in the square with raised fists, ready to tear down whatever they don't understand and had no hand in creating. High Minds call them "citizens" or "constituents," but only if they find them useful. If they don't, they call them backwards. Dangerous.

Some High Minds are envious. Some are sanctimonious. Some are downright pious. But all share the idea that society ought to be arranged. Sometimes they'll move heaven and earth to get what they want, even if it means exploiting a crisis. But it almost always takes more than useful idiots and money to fashion society in one's image.

"The second element," writes Scott of this episode, "is the unrestrained use of the power of the modern state as an instrument for achieving these designs."[15] It's not merely that you needed the smartest people at the rheostat banks of mission control. America's toggles and switches would have to *do something*. And doing something means brushing aside decentralized ways of doing things and going against the objections of the laity.

"The third element," writes Scott, "is a weakened or prostrate civil society that lacks the capacity to resist these plans."[16] The weakening of civil society is central to our collapse thesis, so I will leave a bookmark and devote an entire later chapter to the subject. As we'll see, it's not technology per se that has made us more atomized and alienated. It is, rather, our exorbitant monuments to High Modernism.

In sum, High Modernism provides the desire, the modern state the means to act, and the weakened civil society "the leveled terrain on which to build (dis)utopias." The managerial state has assumed responsibility for everything from the middle class's incomes to the success of large corporations. It found perhaps its fullest expression in Otto von Bismarck's Germany and Mussolini's Italy — yet the High Mind would never admit to anything resembling fascism.

"The foundation of Fascism is the conception of the

State, its character, its duty, and its aim," wrote Benito Mussolini in 1932. Similarly, High Minds prefer declared goals, such as economic development or national greatness, over liberal values such as freedom and charity. They carry out their plans in the name of the public benefit. That benefit might trickle down to the public, but more often it goes to agribusinesses, airlines, and investment banks deemed *too big to fail*. The administrative state ends up choking off the dynamism we find in an unplanned order. Lethargic, wasteful, and well-connected firms exist at the expense of dynamic upstarts.

The columnist Walter Lippmann, writing at the height of the New Deal, reflected on the High Mind as the latter began to intervene in the economy:

> The thinker, as he sits in his study drawing his plans for the direction of society, will do no thinking if his breakfast has not been produced for him by a social process which is beyond his detailed comprehension. He knows that his breakfast depends upon workers on the coffee plantations of Brazil, the citrus groves of Florida, the sugar fields of Cuba, the wheat farms of the Dakotas, the dairies of New York; that it has been assembled by ships, railroads, and trucks, has been cooked with coal from Pennsylvania in utensils made of aluminum, china, steel, and glass. But the intricacy of one breakfast, if every process that brought it to the table had deliberately to be planned, would be beyond the understanding of any mind. Only because he can count upon an infinitely complex system of working routines can a man eat his breakfast and then think about a new social order.[17]

Despite the coordination miracles described in this classic paragraph, these phenomena are invisible to most people. The damage wrought by "the thinker" is even less visible, because the damage usually only shows up as a lack, a generalized socio-economic malaise, or a lagging indicator.

If accounting were just tallying up visible wins, High Modernism is certainly on the scoreboard. The Hoover Dam. The War Effort. The Apollo Missions. Those victories shaped people's ideas for a generation; their enormity put a salve over so many other failures and losses.

THE GREAT RECESSION

The Great Recession was not as severe as the Great Depression, but it was difficult for many. At its worst, the national unemployment rate reached ten percent. A host of factors lead up to this spectacular crash and economic decline. As the United States tried to untangle a mess that had been made over decades, some of those factors became part of our common lexicon: sub-prime mortgages, government-sponsored enterprises (GSEs), FHA loans, mortgage-backed securities, the Community Reinvestment Act, and credit default swaps. I could go on.

The flashback should be familiar by now: Well-intentioned politicians and planners in both parties created policies designed so poorer people could get home mortgages. The trouble is, poorer people are more likely to default; therefore, there is higher risk. Under normal circumstances, few markets would produce loans to such a risky population. But politicians insisted, promising to back or subsidize certain kinds of mortgages. Financial institutions responded with exotic debt instruments.

Then came the game of high-risk hot potato, promising short-term gains and long-term misery. The government's guarantees, both implicit and explicit, created moral hazard among the lenders. Low-interest mortgages were tempting at introductory rates near zero, but could balloon. And balloon they did. More and more people started to default on their mortgages, and it became more and more difficult to pass off the debt-ridden potatoes. Eventually, major financial institutions started to cave, which threatened massive knock-on effects around the economy. Few of the government officials and financial wizards who had set the crisis in motion had stuck around.

But the new officials and central bankers decided that the only way to save the economy was to put together a series of bailout packages for the big banks, as well as monetary and fiscal stimulus for everyone else. The basic narrative was that capitalism was broken. Debates turned into arguments over who broke it, the government or the capitalists, and how it should be fixed.

MACHINE METAPHOR: GREAT RECESSION

Not only do the metaphors we live by shape events, the events have shaped the metaphors we live by. If the 2008 financial crisis hadn't been an object lesson in America's system fragility, it at least revealed a slew of false metaphors. Those who were in the grip of the machine frame are too numerous to count:

- Paul Krugman, interviewed for a *Newsweek* story, once said that what drew him to economics was "the beauty of pushing a button to solve problems."[18]

- *Bloomberg Business* runs this headline for an "expert panel" of leading economists: "How to Fix the Economy."[19]

- Before Barack Obama was elected president, a CNN headline read: "Obama's priority: Fixing the economy."[20]

- Paul Krugman (again) advising President Obama from the pages of *The Guardian*: "This riches-to-rags story is an example for Obama — and the world — of how not to run an economy."[21]

- *Bloomberg* writer Carolina Baums asks rhetorically whether the "U.S. Economy [is] Overheating."[22]

Running. Fixing. Overheating. And don't forget "building": A search of "building an economy that works for everyone" returns too many examples to list. Daily doses of this sort of language add up over time, affecting our collective understanding of how economies actually work. Canned abstractions cause the High Mind to think his intuitions, models, and post hoc rationalizations are all the knowledge he needs.

"Like Midas," writes the British philosopher Michael Oakeshott, "the rationalist [High Mind] is always in the unfortunate position of not being able to touch anything without transforming it into an abstraction; he can never get a square meal of experience."[23]

More often than not, the square meal of unintended consequence lands on the plates of the people long after the High Mind has gone to pasture. It's no wonder most people find it easier to think of the economy more like a machine. After all, it's simpler to borrow from Newtonian mechanics than from Darwinian biology. People fix airplanes. No one has a clue how to fix a coral reef.

One reason is that the economy isn't a thing at all. It's just people trying to do productive things well and serve one another. A much more accurate metaphor for the economy would be an ecosystem. Again, we can no more fix an economy than we can design a rainforest. To say so isn't market fundamentalism; it's a high regard for a rich intellectual tradition whose implications include evolution, complexity, and self-organization. Unfortunately, appeals to self-organization challenge people's desire for certainty. Adam Smith notwithstanding, most people prefer the idea that visible hands are running the show, even if those hands are not their own.

During times of crisis, the Houston control room is the picture most people have in their minds regarding experts, particularly economists. More worryingly, this is how a lot of economists think of themselves. A room full of experts has been staffed with pushing the buttons or turning rheostats and moving resources where they need to go. The result? Prosperity for all! Of course, you have to get the *right* experts. Most people labor under the idea that such experts exist, and that they need to be in the control room. For decades, popular history books have told schoolchildren that President Franklin D. Roosevelt and a team of interventionists — channeling economist John Maynard Keynes — piped in largesse to get America out of the Great Depression. This was referred to as priming the pump.

Interestingly, economist Paul Krugman, defender of Depression-era economics, has tried to defend himself and fellow Keynesians against the charge that they have succumbed to the machine metaphor. Witness Krugman's response to Michael Rothschild's book *Bionomics*:

> Take, for starters, [Rothschild's] assertion that "orthodox economics describes the 'economy as a machine.'" You might presume from his use of quotation marks that this is something an actual economist said, or at least that it was the sort of thing that economists routinely say. But no economist I know thinks of the economy as being anything like a machine. [24]

As noted earlier, Krugman does, in fact, know an economist who treats the economy as a machine: Krugman.[25] Despite his protestations, we find Krugman using the machine metaphor over and over. It goes to shows just how effective this particular mind virus has been.

"Meanwhile," said Krugman, congratulating Nobel laureates Elinor Ostrom and Oliver Williamson, "Keynesian economists, using very simple mathematical models, basically said 'Push this button — we need more G [government spending on goods and services].'"[26]

Paul Krugman is a brilliant economist. So just how does

this sort of metaphor error start to infect so bright a mind?

If it Quacks Like a Duck

In the early eighteenth century, French inventor Jacques de Vaucanson dazzled audiences with a series of eerily lifelike automatons. His masterpiece came in 1739, when he unveiled a "Digesting Duck." The duck could flap its wings, splash in water, and nip grain from someone's hand. It would even poop pre-loaded pellets onto a platter. Inside, the duck, made of gold and copper, was powered by weights which used gravity to turn a collection of levers. First-of-its-kind flexible rubber tubing resembled entrails, giving the impression that the duck could actually swallow and digest food. The duck wowed the people of France, and Vaucanson won widespread praise. When I think of certain High Minds under the spell of the machine metaphor, I am reminded of the phrase, "If it walks like a duck…" But as clever as Vaucanson's contraption had been, it was not a duck. And neither society nor the economy is a machine.

To put all this into perspective, consider that economists built a machine designed to model the British economy in post-war Britain. It's called the Phillips machine.[27] Like the Digesting Duck, the Phillips machine was greeted with much fanfare in 1949 when it was unveiled at the London School of Economics. The machine used hydraulics to model the workings of an economy, but now looks like a mad scientist's work.

"The prototype was an odd assortment of tanks, pipes, sluices and valves," writes Larry Elliot in *The Guardian*, "with water pumped around the machine by a motor cannibalised from the windscreen wiper of a Lancaster bomber. Bits of filed-down Perspex and fishing line were used to channel the coloured dyes that mimicked the flow of income round the economy into consumer spending, taxes, investment, and exports."[28]

Keynes might have been delighted by the device had he lived to see it. By contrast, Friedrich Hayek would surely have shaken his head at such a Rube Goldberg contraption. And maybe he did: Hayek left the London School of Economics for the University of Chicago in 1950.

Few macroeconomists are willing to admit that their models — despite greater sophistication — are infected with the machine meme. Most seem to think we just need better models. Rogue economist Arnold Kling is one of the lone objectors, arguing that mainstream macroeconomics is "hydraulic" and that "there is something called 'aggregate demand' which you adjust by pumping in fiscal and monetary expansion."[29]

High Minds, such as Nobel economist Joseph Stiglitz, have fallen prey to scientism, too. They want to build and run the machine from Washington. Stiglitz argues that we should scrap market entrepreneurism entirely and "recognise that the 'wealth of nations' is the result of *scientific inquiry*...."[30] A more concise definition of High Modernism could hardly be given. But that view is made all the more pernicious by the false promise of economic modeling and its attendant metaphors.

As we move into an uncertain future, it's not at all clear that the High Minds have learned their lessons. An internet search of the phrase "fix the economy" returns too many results to count. "Building an economy" yields even more.

Deus ex Machina

Let's bring back economist Friedrich Hayek for an encore. Having witnessed the technocratic impulse of the twentieth century, Hayek concluded in his 1974 Nobel lecture that so much of economics is afflicted with what we referred to earlier as scientism:

> It seems to me that this failure of the economists to guide policy more successfully is closely connected

with their propensity to imitate as closely as possible the procedures of the brilliantly successful physical sciences — an attempt which in our field may lead to outright error. It is an approach which has come to be described as the "scientistic" attitude — an attitude which, as I defined it some thirty years ago, is decidedly unscientific in the true sense of the word, since it involves a mechanical and uncritical application of habits of thought to fields different from those in which they have been formed.[31]

This critique is as relevant as ever.

"When any theory is treated as sacrosanct," writes Michael Rothschild in *Bionomics*, "its proponents assume the role of high priests, and strange things happen in the name of science."

To recap our earlier discussion, the whole idea of building, fixing, running, pumping, regulating, or designing an economy rests on the idea that society can be ordered by intelligent design. That is, if the right guys are at the buttons.

But there are no buttons. There are no pumps. Neither central bankers nor government bureaucrats can fly in as *deus ex machina* to correct a complex economy without grave unintended effects. Why? Because the relevant forms of knowledge are not concentrated among a few elites but rather dispersed among billions of people and millions of organizations. As such, the economy cannot be engineered. It is dynamic. It is *organic*.

This insight allows us to find out just what's wrong with the language experts use to talk about the economy and our society. Maybe it's time for us to admit that there is no mission control for our living flow systems. Once we accept that, the machine metaphor sputters, then stalls.

Before we turn away from the problematic machine metaphor, we should warn that other language games are being played, and they, too, are misleading. For example, we have *society as a patient* and *technocrat as a doctor*. Have you ever heard the phrase "our ailing economy"? How should we prepare the patient for surgery?

Then there is *society as children, technocrat as parent*. The traditional right provides the paternalistic law and order of a dad. The traditional left provides the unconditional care of a mom. Mom and Dad always fight.

Some view social policy as *an act of creation*. The metaphor here is *government as God*. The latter is omniscient and omnipotent, extending to presidents as messianic figures. While no metaphor works as an exact mapping of reality, some are better at revealing relevant aspects of the truth than others.

Society as living ecosystem is the most truth-conducive metaphor. Sadly, too few use it.

CLIMATE COLLAPSE

The problem of making sense of a complex world doesn't just extend to systems such as economies. It extends to other domains, too. The language we use to explain the world can liberate or constrain our understanding, and this is no truer than in scientific discourse, where false models and metaphors can lead people to abandon good sense.

Climate change is just one example. Despite the incredible emotional and financial investment into what some have termed 'settled science,' uncertainty about climate change's nature and extent remains. We'll discuss this more later. But let me be clear: My position is *not* that climate change isn't happening, nor am I arguing that humans have no influence. I'm taking the controversial position that expertise in this area is limited, and that *collapse* is far more likely to follow the failure of our human systems.

You've probably heard some of the more sensational claims about climate collapse. They've been running for decades.

A Pentagon report leaked in 2003 states: "Disruption and conflict will be endemic features of life…. Once again, warfare would define human life."[32] The report's authors offer dramatic examples in the report, including the claim that "catastrophic" shortages of potable water and energy will lead to widespread war, and Britain will have winters similar to those in Siberia as European temperatures drop off radically, all by 2020.[33]

2020 has now come and gone. In 2017, Yemenis experienced water shortages because of war, but not war because of a lack of rainfall. Britain has undergone a series of milder winters in 2015-2020, and in the five years prior, slightly colder winters.

Of course, these leaked documents were widely reported by a credulous press. We finally got self-driving cars, but we never got catastrophic water shortages and permafrost Britain. How could the authors have gotten things so wrong? To give you a better idea about what I mean, let's zoom out a few orders of magnitude.

Imagine we're in a kind of intellectual low orbit, high enough to get a wide shot, but low enough to still see some detail. From this macro perspective, we want to evaluate a set of claims about climate change that must be connected to form a coherent theory. Put another way: Let's take some familiar premises from what we might term the Climate Collapse Thesis and view them in their totality.

To accept the Climate Collapse Thesis — that climate change ought to be seen as the number one potential driver of collapse — we have to accept all of the following hypotheses:

1. The earth's atmosphere and oceans are warming.

2. The earth is warming primarily due to the influence of emissions like carbon dioxide and methane, which are generated by people engaged in production, trade, transportation, and energy use.

3. Scientists can limn most of the important phenom-
    ena associated with a warming climate, and disen-
    tangle the human causes from the natural ones,
    extending backward well into the past.

4. The data gathered and then aggregated by the
    scientists are overwhelmingly error-free, and the
    scientists operate free of biases when packaging and
    presenting their data. (There is neither peer review
    problem nor replication crisis among this set of
    scientists.)

5. Even though individual scientists are working
    separately on different aspects of climatology and
    related fields, they can stitch these diverse aspects
    together into one complementary dataset, which
    supports a single, coherent hypothesis *up to this point.*

6. Scientists are then able to use computer models to
    simulate most of the phenomena associated with the
    earth's warming and make reasonable predictions,
    within the range of a degree or two, into the future
    about a hundred years.

7. A different group of scientists can repackage that
    packaged information and make certain kinds of
    predictions about the dangers that a couple of
    degrees of predicted warming will make over that
    hundred years, to glaciers, farmland, and sea levels.

8. Social scientists, including economists, can then
    repackage — without loss of accuracy or the intro-
    duction of error — the aforementioned global
    predictions and make yet further predictions about
    the costs and benefits which accompany those
    predictions. Of course, the relevant subset of these
    portends either ecosystem collapse, social collapse,
    or both. (And that subset is, of course, appropri-
    ate to the overall Climate Collapse Thesis in this
    context.)

9. Based on what the world *might* be like if that different group of scientists and the social scientists turn out to be correct, policy wonks can, in turn, accurately predict what the world will be like *if certain climate policies are implemented*. And these policies minimize those effects the social scientists predicted.

10. Policymakers can then take the prior groups' predictions and set policies that will mitigate the predicted warming (and subsequent collapse). Such will ensure what is best for the people and the planet, on net, balanced against other considerations.

11. The policies, once imposed, will be implemented in such a way that they work as intended. And all major emitting nations must in a condition of something close to global unanimity. That means there should be no defections, corruption, or false reporting by such trustworthy authorities as China's Communist Party, or Brazil's Bolsonaro Administration.

12. The abatement of greenhouse gas output has a real effect on the rate of climatic change, enough to pull the world out of danger, including climate collapse.

13. Those policies are worth the costs they will impose on the world's people, especially the world's poor.

I repeat: to accept the Climate Collapse Thesis, we have to accept *everything* above.

Yet the interdependencies are staggering. It's not only possible but probable that one of the linkages will break. A humbler interpretation of climate change science and policy, far from being a conspiracy of people in denial, turns out to be an imperative of reason.

Let's assume the Climate Collapse Thesis is a falsifiable theory. The propagation of uncertainty is something we can calculate. Assuming that on each of the thirteen hypotheses above, the relevant experts were 95 percent certain, compounding the uncertainty would not yield a result of 95 percent. Not even close. My envelope calculation comes out to 51.3 percent that the Climate Collapse Thesis is correct. A coin flip.

The problem is, my envelope method not only accepts the 95 percent certainty per hypothesis at face value, *but treats each hypothesis independently.* The trouble is, the thirteen premises are *interdependent.*

The problems don't stop there. We can zoom down into each of the above claims, as one might a fractal, and check another set of interdependencies. Whether at the level of science or the level of policy implementation, the likelihood of someone introducing error is virtually assured. The chain of claims to "settled science," along with social policy prescriptions, is rather like an enormous telephone game. While it is true that we could spend multiple additional books evaluating each of these interdependencies in depth, it's enough here simply to point out the problem: compounded uncertainty.

At the very least, remaining questions about the state of climate science and policy put us in stark contrast to those predicting catastrophe. Consider the words of sustainability scholar Jem Bendell, who writes that "the field of climate adaptation is oriented around ways to maintain our current societies as they face manageable climatic perturbations.... The concept of 'deep adaptation' resonates with that agenda where we accept that we will need to change, but breaks with it by taking as its starting point the inevitability of societal collapse."[34]

Let's assume that you remain unpersuaded that my critique should knock the Climate Collapse Thesis out of the top issues of global concern. Consider, then, that this book might still be valuable. At the very least, we seek to address a different set of issues. In response, some might offer a variation on Pascal's Wager or the Precautionary Principle; namely, we cannot take the risk because there is uncertainty amid the complexity. We must act to mitigate those risks no matter what, lest we go to Hell.

Isn't it possible, though, that the sort of draconian "action" being proposed could, from a human systems perspective, send us to a different kind of Hell? The point here is that most of climate change alarmism hinges on models of reality that are not, in fact, reality. Questions surrounding climate change are hardly in isolation. Some measure of humility is in order.

RESOURCE COLLAPSE

One of the more persistent — and pernicious — collapse models originates in the ideas of Thomas Malthus, whose narrative returns to modern discourse carried by those we might broadly call neo-Malthusians. Malthus warned that human beings could reproduce exponentially, but people could only produce food and other goods arithmetically. In short: resources are finite and, eventually, populations will have to experience a die-off. This carrying capacity thesis is still widely accepted in ecology, and neo-Malthusians apply this logic to humans on the earth.

Arguably the most famous of this group is Paul Ehrlich. Between the 1960s and the 1990s, Ehrlich predicted that much of the world would experience famine because there were too many people competing for too few resources. To kick off his 1968 book, *The Population Bomb*, Ehrlich wrote: "The battle to feed all of humanity is over."[35] Why? Because according to Ehrlich, by the time of that publication, humanity had already lost. In fact, Ehrlich predicted that by the 1970s "hundreds of millions of people are going to starve to death."[36] There was nothing to be done, and nothing could "prevent a substantial increase in the world death rate."[37] The Stanford Professor of Population Studies earned his fame first by scaring people, then by getting things spectacularly wrong.

Somehow, humanity has found a way out of that particular Malthusian trap. But as with a lot of things, progress wasn't planned; the economy is self-organizing. Of course, we can give credit to singular innovators like Norman Borlaug, the father of the Green Revolution, whose work as an agronomist increased crop yields for the poorest people in the world. But a confluence of associated developments, including transportation, distribution, irrigation, and advanced farming techniques, all worked against famine.

Another famous person of letters has warned of collapse based on the idea of resource depletion. Jared Diamond, in his aptly titled *Collapse*, writes: "Severe problems of overpopulation, environmental impact, and climate change cannot persist indefinitely: sooner or later they are likely to resolve themselves, whether in the manner of Rwanda or in some other manner not of our devising if we don't succeed in solving them by our own actions."[38] In other words, collapse is coming because no one is doing anything to stop it. Diamond omits Ehrlich's error of predicting collapse within a specific timeframe; instead, he thinks collapse will occur "within the lifetimes of the children and young adults alive today."[39]

The problem with neo-Malthusian predictions is that they fail to consider three vital I's: institutions, innovations, and incentives. Such is not to argue that pockets of humanity neither can nor will fall into Malthusian traps. Instead, whenever the three I's are respected and working in harmony, we're *far less likely* to be haunted by the specter of resource collapse:

- *Institutions* are the "rules of the game" in a specific area — that is, what norms, rules, and laws govern resource use and exchange.

- *Innovations* are recipes that allow us to do more with less or to produce something where before we could produce nothing.

- *Incentives*, of course, are what motivate people to change their behavior.

These three forces must work in dynamic interplay to increase carrying capacity. Let's take some simple examples that illustrate how institutions, innovations, and incentives work together to keep us from running out of things.

It used to be that to send telecommunications signals you used copper wiring. So, starting around 1960, there was a steady rise in copper prices as more and more people began using copper wiring. According to data from the CME Group, however, copper prices peaked in February of 2010, at $4.45 per pound.[40] By that point, rising prices had already sent a message to innovators: *Find a substitute.* And they did. Today's fiber-optic lines are made of glass polymers that function sort of like mirrors within the line. These have become ubiquitous. Even though copper has many other uses, for example, in building construction, the price of copper in July 2019 was only $2.53 per pound.[41]

Some would argue that even sand, the silicon used to make fiber optics, is becoming scarcer.[42] But if prices continue to send knowledge wrapped in incentives, people will seek out substitutes for sand. When it comes to fiber optics, they already have: Satellite internet requires no lines at all. Neither do wireless broadband networks.

But what about buildings? Surely they'll always need stone and sand. Won't these resources also eventually run out? Not if innovative designers like CO-LAB in Tulum, Mexico, have anything to say about it. Long ignored by most wealthy nations, bamboo has the compressive strength of concrete and steel's tensile strength.[43] "But unlike those materials," writes Zach Mortice, "bamboo sequesters carbon as it grows instead of emitting it while it's made."

Because bamboo is a grass and not a tree, it grows fast, sometimes shooting up by as much as three feet in a week. Because bamboo is so light, a handful of people can build sophisticated structures without the need for heavy equipment. Travel to Tulum, and you'll see bamboo construction everywhere, from the smallest hut to the most palatial hotel.

In the broader institutional framework, we have learned some exciting things. First, we can make a stark distinction between an unmanaged commons such as the ocean and private property such as a grove of peach trees. The former almost always results in tragedies of the commons. The latter almost always results in better stewardship of resources. Such is especially the case when we're talking about consumption rivalry: *If I eat a peach, you can't.*

Notice how there are no shortages of peaches (or goats or chickens) in developed countries, but there are shortages of ocean fish. That's because economic actors who extract unowned resources do so in a race to exploit: *I'd better get it before someone else does.* As the resource price goes up due to scarcity, more people are encouraged to exploit the resource, which can result in a collapse of the stock. However, when someone owns a resource, they have incentives to restrict access (conserve), even if that incentive comes from the expectation of future returns. Solutions to resource conservation needn't always be narrowly self-interested: They can include models such as conservation trusts, cap-and-trade systems, and even hybrid systems that treat resources as club goods.

In some cases, though, there are pragmatic reasons to keep resources in the commons. Often it's because ascribing private property rights isn't feasible, as with the ocean, or air. In other cases, community ownership and management just makes more sense. That's why so-called Ostrom solutions to resource management (named after Nobel laureate Elinor Ostrom), can also help us become better resource stewards. Ostrom solutions are ways that communities can manage commons locally, using context-relevant, transparent, and agreed-to rules. The operative word here is "local."

Ostrom's field research in a Swiss village is well-known among economists and conservationists alike. In this village, farmers tended private plots for their crops but allowed their cows to graze communally. Usually, this situation would create a tragedy of the commons — but Ostrom discovered the villagers had no problems because they respected a community agreement from 1517, which means that one can graze more cows on the meadow than they can care for over the winter. Ostrom has documented similar practical examples of locally-evolved governance elsewhere in her research, including such far-flung places as Kenya, Guatemala, Nepal, Turkey, and Los Angeles.

These systems stand in stark contrast to far-off, bureaucratic resource management schemes. Ostrom solutions may continue to improve and evolve right along with private property solutions, but suggest that we can avoid resource management proposed by politicians and distant experts. History has shown that bureaucratic systems are ineffective and too easily captured by special interests. Wealthier countries with robust property rights and local commons management find, increasingly, that they can do more with less.

MIT economist Andrew McAfee agrees. Even when it comes to that bastion of extractive capitalism, the United States, he writes in *More from Less* that "we have finally learned how to tread more lightly on our planet."

> In America — a large rich country that accounts for about 25 percent of the global economy — we're now generally using less for most resources year after year, even as our economy and population continue to grow. What's more, we're also polluting the air and water less, emitting fewer greenhouse gases, and seeing population increases in many animals that had almost vanished. America, in short, is post-peak in its exploitation of the earth.[44]

One might quibble with McAfee in the sense that so much of America's extraction has simply been outsourced to dirtier countries. But even these countries are moving in the right direction, with some even leapfrogging.

The tendency to do more with less as societies grow richer might sound dubious on its face. But Simon Kuznets's growth curve works for the environment, too: The environmental Kuznets Curve is an observed relationship between environmental quality and economic growth. At first, ecological degradation tends to be worse as a developing economy takes off. Until, that is, average income reaches a certain point as the country gets richer. At this point, more people can afford and thus demand environmental goods. The implication of this, contra neo-Malthusians, is that wealthier is healthier. Wealth also offers us an extraordinary ability to do more with less, thanks to waste elimination techniques and advanced technology.

As we come more fully to appreciate the dynamic interplay among institutions, incentives, and innovations, we should be less worried about resource collapse. Before his death, the economist Julian Simon reminded us that there is something special about human beings: Our minds are the ultimate resource. Human ingenuity is the dharma of progress. Using good rules, new tools, and accurate information, we can ward off resource collapse with improved human systems. Institutions like private property and Ostrom Commons create the conditions for good resource stewardship. Better incentives get transmitted in free and undistorted price signals, which tell us when we need to conserve and when we're okay to consume. And innovations allow us to conserve or switch to alternatives when necessary.

Instead of worrying about resource collapse, we should thus be worried about the breakdown of institutions, incentives, and innovations.

Before turning to our attention elsewhere, we should note a paradox in all this prosperity: People in wealthier societies tend to have fewer children, while those living in poorer countries generally have more. So, even if one thinks overpopulation is a problem, the best "solution" is probably economic growth, as the relationship between wealth and having fewer children is stronger than mere correlation.

According to U.N. researchers, global fertility levels have dropped from just over five children per woman in 1950 to around 2.5 children per woman in 2015.[45] According to the late Nobel economist Gary Becker, one of the strongest drivers of this demographic change came from women's empowerment. Becker's work showed that, as women become more educated and enter the workforce, the opportunity cost of having more children increases.[46] We can add that as maternal and infant mortality rates have fallen, necessity drives fewer choices for bearing children.

And yet almost all of the solutions proposed by those concerned about overpopulation and resource scarcity have to do with curbing economic growth and fertility rates. Such includes proposals by advocates of the "degrowth movement," explained here by political ecologist Ricardo Mastini as "the abolition of economic growth as a social objective."[47]

Never mind that these movements frequently turn on a series of confusions about the nature of economic growth. Their policy ideas are just prohibitions; linear thinking in a nonlinear world. Such thinking *seems* reasonable on its face because practitioners believe the only way to *fix* a complex problem is for officials to mandate that people "organize and live differently from today."[48] In other words, to solve problems associated with growth, stop growth. The nonlinear alternative tolerates economic growth and relies on greater faith in emergent systems.

Though they can be a tough sell, the counterintuitive insights of emergent complexity bear out repeatedly. Humanity must show intellectual humility before complex systems because these systems are unpredictable by nature. Who would have predicted that in my lifetime, you could:

- Double the world's population but see the world's forestland remain stable?[49]

- Triple the number of cars on the American road but see major air pollution sources go down?[50]

- Double the world's population but see extreme poverty go from 60 percent globally to less than 10 percent?[51]

If we insist on some rationalistic scheme to confer predictability, we'll end up losing the enormous benefits of emergence. Indeed, sometimes we find out the hard way that the ones keenest to save society are the ones who end up destroying it.

Economist Thomas Sowell warned us about those in the grip of what he termed the *unconstrained vision*. Those snared by this spell believe that authority should be as powerful as it needs to be to make the world just. As long as the right people are in power, authorities can rid the world of problems caused by a benighted subset and then set about architecting a just world. "Justice," in this instance, is whatever the High Mind imagines it to be; according to the unconstrained vision, human nature is highly malleable, but the natural world is not. Thus, morally upright people must have the authority to keep the rest in line. To embrace the unconstrained vision, then, is to imagine some ideal world, then use whatever means necessary to realize it.

What is the opposite view? "One of the hallmarks of the constrained vision is that it deals with tradeoffs rather than solutions," writes Sowell in *A Conflict of Visions*.[52] In other words, to accept the constrained vision is to remain humble in the face of what you don't know and probably *can't* know. Instead, we develop better protocols, which allow certain people to solve problems where they can apply local knowledge. This is humility in the face of complexity. It's the recognition of tradeoffs.

OF MUSHROOMS AND MOONSHOTS

"I believe that this nation should commit itself to achieving the goal, before this decade is out, of landing a man on the moon and returning him safely to the Earth. No single space project in this period will be more impressive to mankind, or more important for the long-range exploration of space; and none will be so difficult or expensive to accomplish."[53]

Nations don't make commitments, of course. People do. But with that speech, John F. Kennedy planted a stark, powerful image in Americans' minds. At the risk of tipping golden calves, Kennedy's is just the sort of language that obscures technocracy's problems. Thomas Sowell reminds us that metaphors which suggest society is a decision-making unit can be misleading because they ignore that "the actual decision-making units face a particular kind of incentive structure."[54]

Kennedy was essentially making a commitment on behalf of two hundred million people with two hundred million different plans and projects. Still, most people don't question the grand designs of soothing orators or national father figures because, well, democracy. And, of course, *a man on the moon!* It puts stardust in your eyes. Most of us never participated in the achievement, much less considered its costs. Yet somehow, most Americans still take pride in it. The event certainly left Americans with the distinct impression that there are no limits to what "society" or the "nation" can do in that halfway house of the technocratic-industrial complex.

This variation on High Modernism is not just a holdover from the 1960s, and we should be fair to the spirit in which the term "moonshot" is used in other contexts, namely, as an ambitious project with a relatively low probability of success. We don't want to dismiss this connotation out of hand. My concern with the moonshot mentality is that it can go too far, transforming into an unreflective disposition to tolerate big projects requiring big plans and big money. One shouldn't get the impression that all big projects are bad projects, or that all small-scale projects are worth trying. Instead, we can all agree that *some* projects are not worth doing, big or small. We can also imagine projects that are simply too big or too expensive to undertake.

So what is the limiting principle? How big is too big? How expensive is too expensive?

Because large projects require a lot of capital, we always have to be aware of that niggling lesson from Econ 101: *opportunity costs*. That's a way of asking what alternatives can't exist because resources went to another use. It's easier to gauge opportunity costs when planning with your own resources. At least with investors' resources, you're careful because you owe them a return. When one plays with other people's money — or borrows from people in the future — one can lose all sense of priority.

Space exploration is inspiring. Elon Musk is cool. But out of a billion different human priorities, a lot of people get floored by the whiz-bang nature of great technocratic plans. They fancy that technocracy can be applied anywhere to positive effect — including shaping society itself. In this regard, we have to consider just how many industries are in Hayek's halfway house. You may recall that these are private companies, but use the government to become parasitic on the wider order.

We have to grapple with the probability of failure. Just starting a small business of any kind, and keeping it alive, is hard. According to data from the U.S. Bureau of Labor Statistics, twenty percent of small businesses fail within their first year. After five years, about fifty percent have failed. After a decade, sixty-five percent are dead. And it's not just businesses but communities we might want to enter to realize our ideals. "Generally, intentional communities fail at a rate slightly higher than that of most start-ups."[55]

Despite booms and busts, these failure rates remain pretty consistent over time. The lesson here is that the failure rate of moonshots is not likely to be any better — unless the moonshot organization can be propped up in some manner. But that, too, comes at a cost.

Peter Diamandis, founder of XPrize, though brilliant and successful in his own right, has been a visible propagator of the moonshot mentality. Time and again, he's said that what we really need to push humanity forward is "10x" thinking. People pay Diamandis a lot of money to speak in front of throngs of adoring fans. Diamandis's idea is to imagine a solution that's ten times as big as anything you might typically think of, then start reverse engineering from that audacious vision. Diamandis also describes this as "exponential thinking," which he says Elon Musk has in spades. He suggests young people follow in Musk's footsteps. Young people should pursue their passions and focus on projects that will have an enormous impact, *if successful.*[56]

That's a big if.

No one wants to be the guy who gets on a stage after Diamandis and asks the audience to consider the invisible costs of a hundred failed moonshots or a million foregone dreams. But that's what happens when someone like Elon Musk puts other people's money towards his moonshots. In a world of scarce resources, you only get so many times at bat. You'll have even fewer if too much of your time and money and energy is going into moonshots. So, even if we agree with Peter Diamandis about 10x thinking, the only responsible thing is to add the advice of futurist Chunka Wui, who cautions us to "think big, start small, learn fast."[57] In other words: be visionary, but fail early and cheaply.

Alas, not everyone in the technocratic-industrial complex operates at Wui's level of humility. Perhaps it's because those blinkered by High Modernism or the Moonshot Mentality are simply less concerned about failure. Some are shielded from it for a time. But as Thomas Sowell reminds us, "The godlike approach to analyzing 'society' and its (metaphorical) behavior often overlooks risks, the subjective nature of risk, and/or the wide variation of its cost among individuals."[58]

The simplest way to measure the success of a Musk enterprise is not to delight at videos of Starman orbiting in a Tesla Roadster, but rather to ask whether any of his companies can survive without subsidies. (In case you needed reminding, subsidies are your money transferred to corporations without your consent.) Denmark's experience offers us a warning. After the small Scandinavian country repealed its tax incentives for electric cars, Tesla's sales dropped from nearly five thousand in 2015 to around seven hundred in 2017.

Despite the U.S. electric car tax credit expiring in 2020, Tesla Motors still holds eighty percent of the electric car market in America. Critics say that the company consistently resorts to accounting tricks to show profits. The question is, can the company create real customer value above costs?

People have understandably gone gaga over Elon Musk. He is, after all, a creative genius. He dazzles us with all manner of moonshot ideas, even if most of them require massive taxpayer support to exist at all. But it's precisely in this sort of dependency that we can take the moonshot mentality too far. Big, audacious projects can suck resources away from thousands of more modest, more profitable forms of human action. Instead of 10x thinking, we need to operate within the bounds of iteration, testability, and affordability. We don't have to throw away creativity.

Like Kennedy, Musk is good at casting a spell over those from whom all the largesse is funneled — especially as these kinds of projects can end up costing a lot more than initially proposed. But being under that spell can amount to a failure to grok the systems-wide implications. After all, most moonshots are wasteful. The ones that get completed create a dubious relationship between cost and benefit, as proponents play up the gee-whiz aspects and downplay the less visible costs.

"$110 billion (in today's value) was spent on the Apollo project," writes technology analyst Andrew Stover. "This is a massive investment in what was essentially an enormous geopolitical pissing match between the United States and the USSR; however, as soon as the USA no longer needed the marketing campaign of moon travel, the entire lunar project withered and died."[59]

With a nod to eighteenth-century political economist Frederic Bastiat,[60] we have to ask: What sorts of things never sprang up from all those resources that were taken out of circulation? What innovations, even if they started small or mundane, never got to bloom into the next Apple, AirBnB, or great medical breakthrough?

Humans need to solve big, expensive problems. Most of the time, we have to solve big, expensive problems together. But can we collaborate on big things without succumbing to the temptations of High Modernism, with its emphasis on the unrestrained use of state power?

MYCELIAL THINKING

A few years ago, I attended a conference dedicated to finding ways to help Puerto Rico in the wake of Hurricane Maria. I was honored to participate with a small group of futurists called the Moonshot Group. Some in that group were under the spell of the moonshot mentality. One man, in particular, suggested a hyperloop between the Port of Ponce and San Juan. When one considers that estimates for hyperloop construction range anywhere from $84 million to $121 million per mile (let's say $100 million)[61], with seventy-five miles between the cities, it would cost about $7.5 billion to build. That doesn't include the costs of ongoing maintenance. The government could buy every citizen in both cities (about five hundred thousand people) a compact car for the same cost. Admittedly, this was a back-of-the-envelope calculation. But something didn't seem right.

I turned to the man who had assembled the group, James Hanusa, and said: "This is going to sound weird, but I wonder if thinking on Puerto Rico's recovery needs a different guiding metaphor than moonshot — something more like mushroom spores."

"You mean like a mycelial network?" Mr. Hanusa said. Exactly. BBC's Nic Fleming describes the process:

> While mushrooms might be the most familiar part of a fungus, most of their bodies are made up of a mass of thin threads, known as a mycelium. We now know that these threads act as a kind of underground internet, linking the roots of different plants. That tree in your garden is probably hooked up to a bush several metres away, thanks to mycelia.
> The more we learn about these underground networks, the more our ideas about plants have to change. They aren't just sitting there quietly growing. By linking to the fungal network they can help out their neighbours by sharing nutrients and information...[62]

Mycelial networks are not centrally planned, but are nature's peer-to-peer processors. And like other natural phenomena, mycelial networks are products of evolution and emergence, not intelligent design. It's the network *protocols* we have to design.

Mycelial thinking means, rather than figuring out what big thing we're going to do, one asks: within what simple ruleset are the agents' autonomous goings-and-doings likely to be the most robust and generative? These systems are about organic growth from the bottom up instead of engineering from the top down. Such thinking (again) involves a biological metaphor, whereas moonshot thinking is a holdover from the Machine Age.[63]

Let's juxtapose these two thinking styles:

Moonshot Mentality. Big problems require big projects. Solutions must be as bold as the severity of the issues they seek to address. Want to power the masses' homes and businesses? Build the Hoover Dam. Want to cure what ails Puerto Rico? Build a hyperloop. Want to show the Soviets who's boss? Build a rocket ship which will carry Americans to the moon.

We need brilliant engineers to think in complicated ways until a complete solution can be fully conceived, blueprinted, and built. How much it will cost and where the money will come from is a tertiary consideration at best. Creating something big will bring benefits, which, though hard to measure, represent the best in humanity. Often, these projects are considered "too big to fail."

Mycelial Thinking. Big problems require many different experiments, most of which will start small but can scale to the level of the problem. Such experiments will be carried out in networks of experimenters with superior collective intelligence. These networks attack problems from various angles. Indeed, sometimes the "problem" is really a cluster of interrelated problems.

Mycelial thinking gives rise to a cluster of interrelated solutions. We need brilliant people to think about protocol-level rules, so that complex, multivariate solutions can emerge and be replicated — even if we don't yet know what they are. Often, these projects fail early and cheaply. But when they succeed, we can measure their success exponentially.

Mycelial thinking, as we suggested above, is about starting small and failing cheaply. Mycelial thinking means getting the rules right and running a series of small experiments to see which ones get traction. It might be that only two in ten do, and they might not seem all that visionary. Some might be positively mundane. Others might turn out to be fascinating in ways we didn't expect. Ultimately, mycelial thinking is just as much about letting a thousand flowers bloom as shooting for the moon.

At this point, you might wonder: Are we expected to anticipate prosocial solutions from mycelial thinking even if we don't know what they are? That's where we simply have to have some faith in the entrepreneurial spirit. No wonder moonshots get all the bureaucrats and budgets! A massive project with a visualizable end state is far sexier and easier to sell — especially when we can put it on the national credit card. Most people have a hard time grokking the difference between $100 million and $100 billion. It's just zeros, after all. But everybody can imagine a man on Mars.

Try getting similar support for something abstract and prosaic, such as a diverse, thriving, anti-fragile society. The closest case I can think of was made by President Ronald Reagan, of all people, near the end of his second term:

> I've spoken of the shining city all my political life, but I don't know if I ever quite communicated what I saw when I said it. But in my mind it was a tall, proud city built on rocks stronger than oceans, wind-swept, God-blessed, and teeming with people of all kinds living in harmony and peace; a city with free ports that hummed with commerce and creativity. And if there had to be city walls, the walls had doors and the doors were open to anyone with the will and the heart to get here. That's how I saw it, and see it still.[64]

It's not bad. But is it as captivating as Kennedy's image of a man on the moon?

SPECIALISTS AND SUPPLICANTS

Elon Musk fans might already have thrown this book away. But if you're still with me, I want to make our concerns a bit more explicit. The idea is that too many supplicant organizations like SpaceX could hasten our collapse. But NASA and SpaceX are only a tiny fraction of the extent of the problem, as we'll soon see.

"Supplicant" is my term for a class of companies that wouldn't exist without subsidy, debt, or favoritism by the political class. These companies become dependent as the government functions as a monopsony, or single buyer. Their complication and extent mean layers of dependency, making them fragile. Why should anyone care? Because a single buyer is a single point of failure.

A "specialist" is my term for a class of companies that enjoy no subsidy, debt, or favoritism. They exist because they create value for people willing to pay them to keep providing that value over time. A specialist's enterprise is sustainable.

The discerning reader may have noticed that I made a couple of jabs at economist John Maynard Keynes. One reason is that Keynes made no real distinction between specialists and supplicants. I won't spend too much time taking apart Keynes's theory here. Instead, I'll suggest an alternative. My favorite comes from the rogue economist I mentioned above: Arnold Kling.

Instead of the "hydraulic" concept of aggregate demand, Kling looks at the economy differently. He calls it PSST, which is an acronym for Patterns of Sustainable Specialization and Trade.[65] The key to understanding Kling's approach is to scrap the machine metaphor entirely. As we have suggested, the economy is an evolved ecosystem. And as with evolution, Kling puts the process of discovery, rediscovery, and specialization at the center of economic analysis.

In short, so much of the socio-economic order is like a rainforest. And in that rainforest, there is "almost nothing we consume that we can make for ourselves."[66] Note that Kling isn't saying we ought never to make things for ourselves — although he wouldn't suggest making a toaster from scratch. Instead, he's pointing out how our economy has evolved, especially away from one based almost entirely on agriculture.

> Suppose that we had with us a time traveler from
> 1800. Imagine taking a random sample of a dozen
> people working in different office buildings and
> explaining to our time traveler how those people
> contribute to the production process. Try to convey
> the role of a web programmer, a graphic designer, a
> data analyst, or a social media marketing specialist.
> Try to explain how in the United States fewer than 2
> percent of the labour force is engaged in agricultural
> production and less than 6 percent of the workforce
> consists of manufacturing production workers.[67]

This complexity comes despite technocracy, not because
of it.

Innovation constantly shifts the patterns of specialization and comparative advantage, such that Adam Smith's
pin factory would be digitized and automated to a shocking
degree. And that self-same factory might just as well spring
up in Vietnam as in Vancouver, thanks to gains from trade.
But we must take care: When the patterns of specialization become unsustainable, those affected can face periods
of unemployment. "They are like soldiers," Kling wrote,
"waiting for new orders, except that the orders come not
from a commanding general but from the decentralized
actions of many entrepreneurs testing ideas in search of
profit."[68]

The specialist entrepreneur is continually looking for
ways to produce more at a lower cost. And so are her
competitors. Some people think this process is bad, especially when one considers the acute pain of displacement.
In the long run, though, we get increased variety, complexity, and interdependency.

For now, let's leave aside debates about whether innovation and automation will hit escape velocity, unfolding
at a rate that will outpace the economy's ability to recruit
new workers to new positions. The point here is to reinforce

what Kling thinks is the central process of economic development: not big plans, nor aggregate spending.

Technocracy, even the sort that inspires us with grand visions of Mars colonies and supercolliders, pushes us from sustainability to dependency. From anti-fragility to fragility. When firms — a few large, several mid-sized, and many small — engage in the process of discovery, they are working tirelessly to remain profitable. That means that each has to work within the confines of scarcity and risk to create customer value against competitors who are doing the same. They are specialists because, unlike supplicants, they must create direct-but-distributed customer value in the ultimate democracy — the one in which you vote with your dollars. Profit is earned. Losses are death.

Economies function with scarce resources that have alternative uses. There needs to be a rational way to get the most valuable output from the available inputs. Supplicants, like Lockheed Martin or SpaceX, can be run by brilliant visionaries with highly specialized operations, but their enterprises subsist in the distorted reality of politics. Supplicants play a zero-sum game. The bigger the supplicant, the more it needs taxpayer largesse. While it's tempting to think that they'll never fall due to the unlimited supply of tax dollars, as we'll see, the money runs out.

In America, it already has.

EVONOMICS

One would think that a full appreciation of evolution and emergence in the context of modern economics would be enough to mute the temptations of High Modernism. But there's a new way to smuggle technocratic aspirations in the back door using the language of evolution: enter "Evonomics." The term was first popularized by evolutionary biologist David Sloan Wilson, who thinks that the original idea of the invisible hand is "old and erroneous" and should be replaced. He suggests instead a new version:

> The new version is based on examples of the invisi-
> ble hand that exist in nature, such as cells that benefit
> multi-cellular organisms and social insects that
> benefit their colonies. These lower-level units don't
> have the welfare of the higher-level units in mind.
> They don't even have minds in the human sense of
> the word. Instead, according to Wilson, they exhibit
> behaviors that have been winnowed by higher-level
> selection to benefit the common good. Higher-level
> selection is the new invisible hand.[69]

Remember, nowhere in Wilson's discussion of ants and
bees does he suggest that *nature's* higher-level selection is the
product of *intelligent design*. Nor at any point does he ascribe
a mental life or agency to these creatures. Instead, he sets
forth a theory of group or "multi-level" selection. Then he
concludes:

> We must learn to function in two capacities: 1) As
> designers of social and economic systems; and 2) as
> participants in the systems that we design. As partic-
> ipants, we need not have the welfare of the whole
> system in mind, in classic invisible hand fashion. But
> as designers, we must. The invisible hand must be
> constructed...[70]

The bizarreness of this claim, like Wilson's preferred
theory of selection, is multi-level.

First, we should note that relatively few evolutionary
biologists believe in multi-level selection. That doesn't mean
Wilson is wrong, of course, but it's worth noting because
Wilson appeals to one controversial theory to derive yet
another. The vaguely plausible idea of group selection is
that whole species benefit from certain behaviors. Wilson
thinks that these behaviors could have evolved at the level
of the entire group, rather than at the level of the individual. One source of trouble for group selection theory lies

in the fact that the group-level phenomena Wilson points to can be explained entirely by orthodox Darwinism (for example, by running genetic algorithms). Again, this doesn't mean group selection is wrong, but it does mean that Ockham has gotten out his strop.

Second, the analogy here seems to be that *because* group selection is needed to explain behaviors that benefit the whole species, humans *ought to* develop altruistic super-systems that benefit the whole species. Wilson's "new invisible hand" is short on details. Still, he claims that enlightened "designers" will be able to architect socio-economic systems better than all this crude business of truck, barter, and exchange. But, just as we can explain group traits through individual selection, we can also show that the common good can and does arise through individuals' self-interest. The great economic journalist Frederic Bastiat did just that when, 175 years ago, he rhetorically asked: "How does Paris get fed?"[71] Even if you're not a Francophile, you might consider people having food as something beneficial to the species, never mind that the man who originally came up with the term "invisible hand" wrote another book, *The Theory of Moral Sentiments.* This leaves plenty of room for acts of altruism among consenting adults.

Third, Wilson's approach seems close to yet another deus ex machina. When applied to biological diversity, arguments for intelligent design closely parallel arguments for High Modernism applied to economic theory. Wilson is willing to unleash the High Minds in the latter domain and not the former, even though neither is immune to Darwin's dangerous idea. If Daniel Dennett is correct in saying that natural selection is "the best idea that anyone ever had,"[72] the idea of the invisible hand can't be far behind. We don't need species-level selection any more than we need society-level designers.

"Welfare" is subjective and contextual. And that might be the biggest problem with Evonomics.

None of our responses to Evonomics mean that people can't or shouldn't experiment locally, that altruism can't be effective, or that new institutional forms can't evolve. But experimentation is just conscientious mutation. Ostrom's managed commons and mutual aid organizations emerge just fine in the extended order — that is, until High Minds plan them away. The subtitle of Ostrom's seminal *Governing the Commons* is, after all, "The *Evolution* of Institutions for Collective Action" (emphasis mine). Our critique of Evonomics doesn't imply that humans are just selfish *homo economicus* operating in a world of perfect information. But it does mean that everyone should stop trying to argue from a God's-eye perch and resist the urge to design whole societies as if anyone has the requisite knowledge to do so.

We do have to respond, though, to curious statements like this from entrepreneur Peter Barnes, who, in an interview with Wilson, said: "We need to re-rig our economy as intelligent designers, using a complex systems perspective."[73] I suspect that many of the things Peter Barnes doesn't like about our economy are the unintended consequences of rigging. Neither Barnes nor Wilson has shown how their re-rigging represents an improvement over all of the prior rigging. Until Barnes can tell us how one might "re-rig" the Great Barrier Reef or the Amazon jungle, we should be as suspicious of this whole line as one might be of the Discovery Institute.[74]

A more up-to-date way to describe the original invisible hand is as follows:

1. Voluntary exchange of goods and services among individuals leads to a division of labor in which people specialize in what they're relatively better suited to.

2. Asymmetries of knowledge start to form, which means more and more people have to trade with specialists and become specialists themselves.

3. Thanks to increasing gains from this exchange, people gravitate towards doing the things that they are more productive at doing, which is a constant process of learning and improving. Whether alone or in teams, people use their lights to judge what they are good at doing, in a way central authorities never could.

4. The resulting prosperity encourages more special-ization and more trade. As more producers special-ize, they produce more highly specialized things, yielding a diverse cornucopia. Each person might produce fewer things but can consume more things.

5. People try new things, formulate new recipes, and combine existing ideas to make new ones. Such allows them to specialize and produce. It's called innovation, and it's probably the single greatest driver of prosperity. The more people innovate, specialize, and trade, the more opportunities they have to serve each other better.

6. The more they serve each other, the higher their living standards.

Skeptics might argue that the original view doesn't make room for certain kinds of values. This is an open question. Suffice it to say that the degree to which produc-ers or consumers are able to displace their costs onto others is the degree to which the Common Law can help. Other-wise, the overall good might not come uniformly or be agreeable to any given person. But it comes, just as it does in the rainforest.

Like many under the spell of High Modernism, Wilson thinks that there is a "middle way" between decentralized experimentation and central planning. Supposedly, it will give us better results than an economy in which people self-organize in the service of different missions. Odd that Wilson doesn't think that we are already trying to live with this middle way. He is consistently short on details regarding his new version of the mixed economy, the status-quo version of which is a source of both confusion and corruption because its adherents assume one can reconcile the approaches that are being mixed. They cannot. As we will see, the systems are incommensurable. (Hint: one operates using persuasion, the other using coercion.)

Most of us want to see the world improve. Only the most heartless sociopath will delight in the thought that future generations will endure terrible hardship, environmental degradation, or humanity's end. But in our desire to leave our children a world better than we found it, we must recognize our limitations. In the past, authorities indulged the urge to fix their societies with visible hands. Thus, they left their societies in ruins.

THE POST-SCARCITY ECONOMY

Even if you think David Sloan Wilson's ideas are misguided, they're not completely crazy. Indeed, there is much to recommend in upgrading the invisible hand to include vital information that the price system alone cannot capture. But sometimes, even zany ideas get traction. I'll discuss a couple of these ideas long enough to acknowledge that they're out there in the memosphere. Bad models and metaphors continue to pollute our sensemaking.

Fully Automated Luxury Communism. If it wasn't possible before, technological advance will soon allow humanity to "undermine the key features of what we had previously taken for granted as the natural order of things," writes author and space communist Aaron Bastani in *The New York Times*. "To grasp it, however, will require a new politics. One where technological change serves people, not profit. Where the pursuit of tangible policies — rapid decarbonization, full automation and socialized care — are preferred to present fantasies." [75]

Here we are to imagine technology so advanced that lab-grown meat, solar panels, AI, and automation provides for everyone on earth at *no cost*. According to Bastani, there's only one thing standing in the way: global markets. "Ours is an age of crisis. We inhabit a world of low growth, low productivity and low wages, of climate breakdown and the collapse of democratic politics. A world where billions, mostly in the global south, live in poverty." [76]

An age of crisis?

Nicholas Kristof, writing in the same publication, concludes that "every day for a decade, newspapers could have carried the headline 'Another 170,000 Moved Out of Extreme Poverty Yesterday.' Or if one uses a higher threshold, the headline could have been: 'The Number of People Living on More Than $10 a Day Increased by 245,000 Yesterday.'" So much for the age of crisis. It would seem that global markets are doing fine — so much so that the period from 2010-2020 was the most prosperous decade in human history. (It will be a shame to see sovereign debt wipe out so many of these gains. But I digress.)

The Venus Project. The late structural designer Jacques Fresco gained throngs of admirers in his visual depictions of a resource-based economy, a form of utopian scientism. In a resource-based economy, all goods and services are available to anyone, without the need to pay for it. "For this to be achieved all resources must be declared as the common heritage of all Earth's inhabitants. Equipped with the latest scientific and technological marvels mankind could reach extremely high productivity levels and create an abundance of resources." [77]

Fresco painted, quite literally, pictures of massive solar arrays and towers that excite the technocratic imagination. But he leaves the question of means, costs, and tradeoffs for someone else's imagination.

Much of this fanciful thinking comes from the half-baked idea of a "post-scarcity" society. Though ideas such as luxury communism and Venus projects seem to be all the rage, they depend on the idea that technological abundance will eventually suspend economic laws. The origins of this sort of fantasy extend back to social theorist Jeremy Rifkin, political theorist Herbert Marcuse, and, eventually, to Karl Marx himself.

In a text known as the "Fragment," Marx imagines an economy in which machines produce stuff, and people supervise the machines. He appreciated that the primary productive force in such an economy would be information; for example, a steam engine's productive power doesn't depend on the amount of labor it took to produce it but rather on society's state of knowledge at the time. Knowledge and organization, therefore, are more important than making and running the machines. [78]

Marx is right that knowledge and organization are important. He just didn't know *why* they are important, much less in what configuration that importance is manifest. We'll come back to this in a moment. Right now, let's stipulate that things will soon be different. Production costs will continuously approach zero, and robots will do a lot of the work for us.

And we'll still have the good old economic calculation problem first articulated in 1920.

In his essay "Economic Calculation in the Socialist Commonwealth," economist Ludwig von Mises explained that one of the biggest challenges facing any economic order is the deployment of capital goods designed to make things for consumption. How does anyone decide *what* goods to produce, *how much* should be produced, and *how* these goods should get produced?

For example, if the Servant Robot Company wants to introduce a new robot, what kind of microchips should the company use? Both chips are technologically feasible, but only a working price mechanism conveys that, at the margin, one chip is more expensive than the other.

Because one processor is dedicated to robot movement, the company should only use the more expensive chip for "neural" modules. Techno-socialism seeks to collectivize the ownership of those capital goods. But when? By definition, collectivization eliminates the markets in which these goods get exchanged. Rational economic calculation becomes impossible as soon as the collective removes all the relevant market perspectives.

Think of scenarios in which people can manufacture their own goods with 3-D printers or nano-manufacturing devices that can replicate themselves, requiring only energy and simple slurries as raw inputs. The collective would provide these devices.

Which slurries? What energy? From where and at what cost? And do the first of these future printers and nano-manufacturing devices have no cost or alternative uses? What about services? Will the supercomputer be funnier than Richard Pryor? Weirder than Wes Anderson? And what about services one might *want* to be carried out by humans? What about a vase with wabi-sabi handmade by a single craftsman in Kyoto? What about storytelling in the voice of Morgan Freeman at my kid's birthday party, not a simulacrum, but *the* Morgan Freeman? Won't artists be allowed to price their time and services? Or should we enslave the artists?

Okay, so, services by humans will be an exception. But a super-computer possessing godlike powers will replace entrepreneurial markets for various goods. And that will be enough for Luxury Communism.

Sounds wonderful. If it arrives somehow, I'm all for it. But it seems that a resource-based economy can only arrive *after* certain conditions are met, namely, when a functioning system of property, prices, and profit/loss is no longer necessary. If Luxury Communism is possible at all, it'll take the market's economic calculation to get there.

Those imagining a world without market prices are appealing to a future in which there are self-replicating nanomachines and unlimited energy. Let's pass over the speculative horror that these nanomachines could mutate. Conversations about a world in which people are no longer needed to produce anything seem as distant as a world in which people no longer need each other. Maybe some sophisticated AI overlord will host us as we subsist and dream our realities, as in *The Matrix*. Life wouldn't be so bad if we could experience steak and sex on demand. Perhaps nature will grow up around our energy-harvesting cocoons while we dream. Dystopian stories can scare people into Luddism, dirigisme, or both. When it comes to tech-no-socialism, is turnabout fair play?

For the foreseeable future, without markets for production goods, there are no prices for those goods. Without prices for production goods, there's no way to determine which lines of business are profitable. Indications of scarcity remain distorted at best. In the absence of accurate information signals, nobody has a clue which goods to produce or how to produce them. Such information problems make it impossible for collectivized economies to generate the fantasyland abundance associated with techno-Marxism. Unless someone figures it out, these ideas remain the stuff of science fiction.

2

THE BREAKDOWN OF HIERARCHIES

By lessening the natural tendency for rest-
lessness and by meditating on the infinite,
posture is mastered. thereafter, one is not
disturbed by the dualities.
　　　　　Patanjali, from *the Yoga Sutras*

Life and death. Male and female. Ruler and ruled.
Simple dualities can often describe the world around
us — but they are not always enough in the age of scientific advances. And yet the whole truth and nothing but
the truth of, say, unified field theory can be, as philosopher
Nelson Goodman, put it "too vast, variable and clogged
with trivia."[79] Is there a useful in-between?

Some dualities are hard to deny, because they are simple
and clean: off and on. Cathode and anode. Beginning and
ending. Others blur together in shades, as white does to
black. Poles that are salient enough to notice and simple
enough to use are ours for the taking. Learning to pick out
dualities can offer us clues toward life's mysteries. But we
had better know the difference between description and
ascription; otherwise, we might invent trouble where none
exists, or fail to see the gray.

Let's begin with a duality that lives deep within us.

Sigmund Freud must have contemplated this as his patients lay upon the famous couch in Vienna. In "Beyond the Pleasure Principle," Freud wrote of Eros and Thanatos, which he said are human drives that are not strict binaries but rather move together in the dance of our existence.

Eros drives us to live, to create, and to procreate. We exert ourselves through passion, or we offer ourselves through nurturing. Eros can take the form of ambition or yearning, but what we long for is a *genesis*. It is early spring, the wellspring of anticipation. Thanatos, on the other hand, is the death drive. We seek to dissolve, to destroy, or to die. And though Thanatos can take an aggressive or depressive form, what we long for is a *terminus*. It is late fall, the expectation of absence. Let's suppose that Freud was right about this duality, even though he was wrong about a great many things. Draw a line in your mind that goes from Eros to Thanatos, which, if you like, you can also call *generative* to *destructive*. An *x*-axis.

If Eros to Thanatos is one dimension, now imagine another dimension, a *y*-axis of energies, which goes from Masculine to Feminine. Masculine energy comprises *fuck-fight-force* dispositions, which can motivate our actions; feminine energy includes *flirt-fawn-facilitate* impulses, and these can animate our behavior, too. Men tend toward the Masculine and women tend toward the Feminine, but both dispositions live in men and women alike, as Carl Jung reminded us. Endocrinologists and anthropologists can debate about the nature of these tendencies, but they should be familiar.

The point is, human beings have the drive to create and the drive to destroy, *and* human beings are bundles of masculine and feminine energies. Now we have a two-by-two matrix, which makes four quadrants. Eros and Thanatos now have dual aspects, which are Masculine and Feminine:

Eros Masculine is the urge to control. If things aren't

going your way, you have to *make* them go your way. It's
the way of force. It's the way of steel. Steel can be used to
defend the weak, to jail the criminal, and to build where
before there was nothing. *Have we run out of space in the city?*
Let's build something tall, phallic even, right into the sky. Think yours
is tall? Mine will be taller. Eros Masculine is about competition
and especially compulsion. *Do it, or else. Exert control.*

Thanatos Masculine is the urge to annihilate. If things
aren't going your way, you have to destroy whatever is in
the way. It's the way of aggression. It's the way of fire.
Within the circle of stones, the fire warms our camp, but
if the stones are removed the camp is in danger. Thanatos
Masculine scorches the earth. Their way of life is at odds
with ours. They are the enemy. Bring fire down upon their
village. Thanatos Masculine is a white-hot rage that takes
us to war, or at home, a passion that threatens even those
we love. Thanatos Masculine is about destruction. *Burn it all*
down. End it now.

Eros Feminine is the urge to flow. If things aren't going
your way, it's okay if they go another way. Or maybe they'll
come around to your way in time. It's the way of rhetoric.
It's the way of water. The surface of the earth is seventy
percent water, as are our bodies. As the moon tugs the tides,
we are but complex extensions of life's flows. Eros Feminine
facilitates, perhaps as a fluid that lubricates the necessary
parts. It fawns, nurtures, and tames. Eros Feminine is about
care, and especially about persuasion. *Try it. You'll like it. Let*
things flow.

Thanatos Feminine is the urge to rest. If things aren't
going your way, just go to sleep or stay in bed. It's the way
of withdrawal. It's the way of the night, when we sleep to
recover from the day. But our final rest is in death. Melan-
choly wraps us in times of sorrow, as we grapple with
absence or grieve in loss. Thanatos feminine is sleepiness
after a weary struggle or the torpor of depression. It weak-
ens us but still impels us to lie down. Thanatos Feminine is

about endings. *Goodnight, my love. Let things go.*

As we suggested, the tendency is for men to be motivated primarily by the masculine energy and for women to be motivated by the feminine energy, thanks to hormones. But again, both energies are present in each of us, by degree. So are the drives to create and destroy. The wise among us seek to bring them all into balance, recognizing that all such energies have healthy and unhealthy expressions. At this level of description, we don't need neuroscience. We recognize the patterns.

A healthy home, then, is one in which the couple strives to become like the Hindu god Ardhanarishvara, the *unified* manifestation of Shiva and his consort Parvati, a being who is both male and female. A healthy society is one that balances those self-same energies. And yet another manifestation of Parvati is Kali, the goddess of time, death, and endings. And, of course, Lord Shiva shows up from time to time as the destroyer. In the fullness of time, the cycles of beginnings and endings will turn.

THE IMBALANCE

I find myself agreeing with radical feminists: America is, in a certain sense, a patriarchy. That means that, for too long, American society has exalted the masculine paradigm with its emphasis on power politics. America has also suppressed and subordinated the *flirt-fawn-facilitate* energies of the Eros Feminine. In another way, though, radical feminists are wrong. Most don't seek to replace the masculine power structure that is composed predominantly of men. They simply want to replace men in that masculine power structure, Animus gone wild. Perhaps they should heed the warnings of peace brokers like Scilla Elworthy, who thinks that, "To shape the future that is needed in our world ... we must bring the feminine back into balance with the masculine."[80]

Elworthy cites two examples of feminine power: Aung San Suu Kyi of Burma, who had faced down soldiers with rifles; and Nelson Mandela, who developed compassion for his captors during Apartheid. Though Elsworthy is correct to identify their feminine power, both Suu Kyi and Mandela were eventually assimilated into corrupt, decidedly masculine power structures. Elworthy is right, though, that more of our leaders need to reach for the "deep feminine qualities" which include "empathy, grace under fire... and the insistence that we are all connected." And yet these qualities can only form a layer atop the fundamental structural problems of state power, which are inherently masculine.

At the risk of oversimplifying, we can refer to the masculine and feminine paradigms simply as coercion and persuasion. Coercion is masculine. Persuasion is feminine. We architect our human systems around these paradigms.

Economic historian Dierdre McCloskey agrees. She writes: "About a quarter of national income, to be statistical about it, is earned from merely bourgeois and feminine persuasion: not orders or information but persuasion, 'sweet talk.'"[81]

Maybe this is why women hold more than 80 percent of marketing jobs. I dare say it's no accident that McCloskey gave us this insight, either: she was assigned the male gender at birth. Despite all the pain and uncertainly that comes with any decision to transition, transgender people must at least have a dual perspective most of us lack. McCloskey's perspective is unique in American letters. An interviewer once asked her what sets her apart, say, from a progressive or conservative.

"I think it's easy," she replied. "A liberal is someone who believes that there shouldn't be any masters, no tyrants. Not husbands over wives, not masters over slaves, not politicians over citizens, no hierarchies. Whereas the other two, in their own charming way, delight in coercion, in masters."[82]

At this point, it might strike us as odd to suggest that liberalism is feminine, especially as the most famous liberal philosophers throughout history were men. Still, these energies live in all of us, whatever our sex or gender. We are evolved beings, and evolution has programmed us with particular dispositions. There's no getting around that fact. As a parent, one can watch the programming become activated in their children in times of fear. If they are sick or hurt, they go to their mother without prompting. If they hear a thunderclap, they pass right by their mother and go straight to Dad. Every time.

And so it is when we grow up. Humans turn to the Masculine when they are afraid, but that comes with risks. The Masculine is about control. And in a system of control, you're either the controller or the controlled. The ruler or the ruled. Identification with the controller through partisan affiliation or ideology doesn't change the fact that you have let fear subordinate you to a system with the power to protect and oppress. In America, both things are true: the U.S. government protects and persecutes, much like a father. For too long, we have turned to daddy, which doesn't allow us to grow up. And it's in this dynamic of paternalistic subordination that we find hierarchy.

DOMINANCE HIERARCHY

A dominance hierarchy is a social structure in which control is realized through the threat of violence. In humans, control starts in the form of a command. These commands must be backed by the use of coercion. In such systems, there are a few rulers, and many ruled. As the system normalizes, the rulers extend the reach of their authority. Rulers employ a mix of sticks, carrots, and propaganda to maintain their authority through time. In America, these mechanisms fall under the moniker of a *democratic republic*, which means that the structure sways in the winds of electoral politics. A dominance hierarchy is masculine. Submission to it is feminine. America is, thus, a patriarchy. But it's not quite a patriarchy where men have all the best jobs or hold all the positions of authority, though that's the way things used to be. Instead, America is a coercive power structure that men and women alike are happy to treat as a temple to power. In this way, we are no different from vervet monkeys. Our palaces are just prettier.

Why do primates and other animals organize into dominance hierarchies? Resources. In a world of scarcity, stronger, smarter group members get greater access to food, mates, and other desirable commodities. This also has the effect of ensuring a certain degree of genetic fitness, as the stronger, smarter group members are more likely to survive to pass their genes to successive generations. Humans aren't living in the bush anymore, but we have inborn toleration for hierarchy, even dominance hierarchy, because we are primates. But we have other inborn drives, too, like the desire for autonomy and equality. Unlike our more primitive cousins, we have the wisdom to determine whether and to what degree domination ought to be part of the modern social order.

I don't want to leave the impression that governments are the only kinds of dominance hierarchies. Most corporations are, too. Instead of threatening you with fines, guns, and jails, managers threaten you with your job. The control mechanisms are more or less the same: sticks, carrots, and propaganda. We'll discuss corporations later. We've already noted the strange irony that modern feminists embrace the dominance hierarchy. Such is true for most ideologues. The question in the mind of an ideologue is almost always about *who* should be in control. It's seldom about *whether* anyone should be in control. The urge to control, that blessed rage for order, animates all hierarchies, because hierarchies are made up of people who evolved from primates.

THE PROTECTION RACKET

"The state originated as a protection racket,"[83] writes political scientist James C. Scott. His thesis is deceptively simple: Cereal grain surpluses made possible during the Agricultural Revolution provided a ready means of exploitation. This system eventually became formalized as taxation. Grains are "visible, divisible, assessable, storable, transportable," according to Scott. The breakthrough that pushed humanity from the Paleolithic era of roving hunter-gatherers to the Neolithic period of settled agriculture meant that it was suddenly possible to control farming surpluses and the people who grew them.

It all started with opportunistic men.

Strong warriors made growers an offer they couldn't refuse: accept protection but be taxed. Control over the stored surpluses of tax-paying commoners became more sophisticated, as fortified villages and record-keeping systems made more extensive serfdom possible.

The paradox of settled agriculture is that what made these new kingdoms powerful is also what made them fragile. They depended on the threat of violence. The more the king imposed such systems on the producers, the more likely he was to see desertions, defections, or revolts. So he had to find a kind of kingly sweet spot. In other words, the wise king knew how to balance the sticks, carrots, and propaganda in such a way to maintain coherence. But history, goes the cliché, is written by the winners. So we tend to learn more about the societies that blossomed into empires instead of those that maintained modest peace or got ground into the dust. But empires, too, eventually fade. The history of civilization involves cycles of emergence and entropy. Rising and falling. Life and death.

Entropy in physics is the tendency of energy in a system to disperse. In human systems, we can describe entropy as a tendency towards disorder. In the development of an

ancient kingdom, a simple hierarchy forms from a strong
warrior class subjecting a weaker farming class. But that
development requires overcoming social entropy, which can
be described in simpler terms as just leaving people alone.
For many would-be brigands, the calculation was simple:
*I can use my strength and prowess to seize that guy's yields, or I can
learn how to grow crops and try to defend them.* Such decisions
had the macro effect of dividing people into classes. And in
those times, with life being nasty, brutish, and short, we can
imagine that the benefits of predation were high relative to
the risks.

But as predation became more systematic, these hierarchies grew. And so did kingdoms. It can be counterintuitive
to think of hierarchy as an emergent system, because it
requires a high level of centralized planning, management,
and coordination. But a hierarchy is an intermediate form
that develops in a condition of increasing organizational
complexity.

The real need to ward off competing bands of brigands eventually grew beyond the narrower calculation of
a protection racket. Such protections became more of a
necessary evil, justified by a rationale such as one might find
in Hobbes's *Leviathan*: *Sure, we're bullies. But we're going to take
your grain and protect you from these bigger bullies, so we don't all
become their slaves.*

The state's basic architecture, which separates people
into shades of ruler and ruled, came to be formalized
and even sacralized over time. The people, though many
suffered in serfdom, came to see the kingdom as a true
protector, and protection and predation became the dual
mandates of early states. This fact has been with us for
thousands of years. Aristocracy was blessed. Royalty was
divine. We saw these cultural trappings coevolve because
they let people live with the system, overcome entropy, and
keep their social structures from toppling.

Of course, some toppled under their own weight.

Competitors toppled others. Still others evolved.

THE EVOLUTION OF HIERARCHY

Whatever one thinks about modern life, most of us enjoy
a condition that stands in contrast to that of kings, vassals,
and indentured servitude. And yet hierarchy persists. How
did people go from roaming around on the savannah to
looking out from skyscrapers onto Tokyo or Vancouver?
What forces drove such change? And if we can begin to see
the pattern in those forces, do they offer clues about where
we're headed as a species?

In tracing the evolution of hierarchy through time, we'll
use history, complexity theory, and a dash of imagination.
But keep in mind that beneath it all are decidedly human
forces at play: Eros/Thanatos; Masculine/Feminine. What
follows, then, is a series of transitions, endings, and beginnings, which show up as distinct phases. The phases map
onto historical epochs imperfectly, with human progress
lurching in fits and starts. Hopefully, you'll be able to see
how our forebears organized and re-organized themselves
to deal with increased complexity.

Clans. Our ancestors hunted and gathered. We huddled
together in relatively small clans, sometimes grooming
each other, subsisting on whatever calories we could find.
Robin Dunbar's research showed a correlation between
the size of the human brain and the size of a social group,
which suggests that humans can only comfortably maintain
about 150 stable relationships.[84] The now-famous Dunbar's
number offers us a hint about the size of communal societies. As long as humans subsisted on foraged berries, boar
meat, and tubers, 150 seems like it would have been a
pretty reasonable limit in a condition of such scarcity. At
this scale, we might have developed close ties among your
fellow nitpickers. We might have been able to observe and
correct shirking in the group. But as soon as the food ran

low, the group would have had to divide up and move on. That is, until people realized you could plant some seeds and wait around for them to grow.

Kingdoms. Enter agriculture. Instead of wandering around as nomads or following herd animals, people planted crops and settled. Not everyone adopted agriculture simultaneously, which meant that some clans enjoyed sedentary plenty while others continued hunting and gathering in relative scarcity. But as populations grew, competition for resources intensified. The roving clans saw opportunities to raid. Clan collided with clan in bloody conflict. These deadly food fights meant that tribesmen needed to become mighty warriors able to act as a swift, single unit. Organizing for unitary action meant organizing as a hierarchy. With the shrewdest, most powerful warriors in command, your clan might just win. In the fullness of time, the victorious had to develop protection and subordination systems commonly referred to as kingdoms.

One wouldn't want to suggest people in the age of kingdoms didn't trade with one another; many did. But those who weren't traders were raiders. Such dangerous circumstances meant that your kingdom had to develop better social technology to survive. Better social technology just means better ways of organizing people, and the victors transmitted their war stories and successful strategies to descendants. While strength, courage, and superior weaponry went a long way, the right social technology could make or break a kingdom.

Empires. Great civilizations sprouted amid the remnants of war. The clan-king became a god-king. With all that power and glory, you'd think the king would be happy. But before any victory celebrations could subside, barbarian hordes or jealous rivals brought more assaults against them. Beset by hungry brigands, the emperor had to think preemptively. Sometimes emperors would seize more territory just to eliminate the threat of attacks in the future.

Other times it was just about holding it all together to be formidable enough for defense. Imagine Persian Emperor Darius III trying to keep his satrapies in line as Alexander of Macedon encroached.

But it wasn't just defense of the empire that weighed on the emperor; it was also all of the administrative decisions. More complex administration required more complicated layers of hierarchy, which meant delegating power to governors who would, in turn, delegate tasks to others. The emperor issued commands to his subordinates. Those down the chains of command carried out the orders.

As empires expanded, patronage relationships became the norm. Man lording power over man took on religious dimensions. Cultural values such as loyalty, honor, obedience, and patriotism firmed up the hierarchy. Without culture, the structure could be weakened either from internal dissent or from better-organized enemies.

In the interests of security and continued flourishing, the king delegated more and more responsibilities. Some trusted second-tier hierarchs with powerful armies. Julius Caesar had been given such an army, which he used to advance on Rome. Eventually, it became clear that the kingdom would have to bring the barbarians to heel and occupy their land, both to protect the realm and gain more territory for taxes. There is security in might, after all, and some empires stretched across whole continents. But an empire is complicated and costly to maintain.

RULES: A DETOUR

To this point, we have explored up to the age of empires. But let's pause these developments for a moment and talk about something that, though it risks being boring, is of enormous importance: rules. Maybe you remember the rule *raise your hand to speak*, from the third grade. But rules are far more important to order than ensuring kids fidget.

With the rise of rulers, we can see how people came to adopt formal hierarchies in which a king or emperor achieved order through dictates. But somewhere along the way, people started to organize themselves according to more generalized rules. Rules that get codified and enforced are called laws. Even emperors could appreciate those.

Diorite is a tough carving stone, but that's the idea. If you can manage to chisel into it, the image isn't going anywhere. The black stone stele inscribed with Hammurabi's Code was carved from that substance, and sat atop a two-and-a-half-foot relief carving of a standing Hammurabi receiving the law — symbolized by a measuring rod and tape — from the seated Shamash, the Babylonian god of justice. The entire seven-plus foot monument is covered in cuneiform.

Hammurabi's ancient code is more a record of legal precedents than anything. It confers consistency, primarily in meting out punishments. Depending on the crime, you might have to lose a tongue, an eye, or a hand. If you steal an ox, you have to pay back thirty times the ox's value. And so on. But even as Hammurabi's code stabilized Hammurabi's empire, it exposed the power of rules.

Good rules, evenly applied, can make a big difference to the overall social order. But they need not be like the grand maxims of Lockean Natural Law; they can be as simple as *drive on the right* or *yield to the left*. When everyone obeys these rules, they get to their destinations more quickly and avoid collisions. The resulting order is not something that any individual could achieve by issuing specific commands. Rules offer a regularizing function, and regularity helps people make plans over longer time horizons.

THE EVOLUTION OF HIERARCHY II

Now, the histories of empires seem always to come with a rise and a fall. One of the ways civilizations have coped with this has been to introduce new rules. Though neither perfect nor uniformly applied, the introduction of rules has meant that the rule of law could start to operate. Though the transition away from empires has come in fits and starts, more societies have turned away from tyranny.

Democracies. Humanity's first known democracies were born out of conflict. As much as we might like to think of this watershed moment in history as a product of the agora's philosophers, it turns out this system was the product of a negotiation, a kind of proto-social contract. In the 5th century BCE, the Greeks were doing well economically, trading wine and olives. Competitors, of course, saw the islands as an opportunity to gain through conquest.

"Athens was at war," writes author Paul Vallely, "for three years out of every four over almost two centuries. More than that, the latest military technology was the trireme, the fast warship of the time, whose three banks of oars needed lots of men to row them."[85]

Suddenly, ordinary citizen crewmen had political heft. The poorest sections of society wanted to have a say if they were going to defend the islands. So they instituted a simple rule: majoritarian decisions. The idea of *one man, one vote* enjoyed a golden age among Mediterranean city-states. Though the people's majoritarian power was not absolute, the development was successful enough to emulate it to this day. Greek democracy was arguably more direct and participatory — at least among those males with suffrage rights.

Though these democratic experiments succeeded in containing despotism, the people were still vulnerable to demagogues who could play on their fears and prejudices to gain power. And indeed, democracy ran the risk of legitimating mob rule, as minorities could be left powerless. It would take further developments to prevent tyranny of the majority.

Republics. The earliest republic was, like many that came after, a product of violent overthrow. The earliest republicans had simply had enough of brutal power being lorded over them, and yet they needed leadership. Romans, having expelled their Etruscan kings, tried to establish a peaceful kingdom. But that also ended in violence. Finally, they established rule by the three hundred-person senate. The senators jockeyed to become consuls, but all represented the people.

Quite apart from the unsavory history of kings issuing fiats, the senate could successfully process more information. In other words, the system – a deliberative body – was better able to handle increasing complexity from around the realm. The republican model also enabled a relatively more complex form of society to spring from the detritus of prior kingdoms. At the center of their representative system lay the social technology of making and recording laws, markedly different from the rule of a king. The Roman Republic's economic and social life was predictable and peaceful for nearly five hundred years.

Most of us are aware of the sorry story of Rome's step backward into empire. Such is a risk any time lawmakers delegate power, and especially military power. After the end of the Roman Republic, it would be another thousand years before the rule of law would return to Europe. Only this time, it would arise in the wisdom of adjudicators resolving tensions among people (English Common Law) instead of legislators writing statues to regulate people (Justinian Civil Law). Had the more masculine Justinian Law not so thoroughly suppressed the spread of the more feminine Common Law, the latter might have become the most resilient and flexible form of governance yet devised. Each of these forms of law would inform the next phase of our evolving institutions, and even today, these two forms of law operate in modern societies.

Constitutional Republics. The achievements of past republics were impressive but not sustainable. Most of the world continued in systems of hierarchy and patronage that lasted for nearly two thousand years. Still, revolutionary fires burned in the minds of those who were wary of kings and empires. Only this time, the revolutionaries set in motion a couple of experiments that would reshape much of the world. More and more of the world moved towards what political theorist Francis Fukuyama famously called "the end of history."[86]

Stitching together features of past democracies and republics, the revolutionaries designed a new social operating system. This experiment's genius included various means to devolve authority and set political power upon itself to contain it. Whether in the separation of powers, checks and balances, or enumerated rights, it became clear that it was possible to rein in the excesses of power through constitutional design.

The commercial activity and human improvement these systems unleashed set humanity on a trajectory towards unprecedented material abundance and scientific advancement. One could argue that these social operating systems successfully constrained the imperial ambitions of despots and ideologues. Constitutions allowed beleaguered nations like Germany and Japan to reconstitute themselves after the devastating World Wars. In some instances, constitutional republics have enabled hierarchies to begin the transition to the next phase. Along with its new rules, a new culture emerged; equality, toleration, and civil rights expanded under these regimes, sometimes with culture as a leading indicator, sometimes not. But as successful as the constitutional republic has been, it is not the end of history.

Despite eighteenth-century revolutions in France and America, hierarchy is still the dominant form of social organization throughout most of the world. That is to say, much of the world's people are still stratified like medieval Europe or feudal Japan as compared with modern Switzerland. Even the United States — that once great beacon of freedom — now bears a striking resemblance to Imperial

Rome. The American Founders had made improvements by creating institutional checks on power. Yet the checks are weak. The hierarchy has grown. The paradox here is that as checks weaken further, hierarchy will continue to grow. But as the hierarchy grows, power becomes unstable. Society is vulnerable.

THE LIMITS OF HIERARCHY

What we have just described, then, is a series of transitions. But why did these transitions take place? Remember that, though dominance hierarchies are moderately sophisticated human systems, they originate by simple means: men being assholes. More tactfully, people use threats to get others to do what they want.

We began this chapter by discussing one particular social force: Eros Masculine. This urge to control, which creates a coercion paradigm, ends up growing to protect and perpetuate itself. We bolstered that claim by citing the anthropological evidence of early states. James C. Scott, for example, teaches us that governments started as protection rackets. After that, you had to figure out how to manage the increasing complexity.

Now that you can see how hierarchies appear and evolve, we need to understand how they break down. To lubricate understanding, we have to recognize that human systems, like other parts of nature, operate according to physical laws. From there, following complexity science, we can discover real theoretical limits to how we organize ourselves. Then we can look for evidence that we are reaching the limits of hierarchy.

The easiest way to illustrate that human systems are subject to physical laws is to think of them as information processors seeking to overcome entropy. The *individual* processes information and energy. The *collective* also processes information and energy. *People* process information to do work. *The system* processes information to exist.

If we imagine that each individual is a kind of node or router to which other nodes can respond, it's easy to see that there are limits to what any given node can process at any given time. We know, at least, that every byte of information in the universe would fry the neural circuitry of any single person, no matter how smart or capable. Likewise, as consumers, it's easy to see practical limits to the number of calories one can consume, the number of decibels one can listen to, or the number of watts one uses to power a smartphone. When we organize ourselves into different kinds of human systems, information gets processed in different ways.

But all systems must respect their physical limits.

In the earliest days of the clan kingdom, the relationship between the individual and the collective was simple. Eventually, though, a single king might direct the actions of a significant number of people, such as men conscripted to build a temple. Then, as smaller kingdoms got subsumed under larger organizations, the collective's complexity increased. But that meant a *decrease* in complexity for any given individual in the system. In other words, the more layers of management you added, the simpler the orders became. For a slave working in the clan kingdom, the task might be: *dig up slabs from the quarry and organize them by size and color.* For slaves working in an empire, the task might only be *dig up slabs from the quarry.* A separate task, *organize them according to a plan*, would go to another slave.

"Large-scale human systems executed relatively simple behaviors," writes complexity scientist Yaneer Bar-Yam, "and individuals performed relatively simple individual tasks that were repeated by many individuals over time to have a large-scale effect."[87] So you could have a whole lot of people working on large-scale projects, such as a construction project or farming.

But in time, the behavior of the individuals became

more varied, as did the collective tasks. Diverse individual actions imply the system overall is becoming more complex. The work of building a temple would be far more straight-forward than managing a distant satrapy.

"This required reducing the branching ratio by adding layers of management that served to exercise local control," Bar-Yam adds. "As viewed by higher levels of management, each layer simplified the behavior to a point where an individual could control it. The hierarchy acts as a mechanism for communication of information to and from management." [88]

We can imagine messages passing up and down the chains of command. Caesar expresses a preference for features in the new coliseum. That message would go to the governor of the Gauls. The governor would discuss matters with the builder, and so on down the line. Those at the site might discuss feedback and report it back up to Caesar, through lots of wax, parchment, and jawboning.

Bar-Yam notes that management starts to act as a filter. Information gets reduced on the way up. Today we call this *briefing*. Executives at the top have to process data to make decisions. Without briefs, executives become overloaded. But as decisions get made, information flows down the chain of command. Directives can get more complicated as they travel back down. Middle management is delegated, with authority, to ensure that simpler executive strategies are sufficiently bulked up and broken down into tactics. Such usually takes the form of detailed plans, divided and subdivided into tasks to be performed by subordinates. As information increases and becomes more varied, the layers of hierarchy stack up.

But when *people* are arranged in this structure, grow-ing collective complexity depends on reducing individual complexity. This can mean making once-rich information thinner, so that subordinates can process it. Whether we're talking about soldiers on the front line or workers on an assembly line, task specialization requires simplification. That means that you need more people doing *different* things, but each person doing *fewer* things. Again, such branching means more collective complexity, but less individual complexity.

Trouble is, the branching can't go on forever. Whether in ancient Rome or modern Washington, something has to give.

THE BREAKDOWN OF HIERARCHY

"The point at which the collective complexity is the maximum individual complexity, the process breaks down," says Bar-Yam.

This is true for anyone in any layer of management, all the way up. In hierarchies, the system retains coherence by having a single person make decisions. But that system is only as complex as its most complex decision maker. Hierarchies can provide no greater complexity. Beyond that, there must be some sort of transition. Either managers and subordinates lateralize, taking on more independent decision-making authority — or the system collapses.[89]

As we start to understand these limits, it's silly to talk about how this or that president handles a complex crisis. More importantly, it is foolish to think they ought to handle such crises.

Nobel Prize-winning economist Friedrich A. Hayek similarly cautioned us. When both central economic planning and make-work programs were all the rage, Hayek saw a fatal flaw: Knowledge is distributed among as many individuals as there are in society. Each person's knowledge is informed by the "particular circumstances of time and place."[90]

Hayek's insight is more important today than ever. In our dynamic world, the circumstances of time and place are not only mind-bogglingly diverse, but changing at a dizzying rate. That's why the great economist urged humanity to put more faith in entrepreneurs than in high minds. Not only do entrepreneurs have incentives to focus on local knowledge, they must respect the knowledge transmitted in market prices. But who cares about prices?

Prices are information wrapped in incentives. That means that prices allow individuals to take action in a vast sea of other minds with different perspectives. Social plans are the purview of experts, but almost always formulated far away from our peculiar circumstances, neither informed nor incentivized by the pheromone trails of price signals. Instead, plans originate in the technocrat's mind based on 'knowledge' contrived in the vapors of abstraction. Knowledge forged in the fires of experience, frequently informed by modest failures, discipline the entrepreneur. Of course, the planner will almost always cite some 'study' that confirms her priors. But studies rarely provide local knowledge. And that's their flaw.

In Scott Shane's book *Dismantling Utopia: How Information Ended the Soviet Union*, the author offers a passage that ought to be taught in every economics class:

> My informal survey suggested that some of the longest lines in Moscow were for shoes. At first I assumed that the inefficient Soviet economy did not produce enough shoes, and for that reason, even in the capital, people were forced to line up for hours to buy them…. Then I looked up the statistics.
>
> I was wrong. The Soviet Union was the largest producer of shoes in the world. It was turning out 800 million pairs of shoes a year — twice as many as Italy, three times as many as the United States, four times as many as China. Production amounted to more than three pairs of shoes per year for every Soviet man, woman, and child.
>
> The problem with shoes, it turned out, was not an absolute shortage. It was a far more subtle malfunction. The comfort, the fit, the design, and the size

mix of Soviet shoes were so out of sync with what people needed and wanted that they were willing to stand in line for hours to buy the occasional pair, usually imported, that they liked.

At the root of the dysfunction was the state's control of information. Prices are information — the information producers need in order to know what and how much to produce. In a market for a product as varied in material and design as footwear, shifting prices are like sensors taped to the skin of a patient in a medical experiment; they provide a constant flow of information about consumer needs and preferences. When the state controlled information, it deprived producers of information about demand.[91]

Shane's observation doesn't extend just to shoes. When it comes to the forces of Eros Feminine, it extends to every desire of the human heart that anyone can serve.

That's why Hayek tutted the tendency to privilege abstract expertise over real feedback. Prices flow in dynamic relationships to different currents of local knowledge, which animate our human ecosystems. Prices are thus liquid, changing, and decentralized — measures of specific flows.

The architects of large hierarchies tend to prize abstraction over local knowledge; that is, unless they can use big data somehow. Big data allows a hierarchy to grow beyond what humans would be capable of if left to their own devices. But the data still have to be interpreted by human brains at some point. Until AI is sufficiently advanced, big data can only do so much. That's because technocratic knowledge still works only in predictable patterns of cause and effect, as some part pulled out of a fuselage. Emergence and evolution simply don't compute with a planner who needs control, even when imagining the universe itself.

"There cannot be design without a designer; contrivance without a contriver; order without choice," wrote Christian apologist William Paley in 1800.

Paley's position is known as the argument from design,

and some use it in theological debates. Paley's intuitions here are not unwarranted, though. Emergent systems are counterintuitive. But if intelligent-design thinking has done damage to our understanding of cosmology and evolution, it has done more damage to economics. Paley would have been just as gobsmacked as the Soviet apparatchiks as they tried to figure out how a million preferences could design a shoe, while a million shoes, contrived by a brilliant contriver, could sit in St. Petersburg warehouses collecting dust.

Through the lens of Eros Feminine, it's easy to see how a Soviet factory could fail to produce the right amount of shoes, or screws, or loaves of bread, all of which most of us take for granted. But this lens should also prompt us to be suspicious of what America's planners are up to today. They're not like the Soviets, exactly. Their plans are more insidious because they're less obvious. Instead of big, nationalized industries, we have a complicated array of dependent industries. They depend on some regulation here, a subsidy there. In the American system, planners can paper over errors for a long time. But in time, the failures accumulate. Authorities simply cannot adequately respond to the decision making challenges.

As Bar-Yam warns, "this is true whether we're talking about dictatorships, or communism… or representative democracies today." [92]

Hierarchies fail because neither self-appointed dictators nor elected officials can identify what is right for a complex society. Never mind that society is composed of diverse individuals; it's all beyond the comprehension of any single person. Regardless of anyone's intended result, the outcomes vary from what planners intend.

In diversity and scale, society has changed drastically since the time of the pharaohs. And yet most people believe that significant decisions can and ought to be made by authorities on everyone's behalf. Maybe it's a plan to build a new nation amid sectarian violence so that democracy will soften the hearts of religious extremists. Maybe it's subsidies for Solyndra solar cells or GE Wind turbines to fashion the energy sector in the image of Bill McKibbin. Maybe it's a scheme to ban worker poverty by setting a price floor on labor, the same rate in Mississippi and Manhattan. Maybe it's a plan to lock everyone down in a pandemic and provide bread and circuses until it goes away. Maybe it's a plan to make healthcare more affordable that somehow ends up making it less affordable.

These schemes burn like fires in the planners' minds, but so often turn into charred detritus. The red ink hides the original blueprints, but they're there somewhere. By the time the errors come to light, the planners have moved onto the next scheme.

As state hierarchy grows, entrepreneurs learn to find a way to survive in the technocratic matrix. Some find that it's good for business because it's bad for his competitors. The paradox here is that these predator corporations become enormous, and their gigantism prompts popular outcries, some of which are justified. Others are just scapegoating. It's fashionable to mindlessly blame corporations and to think authorities are there to save us. Ironically, voters oblige the technocrats to rein in the very behemoths they had a hand in creating. Regulation almost always ends up making these companies even larger as upstarts can't afford to comply. With little competition, the big boys grow bigger. New ventures that would diminish their outsized profits and monopoly growth never come into existence at all. These unborn ventures trace invisible skylines as ghost firms in a parallel universe, a world that never was.

When a technocrat sets plans in motion from some federal agency's top floor, she almost always claims knowledge she does not have and destroys phenomena she cannot see.[93] It's counterintuitive. But it's just one reason why it's rash to centralize anything important. Whenever you hear someone cry 'trust the experts' during a crisis, that's precisely the time to open your eyes, watch, wait, and *question*.

Order emerges from human action and not from human design. Because the technocrats' knowledge is limited, technocratic hierarchies are limited. The knowledge required to *run* the federal government effectively would fry anyone's neural circuitry. Likewise, if a given system isn't equipped to process its own complexity, one of two things will happen: change or collapse.

It's time, therefore, to mount an ardent challenge to technocracy. Make no mistake: we are still living in a technocratic age. But that age is coming to a close. The only question is whether it will go out with a bang or a whimper.

TECHNOLOGY AND PROGRESS

Despite all of these concerns, there has been progress. Even though the Eros Masculine is in control, Eros Feminine flows and grows in the interstices. Returning to our biological metaphor, it's as if society has gone from being something like a clump of ferns to a higher-order ecosystem such as a forest. As societies overcome entropy, they become even more rich and diverse, like a rainforest. All this, despite all the temples to hierarchy pushing up through the canopy.

When I close my eyes, I see the ruins of abandoned pyramids deep in the jungles of Guatemala. The Maya built them up out of limestone, high above the forest, defying the earth. They made blood sacrifices to the gods. A thousand years on, the handiwork of Ix Chel, the goddess of fertility and midwifery, is most pronounced. It is emerald and lush.

I open my eyes. Effort and innovation manage to sprout up from the cracks left in the monolith. Such is the power of the Eros Feminine. Ventures exploit gray areas in the law until massive constituencies form. Creativity, innovation, and sweet talk are responsible for the unprecedented material abundance we currently enjoy. Some estimates put technology's contribution as high as 87 percent, relative to capital and labor.[94] But technological advances don't occur in a vacuum.

The circumstances created by institutions and culture allow for what evolutionary zoologist Matt Ridley describes as "the decentralization of the production and testing of new ideas." Decentralization is a precondition of progress. But why? Why should there be, say, more garage tinkering and fewer Manhattan projects?

If innovation is so vital to human progress, as most economists agree it is, shouldn't the taxpayer be asked to 'invest' more in state-sponsored innovation? Sometimes it's important to synthesize two opposing views. But in this case, we must draw battle lines. Let's call them Centralist and the Decentralist.

In the Centralist corner, we have economist Marianna Mazuccato. She argues that governments need to increase research and development budgets massively. After all, some of the greatest inventions have originated in public-ly-funded programs such as the military or academia. The Centralist view is Eros Masculine.

In the Decentralist corner, we have economic historian Dierdre McCloskey. She argues that humanity has experi-enced a Great Enrichment thanks to "innovism," her term for decentralized innovation. After a century of doubling, starting in 1860, real income increased by a factor of thirty. As the world was liberated, more and more tinkerers participated in enriching it. The Decentralist view is Eros Feminine.

Who is right?

On the one hand, we have GPS technology, thanks to the U.S. government. Commercial advances have certainly come out of public R&D. It's easy to point to benefits, and it's nigh impossible to imagine all costs, including any advances foregone. In other words, when the central state pulls talent and resources from the garage economy, fewer people and firms will have the resources to have a go. If so many advances come from government investments, why don't we see more innovation with more government involvement? As hedge fund manager Michael Gibson quips, "I'd love to hear about all those successful spin-off technologies from the Soviet space program."[95] Why Gibson would want to downplay the contribution of Big Muff distortion pedals or Sovtek tubes, I cannot say.

With the Decentralist approach, all these folks working on their little projects meant some of the little projects become very big ones. College dropout John Mackey's little organic food store in Austin, TX got big. College dropout Steve Jobs's little computer maker in California got big. Garage experimenters and nimble startups test their ideas for betterment. According to McCloskey, political liberalism permitted, encouraged, and honored *innovism*. She prefers that term to the charged and misleading term capitalism, "with its erroneous suggestion that the modern world was and is initiated by piling up bricks and bachelors' degrees."[96]

Later we'll explore what an evolved liberalism might look like in the twenty-first century, bruised and battered as the philosophy is. Until then, our job is to talk about the pathologies of collapse. On that note, when it comes to the wisdom of massive transfers into research and development, I'm taking sides.

The Decentralists win because:

- Innovism is antifragile;
- Innovism is humane;
- Innovism is affordable; and
- Innovism works.

The trouble is, we don't have enough of it.

It's not just that we need more economic decentralization. We need more decentralization within organizations, too. All the hand-wringing about the so-called Fourth

Industrial Revolution misses something fundamental: the corporate form is due for a significant shift. Machine-learning algorithms, big databases, and automation are all changing the business landscape. But the most important innovation comes in changes to the social technology of the firm itself. In other words, how might people better organize themselves in service of missions? The corporation is an artifact of Eros Masculine, a hierarchy. The corporate form itself is due for an upgrade.

The Corporate Form

Even as innovation continues to drive progress, there are areas in which change is much needed. It's not just in the halfway house of corporate technocracy that complicated systems threaten to cause collapse. We continue to rely on outdated corporate forms. Many haven't changed much in two hundred years. Not only does the law bake in certain kinds of structural hierarchies, such as C-corps, but many executives still use the scientific management model akin to that introduced by Frederick Winslow Taylor in 1911.

In Taylor's view, the responsibility of a firm's management — usually a factory — was to determine the most efficient way for the employee to do the job, train the employee in that way, and otherwise offer them performance incentives. Taylor broke each job down into standardized tasks, analyzed these to figure out which were essential, and then timed the worker with a stopwatch. With any unnecessary work eliminated, employees could follow scientific management's machine-like routine and the firm would become far more productive. In certain ways, it worked. As long as managers could increase efficiency, and employees could tolerate being a cog to get a paycheck, Taylor's scientific management worked. But it had limits.

This way of doing things lobotomized the worker. Not only are employees sometimes in the best position to improve a process, allowing workers to seek better ways of doing things offers a level of creativity and autonomy that makes work more fulfilling. Such is especially true today: Executing management's way of doing things can be dehumanizing. It also locks out worker creativity, even as it rewards efficiency at the margin. Author Dan Pink assembles years of research and finds that what workers want is *autonomy*, *mastery*, and *purpose* — and that those workers will perform better with these than with mere sticks and carrots.

In the Taylorite firm, however, *managers think*, and *workers work*. Perversely, this can limit the manager, too. When a manager's responsibilities are primarily to manage — i.e. finding efficiencies, analyzing worker performance, and interpreting executive strategy — they can find that their world is also rather cramped. Workers accustomed to performing assigned tasks efficiently won't be as effective on their feet when problems arise; they can pass the buck straight to management as long as they hew to predetermined policies, procedures, and directives. Managers have to take responsibility for any failure that might have been avoided had the cog been allowed to use her cognition.

In many companies, the whole stratum of middle management creates no direct value, they are simply intermediaries going between the decision makers and the employees. That limits the manager's responsibilities to running a complicated switchboard and sticking their nose into other people's work. But the bigger the corporation gets, the more distant the decision makers are from a reality that ordinary employees see every day. From the perspective of the employee, management can seem clueless, often because they are. The top brass misses the subtlety of detecting problems and tensions beyond their office fishbowls.

Matters are no picnic for executives, either, though. Top-level decision makers suffer decision fatigue because they operate in a structure which requires them constantly to make decisions.

"This sort of decision fatigue can make quarterbacks prone to dubious choices late in the game and CFOs prone to disastrous dalliances late in the evening,"[97] writes *New York Times* columnist John Tierney. "It routinely warps the judgment of everyone, executive and non-executive, rich and poor…"[98] As executives face more internal complication and external complexity, we see burnout at every level.

While Taylorism was seen as an upgrade to the traditional hierarchical firm, the method suffers the same problems that afflict any hierarchy after a certain complexity point:

- *Degraded Information.* Information gets degraded as it passes up the chain of command to the executives, or down to the workers.

- *Bounded Authority.* Limiting workers' and employees' autonomy through zealous systematization means the firm loses collaborators' problem-solving potential.

- *Involuntary Subordination.* If you're paid to take orders and carry them out, there's very little room for autonomy, mastery, and purpose. Subordination can feel dehumanizing.

- *Tedium and Decision Fatigue.* At the bottom of the hierarchy, work can be tedious. At the top of the hierarchy, decision makers frequently have to take on too much.

- *Fragility.* Hierarchical systems are fragile in that if decision-making authority is located at the top among the few, bad decisions can be catastrophic.

In short, Taylorism doesn't scale well. If a transition is upon us, we need to imagine ways more people can be included in the processes of load balancing complexity and making things flow. Some will figure it out, but not before a tremendous corporate die-off.

GovCorp

If you aren't experiencing a little bit of cognitive disso-
nance by now, I'm not doing it right. I expect about half of
readers can see company pathologies quite clearly, mainly
if they work within them. The other half can see the
government pathologies quite clearly, especially if they run
those companies. The goal here is to demonstrate that both
forms are vulnerable. The bulk of the American economy
is composed of hierarchies nested in hierarchies. And most
are dependent on one great big hierarchy.

Now, if you're still laboring under the illusion that
corporations and governments are sufficiently different
creatures, consider this thought experiment from political
philosopher Michael Huemer:

> Imagine that someone proposed that the key to
> establishing social justice and restraining corporate
> greed was to establish a very large corporation,
> much larger than any corporation hitherto known
> — one with revenues in the trillions of dollars. A
> corporation that held a monopoly on some extreme-
> ly important market within our society. And used its
> monopoly in that market to extend its control into
> other markets. And hired men with guns to force
> customers to buy its product at whatever price it
> chose. And periodically bombed the employees and
> customers of corporations in other countries. By
> what theory would we predict that this corporation,
> above all others, could be trusted to serve our inter-
> ests and to protect us both from criminals and from
> all the other corporations? If someone proposed to
> establish a corporation like this, would your trep-
> idation be assuaged the moment you learned that
> every adult would be issued one share of stock in
> this corporation, entitling them to vote for members
> of the board of directors? If it would not, is the

governmental system really so different from that
scenario as to explain why we may trust a national
government to selflessly serve and protect the rest of
society?[99]

It's not just that we probably can't trust these hierarchies not to collapse. It's also that we can't entirely trust
these hierarchies.

THE TAO OF TRANSACTION COSTS

In pointing out the limits of hierarchy, though, we should
offer it due respect. After all, as we showed in our evolution story above, different forms of hierarchy have been a
necessary transitional step. Nobel economist Ronald Coase
put his finger on an important insight when he wrote in
"The Nature of the Firm"[100] that companies organize
as hierarchies due to transaction costs. So as the world
'outside' responds to price signals, allocating accordingly, it
can be cheaper to organize bureaucratically inside. But that
is changing — fast.

With the advent of new management protocols and
collaboration technologies, transaction costs are going
down. It's no accident, then, that as those transaction costs
go down, complexity goes up. As we'll see, one key to life
after collapse is reducing transaction costs. Or, in simpler
terms, making organizations more collaborative and adaptive helps things *flow*. Helping things flow and reducing
transaction costs are, thus, two sides of the same coin.

Note that the hierarchies we have been discussing —
dominance hierarchies — are also *formal* hierarchies. They
include formal titles and transparent chains of command.
We should not trick ourselves into thinking that traditional
hierarchies are the only kind. Some organizations grow
hierarchies of a different sort.

New collaboration tools and management practices
reduce transaction costs. These can give rise to *competence*

hierarchies. For example, most people want to collaborate with specialists. When we are on the basketball court, we want to get the ball to a Jordan because his quotient of balls into baskets is higher than everyone else's. As these specialists earn more influence, they command a higher salary, earn a better reputation, and create more value. Far from being unfair, these more fluid hierarchies seem to be built into nature.

Adrian Bejan reminds us that everything evolves to provide greater access to the currents that sustain life, creating vascular systems.[101] It's no different for organizations.

"When nothing flows through our bodies, we are dead. When the water stops moving through the river basin, it too is dead; when material and information stop flying to and from a business, the business withers and dies. And so it goes, with everything."

But if our human systems can adapt to the currents of flow and change, they live. The question before us is, will they adapt? Bejan argues that a prerequisite is that the flow system, such as the firm, must be free to morph. The unfolding flow architecture is how the organization realizes its mission under constraints. In short, *Freedom is good for design.*" (Emphasis Bejan's.)

But how can freedom be good for *design*? Isn't the very mantra of emergence that an economy is "the result of human actions, not of human design"?[102] It most certainly is. Bejan's connotation is different: The design we see in nature, such as the river system's structure, a human circulatory system, or transportation arterials in cities, exist for a reason. Nature tends to generate structures that facilitate access to flow. They are not a product of William Paler's Intelligent Design. They are consequences of the Law of Flow.

FLOW OR DIE

We can take a perspective in the mind's eye, imagining ourselves just high enough above the world. One who takes this perspective doesn't claim the omniscience of a God or Technocrat. They can see patterns of flow which are expressions of what we might call the Law of Flow.[103] But to recognize its patterns doesn't mean that they can design our highly vascularized world in its totality. The control structures of the Eros Masculine are limited. So to take that perspective, one would have to fly too close to the sun. Indeed, we want to resist the urge to design systems atop flow systems which already exist. That's why here on earth, we are better to iterate, to tinker at the margins. And as we iterate, we figure out what flows better.

"There is a quality even meaner than outright ugliness or disorder," wrote Jane Jacobs, "and this meaner quality is the dishonest mask of pretended order, achieved by ignoring or suppressing the real order that is struggling to exist and to be served."[104]

Everything and everyone must be relatively free to morph to accommodate flow. Then we will begin to see fractals and golden ratios everywhere, for these are the Law of Flow's mathematical signatures. These are the expressions of healthy Eros Feminine. Gigantism has its limits, but in any living system, it is normal. The tiniest tributaries eventually link up to the big river, the aorta, the highway. These flows are dynamic. And though the patterns are recognizable, they are also unique, just as the infinite branches of a fractal create unceasing novelty as we zoom down into its wonders.

The fundamental problem, then, is this: where flow ends, collapse begins.

SATYAGRAHA

Mohandas opened his eyes.

Union Jacks flapped over sacred Hindu sites. Rickshaw drivers pulled ladies, dandies, and Redcoats. Soldiers, metal bedizened, strode on ancient avenues with an air of pomp. This picture somehow lent greater humanity to the lowest among us. Whether it was children shining jackboots in Bombay train stations or women begging for bread on Calcutta's streets, they bloody well had a job to do. Still, soldiers marched, sentinels guarded, and the Company made a rupee on every cup that warmed the bellies of souls far away.

Mohandas closed his eyes.

He saw resplendent Krishna, the eighth avatar of Vishnu, with his azure skin and feminine mien; how his chariot gleamed in the mind's eye. With him was Arjuna, the mightiest and most skilled of warriors, ready to fire arrows from faithful Gandiva. But as Krishna joined him on the chariot, Arjuna let the bow slip from his grasp. Arjuna had become despondent. He was worried about going to war with the blind king and his hundred sons. They were, after all, a part of him.

Mohandas opened his eyes.

He watched the lieutenant governors, chief commissioners, governors-in-council, company men, and functionaries as they moved among structures fashioned by foreign hands. Those structures, some dating back to the Company

Raj, had flattened the lush gardens and Ashoka groves where Brahmins once prayed, the Kashatryia once trained, and the Vaishya once harvested. Wide boulevards, busy streets, and narrow alleys cut organic cities up according to the hierarchy's geometric priorities. The colonizers had superimposed symbols of royalty and aristocracy over an ancient caste system.

Mohandas closed his eyes.

It was as if he'd taken on the body of Arjuna now. His golden armor glinted in the light of Krishna's visage, but sadness still weighed on his heart. How could he go to battle against his own? He sat down in his chariot. Then Krishna reminded him that it is they who have been corrupted. Krishna radiated as he reminded him to do what he was born to do: slay the enemy.

Mohandas opened his eyes.

How terrific and absolute was the British Raj! The Crown seemed so far away, yet it loomed off in the distance like monsoon clouds. Its authority covered the territory from the Veil of Kashmir to the Gulf of Mannar; from Kalat's cold deserts to the Burmese jungles. The Viceroy, who governed both the princely states and lands beyond, roamed a palace that rivaled that of any sovereign on earth.

Mohandas closed his eyes.

Krishna spoke:

> *O mighty Arjuna, even if you believe the self to be the subject of birth and death, you should not grieve. Death is inevitable for the living. Birth is inevitable for the dead. Since these are unavoidable, you should not sorrow. Every creature is un-man-ifested at first and then attains manifestation. When its end has come it once again becomes un-manifested. What is there*

to lament in this?[105]

From this truth, Arjuna opened his heart and his mind to Krishna, who went on to reveal the Royal Path. Once Arjuna accepted this path, Krishna prepared to reveal a glimmer of his divine nature. Such a divine nature includes that of the ocean and the syllable Om, the Ganges' flow, and the flow of time. Krishna is consciousness and the cosmos. Krishna is ahimsa. And in this cosmic vision, Krishna revealed that he is Vishnu.

Arjuna gasped:

> *I see all the sons of Dhritarashtra; I see Bhishma, Drona, and Karna; I see our warriors and all the kings who are here to fight. All are rushing into your awful jaws; I see some of them crushed by your teeth. As the rivers flow into the ocean, I see all the warriors of this world are flowing into your fiery jaws; all creatures rush to their destruction like moths into a flame.*[106]

Mahatma Gandhi opened his eyes.

3

THE BREAKDOWN OF OUR BELIEF IN LIBERALISM

A liberal "rhetoric" explains the good features of the modern world compared with earlier and later illiberal régimes — the economic success of the modern world, its arts and sciences, its kindness, its toleration, its inclusiveness, and especially its massive liberation of more and more people from violent hierarchies ancient and modern.

Dierdre McCloskey

Around 2,700 years ago, the Chinese philosopher Lao Tzu said,

The world is a sacred vessel that cannot be changed.
He who changes it will destroy it.
He who seizes it will lose it.[107]

Lao Tzu is speaking of the natural harmony of nonviolent human interaction, which is a liberal conception. Even though liberalism, the term, gained common currency in eighteenth-century Edinburgh, it has lived at all times within all peoples to varying degrees, waiting to be expressed as morality, justice, conscience, and virtue.[108]

An early species of liberalism animates the Hebrew

Talmud, which welcomes discourse and debate and leaves critical rules for living peacefully among other humans. One such story involves a goy who came to Shammai and provoked him, saying that he would convert to Judaism if Shammai could teach him the entire Torah while standing on one foot. Shammai dismissed the goy. But Rabbi Hillel welcomed him, saying: "That which is hateful to you do not do to another; that is the entire Torah, and the rest is its interpretation. Go and learn."[109] Presumably, Hillel was standing on one foot when he said it. Still, in doing so, he taught us toleration, graciousness in the face of provocation, and an important variation of the Golden Rule. That is liberalism.

Hillel is known for other maxims in addition to the above: "If I am not for me, who will be for me? And when I am for myself alone, what am I? And if not now, then when?"

In other words, your primary responsibility is to yourself, but that is not your only responsibility. You should also expand the circle. So, yes, that means embracing rational self-interest, such as what you might see in Adam Smith's baker and the butcher. But also use compassion and benevolence, such as that of the father and the neighbor, which one might find in *The Theory of Moral Sentiments*. This, too, is liberalism.

In the Vedic traditions, including Hinduism, Buddhism, and Jainism, the yogis speak of *ahimsa*. It is the primary, the basis of everything: nonviolence in speech, thought and action. So even as we leave room for discourse and debate, we should take care not to wound ourselves or others with words. The liberalism of this book is an ethic of respect for persons. And we should certainly not threaten or injure them if they do not threaten us.

I remember reading an account of ahimsa in, of all places, a coffee table book of daily aphorisms by Rolf Gates, a former U.S. Army special forces who later turned to yoga. As a cadet, he had heard a recruiter say that the Rangers specialized in "missions that entailed a high degree of shock and violence."[110] The young Gates thought that was "cool," so joined them.

"As a man of violence, I thought I was doing the right thing — and, so, for that matter, did everyone around me. As a young man, I did exactly what our society tells young men to do, and I performed my service with devotion." Through yoga, which it turned out was more than postures and poses, Gates kept his service and dropped the violence. Instead, he has devoted his life to ahimsa, a way of peaceful being old as Sanskrit.

Ahimsa is the first of the *Yamas*, which are conscious self-regulation practices designed to free us from being victims of our impulses. What might seem curious to the Western mind is the idea that *we are not separated*. In the Vedic traditions, violence is more likely when we cleave *you* from *me*. But why wouldn't we? I have a body. You have a body. I have a self. You have a self. So there is something rather odd in the idea that you and I are somehow one. I, Max Borders, am probably a stranger to you. The suggestion of a unified being seems like something people say after eating magic mushrooms. And yet most Westerners are familiar with the maxim *love thy neighbor as thyself.* Does it matter whether we are speaking in metaphysics or metaphor?

For thousands of years, the sifus, the rabbis, and the yogis have been onto something. That *something* is the essence of liberalism, a philosophy that author Leonard Read summed up in simple terms as "let anyone do anything he pleases, so long as it is peaceful." These don't sound like the words of a man who worked his way up to managing the Los Angeles branch of the U.S. Chamber of Commerce and went on to found an economics think tank.

But Read, as if hearing the echoes of a thousand wise men, offered something of a mystical way to liberalism. He thought, for example, that anyone "who acknowledges an infinite consciousness cannot help respecting fellow human beings as the apertures through whom infinite consciousness flows and manifests itself."[111] Sounds like some kind of mystic. The evocation of an infinite consciousness, of which we are all a part, isn't your run-of-the-mill God-talk in early-'60s America. For Read, it reconciles narrow individualism with a deep respect for others, who are all sacred aspects of a larger self, or set of interconnected selves. This way of thinking is neither individualist nor collectivist, per se, but integral.

The consequence of such integration should not be to make us all pacifists. To the extent possible, it is to keep ourselves from becoming predators or paternalists or politicians who do not know the way of peace. Not only will the predators always be among us, but we will always have a responsibility to defend ourselves and to defend the innocent. It is in threatening or initiating violence that we stray from the *dhamma*, which is the path to liberation.

Of course, one consequence of liberalism might well be a market economy, in which people produce and trade peacefully. And that's good, but that is too narrow a conception. Production and exchange are but a sliver of what it means to live well within a flourishing society. The liberal's preoccupation with economics comes from the idea of society as a vibrant, living system. And as we have seen, living systems are self-organizing — living systems flow.

The idea of society as a living system lies quietly at the heart of our more familiar variants. Adam Smith, among the first to use the term liberal, thought that if societies followed "the liberal system of free exportation and free importation,"[112] they would become a universal empire of abundance. In other words, economics was a science of letting things flow. *The Wealth of Nations* was published in 1776, the same year Thomas Jefferson and a group of seditious signatories held certain truths to be self-evident. If they could only see the human progress that has unfolded since.

The word liberal can be misleading, though. In today's usage, *liberal* sits at one end of a one-dimensional spectrum with *conservative* at the other end. That's not what we're talking about. In our sense, a liberal is one concerned with *liberating* people — from violence, oppression, and poverty. *Libertas perfundet omnia luce.* Freedom will flood all things with light. The liberal project, begun in earnest during the enlightenment, animated a band of polymaths. They drew up the blueprints for the first liberal order in Philadelphia, 1789.

Since the moment of its birth, the experiment has teetered, wobbled, and been threatened from every side. Including the inside. The Republic has been challenged. The Constitution has been eroded. But as of this writing, it's all still here. Americans have endured depressions, wars, and civil wars. *We* are still here — but our collective belief in a liberal order is at a nadir. Steadily, including occasional, punctuated attacks, liberalism has been under siege. Americans have turned their backs on our founding ideals and then blamed them for everything under the sun.

Today, the idea that freedom will flood all things with light is but a candle in a windstorm, shielded by a few. We have come to a point in history that we will have to re-conceive liberalism. When our belief in liberalism breaks down, our belief in each other breaks down, too. When we try to exert too much control over each other, as Lao Tzu saw more than two-thousand years ago, it will bring sorrow. But without "compulsion, men will live in harmony."[113]

THE LEVIATHAN FORMULATION

The breakdown in liberalism originates in the shadow. There is a masculine urge to control in our unconscious minds, which we have suggested comes from fear. We project that urge, then rationalize it, and then try to impose it on the world as a political ideology. Such projections act as a veil of illusion between ourselves and the world, causing us to fail to see reality and tempting us into the mechanisms of compulsion. From these shadow impulses, three powerful concepts have emerged to threaten liberalism.

The first comes from philosopher Thomas Hobbes. Even though Hobbes is considered a liberal when his work is taken as a whole, his Leviathan Formulation threatens liberalism itself. That formulation boils down to this:

1. Assume that sovereignty rule, functions as a kind of monopoly over some territory;

2. People living together can only be a community if they have a common system of rules;

3. A common rule system can only exist if those rules come from a common source, a ruler, which is an authority of such power that it must have the final say.[114]

Rule. Rules. Ruler.

Political theorist Vincent Ostrom says this sort of relationship "must involve fundamental inequalities in society. Those who enforce rules must necessarily exercise an authority that is equal in relation to the objects of that enforcement effort."[115] That is to say, the rest of us.

One day, as if by divine will, a man named Desh Subba wrote to me from Nepal. I had just written the preceding paragraph under the header "The Leviathan Formulation." I had never met Subba, but he wanted to share his philosophical perspectives. I almost didn't pay any attention at all, because it's easy to ignore unsolicited contacts. Still, Subba had at that moment sent me an article he'd written on Thomas Hobbes, which piqued my curiosity. Synchronicity and all that. In the article, Subba concludes:

"To avoid the fear of the state of nature; [Hobbes] created artificial social contract and handed over to absolutely [sic] power (monarchy, government and common-wealth). [sic] Entire political philosophy of Hobbes wandered around the hide and seek of fear."[116]

Desh Subba also put fear right at the center of the Leviathan Formulation. And he is right. Hobbes himself wrote the rudiments while in France, having fled the English Civil War. Our formulations and philosophies are just architectures we construct around raw emotional centers we evolved more than 100,000 years ago. Since then, humanity has built Leviathan out of fear, to varying degrees. In this way, one can say the state is an externalization of our fear. It offers the false idea that the more power we give it, the less fearful we will need to be. Despite my liberalism, I have never so enthusiastically embraced the overwhelming power of Leviathan as I did in the days after September 11, 2001. In time, I came to regret that embrace. I was under the spell of Thanatos Masculine.

Hobbes's rule-rules-ruler formulation has so thoroughly infected our minds that most of us have trouble questioning it. It not only has a persuasive internal logic, but has been our reality for so long that it's hard to think of things any other way. Maybe all those punks and hippies riding around with "Question Authority" stickers were onto something. Maybe we didn't pay enough attention to those hippies and punks. Instead, we listened to our urge to control. Yet it's curious that so much of liberalism — at least, the American founding's legal doctrine — has accepted the Leviathan Formulation from the start. The founders wanted to figure out how to check power while preserving it. So much has changed since 1789.

THE GREAT TEMPTATION

The second concept, though distinct, is related to the first. We can think of The Great Temptation as a psychological outgrowth of the Leviathan Formulation. Once we accept the logic of rule-rules-ruler, we are in a certain kind of intellectual box, one that imprisons our imaginations and mutes our creativity. And in that box, we tell ourselves all manner of stories about the necessity of political subordination. Enter the pundits. The policy wonks. The activists. *Now that we have it, how can it be used?*

The assumed necessity of this necessary evil ends up masking its evil. The Great Temptation forces us into crude binary thinking: *Either authority acts or the worst follows.* And those stories we tell take us down any number of roads, depending on what social problem we hold up as the mother of all problems. Fear's voice whispers in the background.

But the Great Temptation always comes with risks. To fight the war on drugs risks treating half the population as criminals. To fight inequality risks cutting the most productive down to size. To fight a recession risks creating a depression. To fight racism risks racializing everything. To fight climate change threatens society's living systems. To fight terrorism risks creating an imperial surveillance state.

The most insidious part of the Great Temptation is that it's a low-cost proposition in the near term. Once you're tempted, you don't have to do anything except let it happen. You just have to do your duty, which is to put your faith in a supreme authority and forget that behind that authority is a vast apparatus of compulsion. Such a proposition, relative to say *working with our neighbors*, appeals to our inner teenager, who is both indignant and lazy.

I can hear my interlocutors now. *Some problems can only be solved when we all act together,* they'll say. *It would be nice if we could all agree to act together for the good of all, but this rarely happens. There is always a group that is feckless, or ignorant, or selfish. When confronted with problems requiring collective action, their very existence justifies the existence of concentrated power.*

COLLECTIVE ACTION

It would seem, then, that collective action problems are everywhere. These are situations in which all individuals would be better off cooperating, but fail to do so because of conflicting interests. They are therefore discouraged in some way from acting as one.

One classic example might be a streetlight from which multiple parties would derive benefit. My benefiting from a streetlight that I pay for doesn't prevent you from benefiting from the same light, even if you don't pay. Because our access to light, respectively, can't easily be controlled, it can't easily be sold to either of us, as it would be in a normal market transaction. Unlike transactions for other types of goods, such as your giving me $20 for this book, public goods can be more complicated. Goods such as street lights can be underproduced. That's why most people default to authorities to provide such goods.

Concerns about collective action loom large in our explorations. We want to see the mutual benefit that occurs in narrow market transactions extend further out to more people, creating omni-win dynamics. We hope these omni-win dynamics extend to as much of humanity as possible, and to the natural environment. But we don't want to be *forced* into the Leviathan Formulation.

Still, most people think that government authority is justified, primarily to solve collective action problems. Pseudonymous blogger Scott Alexander, in his viral sensation "Meditations on Moloch," asks us to consider the story of a group of fish farmers on a lake.[117] If they sign a compact and no one defects, waste from the fish farms will be controlled, the lake will stay clean, and the fish farms will be sustainable. But if anyone figures out that they can profit more if they defect from using the costly filtration system, they'll all end up defecting, and the lake will be ruined. Therefore, suggests Alexander, bring on Leviathan.

To keep the lake clean, we're going to have to trust a group of people with all the guns and jails and pray they're not a monster. Of course, Moloch dines on K Street, but I digress.

But what if we could find examples of people escaping these multi-polar traps on their own? Elinor Ostrom won a Nobel Prize for doing just that. She explains how people, for centuries, have evolved institutions that help them avoid such traps. It turns out it happens all the time. People figured out that they don't need to pray for good rulers, but instead to devise good rules.

Another classic example of collective action includes levying taxes to provide for national defense. People protected by Leviathan shouldn't be able to free-ride on Leviathan, the rationale goes, especially if the point of Leviathan is to protect us from Behemoth or Ziz. Conveniently, Leviathan is powerful enough to tax. And this fact has a deep history, so much so that most of us follow old liberals like Benjamin Franklin in thinking of taxes as inevitable, like death.[118]

The trouble is, as with many things with which authority is entrusted, there is a point beyond which national defense becomes excessive, wasteful, and offensive (instead of defensive). Today, the United States manages what appears to be a global empire, with some estimates indicating more than 650 non-domestic military bases worldwide.[119] Some see that role as a good thing: the world benefits from a force that has been a de facto global constable, which has protected international trade and kept rogue states in line. To others, America's role is a bad thing, as military adventures carried out in the name of pre-emption have turned into costly quagmires and destabilizing occupations.

But being the bully of bullies is a costly proposition. Almost everyone agrees you need national defense. Virtually no one agrees about how much. And in the absence of market prices, we have fewer ways of determining anything like national defense's true value. Whatever your position, the very idea that voters have control regarding the size and scope of the military-industrial complex is, well, naïve. The U.S. defense budget is gargantuan and growing. And if Rolf Gates is right, that militarism will create — or has already created — a culture of violence.

No Angels

Most government functions exemplify what we have called Game A dynamics, which are win-lose institutions and cultures. One might respond that it depends on exactly *which* government you're talking about, but the reality is that all governments, by degree, are infected with Game A problems. Among them is James Madison's concern, about which he famously wrote:

> If Men were angels, no government would be necessary. If angels were to govern men, neither external nor internal controls on government would be necessary. In framing a government which is to be administered by men over men, the great difficulty lies in this: you must first enable the government to control the governed; and the next place, oblige it to control itself.[120]

We must never forget that the very idea of government self-control involves human self-control. In the absence of both human and system self-control, Game A dynamics infect government, even our vaunted democratic republics, from stem to stern. The following is a veritable laundry list of those dynamics, which is not exhaustive. You might call this list something like *Reasons Why it's Hard for Government to Do the Right Thing Even if Angels Staffed it*:

Negative Sums. Set aside the fact that voting for a party means you're voting for a cluster of policies, and that you have to accept the good, the bad, and the ugly of that cluster. For a national-level party to win control means that all those on the other side of the tug-o-war rope must accept the losses, the blanket policies, and otherwise have their concerns ignored. Almost everyone has to pay the costs of those policies, but usually, only certain groups benefit. In some way, politics is a game of groups gaining advantage at the expense of other groups. It is seldom omni-win.

Rational Irrationality. When people don't directly experience a cost to being wrong, or even get *rewarded* for holding wrong or irrational views, you'll get more irrationality. Economist Bryan Caplan explains[121] that most voters are thus under the spell of being wrong, but for good reasons. In other words, it might be irrational for most people to hold correct views, because to do so would be too costly. This observation calls into question the idea that even informed voters know much about the subject matter of voting, much less go and vote for it.

No Skin. If someone's task is to buy something for themselves using their own money, they usually finds the highest quality at the lowest cost. If one's task is to buy something for someone else using someone else's money, there's no telling what any given person will get, especially if the buyer is shielded from that choice's consequences. Thus, when it comes to government, hardly anyone — except the direct beneficiary of a program or subsidy — has skin in the game. Without the discipline of profit and loss, the government is inoculated from the forces that drive households or firms to manage resources wisely.

Logrolling. Legislators trade favors: If you vote for my bill, I'll vote for yours. Each exchanges a vote on issues they don't care much about for a vote on other issues that are more important to them. The legislators transact in votes, and logrolling nearly always comes at the expense of people who were never involved in the exchange. Of course, they'll read about the pork-barrel project in the news, but they'll rarely think about how the project, say, accumulates debt. Logrolling is a natural consequence of a representative system of government.

Devil's Auction. When it comes to lobbying, political entrepreneurs — those seeking to gain advantage through regulations or new laws — play what game theorists call an *all-pay auction.* This is a situation in which every bidder has to pay, regardless of whether they win; the prize is awarded to the highest bidder, as in a conventional auction. Experiments with people playing all-play auctions show that over-bidding is common. Such is true for lobbyists, too. If multiple lobbyists are courting a politician, each competitor reasons from a sunk cost mentality, which means that they're mitigating losses as opposed to realizing gains after a certain point. In this game, everyone loses — except the politician and a few favored cronies.

Shirky Principle. "Institutions will try to preserve the problem to which they are the solution," consultant Clay Shirky is credited with saying.[122] This principle can be manifested as mission creep, where an agency will slowly change its *raison d'etre* to continue receiving funds. In other cases, an agency will treat symptoms of the problem but ignore the underlying pathology. It's seldom a conscious process, but rather a form of groupthink shaped by Game A incentives. *If we solve problem X completely, we will all be looking for work.* No "institution" is worse in this than the government.

Dependency Networks. Government has network effects, too. Only the network effect of any government policy or program tends to create dependencies. These dependencies are layered. One set of taxpayers, say in a particular state that produces missiles, is dependent on the jobs that spending on missiles creates. But the missile contractor, too, is dependent on the agencies in the Pentagon requisitioning funds. And the Pentagon depends on taxpayer dollars or future debt — and so on — creating not just dependency but layers of it.

Mutually Assured Destruction. Just as in the example of trade wars and cold wars, politics creates arms races. For example, suppose one jurisdiction tries to gain an advantage against some other jurisdiction by paying out corporate incentives. In that case, the remaining states feel they have to play too, lest they miss out on opportunities to create jobs. Politicians are quick to celebrate the companies that move in and cut ribbons. They are reluctant to mention it takes real resources to lure those companies, which everyone else pays for. (Studies show that there is no net benefit to these corporate welfare arms races.[123])

Knowledge Problems. Knowledge is distributed, not centralized. And yet we still centralize and patronize all the "problem solvers" in distant capitals, as if they have the knowledge required to plan various aspects of the society or economy without disastrous unintended consequences.

Violence. For what policies are you willing to threaten or kill? "Every law is violent," law professor Stephen L. Carter reminds us. "We try not to think about this, but we should."[124] Codes, statutes, and bills, churned out by the thousands, require people to submit. Armed men with guns put people into prison for failure to comply. Carter adds: "The statute or regulation we like best carries the same risk that some violator will die at the hands of a law enforcement officer who will go too far."[125]

With the examples above, we are only scratching the surface. And yet our failures of imagination means most people still turn to authorities to solve collective action problems and to address so-called market failures.

THE PROBLEM OF POWER

The breakdown of our belief in liberalism leads us to put our faith in political power. But in doing so, we slide inexorably into the Problem of Power, which goes something like this:

1. Powerful, private entities like corporations can exploit people by taking advantage of information

asymmetries or market power.

2. Currently, only an entity with a monopoly on the initiation of violence (a state) is powerful enough to stop these private entities.

3. A government powerful enough to stop these private entities can keep power by threatening violence or colluding with powerful, private entities.

4. Powerful, private entities routinely collude with government officials who have the power to threaten violence, which allows both colluders to exploit people.

5. Only an entity (or entities) that is something other than a private entity or a government can stop private entities from colluding with governments.

As the ouroboros eats, the question embedded in point five leaves us in paradox. What is that entity or entities? Does anything even remotely like it currently exist? Is it a super-powerful AI programmed by a good and wise person? Or are we, with another nod to Madison, going to expect to find angels among us? Maybe we will find ourselves in some sort of constitutional moment, where someone, somewhere, finds an opportunity to reconfigure the institutions and reboot the social technology.

None of these scenarios seems likely. What if the answer lies not in a single proposal at all but rather in our ability, albeit limited, to unleash a thousand experiments? A few of those experiments could help us to reorganize our human systems. Though we would be starting in a system that can be hostile to experimentation and biased towards the status quo (Game A), it is wrong-headed to think we'll be able to transition to Game B *by doubling down on* Game A. Yet some of the finest minds in the world fall into this way of thinking.

Polymath entrepreneur Jim Rutt is one of the first to articulate the difference between Games A and B. I wrote the following to Rutt in a friendly exchange:

> To the extent anyone can agree about what Games
> A and B are: Game A is marked by systems in which
> the strong can more easily take advantage of the
> weak, the smart take advantage of the dim, and the
> powerful take advantage of the powerless. Game B is
> meant to be "omni-win" and "anti-rivalrous" (which
> works under both economic or game-theoretical
> definitions.) But lemme get this straight: we're going
> to oblige those at the highest echelons of power to
> mute the villainous aspirations of corporate CEOs
> running gigantic corporations with… Game A.
> That's an evolutionary strategy of "if you can't beat
> 'em, join 'em."[126]

I am not alone in thinking about things this way.

Edmund Burke, one of those dead white guys people keep ignoring, figured this out a long time ago:

> In vain you tell me that [government] is good, but
> that I fall out only with the Abuse. The Thing! The
> Thing itself is the abuse! Observe, my Lord, I pray
> you, that grand Error upon which all artificial legisla-
> tive Power is founded. It was observed, that Men had
> ungovernable Passions, which made it necessary to
> guard against the Violence they might offer to each
> other. They appointed Governors over them for this
> Reason; but a worse and more perplexing Difficulty
> arises, how to be defended against the Governors?[127]

Put that in your pipe and smoke it, Hobbes. Burke's question plagued the American Founders, too. And in many respects, human progress — beyond any material gains — is about the quest for an answer to Burke's question.

STRONG'S LAW

Because most people take government and its associated dynamics for granted, it is worth pausing briefly to consider a suggestion from educational entrepreneur Michael Strong. He asks us to imagine "a world in which every aspect of law and governance is designed to appeal more effectively to prospective residents of that jurisdiction…"[128] Call this Strong's Law:

Ceteris paribus, properly structured free enterprise, always results over time in higher quality, lower cost, and more customized products and services.

Strong thinks that our world needlessly suffers because we have excluded entrepreneurs from addressing our species' critical problems. It seems like the more serious the problem, the less willing authorities are to let entrepreneurs have a go. But smartphones are ubiquitous, even among the world's poor. If entrepreneurs supply these goods, maybe we should consider extending the sphere of their activity to serving more human needs. In areas such as law, governance, community, and healthcare, Strong argues that we need *more* entrepreneurship, not less.[129] Yet the prevailing mental model is that entrepreneurial innovation doesn't apply to these human systems. "If we are able to create a framework within which we can allow for the right balance of experimentation, feedback, and re-investment in better alternatives, then we will see the same endless system of refinement in human systems that we have seen in technological systems."[130]

Wait, entrepreneurism? That doesn't sound like the path to liberation, just to greed and attachment. Indeed, one might push back against Strong to argue that enterprise is just another holdover from Game A. But is it?

I remain committed to the idea that Game B, far from being determined *a priori*, will arise from some kind of experimental discovery process. Up to this point, the market's discovery process — which happens when a whole bunch of smart, hardworking people innovate, produce, and trade with each other — is the most generative force on earth. So under no circumstances should we define Game B in a way that jettisons the market process.

We should also remember that *the market* is an abstraction that stands in for real people. Everything you eat, wear, play, and read comes from an entrepreneur. These are people who took risks and managed to organize people and resource in such a way that eventually benefitted you. This living flow system allows you to live and live comfortably. Yes, they took some of your money; the other half of the equation is that they served you in some way. Thus, the entrepreneur is only ever as good as their service to others, which they can only sustain as long as capital flows back to them.

Economist Israel Kirzner reminds us that entrepreneurial "boldness and imagination" drives the market process: "What constitutes that process is the series of discoveries generated by that boldness and alertness."[131] Such qualities rarely exist in a vacuum. So in being alert to those opportunities and grasping them, entrepreneurs are engaged in a kind of Olympics to compete to bring value to us.[132] Those entrepreneurs who are bolder and more alert are more likely to be successful, where success is defined as having profited by creating value for others.

COMPETITION AND SOCIOPATHS

In seeking nonviolence in thought, word, and deed, one might get the idea that market competition is also violent. After all, in natural ecosystems, there is a whole lot of predation. Entrepreneurs can be predatory too, depending on your definition of a predator. But antisocial predation happens when the entrepreneur allows herself to become corrupted by the desire to win at any cost. When the desire to win replaces the desire to create value, they are no longer an entrepreneur at all.

Otherwise, competition is vital to the market process. We should not underestimate the benefits of firms vying to serve us better. Most advocates of a transition to Game B would like to see a situation in which, at the very least, competition doesn't turn competitors into villainous exploiters. Indeed, some like conscious entrepreneur Daniel Schmactenberger worry that a competitive enterprise system, as currently structured, rewards and selects for sociopaths. Let's assume for a moment that it does.

When asked what they would do about corporate sociopaths, most people default to Game A thinking. In other words, they turn to another set of sociopaths: politicians. By now, we should all be familiar with how that story ends. Most people continue to labor under the angels theory of government, which is just the Leviathan Formulation with a halo. We succumb to the Great Temptation that authorities will combat the exploiters when they almost always end up colluding with them. Both win, at the expense of everyone else.

Such is the nature of special interest politics as set out by observers such as economics Nobel laureate James Buchanan, who wrote:

> If the government is empowered to grant monopoly rights or tariff protection to one group, at the expense of the general public or of designated losers, it follows that potential beneficiaries will compete for the prize. And since only one group can be rewarded, the resources invested by other groups — which could have been used to produce valued goods and services — are wasted.[133]

Your representative is playing a game that tends to benefit favored groups and not you. As such, "the growth of the bureaucratic or regulatory sector of government can best be explained in terms of the competition between political agents"[134] promising wealth transfers to favored groups.

Transfers are win-lose by definition, thus, they fall under Game A. Even our vaunted democratic republics, conceived in the minds of well-meaning liberals, are plagued by these dynamics. Until we can think of a way out, we might ask ourselves a somewhat seditious question: Would we rather the most sociopathic people on earth have control over armies, prisons, and territory? Or talent, knowledge, and capital? Because right now, they have control over both.

THE MONSTROUS HYBRID

Earlier, I alluded to the idea that human systems are built around *coercion* or *persuasion*. Jane Jacobs discusses similar ideas in her work, referring to Guardian and Commercial syndromes, which are essentially the ethical frameworks of *raiding* and *trading*. When it comes to America, it looks like we're dealing with what Jacobs calls a "monstrous hybrid" of the two syndromes, with unholy alliances between money and power being the norm. Instead of looking for ways to create wealth, political entrepreneurs invest in transferring wealth. When we get a sense that an entrepreneur has become wealthy through transfer or extraction as opposed to value creation, we start to think of them as Dickensian villains.

But rapper Ice-T offers an under-appreciated insight: "Don't hate the player. Hate the game." [135] Don't try to change the entrepreneur, merely try to change the rules they must live by. After all, the more political power on auction, the more entrepreneurs will be tempted by it. Eventually, more and more get sucked into playing the game. Refuse, and lose to those who will. Instead of calling a consultant, they will have to call a lobbyist. Such a game breeds the wrong kind of entrepreneur.

Returning to the issue of sociopathy, if the question of trading versus raiding were binary, I'd take a greedy CEO over a ruthless dictator any day. That's because I would rather pit the greedy sociopaths against one another in a grand contest to serve humanity better. But the winners could only profit by creating real value for people in society. None would be able to enrich themselves by colluding with authorities, displacing costs, or pillaging the commons. Such a game does exist, in theory: It's called the market. The problem is, today's markets are linked in too many places to political leverage points, which provide entrepreneurs *access* to politics, which, as I've said, is a negative sum game. The more you play it, the more illiberal you become. To unleash real value, we'd have to find a way to get the most ambitious people to play a different kind of game.

Liberalism's Triumph

In two spectacular episodes in the life of a great exemplar, Hong Kong, we have witnessed Hongkongers take to the streets. They're struggling for something. This great city-state, mainly built on a commitment to peace, entrepreneurial markets, and benign neglect, has become a symbol of liberalism's triumph. It's not perfect, of course; nothing is. But despite the mainland's circling sharks, Hong Kong is one of the world's most extraordinary natural experiments in comparative human systems. Sadly, I suspect that by the time these words meet your eyes, Hong Kong will have been swallowed up by Beijing.

But even if the events in Hong Kong turn out to fail — first the Umbrella Movement of 2014, then the street protests of 2019 — these should be early indicators of a Westphalian order entering its twilight. Hongkongers have shown that although any authoritarian interregnum will be hard, the seeds of a new era have already been planted. China's communist party cannot keep Hong Kong in chains forever, because Hongkongers embody a spirit Walt Disney once wrote about: "Once a man has tasted freedom, he will never be content to be a slave. That is why I believe that this frightfulness we see everywhere today is only temporary. Tomorrow will be better for as long as Americans [and Hongkongers] keep alive the ideals of freedom and a better life."[136]

The short-term prospects for Hong Kong are bleak. The long-term prospects are better. The same can be said for America.

There is no end of history, but humanity is zigzagging inexorably towards a new liberal order. Author Jamie Bartlett put matters rather starkly when he reminded us that Leviathan states "rely on control. If they can't control information, crime, businesses, borders or the money supply, then they will cease to deliver what citizens demand of them." And what if they cease to deliver? "In the end," says Bartlett, "nation-states are nothing but agreed-upon myths: we give up certain freedoms in order to secure others. But if that transaction no longer works, and we stop agreeing on the myth, it ceases to have power over us."[137]

Over the last few years, authoritarian collectivism from both the far right and the far left have returned as dark echoes from the twentieth century. If Bartlett is right, neither of these ideologies will suppress the creative destruction that an evolved liberalism will bring. Unfortunately, though, liberalism might have to evolve in a bottleneck,[138] as some liberal regimes could die off due to overwhelming pressure from authoritarian power. No matter how it evolves, liberalism will always be understood as a comprehensive system of social and economic freedoms.

"How do I know that my narrative is better than yours?" Dierdre McCloskey asks rhetorically in response to liberalism's detractors. She answers herself:

> The experiments of the 20th century told me so.
> It would have been hard to know the wisdom of
> Friedrich Hayek or Milton Friedman or Matt Ridley
> or Deirdre McCloskey in August of 1914, before the
> experiments in large government were well begun.
> But anyone who after the 20th century still thinks

that thoroughgoing socialism, nationalism, imperialism, mobilization, central planning, regulation,
zoning, price controls, tax policy, labor unions, business cartels, government spending, intrusive policing,
adventurism in foreign policy, faith in entangling
religion and politics, or most of the other thoroughgoing 19th-century proposals for governmental
action are still neat, harmless ideas for improving our
lives is not paying attention.[139]

Every one of the illiberal doctrines she lists has not
only stuck around, but are back with a vengeance. And
as authoritarianism rears its head again from the left and
right, this passage becomes more salient. Permit me a little
more space for McCloskey's diagnosis:

In the 19th and 20th centuries ordinary Europeans
were hurt, not helped, by their colonial empires.
Economic growth in Russia was slowed, not
accelerated, by Soviet central planning. American
Progressive regulation and its European anticipa-
tions protected monopolies of transportation like
railways and protected monopolies of retailing like
High-Street shops and protected monopolies of
professional services like medicine, not the consumers. "Protective" legislation in the United States and
"family-wage" legislation in Europe subordinated
women. State-armed psychiatrists in America jailed
homosexuals, and in Russia jailed democrats. Some
of the New Deal prevented rather than aided America's recovery from the Great Depression.[140]

When one reads this passage, one cannot help but be
struck by all that illiberalism has left in its wake, as Lao Tzu
warned.

Philosophers and deliberative bodies alike once celebrated liberalism. What remains is gradually disappearing
from our civic consciousness. And yet, its residue continues
to pay enormous dividends for those who have managed

to keep it. A small but technologically savvy vanguard is guarding its ideals. Coders. Scribblers. Students in Hong Kong. And, hopefully, readers of this book.

After the collapse of the Eastern bloc, globalization accelerated. A lot of the world got richer, quickly. Liberalization in India and China has lifted more people out of poverty than any event in human history. Though socialism had been in precipitous decline, most regimes were unwilling to liberalize too quickly, or too completely. A monstrous hybrid between systems was ascendant. The state would tolerate private enterprise — but not without considerable redistribution, licensing, and regulation.

Different degrees of corporatism, state-directed and regulated industry, thus came to dominate the global landscape. The downside of these hybrid economies has been the inevitable collusion between industry heads and state authorities, which exacerbates inequality and leads to corruption.[141] But we must always ask: compared to what? Our only standard of comparison was the decidedly less liberal order that held sway before the transformative events of 1980-90, including the Soviet Union's Collapse, China and India's liberalizations, and the World Trade Organization's Uruguay round.

The upside of more liberalism in the world has been billions coming out of penury.

- Thirty years ago, more than a third of the world lived in extreme poverty, defined as $1.90 per day. Today, less than 10 percent of humanity lives on $1.90 a day or less.[142]

- The average price of fifty essential commodities has declined by more than 72 percent since 1980.[143]

- Child mortality has fallen by 60 percent since 1990,[144] and life expectancy has soared worldwide, from 62.8 years in 1980 to 72.3 years in 2017.[145]

From a purely Maslovian standpoint, these are staggering figures which point to unprecedented improvements to the human condition. Those who ignore them also tend to deny the causal factors that gave rise to them — namely, liberalization.

Despite the astounding progress, detractors smell something fishy.

ILLIBERAL CRITICS

Political philosopher John Gray has been flogging strawmen for a long time. "With all its talk of freedom and choice," he writes more recently, "liberalism was in practice the experiment of dissolving traditional sources of social cohesion and political legitimacy and replacing them with the promise of rising material living standards. This experiment has now run its course."[146] Such persistent confusion drives the illiberal rhetoric we see today.

Gray is right that a grand experiment is now running. The evidence of rising living standards is in. But liberalism was never, as Gray claims, about dissolving traditional sources of social cohesion. It was always about dissolving oppressive means of controlling people, and cultures struggling to exist and to be recognized. Whatever one makes of Gray's notion of "political legitimacy," one suspects he finds it in the illiberal urge to control. What he means by "tradition" is authority. Authority cuts through the bonds of need and love and proximity and culture that tie real people together in community. Political power severs the ties of civil association and replaces them with the shackles of conformity and compulsion. And though we should never forget rising living standards, liberalism's real bounty comes in the various forms of social cohesion that can flower in our living systems.

National conservative Patrick Deneen refers to liberalism as an "anti-culture." Far from our belief in liberalism breaking down, Deneen argues that it has succeeded beyond anyone's wildest dreams, despite the title of his book, *Why Liberalism Failed*. And in its successes, its *excesses*, it has marginalized religious and parochial cultures, tamped down better selves that would otherwise form in these cultures, and failed in its promise to be a "vessel in which many cultures can coexist."[147]

While it's true that pluralism is one of liberalism's promises, Deneen goes wrong by claiming that liberalism is antithetical to culture, much less cultural pluralism. Deneen gets away with this intellectual malpractice by equivocating; a two-step between meanings. In an interview for *The Nation*, Deneen explains how it had been liberal "actions by the Obama administration that require institutions to carry birth control and even abortifacients — my own institution, Notre Dame, being one of those." The trouble is, the liberalism of which I speak doesn't require institutions to do, well, anything, except to practice *ahimsa*. Despite his two-step, Deneen is openly hostile to our brand of liberalism, too, at least when it suits him.

Deneen is not entirely to blame for this conflation. Political theorist Linda C. Raeder notes that the appropriation of the term liberal goes back at least to the 1920s: "The American people generally warmed to the term 'liberal.' Thus they could potentially be swayed to support Progressive proposals labeled as such, even if they were not actually liberal in the classic sense."[148] By the twenties, adds Raeder, "the *New York Times* criticized 'the expropriation of the time-honored word 'liberal'' and demanded that 'the radical red school of thought… hand back the word 'liberal' to its original owners.'"[149]

But the Progressives repeated the word endlessly, and so effectively that today conservatives use it as a term of derision. By the 1950s, the transformation of liberal was a "fait accompli."[150] Some liberals tried to reclaim the term, or at least make a starker distinction. Perhaps the best articulation is the one historian of thought Dean Russell made in 1955: "Many of us call ourselves 'liberals.' And it is true that the word 'liberal' once described persons who respected the individual and feared the use of mass compulsions."[151]

Russell believed authoritarians had co-opted the term. And they had. That left those who believe in equal freedom to explain that they mean something else, something less corrupted. "At best, this is awkward and subject to misunderstanding."[152]

Let this chapter serve as a reclamation. In reordering our words, we reorder our minds. Because it's not just that liberals failed to guard and keep their brand. It's also that they have failed to articulate a better vision of liberalism. With many modern variants, you get what writer Jeffery Tucker calls ideological brutalism.

> It strips down the theory to its rawest and most fundamental parts and pushes the application of those parts to the foreground. It tests the limits of the idea by tossing out the finesse, the refinements, the grace, the decency, the accoutrements. It cares nothing for the larger cause of civility and the beauty of results. It is only interested in the pure functionality of the parts. It dares anyone to question the overall look and feel of the ideological apparatus, and shouts down people who do so as being insufficiently devoted to the core of the theory, which itself is asserted without context or regard for aesthetics.[153]

Between the terminological confusion and the stripped-down analyticity of modern versions, liberalism is a doctrine in a vice's grip between two authoritarianisms, left and right. No wonder it's so simple for right-wing and left-wing intellectuals alike to obfuscate, confuse, and get away with being just plain wrong.

Modern-day Tories and so-called national conservatives such as *Hillbilly Elegy* author J.D. Vance join Patrick Deneen in blaming liberalism for everything from the opioid crisis to unemployment in Pennsyltucky. And they're angry. They're ready to bring back blue laws that force businesses to close on Sundays.[154] They're prepared to expand corporate welfare because they think FDR-style makework programs will get people off disability checks and drugs. Like High Minds, they've divorced themselves from the idea that society is a living system made up of free people capable of self-organizing.

Far from seeing the dangerous centralization going on all around them as the problem, conservative High Minds just want to apply central authority to different national goals. Blame America's woes on open markets, secularism, and China. They'll package it all up and label it with the same bugaboo: liberalism.

NEOLIBERALISM

"We fight for and against not men and things as they are," said Joseph Schumpeter famously, "but for and against the caricatures we make of them." [155]

One such caricature is a form of liberalism made out of straw. Everywhere, to the extent that liberalism has been practiced, it has triumphed. And yet its enemies keep thwacking away at something liberals don't recognize. According to High Minds, there is something insidious hiding in your cupboard. It's darker than liberalism: it's *neoliberalism.*

What is neoliberalism? It's hard to say. Those who oppose it tend to focus on the inevitable setbacks, distortions, and downsides of the mixed economy. Relying on the term's imprecision, political scientist Wendy Brown says:

> So free enterprise is [neoliberalism's] clarion call, and even though it requires a lot of state intervention and state support, the idea that goes with it is usually also minimal state intervention in markets. Even if states are needed to prop up or support or sometimes

bail out markets, they shouldn't get into the middle
of them and redistribute [wealth]. ... That's certainly
part of what neoliberalism is.[156]

Brown is confused, and understandably so. Free enterprise does not require state intervention and state support.
In fact, the extent that a market system requires intervention is the extent to which it is not free. But Brown is no
less confused than her conservative counterpart, Patrick
Deneen, who admits: "Now, people debate whether we
have capitalism or crony capitalism or state capitalism. But
essentially we have what, I think, is market ideology."[157]

All of these things cannot simultaneously be true.
Instead of grappling with the criticisms's inconsistency,
critics simply add *neo*.

We have mixed economies, which are the product of
a mixed-up ideology. In Europe. In India. In China. And
of course, in America: The mixed economy is supposed to
be a compromise between two completely different human
systems with entirely different operating protocols. Far from
being integrated or *integral*, the mixed economy is incoher-
ent. It means muddling collectivism and liberalism, technocracy, and entrepreneurism. Thus, the extent to which
any meaning can be made of the term neoliberalism might
well be a jumble of policies that were at least more liberal
by degree after the fall of the Soviet Union and India and
China's opening.

According to economist Sanford Ikeda, entrepreneurial markets and collectivist technocracies are "organized
according to two diametrically opposite principles —
[emergent] order and deliberate design, they mix as well as
oil and water." Trying to combine these systems too zeal-
ously produces chaos, because their fundamental assumptions simply aren't reconcilable. For example, some firms
have to operate according to profit and loss. Others work
according to subsidy and protection. Some firms exist in a
competitive system of undistorted prices. Others work in an

uncompetitive system of manipulated prices. One system relies on coercion. The other system relies on persuasion. In the end, mixing these dynamics ends up generating chaos or deadweight loss.

High Minds usually go on to say that neoliberalism undermines democracy. Wise elites should regulate or abolish entrepreneurism to reduce inequality and rein in corporate excesses. If that happens, they urge, the demos will be ascendant. It's a funny thing, though. Whatever one might think of democracy, when you look around the world at the most illiberal countries, none of them is democratic.

As of this writing, I'm not aware of a single soul, besides writer James Kirchick[158], who self-identifies as a neoliberal. And even Kirchick is being cheeky. None of the High Minds bother to consider the possibility that what makes neoliberalism different from our more familiar variant is the extent to which the High Minds *got their way*.

And that's why some liberals are pushing back. Political philosopher Jason Brennan writes:

> You complain, perhaps rightly, that corporations are just too big. Well, yeah, we told you that would happen. When you create complicated tax codes, complicated regulatory regimes, and complicated licensing rules, these regulations naturally select for larger and larger corporations. We told you that would happen. Of course, these increasingly large corporations then capture these rules, codes, and regulations to disadvantage their competitors and exploit the rest of us. We told you that would happen.[159]

A more cynical person might say that neoliberalism is a term of derision for phenomena the High Minds neither like nor particularly understand. Despite having a visible hand in the mess, they use the word to detach themselves from responsibility. "Neoliberalism in any guise is not the solution but the problem," writes Nancy Fraser, an academic at the New School. "The sort of change we require can only come from elsewhere, from a project that is at the very least anti-neoliberal, if not anti-capitalist."

But what is this change? Whether you dress it up in democratic finery or religious communitarianism, it's always the same: authoritarian intervention. By degree, government intervention puts the 'neo' in neoliberalism. It always has. Before the term gained currency, liberalism's detractors preferred egalitarian poverty to liberal prosperity. That's because layered deep beneath this hostility to open markets is a paleolithic distaste for unequal wealth distributions. And, of course, there is the urge to control.

And yet, most of the problems that persist as countries liberalize persist to the extent that they attempt to impose burdens that match wealthier states' capacity to regulate, intervene, and transfer. Excessive intervention in developing economies creates what economists Alex Tabarrok and Shruti Rajagopalan refer to as a "flailing state." The alternative, particularly for developing nations, is a higher degree of liberalization:

> Laissez-faire is a step to development, perhaps even a necessary step, even if the ultimate desired end point of development is a regulated, mixed economy. Presumptive laissez-faire is the optimal form of government for states with limited capacity and also the optimal learning environment for states to grow capacity.[160]

In flailing states, state regulators' limited capacity means that classic problems of favor seeking become magnified. Officials see opportunity in taking bribes; the people expedite things by paying them. And savvy entrepreneurs figure out how to game regulations, allowing them to gain an advantage over competitors. Greater inequality follows, as only a few can bribe their way to the top. The rest subsist in the informal sector. But in the absence of the interventions, there would be fewer ways to achieve capture.

In other words, one can hardly blame the ill effects of neoliberalism on its liberal aspects. It boils down to this: When you mix an overweening interventionist state with entrepreneurial markets, you get cronyism. And yet we mustn't forget that to the extent neoliberalism has been liberal, we have seen unprecedented gains in human wellbeing.

PLANNERS AND SEARCHERS

It's one thing to point to the undeniable gains in human wellbeing. It's another to associate those gains with specific reasons and causes. One of the most accomplished researchers on the subject is development economist William Easterly, who distinguishes two rather stark theories of development. He calls their adherents Searchers and Planners. "In foreign aid," writes Easterley,

> ...planners announce good intentions but don't
> motivate anyone to carry them out; Searchers find
> things that work and get some reward. Planners
> raise expectations but take no responsibility for
> meeting them. Searchers accept responsibility for
> their actions. Planners determine what to supply;
> Searchers find out what is in demand. Planners
> apply global blueprints. Searchers adapt to local
> conditions. Planners at the top lack the knowledge at
> the bottom. Searchers find out what the reality is at
> the bottom. Planners never hear if the planned got
> what it needed. Searchers find out if the customer is
> satisfied.[161]

Easterly has marshaled tremendous evidence that Searchers are the driving force of development, and that Planner-based foreign aid has been an unmitigated disaster. Part of that marshaling came from a great debate in the early 2000s with celebrity development economist Jeffrey Sachs. Quite interestingly, the debate was resolved in a way, not by the court of public opinion or by a panel of experts, but by a single journalist who followed up on some of Jeffrey Sachs's results.

Sachs was already known for his obsession to end global poverty "once and for all." Undoubtedly, this is a noble ideal. And in his 2005 best-selling book, *The End of Poverty*, Sachs argued that with the right levels of planning and largesse, extreme poverty could be eliminated by the year 2025.[162] The plan was to design and provide for all the basic needs of some poor areas, including scientifically-informed agricultural reform, sanitation facilities, housing, food, and medicine. The hypothesis had been that these would jumpstart local peoples by allowing them an escape from so-called poverty traps. Before *The End of Poverty* went to press, Sachs had already set about designing the prototypes that would realize his ideals in Africa. Sachs called these "Millennium Villages."

Then Nina Munk, a journalist with little experience in development economics, spent six years following Sachs to sub-Saharan Africa. She would check in on all the projects dutifully, at different stages, visiting on her own in a continuous checking and learning process. What would she discover about these prototypes designed eventually to end poverty worldwide? She recounts all of it in her book *The Idealist*.[163]

The first thing she noticed is that, although Sachs's technocratic solutions bore a striking resemblance to development aid projects of the last fifty years, he was confident, even boastful. Curing poverty a la the Millennium Villages would be a breeze. Maybe that overweening confidence is what allowed Sachs to raise between $25-30 million[164] in aid from various charities and development banks worldwide. But the cure for poverty wouldn't be as predictable or straightforward as all that.

The original plan had been for the people on the ground to preserve a nomadic lifestyle. But as more and more things got donated, people came from everywhere, and all of those goods and services, manna from heaven, induced them to stay put. The original village became a "sprawling shantytown, its streets clogged with garbage."[165] Plans for a livestock market went awry, the water pump broke down, and folks began to fight over donated goods. Droughts, floods, epidemics, and other unforeseen events kept setting the village back. And the locals ultimately failed to adapt to the designs. Instead, there was "theft, malingering, and misreporting."[166]

As disillusionment set in, Sachs became more frenetic and ad hoc. He would change the criteria to claim small victories and seek more funds. He never admitted the project was failing. In short, Sachs was unable to anticipate the complex patterns of life surrounding even the smallest village. The idealist, *the planner*, the High Mind, had failed. William Easterly was vindicated.

So if it wasn't foreign aid and technocratic planning that deserves the undeniable credit for global gains in human wellbeing, who gets the credit? Well, the Searchers, of course. But Searchers, courageous entrepreneurs who serve others through producing goods and services people need, are not as likely to succeed in a matrix without liberalism's essentials:

1. Protected property rights,
2. Low-burden regulation, taxation and corruption,
3. Legitimate and sustainable means of raising capital,
4. A fair system of dispute resolution, and
5. A culture tolerant of innovation, entrepreneurship, and change.

If the above are the keys to development, these keys can be very hard to obtain in most of Africa. And yet the evidence is overwhelmingly clear: those who have managed to liberalize their institutions have improved their living standards.

Anticipating High Minds' objections, let's look only at societies that 1) were not beneficiaries of colonialism, 2) not societies with 'old money,' and 3) have liberalized in the last forty years. We'll use *movement* on economic freedom indices as our proxy for liberalization. People in economies rated "free" or "mostly free" in the 2019 Economic Freedom Index[167] enjoy incomes that are more than twice the average in all the other countries and more than *six times higher* than those in repressed or unfree economies. Of these, many satisfy our criteria 1), 2), and 3):

- New Zealand — Since 1995, New Zealand has more than tripled GDP.
- Estonia — Since 1995, Estonia has tripled GDP.
- Chile — Since 1995, Chile has tripled GDP.
- Latvia — Since 1995, Latvia has tripled GDP.
- Ireland — Since 1995, Ireland has nearly quadrupled GDP.
- United Arab Emirates — Since 1995, the UAE has quadrupled GDP.
- Lithuania — Since 1995, Lithuania has increased GDP nearly sevenfold.
- Rwanda — From 1980 until 2003, Rwanda's GDP was less than $2 billion, but Rwanda's economy grew briskly to $10.2 billion in 2019, a *fivefold* increase in less than twenty years.

Notable countries on this list include New Zealand, which had been on the verge of collapse before liberalization in the early 1980s pulled the island nation back from the brink. The Baltic States, operating after the fall of the Soviet Union, had to figure out how to liberalize — and fast. And Rwanda's growth under the leadership of Paul Kagami has enjoyed stellar growth despite genocides in the early 1990s.

Some economists argue that GDP is an inadequate indicator of growth and development, and they're right, to some extent. But the relationship between improvements in economic freedom and economic growth is robust. According to the Index's authors, the "economic growth rates of countries where economic freedom has expanded the most are at least 30 percent higher than those of countries where freedom has stagnated or slowed."[168] The overall move to greater economic freedom and global interconnection has contributed to a doubling of the world economy in recent decades. That has not only reduced extreme poverty, but made life more bearable for hundreds of millions of people.

Back in the developed world, those who have lost their jobs to offshoring might not appreciate the abstraction of global uplift. The acute pain of regional displacement is front and center. Even regions that have struggled to compete have enjoyed greater overall purchasing power. Those Rust Belt areas which have diversified their economies, places like Pittsburgh in the U.S. or Manchester in the U.K, have come back stronger.

High Minds might argue that recent gains among the global poor are either mere correlation or primarily the result of Sachs-style foreign aid. Others say that the wealthy nations of the world only got rich thanks to exploitative colonialism.[169] Even if reduced poverty and increased life expectancy were primarily the consequence of philanthropy and aid, these sectors are utterly dependent on profit-seeking enterprises for their existence. And colonialism? Plenty of tiger economies had nothing to do with colonialism, many of which we listed above. In fact, Singapore and Hong Kong have thrived *despite* colonialism.

Unprecedented increases in economic growth are due to economic liberalism. According to economist Max Roser: "Before the printing press was invented the only way to copy a book was for a scribe to copy it. Gregory Clark estimates that the scribes who were doing this work back then were able to copy 3,000 words of plain text per day."[170] That means producing one Bible took 136 days of work.

We take for granted that someone can print thousands of books in an afternoon. Millions can read a single article online, instantaneously. Deirdre McCloskey hits the nail squarely when she writes that the "capital became productive because of ideas for betterment — ideas enacted by a country carpenter or a boy telegrapher or a teenage Seattle computer whiz."

Or, as Matt Ridley reminds us, what happened over the past two hundred years is that more people started *having a go* and more ideas started *having sex*. When more people live by better rules, they create better recipes. The rules are the institutions most hospitable to entrepreneurism. Recipes are the kind of knowledge that allows producers to generate greater abundance with fewer resources. In such conditions, Searchers thrive.

LIBERALISM UNDER SIEGE

In some quarters, it would appear that the liberal order is beset by wolves. The High Minds haven't gone anywhere. Neither have the strongmen. Eerily reminiscent of the early twentieth century, authoritarians attack on all sides. Can liberalism survive?

Liberalism is a worldview of integration, but its few remaining adherents sometimes forget the doctrine makes room for diverse values and competing conceptions of the good. In this way, liberalism is a kind of meta doctrine — if it is an ideology at all. By contrast, authoritarian forms are defined by their hostility to pluralism. They always have been. To impose an economic plan or national monoculture, you have to compel others by threat of violence. That is, after all, what it means to be an authoritarian. But that is also what it means to be a High Mind: *my values are all that matter.*

Any evolved form of liberalism will be able to integrate many of the concerns of its adversaries. It will synthesize apparent opposites. Commercial cosmopolitanism can be reconciled with cultural self-determination. Open entrepreneurism does not contradict creating protections for the vulnerable. Economic growth can be better for environmental stewardship. An evolved liberalism will also help people live flourishing lives, not just by allowing them to live in peace and with fair rules but by offering a set of moral and spiritual practices.

People are currently drawn to extremes. Most labor under the notion that disparate values must exist in conflict. Politics as we know it creates a winner-take-all mentality. *If we can just win the next election, we'll do things our way.* Everyone gets force fed *their way,* like pâté ducks.

But liberalism offers a way out. Imagine two teams on either side of a tug-o-war rope. Each side pulls and pulls. Liberalism comes along and says, "Everybody drop the rope." More prosaically, liberalism offers protocols for letting people cluster into communities of consent while balancing different conceptions of the good. No competing doctrines can boast such pluralism — which is why they are doomed. But Americans *are* embracing those competing doctrines — which is why we are doomed.

In the United States, the rule of law is already eroded. Civic coherence around its founding ideals is waning. Fear-based illiberalism is on the rise.

The problem with liberalism in its current form is that people view it as either a narrowly legalistic doctrine or an economic theory. Preoccupation with good rules and economic growth can be a turn off. In this way, today's liberalism offers little to nourish the spirit. If it is to animate us as a people, each of us will have to cultivate it. It's not enough to write rules and charters. Liberalism will have to become a practice, as people practice Eastern traditions, the classical virtues, or any other prosocial habits of mind.

If more people embraced an evolved liberalism, it could stave off collapse. But that's a big *if.* I think that we'll have to settle for humanity evolving to rebuild *after* collapse. A new liberalism will show the way through the darkness. And until that liberalism arrives, the more familiar variant will continue to be misunderstood and forgotten.

4

THE BREAKDOWN OF COMMUNITY AND MUTUAL AID

Therefore combine – practice mutual aid!
That is the surest means for giving to
each and to all the greatest safety, the best
guarantee of existence and progress, bodily,
intellectual, and moral.
Peter Kropotkin, from *Mutual Aid*

Osceola McCarty spent most of her life taking in laundry and ironing to eke out a living in small-town Mississippi. She scraped, saved, and lived austerely, starting when she was a teenager.

In her words, the following was a typical day:

> I would go outside and start a fire under my wash-pot. Then I would soak, wash, and boil a bundle of clothes. Then I would rub 'em, wrench 'em, rub 'em again, starch 'em, and hang 'em on the line. After I had all of the clean clothes on the line, I would start on the next batch. I'd wash all day, and in the evenin' I'd iron until 11:00. I loved the work. The bright fire. Wrenching the wet, clean cloth. White shirts shinin' on the line.[171]

That is, until 1995. That was the year McCarty gave the bulk of her life savings, $150,000, to Southern Mississippi University. For as long as she could remember, she had always wanted to be a nurse. Everything McCarty saved cleaning and pressing the clothes of wealthier folk went into a scholarship fund. She wanted young women to be able to study nursing, even if they didn't have the means.

"Contributions from more than 600 donors have added some $330,000 to the original scholarship fund of $150,000," wrote Rick Bragg in *The New York Times*. "After hearing of Miss McCarty's gift, Ted Turner, a multibillionaire, gave away a billion dollars."[172]

Note that when McCarty made her donation, she didn't give it to any organization. She gave based on what she knew, what she felt connected to, and what held meaning for her. Her goal was to help young women pull themselves up, rather than offering money as a handout. If she had just wanted to give her money away, she could have divided it into envelopes and stuffed it into the mailboxes of poor people along some street in Hattiesburg. Her ethics said otherwise.

"I knew there were people who didn't have to work as hard as I did, but it didn't make me feel sad. I loved to work, and when you love to do anything, those things don't bother you . . . Sometimes I worked straight through two or three days. I had goals I was working toward."[173]

Still, one who works as hard as Osceola McCarty is likely to give wisely and have certain expectations. In McCarty's mind, a gift to young women in her community would need to be an investment in human capital. Today we call that effective altruism — but only because we have forgotten how to give well.

McCarty had not only left a legacy; she had transmitted opportunities to young women in the future. But what did her gift mean? Maybe it meant she would die having lived a life of meaning. Maybe it meant leaving sosme trace of herself after she died.

We know it had something to do with the dignity of work, of which her scholarship has become a symbol. Some people think a life of meaning is about posterity—leaving the world better than you found it. McCarty certainly did.

Her gift was also about strengthening her community. She wanted young women, just like the one who had taken in ironing all those years ago, to treat sick people, which she considered a higher calling. In this way, she wanted to be a force multiplier for the people around her.

Maybe there's a little bit of that Osceola McCarty ethic left down in Mississippi. But all over America, it's disappearing. Communities are fading. A simulacrum has replaced compassion — the hollow activism of moralists.

OF BEING AND BARN RAISINGS

If you have ever been to a barn raising, you are among the last of a dying breed. In rural America, you might find a few. In any case, the idea is that when a fire or severe weather brings down a structure on your property, you and your neighbors work to rebuild it. There's no insurance policy; there is compassion and community.

Soon after the fire, everybody would plan to show up and put up a new barn. People didn't need to reason or deliberate about it. It's what you did. It could happen to you. If it did, you'd get the same help. If it didn't, you'd give help to the less fortunate ones.

Barn building specialists worked on the more critical roles, such as joinery or dowling the beams. If anyone got a little pay it was the specialist, but everyone else in the community was expected to turn up and work. The specialist gave the others assignments based on age and gender. Men built the barn. Women supplied water and victuals. Younger boys watched to learn the work, while older boys fetched parts and tools.[174]

When the work was finished, they would put something, like a wreath, on the highest part of the barn, to celebrate the community's achievement. This was called *topping*. It signified not only the project's completion, but it honored all those who participated.

Barn raisings transmitted knowledge and ethos so that everyone knew what to do when the next disaster struck or the next newcomer arrived. In this way, they could serve as initiations into the community, as much by rite as right.[175]

The communitarian part is knowing what we ought to do while cultivating the disposition to do it. People in proximity to one another develop a shared culture and needs. In America, people once self-organized to create a social safety net. They practiced compassion every day, and they knew what to do in practice. So the knowledge of when and how to engage in communitarian activities ties in with collective intelligence. Normativity and knowledge are connected.

LOSING OUR COMPASSION

What is the twenty-first-century barn raising? Pretty much the only people left raising actual barns, after all, are the Amish and the Mennonites. I use barn raising as a metaphor, but unless one is employed in the shriveled civil-society sector, most of us can only claim to be either taxpayers or donors, neither of whom are barn raisers. Taxpayers are compelled to give to a faraway authority. Donors give voluntarily, but the charity might be a thousand miles away.

It is, after all, now possible to support causes on the other side of the world with just the click of a button. When a tsunami hit Indonesia in 2004, people half a world away sent donations in record sums. Yet when we see poverty or problems two streets over, it's easy to think *that's someone else's problem*. Or we tell ourselves that it's *our* problem collectively, which translates as somebody else's problem. Seldom are we active participants anymore.

Today, most of us outsource our moral commitments to corporate charities or the voting booth. Make no mistake, this comes at a cost: making donations and paying taxes does comparatively little for our development as moral beings, and even less for our communities. To become a moral being, one has to *practice* being good, which includes acts of compassion. Aristotle thought of the virtues as needing to be habituated. To a great degree, he was right.

The paradox here is that a virtue, to be practiced, cannot also be legislated. To encode a virtue into law and policy means giving up the conscious practice. People obey the law out of fear, not compassion. At least you can say, "I pay my taxes." Solving some social problem or helping someone is rarely as important to people as claiming that you did your part. But if genuine compassion prompts us to charitable acts, to make charity into something compulsory destroys it *as a practice*.

When people can outsource virtue to some authority, it makes them less virtuous. Charity as a habit of heart and mind is becoming a lost art. And that is why the breakdown of community and mutual aid is the direct consequence of the lost need to practice compassion.

Generation after generation, Americans have chosen to follow the European welfare state model, in which compassion is outsourced and centralized. But that doesn't mean the total disappearance of the virtuous. It just means we have to look a little harder to find them.

STRANGE PRODUCE

Dwight B. "Whitey" Hord, DDS — my grandfather on my mother's side — never retired. For years, he was pretty much the only dentist in Upper Cleveland County, North Carolina. A lot of people depended on him. But when he was about forty, his joints started giving him problems due to severe rheumatoid arthritis. His fingers were so gnarled he couldn't straighten them.

But it never disabled him. He scaled back his practice when he got into his late 70s, but he knew that he would completely wither if he ever stopped practicing. So he never stopped, and he never completely withered. Eventually, Whitey succumbed to complications of pneumonia, but he practiced dentistry right up until he died. Even as his hands became crippled, he would simply position the dental instruments between his knobby joints so he could work.

Whitey was one of the "Greatest Generation." To be fair, I used to wonder about that term. I understood that living through the Depression and World War II would qualify someone for a nice designation, but as I age, I appreciate the contrasts between his generation and the ones that came after, in the way they thought, how they acted, and what they built. We've inherited their country and some of their wealth, but as they pass away, much of their greatness goes with them.

After WWII, Whitey returned from the Pacific to create a life for himself back in his hometown, in rural North Carolina. When the local high school refused to renew his teaching contract after he taught evolution in his biology classes, he went back to Chapel Hill to study in UNC's first dental class. He might have gotten richer setting up a dental practice in an urban area, but he set up near his parents, who had taken in ironing and worked longer hours at the mill so that he could study dentistry.

Not too long after starting up his practice, Whitey became a man of means. Today we might not think as much of his home atop the pine-covered hill there in sleepy Lawndale. But to the townspeople at that time, it must have been rather like their Monticello. Whitey was a county patriarch, a community pillar, and a deacon of the church. In Upper Cleveland County, he was among the one percent. Doing well for oneself in small-town America is not always about becoming wealthy; there are tacit exchanges and profound responsibilities that go beyond money.

Soon after Whitey got his practice going, he started coming home with strange things. At first, it would be ears of corn or a bag of apples. Another day it might be a giant head of cabbage, a jar of chow chow (pickled slaw), or a block of livermush (cornmeal-based pork pâté). The kids never thought much of it until years later, when even stranger things started showing up.

"A year or so before he died," my aunt Jean recalls, "he showed me a letter he received in the mail from someone who sent him a $10 bill in an envelope. The unsigned note included that this was for services from many years before that the person couldn't afford to pay at the time. Daddy didn't know who sent it. The truth is, it could have been anybody. And that was the beauty of it."[176]

Whitey was known for being private about financial matters. So what he did for the people in his community was really nobody's business. Yet in some way, everybody knew about it. How else would he have ended up with all the strange produce and mysterious letters? And how are his children still hearing things, years after his death, about what he did for people?

Within our family, stories of his frugality outnumber those of his generosity. That's pretty typical of families, or it used to be. We rarely take the time to familiarize ourselves with good things about our loved ones when they're alive. Likewise, because we enjoyed all the advantages of being the children and grandchildren of a successful dentist, we occupied ourselves with Whitey's parsimony. Of course he took care of his children and grandchildren. And he was wise not to spoil us.

Note that Whitey never charged a penny if he didn't have to do any work. No cavities meant no charge. While an exam cost him another opportunity or some free time, Whitey felt a good checkup deserved a reward. Can you imagine a dentist not charging for a visit today?

Every summer, Whitey would spend Thursdays doing dental work for low-income kids. For many of those children, it meant multiple visits to fill numerous cavities. They all left with a new toothbrush, a tube of toothpaste, and whiter smiles — for which Whitey never received a dime.

He also used to pack his tools and do a house call every year to a young woman with cerebral palsy. My aunt Jean, the youngest of his children, used to assist him. "I remember being with him as he tried to clean her teeth while she twisted and jerked involuntarily,"[177] she recalls.

And, of course, there were the bills that came due. In a small town, they're probably people you know. My aunt Ellen, the third-born sibling, helped out in the dental office many times over the years. "When I was helping Daddy with his office affairs," Ellen recalled, "he wouldn't let me send second notices to patients. He told me that they knew they owed him, and they must not have the money to pay. He didn't want to embarrass them by sending additional notices."

Embarrass them? That seems like such a distant consideration in an era of collection agencies. Yet in a genuine community, looking out for every member's dignity is essential to its cohesion. Wherever this social cohesion exists today, it is rare. None of this is to argue that people aren't generous anymore. Nor is it to say that we can't find our way back to being there for each other. It's that our current system has made us complacent. It keeps us from *practicing* virtue.

I should note that Dwight B. Hord, DDS, as benevolent as he was, lived through and supported every significant policy that has brought us to where we are today. By disposition, he was a Barn Raiser. By intellect, he was a High Mind. And this is true for many of the so-called Greatest Generation, none of whom will live to witness the collapse.

THE DECLINE OF MUTUAL AID

"The third element is a weakened or prostrate civil society that lacks the capacity to resist these plans,"[178] writes political scientist James C. Scott of High Modernism.

I promised we would come back to this point because it's in the weakening of civil society that our most intimate ties begin to break with one another. The plans to which Scott is referring are for the administrative ordering of society through the blunt instrument of power. In America, High Modernism gave us the Central Bank and the income tax. Then it gave us the New Deal, with its alphabet soup of programs. Then it gave us the Second Great War, with its almighty industrial policy, followed closely by the Bretton Woods agreement, which made the dollar almighty, too. After that was the Great Society and the overweening regulatory state; soon after, a military empire with status as a nation-builder. In my lifetime, the administrative ordering of American society would extend to the entire world. And this blind apparatus rattles on, pulling everything it can into its great maw, even from the future.

The great fact of opportunity costs means that a dollar spent building a base in Basrah is a dollar that cannot be spent at home. A dollar spent on issuing a social security check to a millionaire cannot be invested in a college fund. An hour of human labor spent realizing the fever dreams of a High Mind is an hour that can never go to building civil society from the ground up.

The society held together by mutual support, tight neighborhoods, and barn raisings is long gone; we're now utterly dependent on the plans and power of people thousands of miles away. Despite the growth of the administrative welfare state, Americans managed to increase their productivity and get wealthier. It seemed for a time, therefore, that the aspirations of High Modernism were feasible and affordable. Today, they are neither. The whole edifice exists through debt. And as authorities have kicked the can, year after year, we have forgotten how to take care of each other. In other words, as the administrative state grew, civil society fell into decline. Whether it's correlation or causation, I cannot say. Either way, the circumstantial evidence is pretty damning.

CIVIL ASSOCIATION IN AMERICA

When Alexis de Tocqueville came to America in 1831, he saw something profound. Maybe you've read the following passage before. But as you reread it, ask yourself whether or to what degree this is an America you recognize:

> The political associations that exist in the United States are only a single feature in the midst of the immense assemblage of associations in that country. Americans of all ages, all conditions, and all dispositions constantly form associations. They have not only commercial and manufacturing companies, in which all take part, but associations of a thousand other kinds, religious, moral, serious, futile, general or restricted, enormous or diminutive. The Americans make associations to give entertainments, to found seminaries, to build inns, to construct churches, to diffuse books, to send missionaries to the antipodes; in this manner they found hospitals, prisons, and schools. If it is proposed to inculcate some truth or to foster some feeling by the encouragement of a great example, they form a society. Wherever at the head of some new undertaking you see the government in France, or a man of rank in England, in the United States you will be sure to find an association.[179]

I suspect that even if you see something of America in the above, it's weakened in the sense that it is no longer at the center of American life.

Reading Tocqueville, one can imagine a time when the

organs of civil association extended to spheres of life such as childhood and old age, which are wholly institutionalized and segregated today. Children are warehoused by the state so that parents can work and pay taxes. The elderly are sequestered and told, more or less, that their participation in society is optional after sixty-five. At that point, they become liabilities to be managed by the Congressional Budget Office.

No doubt, then, a weakened and prostrate civil society includes the lost array of mutual aid societies, lodges, and fraternal orders of which a third of Americans were once members. Historian David Beito painstakingly investigates these:

> The record of five societies that thrived at or near the turn of the century illustrates the many variants of this system. Each had a distinct membership base. Two of the societies, the Independent Order of Saint Luke and the United Order of True Reformers, were all-black. Both had been founded by ex-slaves after the Civil War and specialized initially in sickness and burial insurance. The other societies had entirely white memberships. The Loyal Order of Moose was an exclusively male society that emphasized sickness and burial benefits. It became best known during the 20th century for its orphanage, Mooseheart, near Aurora, Illinois. The Security Benefit Association (originally the Knights and Ladies of Security) followed in a similar tradition but broke from the mainstream by allowing men and women to join on equal terms.[180]

Even as we shake our modern heads at segregation along racial lines, we can appreciate the power of civil association in those days.

Today, if you were to ask the average man on the street to name a mutual aid society, you would be lucky if he could name a single one. But at one time, these organizations were everywhere. They had funny names like the

Oddfellows and the Brotherhood of Locomotive Engineers. They are the forgotten social safety net. At one time, they included health insurance and unemployment support. Because they were a mix of the communitarian and the charitable, surplus dues could go to growth and giving. Because most were organized as local lodges, they featured undocumented acts of kindness and tough love we would scarcely recognize today.

Beito describes all-female societies such as the Knights and Ladies of Security and the Ladies of the Maccabees, which created tremendous works such as orphanages and surgical centers, despite women's continued political marginalization. Women who belonged to these societies thought of themselves as members of fraternal societies. What's striking is an ethos that is virtually absent in American society today: "Fraternity," writes one of the Ladies of the Maccabees, "in these modern days has been wrested from its original significance and has come to mean a sisterhood, as well as a brotherhood, in the human family."[181]

This vast empire of human good was built not by federal largesse but by the moral conviction of people weaving their lives together to guard against hardship and protect the vulnerable. Redistribution and centralized welfare tore apart the linkages of mutual aid. Most Americans are now totally dependent on the plans of people thousands of miles away. Thanks to growth in the private sector, Americans grew rich enough to afford their welfare state for a while. But in time, the system became corrosive and dependent on debt.

With the exception of Greek Week rushes on college campuses, the word fraternity is all but missing from our common lexicon. It is practically taboo even to suggest, much less say: *The rise of the welfare state has all but destroyed our sense of human brotherhood.*

Communities that fraternity once held together have been lost, too. The breakdown of community in America started long ago. Our robust civil society sector was made moribund by the New Deal, and by 1965 had been scorched entirely by the introduction of the Great Society programs. Why? Because mutual aid is participatory, which requires skin in the game and a real commitment to the people in one's community. By contrast, the government program is impersonal. All it requires is a completed checklist of eligibility requirements and the appropriate number of stamps. But it's free. No more Wednesday evenings at the fellowship hall. No more difficult conversations with members. No more membership dues.

Freemasons researcher Justin Arman shares an example of how the Masons built community around compassion in Texas. Here's a passage from the Grand Master Lightfoot:

> It is not only our duty, but should be a privilege to aid in binding up the wounds of our stricken brethren, to feed the hungry, clothe the naked, to give protection to the widows and orphans, and by these noble examples of brotherly love, relief and truth, kindle brighter the fires of Fraternity and Universal Brotherhood, and prevent their extinction among mankind.[182]

When it comes to the Freemasons, most of what we hear are conspiracy theories. No doubt some of them are true. But we rarely hear about the Masons' commitment to helping the peoples of the world, both nearby and far away. The closer you are to the action, the better equipped you are to determine whether your gift is needed and the results of your giving are good. It's simply easier to be mindful if you know the people and the terrain. Social entrepreneur Ron Schultz calls it "adjacent opportunities":

> In practicing this level of engagement, we discover that something rather unexpected happens. When we operate from a mindful image of the world we

encounter, we see things we might previously have
missed. We still bring our causal chain of experience
with us, but as we break through the patterned
behavior and habitual responses that have influenced
it in the past, and add a new and more present way
of looking at the world we encounter, the possibility
space surrounding us enlarges and we see more
within it with greater clarity...[183]

Mindfulness — especially when it comes to those affective bonds we form with our family, friends, and neighbors
— changes the dynamic. It changes us. And it is through
our lived experience of taking care of one another that we
come fully to understand what it means to be human.

Americans are compassionate, giving people. But we
have changed our patterns of contribution over the last
decades. Now, large sections of our very identities have
been blotted out due to gradual transference of our attention away from adjacent opportunities, toward party and
politics. How we fit into our communities, what we contribute, and any sense of common purpose has been reduced
to virtue posturing and political peacocking. Our *agency in
context* has weakened.

For the vast majority of people in the developed world,
the welfare state is charity enough. Paying one's taxes
is compassion. Agitating for more welfare programs *is*
care. Apart from tossing $20 into someone's GoFundMe
campaign, we are hardly barn raisers anymore. The Great
Plans of the welfare state are not only sending us headlong
into insolvency but continue to rob people of opportunities
to practice compassion. *The people can't be trusted to take care
of each other,* we're told; *they're too selfish.* And yet somehow,
among those self-same people, there are angels to be discovered, trusted, and installed at the highest levels of power.

Matters have gotten so bad that millionaires and billionaires make news with open letters: "Tax us. Tax us. Tax
us." they write in an open letter to which they are signato-

ries. "It is the right choice. It is the only choice."[184] Yet not a single signatory I know of has written an extra check to the U.S. Treasury. To sign an open letter calling for an unlikely political change is a way of *seeming* compassionate without having to *be* compassionate. This sort of posturing is another sign of American decline.

The truth is we can all do more, even those of us who are not millionaires. And we should. If we were all just one-tenth the human being that Oseola McCarty was, our society would be stronger and more resilient. We wouldn't need billionaires to posture. Instead, we would need them to bankroll a hundred thousand experiments in effective altruism — not because they were forced to do so by IRS agents, but because it might improve someone's life.

Alas, the welfare state is now a bipartisan megachurch. If you turn the conversation to the impending financial collapse, you might as well be messing with the national religion. We need a new secular religion that does not view free enterprise and mutual aid as political contradictions. After collapse, we will have no choice. We will have to rediscover compassion, fraternity, and virtue in ourselves.

THE RETURN OF 'FRATERNAL INDIVIDUALISM'

These days, one might argue that too many of us are keeping up with the Joneses and working forty-plus hours a week to keep some corporation profitable. That leaves little time or energy for the practice of compassion, beyond feeding the hungry mouths of the nuclear family.

There is, of course, a grain of truth in this. Yet people still find time for all manner of practices, from Ashtanga yoga to political canvassing; video gaming to Zen meditation. Most of these activities are supposed to quell the anxieties of modern life.

We'll return to the question of what a renaissance in

mutual aid might look like in the twenty-first century. For now, it's enough to urge that if it's true that the financial collapse of the federal government is imminent, we will have no choice but to reconstitute the civil society sector. The silver lining is that we will also be able to revive our shriveled identities and bring more balance to ourselves as moral beings. Maybe we will welcome the return of 'fraternal individualism.'

"If self-reliance and thrift were fraternal watchwords," writes Beito, "so too was individualism. The word did not entail Epicurean self-gratification or Emersonian contrariness; instead, it was akin to a winnowing out process for the improvement of character."[185]

In every case Beito studied, the goal for each member was economic self-reliance. Leaders were artful directors and cooperators. Everyone had to exercise self-discipline, which was not primarily selfish. That's why an official of the all-Black United Order of True Reformers held two views without contraction: he thought that "selfish individualism" and "intemperance" should be shunned, but he also supported a program that enabled "people to get homes and means upon which they may independently subsist."[186]

The place where compassion meets self-reliance is sacred, which is why the mutual aid era was about doing what you could to help others in your community while also helping them become self-reliant. None of this is an argument against giving aid to people in distress around the world. By all means, we should fight malaria and help distant peoples access clean drinking water. But we should also turn some of our attention back to the people around us. To practice compassion is to create a *functional role* for ourselves. Sometimes advice, encouragement, and mentorship are more valuable than money.

We can imagine the True Reformer looking a fellow member in the eyes to offer him help with a sick child. We can imagine the True Reformer looking back to take it, clasping the man's hand, and vowing to help cook for the other men as a thank you. These are not the distant abstractions of Washington bureaucracy, nor the Welfare State's means tests, statistics, and plot-points, all of which can only stand in for thinking, feeling, flesh-and-blood people. People in mutual aid make real commitments to each other. Broken commitments are felt. This is no abstract social contract, but real promises people make to each other. Practitioners assume that nearly everyone is capable of community stewardship and personal transformation. It does not treat great swaths of humanity like the target of budget outlays.

Today, the sum of one's moral commitments is to dabble in online activism until that day comes to send your prayers up in the voting booth. But it's not just that people have forgotten how to be barn raisers — it's also that they have lost the requisite knowledge and discernment to be better community members. We have become a people enchanted by controversies far, far away.

THE EXTENDED FAMILY

There is probably something to columnist David Brooks's observation that the extended family has shrunk and that the nuclear family makes us a little more fractured than we should be.[187] To the extent that we can rebuild our most important unit of civilization, we must view our families as sources of connection and aid.

Currently, most people view the extended family as those with whom we sit around the table at Thanksgiving or Passover. But even the original Thanksgiving and traditional Passover had been about opening our homes and tables to others, even strangers. During the Passover seder, Jews worldwide sit together to eat, pray, and love. They raise cups of wine and say words in unison, just as they have done for thousands of years. "Today, as well," Herbert

Bronstein, the editor of *A Passover Haggadah* says, "wherever slavery remains, Jews taste its bitterness."[188]

Eating the bitter herbs from the Seder plate, they recall the bitterness of those once in bondage, and contemplate those still in it. It is a celebration of their freedom. It is the remembrance of sorrow. It is a call to compassion and a reminder that there is always more to do. That call to compassion for and the liberation of others is an ongoing process that is not just intended for them, but is a universal aspiration.

Group
Still we remember: "It was we who were slaves... we who were strangers." And therefore we recall these words as well.

Leader
You shall not oppress a stranger, for you know the feelings of the stranger,

Group
Having yourselves been strangers in the land of Egypt

Leader
When strangers reside with you in your land, you shall not wrong them… You should love them as yourself,

Group
For you were strangers in the land of Egypt.[189]

This kind of compassion, which extends beyond the family and the tribe, is compassion that should be manifested through continuous acts of service. Through these acts, Jews seek to heal the world. And to heal the world requires ongoing commitment, or what we have described as *practice*. Variously interpreted, *tikkun olam* was defined by the Medieval scholar Maimonides as compassionate acts, which bring a continuous "ordering of reality." And though modern Jews engage in service projects and other *tikkun olam* activities they, like their American counterparts in other faiths, have at times come to confuse compassionate action with activism.

The Jews' stranger, which is potentially anyone, is invited to sit at the Passover table. This extension of the nuclear family, though not racial, biological, or genetic, is a path by which humanity can overcome birds-of-a-feather tendencies. The gravity to those we know too often keeps us from extending our compassion outward. There are limits, of course, to widening the circle of community. But it's become clear that our conception of the family has shrunk, and that we have become too atomistic. Nuclear families and atomistic individuals may not be luxuries we can always afford in the future.

THE BLAME

Some will try to argue that it's not the Welfare State that's to blame, but rather the market, with its rabid capitalists and consumerists. Instead of placing value on each other, we place more value on stuff, status, and stuff that helps us be seen as having status. There is some truth in this critique. Even if capitalism shares some blame for our shrunken civil society sector, we have to acknowledge that Americans outsourced their charity and self-sufficiency to politicians somewhere along the way. With that charity went enormous power.

There is thus an unholy symbiosis between the Welfare State and Consumerism. At some level, it's about being able to say *I pay my taxes* as a stand-in for the practice of compassion. The cost has also come in relinquishing to authorities a lever of control no group should possess. Compassion lives in the heart, not in the legislators' lobby. It cannot be horse-traded into existence by political elites with axes to grind.

THE UNHAPPINESS HYPOTHESIS

Americans are less happy in part because they have forgotten how to give well. I realize that's a bold hypothesis, but I think we can support it.

To begin with, happiness is subjective, and so I am generally skeptical of survey data on the subject. There's no good translation manual between questionnaires and subjective states, especially answers reported by different people at different times in different contexts. Still, I rely on positive psychology experiments conducted by Elizabeth Dunn and Michael I. Norton.

Positive psychology is a branch of psychology that deals with questions about why people are happy instead of questions about why people are mentally ill. In their experiments, Dunn and Norton found that when people give, they are consistently happier than when they spend the same money on themselves. Here's an excerpt:

> [B]oth correlational and experimental studies show that people who spend money on others report greater happiness. The benefits of such prosocial spending emerge among adults around the world, and the warm glow of giving can be detected even in toddlers.[190]

But the thing is — and this is important — it's not just any giving that offers this result. Dunn and Norton add that "these benefits are most likely to emerge when giving satisfies one or more core human needs (relatedness, competence, and autonomy)."[191]

Relatedness. Competence. Autonomy. In simpler terms, we can call these *connection, impact,* and *choice.*

Connection. The stronger the tie you have with the recipient, the happier giving makes you. Call to mind those concentric circles of relatedness to others, from your family and closest friends, then to your extended family and acquaintances, then to your colleagues and neighbors, and then outward, to strangers. You're more likely to derive happiness from giving to those closest to you. But what's interesting is, when you give a gift to a stranger, it can be a mechanism for making those closer ties.

Impact. It's not enough simply to give. We want to know that our giving improved someone's life appreciably. That means that one might not derive a lot of positive feeling from giving to a large, faceless organization like the United Way. But when one can see that their contributions are going to specific people whose lives are improved — like helping a neighbor rebuild after a disaster or helping a lodge member's child go to college — that's when the good feelings grow.

Choice. If we don't get to choose where our gifts go, we don't get a good feeling from giving. Most of us have been in a scenario in which we felt pressured to help. Whether you get trapped by a kid selling overpriced candy bars or shaken down by United Way at work, this sort of altruism is no fun. Getting cornered takes the joy out of giving, as do IRS audits.

Some might quibble with the idea that giving ought to make us happier. I'd rather not get into any debates about whether suffering purifies the spirit or whether altruism is a paradox. Let's just say that if we want more giving in the world, it helps when giving makes people happier.

What if the institutions of civil society and mutual aid had continued to develop through the twentieth century instead of being crowded out? Compared with government welfare, which denies connection, impact, and choice, mutual aid's dismantled structures must have been great reservoirs of happiness.

Not just happiness: meaning.

Beware the Universal Basic Income

Not since the carbon tax have we seen a proposal hotter than the universal basic income (UBI). Even Big Tech luminaries like Mark Zuckerberg have expressed support for the idea that some ultra-lean government body cuts everyone a check periodically. No one is left to live in poverty — because once you establish a reasonable poverty line, the UBI ensures no one lives below it.

For the poorest among us, life still won't be easy, but everyone under a UBI can meet his or her basic needs. No matter one's income, each citizen will get (for example) $1,000 a month. And in some ways, it's bipartisan. A UBI combines the economic efficiency favored by the right with redistributive aspects favored by the left.

Bipartisanship is a big reason the idea has gotten legs:

- Those on the right should love a UBI because it would be designed to eliminate welfare-state bureaucracy layers. A cluster of alphabet soup agencies would simply go away.

- Those on the left should love a UBI because it would ensure that no one living under its auspices would have to live below the poverty line.

- Those on the right should love a UBI because it allows people the freedom to spend the money as they choose, rather than having authorities direct the resources.

- Those on the left should love a UBI because people on the lower end of the income distribution would benefit.

- Those left, right, center, and beyond think it has the potential to save humanity from the effects of mass displacement due to AI and automation.

There is much to recommend about the UBI. In some respects, it would be preferable to the status quo. Those enamored of digital ledgers think a UBI is even more promising, because such technology has the potential to protect the system's integrity.

But we should have some deep concerns about a UBI — or, at least, the variation that High Minds are currently floating. H. L. Mencken, perhaps, put it best: "There is always a well-known solution to every human problem — neat, plausible, and wrong."[192]

With the following, I offer some reasons to be wary.

HUMAN HOUSE CATS

As every economist will tell you, incentives matter. The basic idea is that if you *subsidize* some activity you'll get more of it, and if you *tax* some activity you'll get less of it.

So when you pay people to be relatively poorer, they are more likely to remain relatively poorer. Some UBI proponents are convinced that these incentive effects will go away; people who are less stressed about meeting their basic needs will be *more* productive, proponents argue, because they will have the financial freedom to experiment with different career options. And one might find anecdotal cases where that would be true.

But for the vast majority, a UBI could create legions of human house cats. Living on a UBI might not be all that uncomfortable if you can afford a room, ramen noodles, and an Xbox to while away the hours. One need only look at the perverse effects of welfare, which in 1996 led President Bill Clinton to sign a welfare reform bill designed to unwind intergenerational cycles of poverty begun under President Lyndon Johnson's Great Society initiative.

Many people are comfortable with the idea that there will be a massive superstratum of people who simply exist without knowing the dignity of work. A few imagine not work, but more generative behavior such as art. People will gather in the agora to contemplate life and dream up grand theories together. We should be skeptical — but whether you're in the agora or playing video games, you're likely to be generating deadweight loss, for which the productive members of society must pay.

We have a great number of existing experiments that have come along with the incentives of traditional welfare, which have, for the most part, caused house-cat behavior. UBI Proponents say cash transfers will be different. But will they? We have only seen a couple of experiments with UBI, such as Manitoba's Mincome experiment of the 1970s, which is small and dated, and Finland's more recent attempt (2017-2018), which almost everyone agrees was poorly devised. The Finnish government scuttled that experiment prematurely. Some cite the Alaska Permanent Fund as a success story, but Alaska residents get less than $2,000 per year—which is a fraction of most UBI proposals and might not be big enough to affect one's incentives to create value. As long as these experiments are carried out in small but diverse jurisdictions, they're perhaps worth investigating. But is it wise or useful to experiment on 350 million? Since the Welfare Reform Act of 1996, there are too many examples of negative incentive effects of free money or welfare transfers to ignore.

LEVERS OF CENTRALIZATION

Another troubling feature of UBIs currently under consideration is that a large, powerful central government would administer it. Institute a UBI, and suddenly authorities have a massive new level of power. Suppose there is a UBI of $10,000 per year, per person. That's an enormous new system of incentives, a Skinner Box of epic proportions. Let's also imagine the bill that creates the UBI leaves open the possibility for certain conditions placed on citizens that they must meet in order to receive their UBI check each month. According to statute, such conditions can be determined by the administering agency.

Maybe you thought Donald Trump was terrific. Maybe you loathed him with every fiber of your being. Either way: imagine the politician you hate most controlling the levers of incentive for every single American taxpayer. Is that something that sits comfortably with you? A remarkable degree of power now lies in that hated politician's hands. Just think what they could get away with, given the threat to withhold those funds. Consider, for example, laws that require people to take drug tests to collect welfare checks, or any number of paternalist schemes. Drug testing might sound like a good idea to some readers — but maybe the program is something you don't like. Otherwise, a UBI could very well evolve into a central control mechanism that runs counter to your values.

But a UBI should never have conditions placed on it or be used as a lever of control, say its proponents. We must imagine something elegant and unadulterated by politics.

ROMANTIC POLITICS

Romantics about a UBI insist that any such system will be immune from politics. Like Social Security funds, it will be a special fund locked away from politicians and their influence. It will work as an algorithm, redistributing funds like clockwork, without conditions, to everyone — that is, of course, if it can get passed.

1. I would ask the reader to consider what legislative sausage, first ground along the corridors of K Street, has *ever* been ideal. What angels staff the halls of Capitol Hill? In other words: why should we expect that whatever UBI has the political feasibility to pass would be pure in the way UBI proponents hope? It's not a stretch to say that no bill has ever

gone through Congress and come out of the process elegant, simple, and ideal.

2. A UBI is supposed to establish a poverty floor so that people simply get accustomed to poverty, starting at a certain level. Many believe that, in its ideal form, it won't create as many perverse incentives. Whether or not that hypothesis is correct (it most certainly is not), the threat of suspending someone's UBI is both a stick and a carrot, thanks to the human propensity for loss aversion. Politicians know this. And you'd better believe they'll use it to manipulate the electorate.

3. Politics is as much about the art of compromise as the science of corruption. If there is no perceived political advantage to enacting a UBI, it will be a dead letter. Therefore, the only way to get a UBI to pass is when politicians see that it can be an instrument of power. Even if you think free money benefits people, the question is whether the politicians think they will benefit.

Remember, also, that politicians seldom worry about who is going to pick up the tab.

AFFORDABILITY ISSUES

Few people take the time actually to sit down and ask whether or not a UBI is even affordable. A couple of people have done that work for us, though. Robert Greenstein, of the progressive Center for Budget and Policy Priorities, lays it out starkly: "There are over 300 million Americans today. Suppose UBI provided everyone with $10,000 a year. That would cost more than $3 trillion a year — and $30 trillion to $40 trillion over ten years. This single-year figure amounts to more than three-fourths of the entire yearly federal budget — and double the entire budget outside

Social Security, Medicare, defense, and interest payments. It's also equal to close to 100 percent of all tax revenue the federal government collects."[193]

Even if you cut the above UBI in half, it would still "cost as much as the entire federal budget outside Social Security, Medicare, defense, and interest payments."[194]

UBI proponents often respond by suggesting that a UBI simply be made taxable, which essentially makes it not universal. Still, that sliding-scale approach means that the great bulk of Americans who have no tax liability would still fail to offset the cost. Put another way, the savings would only bring a UBI cost down "to something like $2.5 trillion or $2.75 trillion (or $25 trillion to $27.5 trillion over ten years)"[195], according to Greenstein.

Much of the above overlap with our concerns above because it's naïve to think that any significant program would go on the chopping block. Under what circumstances will the Pentagon give up its goodies, or will people be willing to give up Social Security or Medicare? If we are not prepared to *add* to the looming tsunami of debt that awaits Americans due to the Big Three entitlements and Pentagon spending, then we have to figure out where to cut. And spending cuts are the political equivalent of flying pigs.

Some commenters have floated the idea of defunding the police or taxing corporations like Amazon more. Still, such proposals have to find a way to make the math add up to the sums above and find a way not to create more armies of unemployed in the process—as higher corporate taxation risks doing.

COMMUNITY'S CORE

It seems obvious to some that community is rooted in culture; fewer are willing to admit that real, lasting community is rooted in need. The invisible filaments that bind us together as communities almost always originate in the desire for mutual aid. When mutual aid self-organizes, communities can become particularly robust.

When aid is centralized and doled out from distant capitals, it can destroy the invisible filaments that bind people. Like the centralized welfare state of the twentieth century, current conceptions of a UBI likewise dilute fraternity and care structures that arise among people with a common culture and common needs.

HETEROGENEITY

Under the current conception of a UBI, everybody everywhere gets the same amount. But $10,000 in Manhattan is not the same as $10,000 in Mississippi. In other words, the economy, including the cost of basic living expenses, will create a differential treatment for people due to considerations that one might consider arbitrary under most ideas of equal justice. In Jackson, MS, for example, the average monthly rent is $843[196] — compared to $3,629 in San Francisco, CA[197]; $1,089 in Chattanooga, TN[198]; and $3,436 in New York, NY.[199] Notice that in Jackson and Chattanooga, a $10,000 UBI would cover someone's rent almost entirely. In San Francisco or New York, it would certainly not. A higher cost of living is frequently why labor costs are higher in more expensive cities.

Another related problem is that heavy regulation in specific industries versus light regulation in others creates inflation in those heavily-regulated sectors relative to the others. These relatively unregulated areas of the economy mean *better, faster, cheape*r for things we might think of as non-essential, such as smartphones, TVs, and toys. But if we were to add a UBI to those differences, we'd be likely to see a de facto incentive for people to spend more in those areas, where they can get a better deal (which zips us back to the human house cats problem).

The preceding objections should give us pause as we

face what seems to be a daily diet of UBI boosterism. The UBI has its advocates on the traditional right and left. But at the end of the day, we have to ask ourselves whether another distribution scheme is what a collapsing America needs. Like many other schemes, the UBI doesn't deal with the fundamental pathologies of American society. Instead, it would be a perpetual numbing agent, one that legions of people would come to depend on, in the way people come to depend on painkillers.

If collapse is the cliff toward which we are driving, a UBI would be hitting the gas.

What Replaced Compassion

Compassion has an evil twin called *envy*. Whenever compassion is missing, envy will sidle up next to us to whisper untruths. Envy, of course, is the emotional response that arises when you compare yourself to others and find they have something you don't — or, at least, more of it.

Following anthropologist Helmut Schoeck, the impetus toward totalitarian regimes has its roots in envy. "*Who does not envy with us is against us!*"[200] writes Schoek, aping the indignant. If Schoeck is right, too many societies have been consumed by it. In America, envy, coupled with the dogmas of social justice, has given rise to blanket indignation. This indignation, this ersatz morality, has swept through this generation like a contagion.

"My distaste for democracy as a political theory is," wrote the inimitable H. L. Mencken, "like every other human prejudice, due to an inner lack—to a defect that is a good deal less in the theory than in myself. In this case, it is very probably my incapacity for envy."[201] Would that we were all just a little more like Mencken.

One wonders if indignation and compassion are commensurable emotions at all. After all, the former doesn't motivate one to love, to help, or to give. It suffocates wisdom and provokes the inner adolescent to agitate, hector, and shame. Yet indignation functions like a special card that allows its bearer to abandon responsibility to his fellow humans. He is no longer required even to be tolerant. Instead of *being* virtuous, he only has to *seem* virtuous. Such manifests itself in vapid hashtags, virtue selfies, and Twitter mobs.

The indignant care more about tearing down the rich than lifting up the poor. They prefer institutions of compulsion to those of compassion. In other words: only an apparatus of permanent parasitism will do. The idea of growing the giving sector never enters their minds.

The indignant cares less about people of color than they do about getting to speak for them. Their final act of white privilege will be to play Joan of Arc on social media. When they and their friends have pulled down all the statues and looted all the small businesses, they will gather amid the rubble, smeared with soot, and bask in their rectitude.

The poor will still be there, peeking out from a tent city somewhere under a bridge.

At the intellectual rear guard are the High Minds. Together they represent a new puritan army. You are no match for their indignation, which fuels their unending demands. If they ever get what they want, it will mean dark times for everyone.

You can hear sounds of sanctimony in the classrooms, corporate board rooms, and streets of husk cities such as San Francisco. It'll start with a noise that seems off in the distance; a single reference to equity, diversity, and inclusion. But the noise builds. Soon it will be on every daytime television show and news broadcast. It will come to your workplace. It will come to almost every institution you hold dear. Like a locust plague, the wokest will descend. They'll require more and more. But it will never be enough.

Their ultimate goal is not to rid the world of oppression; to do so would deny the indignant their indignance and their identity. In other words, the indignant *define themselves* as *for the oppressed* and *against the oppressors*. Their *raison d'être* is then to oppose, even oppress, those they regard as oppressors. The oppressed serve as props in a performance without end.

When it comes, we'll withdraw at first, waiting for it to all go away. The ever-present noise will distract us, interfering with our ability to practice genuine compassion. But as long as the indignation chorus is there, the sound will get louder.

We can no longer sit by and just wait for it to pass. It won't.

5

THE BREAKDOWN OF
COLLECTIVE INTELLIGENCE

*Without a World Encyclopaedia to hold
men's minds together in something like a
common interpretation of reality, there is no
hope whatever of anything but an accidental
and transitory alleviation of any of our
world troubles.*

H. G. Wells, from *World Brain*

In 2008, British designer Thomas Thwaites decided that he would try to build a toaster from scratch. We're not talking about going to a store and buying manufactured parts to assemble; we're talking *from scratch* as in from raw materials pulled from the earth. Thwaites wanted to go deeper into the process most of us take for granted: What turns the stuff we pull out of the ground into the stuff that fills our homes?

Thwaites set about on a solo manufacturing adventure that demonstrates how removed we are from the collective intelligence that makes our lives better. Thwaites had to find copper and iron ore in mines around the world, then do some in-house smelting. He had to look up patents for rudimentary components. And after a couple of failed attempts to convince BP to fly him out to an oil rig to get crude to make plastic, he ended up using potato starch instead.

The final product wasn't pretty. It wasn't even shiny or spare. It was a haggard thing, the kind of toaster you or I might buy for the price of a decent meal. It took Thwaites nine months, international travel, and lots of creative repurposing to build. It didn't even work. Thwaites did plug his toaster in once, but because he didn't make insulation for the wires, the toaster began to melt after about five seconds. I don't expect that was enough time for the bread to brown.[202]

It's not just toasters (or smartphones, or automobiles) that depend on collective intelligence. It's also the collaboration teams, cooperatives, and communal arrangements that make stuff and do things for us. Because each of us individually isn't smart or capable enough to know everything there is to know, we use ever-improving manufacturing facilities, computing technologies, and organizational models to harness the smarts of a diverse set of minds. Collective intelligence, when it's free to flower and morph but checked by input from reality, lies at the core of our modern living standards. And we pull it, moment to moment, from a billion minds around the world.

Collective Intelligence

The kind of collective intelligence that allows us to buy a cheap-but-functional toaster is a miracle of materialism. But it doesn't represent every kind of collective intelligence. Other forms include shared knowledge in a discipline or sub-discipline, such as medicine or oncology. Another form might be ten million readers simultaneously experiencing an event a thousand miles away. Another form is the rules and norms that spring up within a community to keep harmony and help things work.

I'll use the term, but be the first to admit that *collective intelligence* can be an eely concept. If it means *stuff a lot of people happen to know*, well, that's useful but not earth-shattering. If we define it as some emergent noosphere that has a mind of its own and regards the world as a distributed God-brain, well, that's speculative, weird, and perhaps a bit too spooky to consider. For now, let's assume that collective intelligence is something in between. When people work together to track truth, coordinate, or collaborate, the whole can be greater than the sum of its parts. This process can form useful layers of knowledge that can be higher quality and less prone to error than any produced by any single intelligence.

MINDMELDING

To take a simple example, the words you're reading right now are not the product of a single mind. A talented editor read through a prior version, struck through extraneous words, suggested rewrites, and challenged my assumptions. Another editor came along and did copyediting and proofing, which I hope makes the prose silky smooth for your reading pleasure. Their minds have, in a sense, melded with mine to produce this paragraph, a string of symbols that you process more readily than you might have if I'd been left to my own devices.

But that's not all. Before writing this, I had researched to consume and interpret other people's ideas. And that required poring through books and, of course, Googling, which meant I was coming into cognitive interplay with symbols spilled by other minds. Behind the search, an army of Google's employees, with all their perspectives, biases, and motivations to weight and rank information, had set up elaborate algorithms to control the information that flowed to me when I searched. Undoubtedly that fact shaped my research. Had another article come up, I might have been influenced to write something different, if only slightly.

Finally, I filtered, reconfigured, and synthesized all of

that information into prose before sending it to the editor's desk. That means that this book, for all I know, could be the product of a million minds. In certain respects, we authors are, and always have been, masters of repackaging collective intelligence. We stand on the shoulders of giants, while functioning as tour guides around the Library of Babel. Despite my mixed metaphors, one thing is sure: We could never do it alone.

EXPERTISE VS. COLLECTIVE INTELLIGENCE

Before we proceed, it's important to distinguish between expertise and collective intelligence. When one has knowledge in a given field, we call that expertise. It's only when experts try to build walls around that knowledge — or obscure the limits of their understanding — that expertise gets a bad rap. Indeed, it's the mediated or gated aspect of some expertise that makes it restrictive at best, wrong at worst. If, for example, a claim is shielded from questions or revisions — or is otherwise difficult to integrate into a more comprehensive conceptual framework — then it might be the wares of a knowledge cartel. Such cartels benefit the purported experts, whether in their authority, income, or influence. For example, universities tend to generate expertise, which gets published mostly in gated journals.

By contrast, collective intelligence uses open knowledge networks that are, in principle, available to everyone. The internet is designed primarily around open access, so it provides a basic infrastructure for collective intelligence. Alas, Sturgeon's Law says that 90 percent of everything on the internet is shit, so we will only improve our collective intelligence when open-access networks have built in mechanisms for truth tracking and reliability. That means that for the 10 percent to be useful to anyone, there needs to be a way for multiple concurrent collaborators to draw upon the good and come to reasoned, intersubjective agreement. As of this writing, there is no complete mechanism for gaining such. And so our collective intelligence muddles along.

The other crucial insight about collective intelligence is that any given member of some knowledge community might only have part of the relevant knowledge set. Members are holding pieces of a bigger puzzle that none could hold in its totality. Experts, on the other hand, claim to know most of what can be known in their field. There is no bright line between expertise and collective intelligence, so it can be hard to orient oneself as different parties make different kinds of knowledge claims.

It certainly makes it easy to confuse expertise with collective intelligence. For example, when experts deliver news, rules, or heuristics in, say, a global pandemic, we might mistake the herd's assent to the expertise for collective intelligence. You might say that when expertise is both known by virtually anyone and is useful to the relevant party, then it is being transformed into a form of collective intelligence. That's why we have to find the sweet spot between complete faith in experts and the idea that any given person has to *become* an expert to contribute to collective intelligence. What lies in between is a mutually beneficial discernment that makes some knowledge sets useful to a group of some significant size. We have to become better at evaluating such intersubjective agreement within a knowledge community. We have to take care to spot the difference between gravitas and groupthink.

COLLECTIVE INTELLIGENCE IN CRISIS

Collective intelligence also has something to do with crises. We have first to determine whether and to what extent we are in a crisis. We have a responsibility to figure out the nature and magnitude of a problem before we do or say *anything,* even as the clock ticks. After all, one bad narrative can generate an information cascade. And when a bad narrative gets propagated, that's hard to undo.

Then, once a narrative is determined to track the truth, we have to decide whether we need to do something *collectively*. Experts and authorities have an even greater responsibility to these determinations because, whether we like it or not, they sometimes make decisions on our behalf.

During the 2020 pandemic, writer David Cayley, reflecting on the work of philosopher Ivan Illich, had this to say about the quality of our collective intelligence at the close of the twentieth century.

> Illich had a sense, during the last twenty years of his life, of a world immured in "an ontology of systems," a world immune to grace, alienated from death, and totally convinced of its duty to manage every eventuality – a world, as he once put it, in which "exciting, soul-capturing abstractions have extended themselves over the perception of world and self like plastic pillowcases."… Illich was *talking about modes of sensing, of thinking, and of feeling that had crept into people at a much deeper level.*[203] (Emphasis mine.)

Illich's modes include deference to the graph, the expert, or the stat, which forms a sort of ersatz collective intelligence. One finds comfort in the confines of the *measurable*, but that's only an illusion of understanding. We end up reducing complexity to convenient abstractions, real people to plot points.

So to mitigate the COVID-19 death rate, a great many people embraced the plastic pillowcase of curve-flattening lockdowns, which instantly suffocated 30 million jobs. High Minds could afford to sit tight and watch the curve get flatter from the bosom of home. Not as easy to think about Jane, the single mom who used to work at the flower shop; or Jose, who used to work in the restaurant kitchen. To watch CNN, you'd think the only people demanding a return to work were troglodytic Trump voters. *Who cares about them. I'm sitting here posting on Facebook. Science says I'm right.* Instead of better collective intelligence, we ended up with abject faith in statistical models rendered by a boffin at Imperial College London.

These models turned out to be gross exaggerations, which the media, in turn, grossly exaggerated. Once authorities lifted lockdown orders and more testing became available, there were more apparent transmissions. Death rates spiked, then dropped, then remained fairly flat for a time. New cases penetrated more remote areas, so aggregated first wave data looked like a second wave. As collective intelligence improved both inside and outside hospitals, new cases started to decline in most places until the cold weather returned. Maybe the pretext for lockdowns, preventing hospital overwhelm, worked to some degree. But so also did conscientious use of masks, hygiene, and social distancing, which seemed to wane as people let their guard down, arguably due to unhealthy Thanatos Feminine. Still, it was astonishing how easily politicians were able to shut down almost every aspect of life and how deferential people had been in the face of uncertainty.

A few brave souls spoke out about how panic played neatly into an agenda of control. Many got accused of wearing tinfoil hats, but some were right to be concerned. Fear seizes people, forcing them to accept abridgments to their civil liberties that would be impossible to justify under normal circumstances. Shutting down businesses. Quarantining the well. Censoring minority or amateur opinions. I could go on. But concern for civil liberties almost always takes a back seat to fear — at least, for a time. The apparatus of control succeeds in bringing a pliant people to heel. *The authorities have spoken.* By November, new lockdowns were being imposed at a time when the costs of rapid testing had dropped to less than $5. These could have been taken at home for months had at-home tests been legalized. Vaccines that took nine days to be developed queued up for nine months for approval. As deaths mounted, authorities demanded proof of 'efficacy.'

Whether it's the War on Drugs, the War on Terror, and now, the War on Death, the submission instinct becomes an instrument of social control. In that period of chaos before our collective intelligence improves, authorities can take illiberal measures with relative ease.

Noble Lies

Whether it's a global pandemic or a cluster of terrorist acts, one has a responsibility to consider the fragile, interconnected nature of peoples before spreading fear. One also has an obligation, where possible, to offer people better heuristics instead of blunt-force directives. Heuristics — which are just rules of thumb for people to take action — help us adapt to local circumstances. And, hopefully, they allow us each to get through the worst.

But heuristics can compete, and adjudicating between competing heuristics is rarely easy. For example, early on in the 2020 pandemic, two different competing heuristics emerged:

1. *Wear a mask to protect yourself and others.*

2. *Don't wear a mask.*

Note that both of these rules were delivered to us from the top down by experts. It's intuitively obvious that viruses can penetrate porous cloth and mask materials. It should also be common sense to think that reducing the viral load that enters the body at any given time would likely be beneficial — especially given that COVID-19 can be aerosolized and linger in the air. Some aerosolized viral droplets will cling to the fabric of the mask. To be fair, we needed hard data to make a definitive claim one way or the other. Until such time, it seemed fair to assume that masks can slow the transmission of the virus, and we probably ought to wear them if we care about others. Unlike lockdowns, masks and responsible practice don't come at such a great expense to people's lives and livelihoods.

We'll never know whether things would have been different had we all simply acted more like the Swedes, whose authorities never instituted lockdowns. A survey of international mortality rates indicates that jurisdictions with more draconian lockdowns simply pushed new infections and mortality into the future. In other words, as Sweden's new infections and deaths approached zero, cases were still climbing in other countries, such as those in the rest of Europe.[204] Yet Sweden's Scandinavian neighbors saw a more modest uptick, and they managed to keep their death rate down. Interestingly, Sweden's year-prior period was nearly identical in terms of overall deaths — which itself was virtually identical to the prior ten years (even with COVID). My point here is not to claim expertise I don't have, but rather to suggest there are plenty of contradictory results, as well as evidence that runs counter to any admonition to listen to the experts.

What we do know, however, is that Hong Kong used more collective intelligence at the start of the pandemic, bolstered by a strong sense of community. Techno-sociologist, Zeynep Tufekci, offers a first-hand account:

> In response to the crisis, Hong Kongers spontaneously adopted near-universal masking on their own, defying the government's ban on masks. When Lam oscillated between not wearing a mask in public and wearing one but incorrectly, they blasted her online and mocked her incorrect mask wearing. In response to the mask shortage, the foot soldiers of the protest movement set up mask brigades — acquiring and distributing masks, especially to the poor and elderly, who may not be able to spend hours in lines. An "army of volunteers" also spread among the intensely crowded and often decrepit tenement buildings to install and keep filled hand-sanitizer dispensers.

> During the protest movement, I had become accus-
> tomed to seeing shared digital maps that kept track
> of police blockades and clashes; now digital maps
> kept track of outbreaks and hand-sanitizer distribu-
> tion.[205]

To be sure, Hongkongers have had more recent experiences with pandemics. But they have also demonstrated the
ability to organize more effectively as a hive mind, one that
seems comparatively superior to the mainland and its party
mandates, or America's technocratic approaches. In short,
Hongkongers are more civic-minded in their freedom.

The U.S. Centers for Disease Control (CDC), which is
supposed to be composed of trusted experts and authorities
on, well, disease control, issued early guidelines indicating
that masks would *not* help slow the spread of the virus.
Thus, people listened to the experts and wore no masks.
Digital insurgents — *amateurs* — looked at data from countries with widespread mask use and began to question those
experts. Eventually, the CDC revised its heuristic after
coming under enormous pressure. One wonders how many
people lived thanks to the digital insurgents' skepticism.

In fairness, the CDC's initial guidelines had probably
been a noble lie. That is, the experts conspired to tell people
that masks don't work so that they would be more likely to
shelter in place and keep equipment for healthcare workers.
To acknowledge masks as slowing transmission might have
created what is known as a moral hazard, that is, a perverse
incentive to take undue risks; in this case, to think *it's okay
to be outside in large groups as long as I'm wearing a mask*. And
concerns about moral hazard are plausible but wrong. The
noble lie backfired.

Ultimately, anyone seeking to avoid panic in a crisis
has to be circumspect and patient. One should learn what
she can, piecemeal, and contribute only good information
to the discourse; otherwise, there is wisdom in silence. But
it's not easy. We want to be able to track the truth, which

means we try to figure out what is going on first. Then we take care to separate signal from noise; plausible narratives from implausible ones. When people spread fear, hyperbole, or falsehood, it can have terrible ramifications. But the thing is, it's a difficult thing for anyone — including experts — to claim a monopoly on truth. Whether in pandemics or economics, tracking truth can be an ongoing quest amid shifting circumstances. It's neither a fixed moment in time nor a point on a graph. It's an endeavor without end.

Experts and authorities get to be experts and authorities for all kinds of reasons. The primary reason is that the expert is supposed to possess more knowledge in some domains than others. That's the idea, anyway. The problem is that, far too often, a thousand amateurs are more effective than a single expert.

Irrelevant Experts

Expertise can be designated for all sorts of reasons, many of which are irrelevant. Some people get to be experts because they have silver tongues; others, because they are members of a guild, or a university department mints their laurels. Some qualify because they have a reputation for saying inflammatory things on TV; others still count as experts because they have some credentials, but in reality, know only slightly more about a subject than the rest of us, which creates only the thinnest veneer of credibility. The funny thing is, add up all these irrelevancies, and it's far too *easy* to find an expert.

People will write entire books about this or that subject just to position themselves as an expert, as if the mere fact of writing a book confers magical insight. *Isn't that what you're doing right now, Max?* I am aware of the irony. Still, if I leave you with nothing else beyond this point, I hope it is this: All God's children need a skeptic. Indeed, one of the most dangerous phrases that ever got turned into a meme is 'trust the experts.' This admonition is the modern-day equivalent of keeping a thousand Galileos under house arrest. *Jesus take the wheel* makes more sense — which is a hell of a thing to say when you're not particularly religious.

None of this is to argue that expertise is useless. I certainly wouldn't pay an untrained professional to fix my car or operate on my body, and I certainly don't want to open the door to quackery. But the difference between a quack and a crackerjack is skin in the game and a verifiable track record of success in a fairly restricted sphere of expertise. At least with someone you pay, you have the option of not taking their advice, or not paying them anymore.

EXPERTISE TRAPS

One of the through-lines of this book is that the urge to control originates in fear. Humans, I've suggested, seek to take control or cede control when they are afraid. There were probably evolutionary advantages to this programming in the distant past, and some of those advantages persist. Our forebears frequently found themselves in dangerous situations; the tribe could quickly reduce its coordination costs if everyone had an instinct to rally behind a strong leader. And because that strategy worked in those ancient contexts, the germ line survived. We inherited those instincts. We're still cave-people. But the world around us has changed considerably, and our instinctive strategies are not always appropriate to a modern context.

In many cases, experts are helping set policies for hundreds of millions of people. And that's where illusions of expertise are the most dangerous. Let's go through some ways that fear can lead to fallacy when it comes to experts.

The Fallacy of Adjacent Expertise. It's tempting to believe that people who might be effective in some areas will also be effective in a similar or nearby domain. When we are so tempted, we transfer their expertise across domains as if it's transferable.

> *He is a good CEO, so I trust his opinion on economics.*
> *He is a doctor, so I trust his opinion on healthcare policy.*
> *She got a lot of people to vote for her, so she must be good at*
> *making important decisions.*

Expertise in one field that is loosely related to another does not make someone an expert in the adjacent field. It's easy to fall into this trap, though, especially when we are desperate to believe.

The Signal Fallacy. Sometimes the credential signal creates the illusion. If there is some affiliation or designation that confers an air of validity, it's easier and lower cost to let that signal stand in for validating the individual's expertise. Some examples include:

> *She is a professor at Harvard, so she knows what's good for*
> *people.*
> *They've been studying this stuff for years, who are we to*
> *question?*
> *X percent of experts polled believe Y, therefore you should*
> *believe Y.*

Not only are human beings naturally inclined to accept indicators of status, but we are also inclined to put faith in scholars dedicated to some discipline. But a signal itself is not evidence of efficacy, fact, or predictive capability. Nor does it mean one has skin in the game. At best, the credential signal is a stand-in, a kind of intellectual peacocking.

Indeed, far from signaling that someone possesses a good opinion, one's position at an Ivy League University can make them *less* likely to understand the society around them. Not only do university faculty operate with very little skin in the game (in that they are insulated from the forces that make people more responsive to customer feedback), but many universities are disconnected from the wider societies upon which they are parasitic. After all, most depend on federally subsidized student loans, state budgets, grants, and endowments. Such a system can leave less room for truth tracking. Instead, they have strong incentives to play the publication game. If anyone could figure out whether anyone reads the majority of journal articles that get published, they might be able to find out just how wasteful a game it is. So controversy abounds.

A 2007 Indiana University study concluded that as many as half of the published academic papers are never read by anyone other than the authors, their referees, and the journal's editors. This sounds plausible, given that scaling laws probably operate in large numbers of papers.[206] But the Indiana paper has since been taken down, and the sources are either disappeared, dated, or discredited.[207] Nearly fifteen years on, no one has been able to paint any sort of definitive picture of the state of American scholarship. If taxpayers, parents, and students are being asked to pay for research, to what extent is that research being engaged or cited? It would seem that no one has any real incentive to seek out that particular truth — especially not recipients of higher education funding.

Replication in science and social science is meant to be the gold standard of research. If you can't reproduce at least similar results, the research is dubious. But the news isn't good for the state of research: recent meta-science studies have shown that only half of researchers in psychology could reproduce their results[208], with similar issues plaguing other social sciences.[209] The twin crises of peer review and research replication have raised doubts about these institutions' value. With so much rot in higher education, we have good reason to be suspicious of its experts.

The Study Fallacy. One of the stealthiest fallacies is the careless (or deliberate) use of "study" or "report" in a headline. Few people take the time to find the study and evaluate its data or methods. *Someone else has checked the work*, the reader thinks — if they think at all. Most people just assume that a report is valid and that the journalist checked into the original. In some cases, journalists and researchers collude in advance of a study, as if the conclusions are foregone.

NPR science writer Richard Harris explains the different forms of bad science that passes for research. Far from being some definitive gotcha moment, the phrase "study finds…" or "science says" should be greeted with suspicion. "Each year, about a million biomedical studies are published in the scientific literature," says Harris. "And many of them are simply wrong. Set aside the voice-of-God prose, the fancy statistics, and the peer review process, which is supposed to weed out the weak and errant. Lots of this stuff just doesn't stand up to scrutiny."

In other words, researchers unconsciously *will* data to tell a story that's simply not true. Other times, laments Harris, there's outright fraud. Either way, a large share of what gets published is wrong — yet people still eat it up. And because they do, journalists have learned they can invoke our blind faith by appealing to the enterprise of science itself. Science sometimes appears as an omniscient being. Of course, 'science' itself doesn't say anything. *Scientists* do. And each scientist is a fallible human with biases and shortcomings. Some even stake their entire careers on a single line of inquiry.

Whenever writers tell us to "listen to the science" or otherwise tell us what "studies show," someone with an agenda is invoking a dangerous power. But there is no such thing as the god Science. There is only the sciences and their human practitioners. Each has its unique uses, limitations, and language games. When we abstract *science* away from all the vicissitudes of knowledge production, we are not truth tracking. When we turn science into an oracle whose priests can be identified by their frocks or impressive letters, our judgment suffers. As Ivan Illich suggests, we no longer respond to what seems right to our sense of how things are down here on the ground. Instead, we parrot what science says.

NPR fallacy. The National Public Radio (NPR) is a fallacy in which, over time, listeners or viewers turn off their critical thinking because they have come to think that a source no longer requires scrutiny. NPR is just one example, of course. It can be exhausting to be skeptical day in and day out. When NPR has one of its quarterly fund drives from listeners, they say, *You want news and commentary you can trust.* And that is another way of saying *turn off your brain.*

Here are just a handful of ways NPR and similar 'trusted' news sources distort reality.

- Write the story and read the news as if the listener already agrees with you and accepts your assumptions.

- Omit information or perspectives that would show the issue in a completely different light.

- Play it straight or even semi-skeptical as the writer or host, but invite a guest expert, or otherwise quote someone who is partisan.

If there were ever thirty-seventh-level wizards of distortion like those discussed above, it would be NPR journalists. To them, fallacies are strategies, masterfully executed and flawlessly delivered, which makes them easy to digest on your way to work.

The Government Fallacy. Perhaps one of the oldest and most intractable fallacies is that government research, data, or expertise is unassailable. People blindly trust the government because, supposedly, their missions are to deliver accurate information without bias. Undue influence or corrupting incentives comes from other sectors, not from public servants. Or so the story goes.

No organization is immune to bias and corrupting incentives. *None.* Some might argue that, by degree, government experts are more trustworthy than corporate or university experts. And yet such notions are just blind faith.

It's comforting, yes, to think that there is an authority out there charged with looking out for our interests. But experts in bureaucracies have their agendas. They operate within different sets of incentives, but the incentives are there. Remember Shirky's Principle? *Institutions will try to preserve the problem to which they are the solution.*

Operating in the background, some force like this must have been responsible for the experts who testified that:

- There was hard proof of WMDs in the lead up to the second Iraq War;

- We should eat a diet like that pictured in the USDA Food Pyramid; and

- Taxpayer dollars to corporations "stimulate" the economy and ease boom-bust cycles.

Can we count on the data from the Bureau of Labor Statistics or the Census Bureau? It's hard to say. The questions they ask and the data they reveal are only part of the story. But these statistics become the paint that pundits use to color our reality.

The Amateur Fallacy. Any number of the above fallacies can leave one with the sense that experts have a certain kind of privileged status. This status is important enough that we must systematically exclude amateurs from discourse and decision making. Just as we should be skeptical of the credentialed class and its claims, we should not ignore the amateur's claims.

- Economist Art DeVany was a principal founder of evolutionary fitness and the paleo diet, despite not having any diet and nutrition degrees. Devany and other amateurs such as Mark Sisson and Gary Taubes helped overturn decades of nutrition orthodoxy involving the proper role of carbohydrates, fats, and sugar.

- Biohackers, gene editors, and amateur CRISPR

researchers work out of their garages and learn from each other online. Their work sometimes involves cracking proprietary formulae and gene therapies in order to make them more accessible for the least advantaged.

- In 2012, a group of amateur astronomers discovered forty-two planets; while in 2013, Michael Sidonio sighted a new dwarf galaxy, NGC 253-dw2. And in 2016, two amateur astronomers — John McKeon from Ireland and Gerrit Kernbauer of Austria — filmed an asteroid impact on Jupiter in 2016.[210]

- Citizen stringers and civic journalists routinely film, blog, and report first-hand information in ways that allow stories to break. Famous examples include films of police abuse and video taken by the infamous right-wing provocateur, James O' Keefe, whose work has exposed voter fraud and toppled media executives.

- Teen software developers are notorious for becoming millionaires after working on applications in their bedrooms and basements. Tech giants now routinely hire coders without advanced degrees.

As we continue to connect with others around the world, we have the opportunity not to see ourselves as merely passive consumers or sharers of information but also as active participants in the creation of a great, ever-shifting mosaic of understanding.

LAYERS OF DISTORTION

If the fallacies of expertise weren't enough, there is also a minefield of distortions. Those of us involved in questions about how we make sense of the world, which ought to be just about everybody, will do well to look at some of these layers. What stands in between us and the truth is vast and can be enormously problematic to truth tracking. Although the following list is not exhaustive, it reveals plenty:

1. *Subjectivity.* First comes the fact that one's relationship to the truth is always subjective. What we imagine is the case always *appears to us* in a certain way. That means our perceptions and our minds mediate our perceptions, which might get mined later as memories. The way we experience perceptions and memories is subjective, too.

2. *Cognitive Biases.* To be human is also to have biases. These biases probably helped us survive in some caveman context, but not all of them allow us to track the truth or be more discerning in the digital age. Your window on the world gets filtered and distorted by any number in a very long laundry list of these biases, including framing effects, clustering illusions, and status quo bias.

3. *Representation.* Words, data, and pictures are, at best, representations of reality. No matter how accurate the news story, how data-driven the study, or how detailed the video resolution, a representation is not the thing itself. Not only can we omit relevant information, but we always take words, data, or pictures from a perspective. That means it excludes *other* perspectives. A single perspective is a low-dimension slice of a high-dimension reality. Indeed, representing reality from a certain point of view means that misperceptions are unavoidable.

4. *Is or Ought.* Human beings have a hard time respecting this stark divide between two different classes of phenomena. One class includes *that which is true* (let's call them facts), and another class consists of *the way we wish things were* (let's call them values). Both of these classes are important, but it's easy to muddy

them up.

5. *Truth Decay.* The further we move away from some event in time, the greater the chances our representations of reality will become distorted. Our memories can fade or become degraded by new memories. Our ability to piece together available evidence degrades. Of course, though there are exceptions to this tendency of truth to decay in time — such as technological advance affording us new evidentiary tools like smartphone video or DNA testing — truth decay is the norm.

6. *Metaphors.* There are times when our use of figurative language gives us greater access to truth. Other times it can distort or hide the truth. As philosopher Max Black wrote, "A memorable metaphor has the power to bring to separate domains into cognitive and emotional relation by using language directly appropriate to the one as a lens for seeing the other."[211] Such power can be used or abused. Metaphors can shed light on the truth or 'reframe' a truth to be more palatable to some in-group, or misleading to some out-group.

7. *Statistics.* Numbers and data are indispensable to the necessary projects of fact-checking and truth tracking. And yet it's easier to create multiple competing narratives with the slightest sleight of hand. Statistics, insofar as they are designed to mediate between some phenomena and us, can also lead us astray.

8. *Chinese Telephone.* Recall the childhood game where you whisper a message into your neighbor's ear, then the neighbor whispers the message into their neighbor's ear, and so on until all the children have transmitted the message. When the phrase comes out on the other end of the transmission line, you can get hilarious results that don't resemble the orig-

inal in any way. But as information narratives travel through networks only to be retold in different ways, a narrative can become similarly degraded.

9. *Missing Context.* You've probably seen a news clip. Typically, they give you just enough information to cause you to form a particular opinion on some matter. But sometimes one's opinion can change when you see more of the footage. Likewise, journalists routinely quote people out of context. Both of these are examples of context that, if returned, would completely change our perceptions of some purported event.

10. *Echo Chambers.* The temptation to surround ourselves with people who share our values is understandable. But when we silo ourselves, retaining select perspectives and rejecting others, we can fail to challenge our closely held assumptions. When perspectives interlock around a group's wishes, echo chambers can form and grow into unhealthy groupthink.

11. *Mendacity, Forgery, and Deep Fakes.* Sometimes people purposely mislead, and technology is making it easier not only to lie or deceive but to do so via multiple media channels in a way that's hard to trace. Some have incentives to hide the truth. Others just get a kick out of it. But if one's authority depends on hiding some truth, that's when we're most likely to see smokescreens.

12. *Appeal to Central Authority.* As we suggested above, any authority wants first to survive. If that means lying to the public, putting out disinformation, or suppressing information, some will be willing to traffic in falsehoods.

Each of the above items can be problematic, even if the distortion is inadvertent. We could create a separate list that unpacks all the ways media elites purposefully hide the truth. Whether people are simply unaware of the rhetorical devices they use or consciously apply them to win, fallacy can be much more potent than fact. That means discourse that was once predicated on the pursuit of understanding has become something of a relic. Just about everything you read today is *designed to get your attention*. 'Truth' is a secondary consideration — at best.

THE AVAILABILITY CASCADE

Have you ever looked at some part of your body under a magnifying glass or microscope? It can look weird, or gross. In some cases, it can change your perception entirely. Now imagine you could do that — metaphorically, anyway — with some aspect of society. You might not see the whole picture, or be able to take on a perspective that would balance against a more horrible point of view. Your inference system might kick in, leading you to think that this is the entire truth, revealed finally through modern media. Behavioral economists Timur Kuran and Cass Sunstein call this phenomenon an *availability cascade*.[212]

An availability cascade is a self-reinforcing cycle in which a certain position or narrative gains increasing prominence. Often this occurs within an earnest but inflamed national conversation, which increases its availability to any given person, making the issue seem more pressing or widespread. Such causes the receiver to propagate the narrative. Often, a news story or smartphone video of something horrific triggers a wave of public discussion.

This leads to more focus, more stories, and more discussions on the topic. The narrative gets magnified, distorted, and transmitted through social media. This process culminates in a call for legislation to deal with the topic at hand. In some cases, digital mobs ruin the lives and careers of people who might have said something ten years ago that is somehow at odds with the tenor of the national conversation today. Because the original event is sensational, it causes emotional earthquakes that fracture people into tribes, often along partisan lines.

Because people are more likely to believe whatever is readily available to them, they get swept up, more likely to accept the narrative and to spread it to others. This, in turn, makes the narrative more available, leading to a massive, self-perpetuating cycle that shapes public opinion and sets agendas. These cascade agendas end up sucking the oxygen out of far more critical matters. The matters from which we are distracted don't have a tidal wave of emotion behind them. So, more and more availability cascades wash through the public discourse and push aside other priorities.

Of course, the most cynical among us will learn to *create* availability heuristics. Some of those cynics include journalists. And a shift has occurred: Instead of journalists tracking truth, they write propaganda or butter their bread on demand for sensation and outrage. Either way, the effect is the same.

THE BLUE CHURCH

Another particular wrinkle of modern life is that we try to understand through a mediated set of words and images. In the twentieth century, information got pumped out from enormous content factories, such as ABC and CBS on television, or *The New York Times* and *The Washington Post* in print. The people were mostly passive consumers of these corporate media giants. Like it or not, it was the age of propaganda, but at least that propaganda meant a high degree of social coherence. It was propaganda we trusted. And it worked to a great degree, at least if social coherence is the goal.

Specifically, in the United States, we saw the rise of what polymath entrepreneur Jordan Hall refers to as the "Blue Church":

> The abstract is this: the Blue Church is a kind of narrative/ideology control structure that is a natural result of mass media. It is an evolved (rather than designed) function that has come over the past half-century to be deeply connected with the Democratic political "Establishment" and lightly connected with the "Deep State" to form an effective political and dominant cultural force in the United States.[213]

You might say the Blue Church symbolizes all the institutions of High Modernism. If so, what are its origins?

> We can trace its roots at least as far back as the beginning of the 20th century where it emerged in response to the new capabilities of mass media for social control. By mid-century it began to play an increasingly meaningful role in forming and shaping American culture-producing institutions; became pervasive through the last half of the 20th and seems to have peaked in its influence somewhere in the first decade of the 21st century.[214]

It's pretty easy to grasp the basic configuration of the Blue Church's control structure, says Hall. And when you do, you start to see it everywhere: "There is a basic bi-directional flow. In the upwards direction there is the flow of 'credentialed authority.' The 'experts' who are authorized through some legitimizing process to be permitted to form and express their opinions through some form of broadcast media. In the downwards direction, these 'good opinions' which anchor and place boundaries around our collective social coherence."[215]

As we have suggested above, it's not just the media; academia is set up this way, too, with students as the audience. Credentialed experts broadcast good opinion and right action. Thus, students must listen and learn. Let the professor pour information into your brain like a bucket, or write canonical knowledge upon your blank slate. To get an A, approximate it and regurgitate. If not, you will fail. Remember, this is how you got to this point; you filled in the right bubbles. For twelve years? Sixteen?

"Regardless of the specific subject matter, every class is a lesson in how to play the Blue Church game," says Hall. And in many respects, it is an intergenerational game. Remember, the professors got where they are because they did a good job being students, and eventually got invited into the Blue Church hierarchy. Stray too far from orthodoxy, and you will see inquisitions, ex-communications, and other forms of ostracism. Maybe you'll never get tenure.

The Blue Church broadcast control structure extends to the government and mainstream media, too, of course. But by the twenty-first century the media, at least, had become far more fragmented and decentralized. We have witnessed the rise of digital insurgencies that have made cracks in the Blue Church, which means it is no longer the dominant force for social coherence. With the breakup of any sense-making cartel, autodidacts, checkers, and capable amateurs will rise to fill the void.

There is a major downside of this process. Expectedly, online echo chambers and destructive meme factories come out of the woodwork. These can pollute our collective intelligence, because they shield people from the consequences of false beliefs. Such a system accelerates the transmission of biased reporting, fake news, and a la carte ideology. There is much to celebrate and much to lament in the fall of the Blue Church. Still, for better or worse, here we are. Until the next wave comes, we are in transition.

And to some of us, that looks like chaos.

THE SCREEN OF GYGES

At an individual level, at least, digital media allows us to create our own brands. We select snapshots of our lives to maintain an image of ourselves that we want others to see, though it is often a simulacrum of who we actually are. Ordinary people, armed with smartphones, can gain millions of followers. Like some supernatural gift that confers new powers, these new tools can be abused and distort our identities. We have become a society of specialization, signaling, and spectacle, rather than one of community, craft, and collective sense-making. Disillusioned, some want to walk away from these new powers. And it's no wonder: If we don't find a way to use modern media to build collective sense-making, many of us will continue to feel alienated.

By 'alienation,' I'm not referring to Marx's idea of the worker being separated from his handicraft and the fruits of his work. Instead, modern media can alienate us from the way in which we make our meaning. Online avatars can remove us from the world and our contextual meaning, which is how we function in our communities. These online identities can also shear off our authored meaning, which is how we cultivate our best selves independently of how others perceive us. Instead, we fragment our identities by wearing a series of masks, acting in a series of plays. We might display a pattern of behavior online that we would never exhibit at work. Some people have multiple online identities.

When we hide behind online avatars, we wear something akin to the Ring of Gyges, of Plato's *Republic*. The ring makes the wearer invisible, which gives him the power to act with relative impunity. In the case of our pseudonymous selves, we are, as it were, fondling the ring. At least we are separating ourselves far enough from our interlocutors to act either like vicious shits or virtue signalers. We find ourselves completely different people when we are among our loved ones. To the extent that we can make sense of the idea of being a more 'genuine self,' the test comes in being a better version of ourselves, even when we're fondling the Ring — er, the smartphone screen.

THE HALL OF MIRRORS

The internet creates a paradox: Reality is abundant; Reality is scarce. The more we live online, the more we occupy the hall of mirrors. The more disconnected we become from meatspace, the more we lose ourselves in an information landscape that is synthetic, approximate, and prepackaged. You can't taste, touch, or smell it. We evolved brains designed for survival among rocks and animals and trees and waterways, yet we spend so much time in elaborate symbol systems composed of video and audio and images and text. This *must* affect us. And it must affect our human systems, too.

Earlier, we explored the idea that information and knowledge animate human systems. For any individual operating within a given system, good decisions rarely come from bad information. The more bad information there is, the more bad decisions are likely to be made. Bad decisions, especially in fragile systems, are the handmaidens of collapse. Unless we figure out how to both incentivize and sacralize truth tracking, disinformation will continue to pollute the information landscape. It's not just that we need to set up new systems that track truth; we need to *set ourselves up* to better track the truth. We must make a quantum leap in collective intelligence.

Expertise can break down in several ways. As I said before, it's essential that all people feel the direct sting of being wrong. For example, voters are almost always rationally ignorant and rationally irrational. Otherwise, it's too hard and too costly for most of us to be anything more than a Thomas Thwaite on most matters relating to a complex world. So when some populist politician promises impossible things, people get an immediate reward for believing them. The cost of being wrong unfolds over decades.

GROUPTHINK

Ignaz Semmelweis was both a physician and an empiricist, so when he landed his new job in the maternity ward in Vienna's General Hospital, he started collecting data. Semmelweis wanted to figure out why so many women in a particular maternity ward were dying of childbed fever. One was staffed by all-male physicians and students; the other, female midwives. When Semmelweis counted the number of deaths on each ward, he discovered that women in the clinic staffed by physicians died at a rate almost five times that of the midwives' ward.[216]

Semmelweis then set about looking for differences between the two wards — and discovered a big difference straight away. Among the physicians, women gave birth on their backs; among the midwives, women gave birth on their sides. Thus, Semmelweis instructed the women in the physicians in the women's ward to give birth on their sides, too. Sadly, this had no effect.

Semmelweis tried a couple of other things, too, which also had no effect, and so he became despondent. He decided to take a leave of absence, hoping that the time would help him clear his head. When Semmelweis later returned to the hospital, some news awaited him: a colleague had died. The colleague had pricked his finger while doing an autopsy on someone who had died from childbed fever. He ended up contracting it himself.

Semmelweis studied the colleague's symptoms and realized that the pathologist had died from the same disease as the autopsied women. Up to this point, it had never occurred to him that other people in the hospital could get the same illness.

Still, Semmelweis wanted to know why more women died in the physicians' clinic, and the death of his colleague offered a clue. Eventually, he figured out that the doctors and students were performing autopsies, and the midwives were not. So, Semmelweis thought — correctly, more or less — that students must be getting cadaver particles on their hands. If they then immediately went to deliver a baby, they would bring these particles to the women, who would, in turn, develop the disease.

Semmelweis ordered the physicians' staff to start cleaning their hands and instruments with a chlorine and lime solution. We now know that bleach is an excellent disinfectant, but Semmelweis used it mostly to get rid of the odor. In 1847, germ theory wasn't around yet, but Semmelweis's new protocol cut the rate of childbed fever to below 1 percent.[217] To this day, we know that hand washing is critical to keeping a hospital environment disease-free. Despite publishing his findings, Semmelweis's observations conflicted with the establishment's scientific and medical opinions. And in the absence of a full explanation for his results, his recommendations were greeted with ridicule.

Indeed, many of his colleagues thought that Semmelweis's claims made them look bad, like they were the source of the problem. Having seen the results, Semmelweis made no bones about his approach, and insisted quite publicly that everyone stick to the regime. But in the process, he created enemies. Eventually, the doctors not only gave up the chlorine solution protocol, they got Semmelweis fired. The physicians' willingness to abandon Semmelweis's protocol is a good example of groupthink. It took decades before the profession figured out that he was right and resumed saving lives.

Even though we've made a lot of progress in our knowledge about microorganisms and disease pathology, examples of groupthink abound to this day. Whether it's the political tribalism of the anti-mask movement during the 2020 pandemic or statistically unsubstantiated narratives of the Black Lives Matter movement that same year, human beings are still susceptible to in-group herd psychology. In these cases, it seems like errant populism driving the groupthink. But, as we saw in the Semmelweis case, the experts themselves were the groupthink victims.

Sometimes the experts are gloriously wrong, and are indeed all wrong together.

THE ROLE OF EXPERTS

What, then, is the role of experts? And how much should they figure into our collective intelligence?

Thomas Thwaites, the one-man toaster manufacturer, is a brilliant designer — but he could not make a toaster. Human society is, of course, infinitely more complex than a toaster, so the expert's expertise is often as useful to solving social problems as a Thwaites' toaster is to toast making. The difference between Thwaites and the political elite is that Thwaites has the humility to see his limitations, even if that humility comes in learning from his mistakes, the costs of which he bore directly.

Political elites are rewarded for their expertise. But how many of those rewards accrue to the expert for being right? Most are shielded entirely from the consequences of being wrong. And some are even given a column in *The New York Times*! Experts driven by ideology are even more dangerous because they seek to fashion society according to some ideal or other, which requires their Grand Plans to be tested on millions of people, each of whom might well have individual plans of their own.

To devise a simple heuristic for evaluating the role of an expert, consider a couple of dimensions. The first one, we'll call the degree of skin in the game; the second, the degree of local knowledge. More skin in the game means that the expert has something significant to lose if they predict in error or make a falsehood. Greater local knowledge has to do with real experience, that is, how close the expert is to particular circumstances. If the purported experts can have significant skin in the game and have a high degree of local knowledge, it's probably safer to believe their claims.

Sadly, most of what passes for expertise is carried out by those who have neither local knowledge *nor* skin in the game. We can think of hill staffers in Washington, D.C., who are responsible for drafting thousand-page bills that their Members of Congress never read. On the policy side, bills must be interpreted by experts in various bureaucracies of the executive branch. In the whole nexus from legislation to regulation, these so-called experts will probably never have had any experience working in the industries they have been charged with regulating.

Government functionaries are a particularly nefarious kind of expert because they flatten the delicate shoots of self-organization with their Grand Plans. The Rexford Tugwells[218] of the world have moved along by the time things have come to ruin, long after integrating themselves into some brain trust.

What experts were responsible for the plight of Britain in 1978? New Zealand in 1982? Or of Greece in 2008? These governments were staffed with people who, though probably very bright, weren't smart enough to design society. The United States government in 2020 is no different and no better. The capitals are filled with brahmins, bureaucrats, and High Minds possessed by the urge to control. Almost none of them have local knowledge or skin in the game.

FOXES AND HEDGEHOGS

"The fox knows many things; the hedgehog one great thing," said the Greek poet Archilochus. Later, philosopher Isaiah Berlin expanded on this insight, and political forecaster Philip E. Tetlock turned it into a research program called the Good Judgement Project.[219]

As Tetlock sees things, Hedgehogs have one big theory or predictive model. They're happy to apply this grand theory in most contexts and tend to express their views with great confidence. But the Foxes are different. They're skeptical of grand theories and tend to be more modest and tentative with their forecasts. Foxes are ready to adjust their ideas based on feedback from the world.

While no one always predicts with 100 percent accuracy, Foxes significantly outperform Hedgehogs. Tetlock finds that Hedgehogs are, indeed, particularly bad at long-term forecasting, despite their extensive expertise. Foxes not only have more accurate predictions but are more accurate in the *likelihoods* they assign to their predictions, for example, as they assign percentages.

That's not to say that Hedgehogs are never right. When they are right in their big, far-reaching predictions, the win tends to be highly visible. These highly visible stopped-clock-twice predictions tend to outshine a great many instances of getting it wrong. Note that Hedgehogs tend to be partisan or monolithic, while Foxes tend to be equal-opportunity forecasters, often cherry-picking from several different Hedgehogs.

Famous Hedgehogs include futurist Ray Kurzweil, who sees most everything through the lens of Moore's Law; economist Paul Krugman, who sees most everything through the lens of Keynesian aggregate spending; and biologist Paul Ehrlich who sees most everything through simple Malthusian overpopulation formulae. Famous Foxes include economist Bryan Caplan, who is fond of making bets on his predictions and has a remarkable track record for winning those bets; investment guru Charlie Munger, who disciplines himself to destroy his cherished ideas and priors while knowing the other side of an argument as well as those who hold it; and Nicolas Taleb, who though he arguably has Hedgehog moments, is known for his black swan theories that prepare us to expect the wildly unexpected.

I'll leave it to you, Dear Reader, to decide whether your

humble author is a Fox, a Hedgehog, or something else altogether. I certainly don't speak in granular percentages as Foxes do, and I can be as much a theorist as a Bayesian. But I am also deferential to people with both local knowledge and skin in the game.

One way to improve collective intelligence might be to find ways to harness each style's best and look for patterns where appropriate. Instead of making too many predictions, try on different predictive lenses. I don't see *a priori* and *a posteriori* as incommensurable styles, but tools to be used in dynamic interplay.

Another problem of expertise is, of course, that much gets politicized. The political class selects the experts it wants to hear from, rather than the ones that might deliver unpleasant truths. But when an expert presents unpleasant truths, the centralized apparatus of sense-making (The Blue Church) will sometimes eat its own. Research goes down the memory hole.

In one example, the authors of a controversial paper analyzed government data on race and police shootings. They concluded that there is "no evidence of anti-Black or anti-Hispanic disparities across shootings, and White officers are not more likely to shoot minority civilians than non-White officers."[220] But when the filmed killing of George Floyd became a flashpoint in the debate about police abuse and race, the authors sought to retract their paper less than a year later. Why? Those authors, Joseph Cesario and David Johnson, claim they were "careless when describing the inferences that could be made from our data."[221]

The more likely truth is that they were pressured by activists within their universities to retract the paper after it was cited fourteen times in major publications, including the *Wall Street Journal*. Because the Cesario and Johnson paper offers evidence that counters a prevailing narrative that law enforcement is an institution shot through with conscious and unconscious racial bias, those propagating the narrative would simply rather make any countervailing evidence go away. Even if Cesario and Johnson felt guilty that their research was being cited by the Other, does that justify having it erased?

The memory hole is no place for the truth. And yet corporations responsible for search data and social sharing are figuratively disappearing people through de-platforming. Their bodies of work are censored. Such censorship is not at odds with the First Amendment, because these platforms are private. Censorship is at odds with the fundamental liberal value of tolerating speech in the pursuit of truth. The erasers claim to be scouring the web of fake news. But too often, they are purging our awareness of unpleasant truths. Moral psychologist Jonathan Haidt argues that we have a stark choice before us: we can pursue truth. Or we can pursue social justice. But if we pursue the latter at the former's expense, there will be neither justice nor truth.[222]

6

The Breakdown of Discourse and Civil Order

Turning and turning in the widening gyre
The falcon cannot hear the falconer;
Things fall apart; the centre cannot hold;
Mere anarchy is loosed upon the world,
The blood-dimmed tide is loosed, and
everywhere
The ceremony of innocence is drowned;
The best lack all conviction, while the worst
Are full of passionate intensity.
  W. B. Yeats, from *The Second Coming*

Whenever there is conflict in the world, you'll hear someone make a plea to recognize our "common humanity." That person is usually roundly ignored, either because the appeal gets lost in the heat of friction and faction or because it interferes with a collective desire for revenge. But in this refrain, however platitudinous, lies an important truth: Our common humanity forms the basis of our creation stories and secular humanisms alike. It is how we say *we are not so different, you and I.* It is a call to civility.

Today we are again witnessing the breakdown of civility

and civil order. I say *again* because it's never really left us. It would be dishonest to claim there has ever been an era in which civility was a mainstay. War is uncivil, but our Civil War was fought over that most horrific form of disrespect for one human being by another. Slavery was instituted well before America became a nation. Despite the stirring words of the Declaration, its very fact adulterated the Constitution. What then does the Declaration mean in the twenty-first century?

"It's 244 years of effort by Americans — sometimes halting, but often heroic — to live up to our greatest ideal," writes columnist Bret Stephens. "That's a struggle that has been waged by people of every race and creed. And it's an ideal that continues to inspire millions of people at home and abroad."[223]

Even after the bloody mess of 1860, almost a century passed before federal troops escorted the Little Rock Nine into their Arkansas high school. Before that day, there had been chain gangs, lynchings, and countless other indignities. Troubles remained well after a Memphis shooter made Dr. King a martyr for the cause of civil rights. Still, little by little, things got better. Not perfect, but better.

If we think of our common humanity as the trunk of a Great Tree, we know that a few limbs must grow from the trunk, each finding its direction as it pushes outward or upward. Maybe these are broad ethnicities. From the limbs, large branches grow and hold the world's major cultures. But the large branches divide into medium-sized branches, which are subcultures, and so on into small branches, which are even more distinct. These, in turn, divide into twigs of linguistic or regional variation on which you'll find the buds, leaves, and blossoms of wild diversity and local color. It can be easy to forget that a Siberian Inuit has anything to do with a tuba player from New Orleans. And yet everyone knows what happens to a tree branch if you saw it off.

In this chapter, I want to explore some of the root

causes of social fissuring in America. Issues of race are so comprehensive as to be a through-line, but the lessons here extend to the division based on party or religion. Note also that the breakdown of civility and civil order almost always appears the further away we get from liberalism, which includes recognizing our common humanity.

"Power based on love is a thousand times more effective and permanent than the one derived from fear of punishment," wrote Mahatma Gandhi. But this is a lesson that must be retaught and relearned with each generation.

PEOPLE WHO HURT, THEY COME FROM HURT

Ann Arbor, Michigan, is a university town full of people you wouldn't think of as having many racists. All that changed one day in 1996, when the Ku Klux Klan came to town.[224] Keshia Thomas was among the protesters who turned out to express her disapproval. Thomas, an eighteen-year-old black high schooler, had had her own experiences with racism. So she wanted to join the protest.

According to reports, local police had organized the scene to keep the peace, which is to say they kept protestors and marchers separated. All parties had stayed in control, despite tensions running high. A procession of men in white robes and coned hoods walked along the thoroughfare. Far enough away, protestors aired their resentment. Then events took an unfortunate turn: "There's a Klansman in the crowd!" said a woman with a megaphone.

Thomas and her friends, black and white, had been standing next to a fence designed to separate the groups. They turned around to see a middle-aged white man wearing a shirt emblazoned with a Confederate flag. His arms bore tattoos of neo-Nazi symbols. The man tried to walk away from the group, but the protesters, including Thomas, pursued him. Mob mentality took over.

"Kill the Nazi!" someone cried out. When the man tried to run away, the crowd gave chase. A group surrounded him. They began kicking him and beating him with their placard sticks. Keshia Thomas jumped into the fray, using her own body as a shield to protect a man who, if outward appearances were any indication, hated her. She wept and cried out for the protestors to cease their violence. And they did.

A student photographer managed to capture images of the scene. In revisiting this story and the photos, now decades old, they prompt us to ask a series of essential questions. Foremost: what would possess Keshia Thomas to risk injury or worse to protect someone like this? When she recounts it, she credits her religious faith. And who knows? When everyone around her was caught up in a flash of anger, it's hard to imagine it could have been anything other than a divine hand guiding her. Still, had something else motivated Thomas? We can find a clue in her own words: "For the most part, people who hurt... they come from hurt. It is a cycle. Let's say they had killed him or hurt him really bad. How does the son feel? Does he carry on the violence?"[225]

One rarely hears such wisdom in the words of teenagers. And yet it had come forth from deep within her in an instant.

Fast forward a quarter-century. Whatever forces led Keshia Thomas to act so bravely, lovingly, and utterly without judgment, there seems to be decidedly less of it in the world today.

DAY OF ABSENCE

2017. At Evergreen State University in Oregon, students declared a People of Color Day. In previous years, this day had been set up so that people of color could stay home from class voluntarily, purportedly to signify how their value to the campus would be missed. To my knowledge, no one at Evergreen had up to this point registered public concern about a de facto day of segregation, a condition against which so many in the Civil Rights Movement had struggled. It would just be for a day, after all, and it could all be explained by reference to a play.[226]

But this particular year, the policy had changed. White students and professors were required to stay away from campus in a symbolic act of self-abasement. The change had come in the wake of Evergreen's hiring a new president, George Bridges. According to various accounts, Bridges almost immediately expanded university administration and allied himself with factions obsessed with race and 'social justice.'[227] Some months before People of Color day, there had been a meeting of the 'Equity Council,' whose stated purpose under Bridge's charge was to "[advance] Evergreen's commitment to and aspirations for greater equity, diversity, and inclusion of underrepresented populations in our campus community." How, exactly? Through "proactive, strategic, and sustained initiatives for progressive institutional change."[228] In other words, a taxpayer-funded group dedicated to political activism and indoctrination now had authority over important aspects of campus life.

Once the Equity Council had convened, faculty members were notified of the council's new manifesto and told that they were either allies or enemies of its contents, binaries eerily reminiscent of puritan America, when people believed they were either on the side of God or in league with the Devil. Of course, to be aware of such history, one would likely have to have been taught it.

In any case, one professor of evolutionary biology, Bret Weinstein, objected to the new policy, which he explained in an email to a staff member:

> There is a huge difference between a group or coalition deciding to voluntarily absent themselves from

a shared space in order to highlight their vital and under-appreciated roles... and a group or coalition encouraging another group to go away. The first is a forceful call to consciousness which is, of course, crippling to the logic of oppression. The second is a show of force, and an act of oppression in and of itself.[229]

Neither the Equity Council nor the student groups who bought into their manifesto saw things this way. Weinstein's patient voice of dissent would be unwelcome, both in the infamous email and in general — not just because the other side disagreed, but because the university environment at Evergreen State had become intolerant of dissent.

As it happens, students who shared Weinstein's concerns confided that they were afraid to speak up. Most thought that they would be branded as white supremacists. The message was clear: *if you are white, it's not enough to acknowledge the marginalized struggles. You must also feel the sting of exclusion. Otherwise, how will you atone for your white privilege? If you disagree, watch out.* Through the equity manifesto, the administrators had essentially sanctioned a group of students to use unreason and intimidation in response to a tenured professor with grave concerns about, you know, forced segregation. Weinstein, a mild-mannered Jewish liberal with an excellent teaching and publishing record, would be branded a racist. Why? Because *you are an ally or an enemy.* In the Manichean minds of the woke student body, Weinstein was *other.*

Weinstein refused to stay home on People of Color Day, and things quickly turned south. A group of students, long since steeped in messages of victimhood, found Weinstein and surrounded him. Some cursed at him. Others menaced. At one point, he was unable to leave. He would have to wait for the campus police to arrive to get out. Until then, he tried to reason with the students — but that assumes reasonable listeners. The students surrounded

Weinstein like some scene out of *Children of the Corn*, record-ing with their smart devices, shouting over him as he sought calmly to engage.

The same group of students would also surround President Bridges. They shouted the meek president down, called for Weinstein's ouster, and insisted the university president "shut the fuck up" whenever he offered any sort of half-hearted defense. Because he had not purged the university of the enemy (Weinstein), Bridges had become the enemy. The irony is most pronounced in the videos of the president. One can't help but see a man neutered by his political allegiances and a masochistic fidelity to a world-view. Even in interviews after the encounter where students treated him with utter disrespect, Bridges defended their behavior.

Weinstein, by contrast, came across to outsiders at least as a picture of calm. Eventually, Weinstein resigned. He settled for $500,000 on condition that the University admit-ted to no wrongdoing.

THE RECOGNITION

The wisdom traditions tell us to recognize our common humanity because a failure to do so is often the first step towards suffering. Deconstructed, the process goes: We forget our common humanity; this leads to incivility; which, in turn, leads to civil disorder or bloodshed. One, two, three. It's almost a tautology to say that there will be differ-ences among people. Why else would we need to cultivate the virtue of tolerance, which is necessary to living together peacefully? Otherwise, we otherize.

In 'othering' we are tempted to emphasize the inevita-ble differences in other people and use those differences to place those others in categories of moral or cultural inferi-ority. Ironically, the concept of othering comes from many of the self-same philosophers whose ideas have given rise to much of today's incivility. No matter: Even if one doesn't accept postmodernism or critical theory, we should understand othering. In othering someone, it's easier to justify harming them, ignoring their suffering, or regarding them as irredeemable.

Evolution probably gave humans the wiring to otherize. Psychologists Catherine Cottrell and Steven Neuberg argue that prejudice evolved as a function of living in groups. Group living allowed humans to collaborate to access resources necessary for survival. Group living also offered advantages such as protection and assistance with child-rearing. But given the limits to the benefits of group life, groups soon became wary of outsiders. In a fierce competition for resources, outsiders might kill to take yours. To protect ourselves, we evolved ways of identifying who is a group member and who is not. Over millennia, this process would have become so immediate and instinctual that it became a generalized unconscious mistrust. Differences in skin color would simply expedite this subliminal process.[230]

But as with many instincts that might be natural or evolved, we have to overcome them. Just because something is natural doesn't make it right, or good. And racial prejudice is neither right nor good. If we care about living together in peace, we can and should have a more cosmopolitan outlook. We have to do more than mouth the words:

> *I have a dream that my four little children will one day live in a nation where they will not be judged by the color of their skin but by the content of their character.[231]*

In 1996, Keshia Thomas didn't just mouth the words. But by 2017, the call to recognize our common humanity had become somewhat fainter. After all, it's hard to hear that call over the cacophony of a mob.

If we think of that mob as being like an organism, then what animates it is a kind of religious zeal — but it's a religion that glorifies nothing. Its very existence depends on the presence of an evil against which it defines itself. The less one can find that evil, the more one must look for it around every corner. Or one must 'do the work' to discover that even the most dedicated ally to the oppressed is irredeemable at some level. If we could finally overcome, working, say, to a condition of colorblindness, this would deny the zealot their *raison d'être*, their source of moral superiority, and in the case of many in the academy, a paycheck.

BENEVOLENT OTHERING

In 2020, administrators of the Smithsonian Institute's National Museum of African-American History and Culture put up a poster that was meant to represent the black perspective on race matters in today's society. The poster, titled "Aspects and Assumptions of Whiteness and White Culture in the United States," listed characteristics that included:

1. Objective, rational linear thinking
2. Values cause and effect relationships
3. Quantitative emphasis
4. Emphasis on the scientific method
5. Hard work is the key to success
6. Work before play
7. Plan[ning] for the future
8. Delayed gratification
9. Values being on time

By implication, people of color would and perhaps should not generally share these values. Most commenters observed that such a bizarre list of attributes would more likely come from white separatists than anyone who had ever had any passing association with the Civil Rights movement.

My friend, entrepreneur Magatte Wade — who is Senegalese — was horrified upon seeing the poster. She wrote a lengthy response, from which I will liberally quote:

> As a proud black African, I regard many of these
> characteristics as mine, either by birthright or
> adoption. My Mourides culture in Senegal is firmly
> committed to hard work, planning for the future,
> and delayed gratification for generations — and it
> is an insult to our people to imply otherwise. As a
> proud African immigrant to the U.S. who is eager to
> support the people of Africa in becoming co-creators
> of global prosperity and innovation, I passionately
> advocate for objectivity and rational thinking, under-
> standing cause and effect relationships, quantitative
> thinking, effective decision-making, and more.
> Anyone who promotes "blackness" as somehow
> opposed to or not aligned with hard work and
> rationality is perpetuating the most degrading racist
> stereotypes — in essence, black people are once
> again regarded as savages.[232]

Wade goes on to explain that so-called 'antiracism'
not only reinforces dangerous stereotypes, but reinforces
them in the minds of black people, "especially among our
youth." And it is in this last point that Wade's words should
cause any conscientious person to shudder — because too
much of so-called antiracism engenders an unproductive
victimhood mentality.

Strangely, white 'allies' foment most of the racial incivility in the twenty-first century. For example, in her bestsell-
ing book *White Fragility*, Robin D'Angelo calls upon white
people to confess the sin of whiteness and "do the work"
of purging it.[233] D'Angelo herself is white. The majority of
so-called racial justice advocates are educated and white.
Their support for the marginalized comes across at times
more like a collective pity party than anything resembling
civil rights. If a black person is looking for inspiration for
personal empowerment, they won't find it in this movement.

Antiracism feeds condescension on its best days, cancel

culture on its worst. To some people of color, antiracism can come across as a dehumanizing form of ventriloquism. Many have spent the last fifty years climbing out of victimhood, and they know good and well how to speak for themselves. Due to all of the white paladins who purport to speak for blacks, it's no wonder that author John McWhorter writes, "In 2020 — as opposed to 1920 — I neither need nor want anyone to muse on how whiteness privileges them over me. Nor do I need wider society to undergo teachings in how to be exquisitely sensitive about my feelings."[234]

THE DREAM DEFERRED

As Chicago was roiled by protests and looting in the wake of George Floyd's murder, eighteen people were killed six days after Floyd's death, on June 1, 2020, making it the single most violent day for Chicago in sixty years. The victims and suspects were all blacks. Similar violence waxed and waned throughout major U.S. cities throughout the eighties, nineties, and aughts. Though violence declined steadily through those three decades, it is resurgent now. Back in the '90s, the nightly news carried far more frequent reminders of violence within black communities. I remember regular news reports of mothers crying over their dead children, caught up in gangland crossfire; or over a son killed in a drive-by shooting. Few seemed to notice the parallels with Prohibition, a time when whites killed whites. This time, there would be no repeal. Americans had become inured to the violence, so much so that the only thing that would be unusual or sensational about a Black person's killing would be if the killer were white. *Then* all hell would break loose.

But why?

It's one thing to have a drug dealer kill another drug dealer. It's quite another to have the police themselves become predators. If those charged with upholding the peace and protecting the community are mostly white, that fact alone can create a particular perception. When there is a violent crime, people want to turn to the police to patrol and reduce crime in their neighborhoods. But when there is a perception that they can't, they'll feel unsafe, desperate, and betrayed. Indeed, depending on the statistics one uses, there is evidence that police abuse falls disproportionately on blacks. Whether this is due primarily to racism or to the focus of police resources on the Drug War, it should be important to find out. Otherwise, how is one reasonably and *proportionally* to direct one's outrage?

It could also be that poorer people have far more encounters with police because they are more likely to be pulled over for simple infractions, as poor people often lack the resources to come into compliance.[235] All of these factors are at play — but we have to know *which* factors are *primarily* at play. Otherwise, our collective responses to different forms of violence might be wildly out of propor-tion. In other words, if black lives matter, then *all* black lives ought to matter.

To put this into perspective, consider that in the period between 2013 to 2019, 336 unarmed black people were killed by police, according to a project called Mapping Police Violence, which uses government data.[236] In that same date range, 452 unarmed whites were killed, as well as 201 unarmed Hispanics. Because blacks represent only 13.4 percent of the population, they suffer a more signifi-cant share of the violence than whites, who comprise 63.4 percent of the population. If there is any meaning in the idea of *proportional* police violence, such violence against unarmed whites should be around 4.75 times greater than against unarmed blacks, given that is how many more whites there are than blacks in America. But there is only 1.35 times the violence against unarmed whites, relative to the population. You might think this paints a picture of racism that should send people running into the streets.

Let's look at overall violence by race/ethnicity.

In just one year, 2018, 7,407 blacks were killed compared to 6,088 whites, which means that there was *more* black violence, and much more violence *against* blacks as a percentage of the population. Now let's consider a confounding factor: Blacks comprised 54.9 percent of all homicide offenders, compared to 42.4 percent for whites. Blacks were 13.4 percent of the U.S. population, yet they accounted for more than half of all murders. And according to the FBI's National Incident-Based Reporting System, 61.5 percent of all offenders were male.[237] According to the FBI's Crime Report for 2018, 87.7 percent of murderers were male.[238] That means about 6 percent of the U.S. population, black males, committed approximately half of all murders that year.

We should note here that the above statistics are only for instances in which the killer was caught and found guilty. One might argue that there is racial injustice because a disproportionate number of homicides go unsolved when the victim is black. Let's assume this is accurate. It's reasonable to think that the perpetrators of unsolved homicides won't have a vastly different racial composition than those of the solved cases. (Never mind that black witnesses to violent crime are frequently afraid to report anything lest they be branded as 'snitches.') So the idea that a disproportionate number of black-victim homicide cases go unsolved probably doesn't cast the data on black-offender murder in a better light, even as it hints at some disproportionality in serving justice for black victims and their families.

What about the fact that blacks are 50 percent more likely to be wrongfully convicted of murder?[239] Groups like the Innocence Project work tirelessly to undo problems created by the U.S. criminal justice system, which fall disproportionately on blacks. But we still have to ask ourselves whether the riots of 2020 were based on accuracy and proportionality. As with many phenomena, the narrative of comprehensive white racism and black victim-hood falls apart under scrutiny. To point this out is not to deny the existence of racism, but rather to make a plea for reason in civil discourse. The current narratives threaten to divide Americans more deeply along racial and political lines.

Behind every data point is a story of real people in unique circumstances. And data can, of course, paint a misleading picture. But if policing has *anything* to do with violent crime prevention, it would be logical to target more law-enforcement resources in areas in which there is more violent crime. And that will always create more interactions between cops and citizens. None of this is to say that racism isn't a factor in police violence. It is rather to argue that it is highly unlikely to be the main factor, or even a significant factor. Whether you're black or white, if your job requires mopping up blood in the black community day after day, you might start to associate bloodshed with race in that community.

Things get worse for the black victim narrative: According to a Bureau of Justice Statistics study of the year 2018[240], blacks committed 15.3 percent of crimes against whites, for a total of 547,948 crimes. In contrast, whites committed 10.6 percent of crimes against blacks for a total of 59,777 crimes. That means that blacks committed more crimes against whites by an order of magnitude. Does that mean whites should be marching against black racism? Of course not. It means that there are a host of factors that run counter to popular narratives of 'anti-racist' orthodoxy. These include the number of fatherless black children, the illegal drug trade, and the prosecution of the Drug War, as well as various other root causes of black poverty.

One might even be courageous enough to mention themes of violence, documented and celebrated in rap culture. Consider this passage from the Grammy-nominated "Love it or Hate it" by rap artist, The Game:

> On the grill of my lowrider
> Guns on both sides, right above the gold wires
> I'll fo'-five 'em, kill a nigga on my song
> And really do it, that's the true meaning of a ghost-
> writer
> 10 G's will take your daughter out her Air Forces
> Believe in me, homie, I know all about losses
> I'm from Compton, wear the wrong colors, be
> cautious
> One phone call'll have your body dumped in Marcy
> I stay strapped like car seats
> Been bangin' since my lil' nigga Rob got killed for his
> Barkleys[241]

There are thousands of songs like this in existence. Here's another lyric from Mobb Deep, in a song called 'Kill that Nigga':

> My hammer will knock sense in the nigga real quick
> Nail a nigga tongue with the four fifth
> Nigga you in violation of that code of silence
> Niggas like you get real niggas indicted[242]

There is no doubt that gangsta rap songs like these are a means of expression for those whose lived experience is one of troubling circumstances and perpetual violence. But these songs also reflect a set of truths that might be uncomfortable for suburban elites raised in denial about deep social problems that have only the most tenuous connection to white racism.

Of course, anyone can look at statistics and question their validity. Maybe racial bias is so widespread that certain kinds of crimes are undercounted, while others are overcounted. But such a claim needs to be supported with evidence, not merely asserted. Thus, anyone with objections must use 'objective, rational thinking,' see 'cause and effect relationships,' and place an 'emphasis on the scientific method,' which critical race theorists claim is the very definition of whiteness. Brown University economist Glenn

Loury, who is black, is famous for applying these tools of inquiry. His conclusions are wildly different from popular race-based victimhood narratives. Are we to believe that Loury is not white enough for critical thinking? Of course not. But such is the circular nature of critical theory.

CRITICAL THEORY VS. CRITICAL THINKING

Not only has it become fashionable to abandon critical thinking and the basic rules of inquiry, it has also become fashionable to deny that third-wave Critical Theory is primarily responsible for this abandonment. At the risk of using a tool of oppression, let's look at the evidence. According to James Lindsay in his excellent essay, "No, the Woke Won't Debate You. Here's Why,"[243] Lindsay simply quotes from critical theorists. Here's one from philosopher Alison Bailey:

> The critical-thinking tradition is concerned primarily with epistemic adequacy. To be critical is to show good judgment in recognizing when arguments are faulty, assertions lack evidence, truth claims appeal to unreliable sources, or concepts are sloppily crafted and applied. For critical thinkers, the problem is that people fail to "examine the assumptions, commitments, and logic of daily life... the basic problem is irrational, illogical, and unexamined living." In this tradition sloppy claims can be identified and fixed by learning to apply the tools of formal and informal logic correctly.
>
> Critical pedagogy begins from a different set of assumptions rooted in the neo-Marxian literature on critical theory commonly associated with the Frankfurt School. Here, the critical learner is someone who is empowered and motivated to seek justice and emancipation.[244]

Rational inquiry will never, as poet Audre Lorde says, help you tear down the "Master's House."[245] Instead, according to some critical theorists, to make social change, you have to abandon rational inquiry in favor of motivated narratives. They used to call this the dangerous game of letting the ends justify the means; when the question of truth or falsity never enters the picture, we've entered the realm of fiction and lies. If rational inquiry is a tool of racism, just-so stories are the tools of social justice. As Bailey readily admits:

> Critical pedagogy regards the claims that students make in response to social-justice issues not as propositions to be assessed for their truth value, but as expressions of power that function to re-inscribe and perpetuate social inequalities.[246]

Critical theory can thus be reduced to this: *Do whatever you have to do to get power, even if you have to make things up. And if someone challenges you based on rational inquiry, call them racist (or sexist or transphobic), change the subject, and agitate.*

The use of unsupported assertion, otherizing, and the expectation of blind obedience should be familiar to us: Hitler, Stalin, Mussolini used similar devices. Ironically, Donald Trump came to power on them, as well. And they are destroying the very rules of rational discourse we use to pursue truth, or at least informed intersubjective agreement.

Human beings ought to put truth instead of politics at the center of inquiry because there can be no justice without it. Can you imagine the intrepid lawyers at the Innocence Project working to exonerate prisoners using chants and slogans? No, they use exculpatory evidence like DNA samples. Prosecutors likewise have a very high burden of proof, which is evidence beyond a reasonable doubt. Why would we want to suspend reason and evidence at the scale of society? Yet the presumption of guilt is just what many social justice advocates expect.

THE PURSUIT OF UNDERSTANDING

Stephen Hsu is a brilliant physicist with a penchant for crunching and analyzing data. But in 2019, Hsu was forced to resign from an administrative post after activists sent a petition around Michigan State University where Hsu taught. You see, Hsu had decided to pursue truth instead of social justice.

Hsu, a Chinese American, made the grievous sin of looking at evidence to see whether narratives about racism held up on questions having to do with income disparities in society. On one such instance, Hsu made an appearance on a controversial podcast, where he claimed IQ was by far the strongest predictor of income and opportunity. Whatever one thinks about Hsu's wisdom in appearing on a controversial podcast, it has no bearing whatsoever on the validity of his claims. Specifically, Hsu claimed IQ predicts "underrepresentation." One could simply look at people's self-reporting on ethnicity and match that against their IQ scores. If there were systemic racism, Chu would expect to find high IQ minorities in low-paid jobs, or those same minorities restricted from academia. But he did not. Instead, he found that the distribution of opportunities tracks ever-so-closely to the distribution of IQ, race be damned. Of course, this type of inquiry is taboo because it virtually obliterates claims about systemic racism, at least as those claims apply to questions about how opportunities are distributed in society.

There is undoubtedly controversy about 'race science,' especially given the idea of race and that reporting on race can be a somewhat nebulous exercise. That had not been Hsu's concern in this case. Still, the mere accusation of 'race science' was enough to ensure Hsu's resignation from a graduate studies administrative post. Few involved in the

affair ever seemed concerned about whether Hsu's research
methods were reliable, much less whether his claims might
have been valid. The university had to trump up other
charges to justify firing Hsu. Still, the discovery of alleged
"conflicts of interest" only came after Hsu's notorious views
on IQ became widely known. Instead, the implications of
Hsu's work were simply too taboo to abide. This statement
from the MSU Graduate Employees Union says it all:

> The GEU recognizes that academic freedom entitles
> a scholar to express ideas without professional disad-
> vantage. However, the VP of Research and Grad-
> uate Studies has tremendous power in determining
> research budgets and therefore tremendous responsi-
> bility in doing so in agreement with University values
> of diversity, equity, and inclusion.[247]

Diversity. Equity. Inclusion. These values seem benign
enough, until you realize that they are intended to circum-
scribe all other values. In other words: no one is ever to
question diversity, equity, and inclusion. Instead, facts are to
be replaced by values. Science is to be replaced by activism. Civil society is to be replaced by assertions of political
power.

Nita Farahany, a professor of philosophy and law, said
of the Hsu affair: "I do think that researchers have a duty
to consider how their research will be used, to understand
the implications of their research for society and to help
safeguard against scientific misuse."[248]

I don't want to misinterpret Farahany, but appeals to
duty offer justification for those stifling free speech and open
inquiry. Even if we were to stipulate that Hsu's conclusions
were mostly false, we might ask: *What is the limiting principle
for such a duty?* Under what circumstances should evidence
be suppressed? When should a claimant be muzzled? After
all, science depends on truth trackers presenting countervailing evidence in a process similar to philosopher Karl
Popper's theory of falsification. It's too easy for anyone to

claim "scientific misuse" whenever evidence contradicts some favored power narrative.

In Hsu's case, it's not merely that his research runs counter to the narrative that *everything I don't like about America is because of racism.* It's that an entire secular religion depends on waging war against inquiry. Stephen Hsu is collateral damage.

THE LONG MARCH

The gains made in the Civil Rights movement are being rolled back; the waves of incivility are worsening. It need not be that way. But just as the fires of racism were being tamped into embers, Marxism's intellectual and cultural remnants sought refuge in the academy. These activists set about fanning the flames again, blending the grand narrative of class warfare into a grand narrative of racialized warfare.

Of course, class warfare never really went away. So what we were witnessing throughout the 1990s and 2000s was the slow and deliberate inculcation of illiberal ideas. This has come to be known as the "long march through the institutions."[249] Adherents have successfully programmed these ideas into much of the educated elite. Recent events just go to show, for better or worse, how much ideas still matter, decades after the fall of the Berlin Wall.

In 1930, Italian Marxist Antonio Gramsci likened the strategy to preparation for trench warfare. You don't want to try a frontal attack, thought Gramsci, you want to weaken civil society. He saw civil society not as the bounty of freedom, but rather as the ruling class's cultural hegemony. Gramsci writes:

> The massive structures of the modern democracies, both as state organizations, and as complexes of associations in civil society, constitute for the art of politics as it were the 'trenches' and the permanent

> fortifications of the front in the war of position: they render merely 'partial' the element of maneuver which before used to be 'the whole' of war...[250]

Higher education, then, became the primary beachhead for those with illiberal agendas. But Gramsci had taught them to be patient in their strategy. To transform a generation, those purveyors would have to undertake a multigenerational effort to occupy the university and spread a particular mind virus to students, year after year. But that meant *the university would no longer be dedicated to the pursuit of truth. The university would be dedicated to social justice.* Year on year, that idea metastasized, until an institution once dedicated to learning would become dedicated to activism. Universities were transformed into reeducation camps.

Education entrepreneur Michael Strong argues that academia is the "world's leading social problem,"[251] due to how thoroughly bankrupt ideas have taken hold. "Because of the current sad state of higher education," he argues, "we must create a new institution in order to create a new, freer social and intellectual order."

THE DEATH OF DISCOURSE: VICTIMOLOGY

As the chaos of memetic warfare enters its third decade, two particularly virulent illiberal strains stand out. One is based on identity politics and critical theory; the other is more or less a reactionary movement that evolved, rather grotesquely, to answer it. For our purposes, let's call them victimologists and reactionaries.

Victimologists are part of a sociological phenomenon that likely had its origins in the 1970s. Perhaps the best explanation of "victim culture" comes from sociologists Bradley Campbell and Jason Manning, who identify three primary cultural types: *honor culture*, *dignity culture*, and *victim culture*.[252]

Honor cultures evolved more or less due to the relative absence of mediating institutions. In effect, people in honor cultures had to send a message that they were willing to be friendly and even gentlemanly to avoid conflict, but would tolerate no insult that could invite anyone to test opportunities to take advantage. This culture historically predominated in Southern U.S. states, where mediating institutions were underdeveloped as compared with the North.

"In honor cultures, there's a much greater sensitivity to slight," write Campbell and Manning. "Insults demand a serious response, and even accidental slights might provoke severe conflict. Having a low tolerance for offense is more likely to be seen as a virtue than a vice."[253]

Within honor culture, you might be challenged to a duel or a bar fight. What kind of reputation would you get if you called the cops every time someone hurled an insult? People would see that you might be weak or afraid, then make note of your fear. When brought up in honor culture, you tend to value your own courage and capability. Some will forego reliance on legal authority even when it's available, because to do so risks lowering their standing.[254]

But as mediating institutions developed more fully, people started to get a sense that it wasn't worth it to get into a dust-up or duel every time someone slighted you. Dignity culture emerged. Within *dignity culture*, one relies far more heavily on mediating legal structures.

"It is even commendable to have 'thick skin' that allows one to shrug off slights and even serious insults," write Campbell and Manning. And in a dignity-based society, "parents might teach children some version of 'sticks and stones may break my bones, but words will never hurt me' — an idea that would be alien in a culture of honor."[255]

Dignity culture says that we should avoid insulting others, too. In general, an ethic of restraint prevails. The more people who start to reason this way, the more there is a measure of peace for everyone. It amounts to a kind of multilateral disarmament.

But what if mediating institutions are perceived to apportion justice unfairly or disproportionately? With blacks, from the time of emancipation through the Jim Crow years and up through Rodney King, Eric Garner, and George Floyd, it appears that mediating institutions have not worked for a large segment of the population. Indeed, it seems that these institutions actively work against blacks. Because there is more than a grain of truth to these perceptions, it has become a simple matter to build a contemporary narrative of racial injustice around comparatively rare anecdotes—comparatively, that is, relative to America's dark history of oppression.

So, a new culture emerged, starting roughly in the early 1990s: victim culture. Bizarrely this culture did not originate so much among the victims themselves but rather the academic elites. Such is not to argue that no minority groups have taken up the mantle of victim culture. Still, it resembles the claptrap of critical theory more than a genuine, endogenous cultural shift.

Victim culture, according to Campbell and Manning, is a hybrid of honor culture and dignity culture. People in a victimhood culture are like the honorable in having a high sensitivity to slight. They're exceptionally touchy and stay vigilant to perceived offenses. Insults are serious business, and even unintentional slights might provoke a severe conflict. But, as in a dignity culture, people generally eschew violent vengeance in favor of relying on some authority figure or other third party. They complain to the law, to their company's Human Resources department, to the university administrators, or — perhaps as a strategy to get attention — to the public at large. All of this puts things mildly.

The dynamics track closely with what transpired at Evergreen State involving Bret Weinstein. Other high-profile cases include the Nikolas Christakis episode at Yale, where students surrounded Christakis and berated him for refusing to censor students' Halloween costumes.[256] Invariably, these events end up associated with some petition or other that begins: *In order to create a safer and more inclusive environment for marginalized students, we demand...*

It's one thing to have victimhood culture develop to a healthy degree. For example, we might want to raise awareness about police abuse or sexual harassment. It's quite another to have it morph into unhealthy extremes that work at odds with healing and humane progress. Interestingly, those in the thrall of victim culture rely on hyperbole. Or as Campbell and Manning conclude:

> The combination of high sensitivity with dependence on others encourages people to emphasize or exaggerate the severity of offenses. There's a corresponding tendency to emphasize one's degree of victimization, one's vulnerability to harm, and one's need for assistance and protection. People who air grievances are likely to appeal to such concepts as disadvantage, marginality, or trauma, while casting the conflict as a matter of oppression.[257]

It's hard to untangle strategy from sentiment. It's no doubt true that people will attempt to use emotionally-wrought accusations for political ends. After all, the mere appearance of impropriety is often enough to get someone canceled. But on the other end of the spectrum, Jonathan Haidt and Greg Lukianoff detail the degree to which a generation of children has been raised to suck their thumbs in safe spaces.[258] Couple this with the belief on the part of many that they are victims, and that their victimhood is an inescapable prison of horrors built by white cisgender males, and political activism blurs with cognitive distortion. If someone tells you that you are a victim often enough, you will start to believe it. Suddenly, there are bogeymen around every corner. Every ex-president is an insult. Every piece of literature is a traumatic trigger. Every statue, a Satanic symbol. Gramsci's strategy is more effective in a river of crocodile tears.

Author Uri Harris identifies related mechanisms of victim culture, which he shrewdly observes at Evergreen State.[259] I'll cite Harris's mechanisms using italics, then offer my interpretation of each:

> *Mechanism 1: A binary classification of allies and enemies that's vaguely defined but emotionally and morally charged.*

This sort of Manichean thinking shuts down discourse. It divides people along lines that have little to do with the subject matter and everything to do with forced allegiance with some purported good or evil. Whether in one's complicity with empty symbolic gestures or unreasonable demands, the 'privileged' must self-flagellate and sacrifice all reason to the angry gods of 'social justice.' Nothing else will do. Discourse is for the privileged. 'Allies' are left with two remaining options: keep quiet or grab a placard and take to the streets to make demands. Everyone else is the enemy, benighted by some ism or false consciousness.

> *Mechanism 2: A notion of multiple truths and the sanctity of subjective experience that's selectively applied.*

Victim culture found its roots in critical theory and postmodernism. Psychology professor Jordan Peterson and others who have pointed out this fact have found themselves mired in controversy. And yet when the critical theorists of the seventies and eighties began to test what would become the mind viruses of political correctness in the nineties, the pared-down postmodernism never went away. It simply evolved. Stripped of its obscurantism, what remained is the idea that truth is entirely relative, and that the victims' 'truth' should be exalted, even sacralized (#believeallvictims). Oppressed peoples are not individuals but whole groups of people who must see themselves as such.

Mechanism 3: A notion of an extremely powerful but intangible power structure.

When seen through the lens of victim culture, all social problems somehow trace back to a single binary: oppressor and oppressed. Though the words 'good' and 'evil' rarely get used, victimology's binaries have the same effect as puritanism of 1690s Salem, when everything was black or white and there were witches to burn. Of course, where you find oppression, there is also 'power.' *Power animates all of life like a contagion which must be eradicated.* And those who wield power — whether in holding wealth or in being born a certain race — are irredeemable villains. Privilege is Original Sin.

The irony of victimology is that it was begun and propagated among the privileged. Generations of young people have been inculcated now for two generations. Part of our unfolding story of collapse must include the rot in higher education, which has begun to infect primary and secondary education, as well. The watchwords of victimology are terms like *structural* or *systemic* and tie to charged terms like *racism* or *oppression*. These words are strong enough to create a sense that oppression is everywhere, but they are unspecific enough to let the wielder moralize with impunity. Consider this definition of structural racism offered by the Aspen Institute:

> A system in which public policies, institutional practices, cultural representations, and other norms work in various, often reinforcing ways to perpetuate racial group inequity. It identifies dimensions of our history and culture that have allowed privileges associated with "whiteness" and disadvantages associated with "color" to endure and adapt over time. Structural racism is not something that a few people or institutions choose to practice. Instead it has been a feature of the social, economic and political systems in which we all exist.

Sounds plausible enough. But like many byproducts of critical theory, it is difficult to falsify and easy to parrot. The extent of structural racism amounts to a set of anecdotes that seem to indicate the tip of a great iceberg. Instead of doing the work of empirics, most evoke the term as a trump card to remind you that *people of color are victims and whites are oppressors.*

Thus we have victim culture — and quite a lot of it. Some dispassionate observer might argue we have too much of it. As the 'mechanisms' of victim culture eat through the population with each successive generation, essential things — even good things — are weakening, faltering, and fading. For like all cultures, victim culture has its unhealthy extremes. It's one thing to raise consciousness among those who remain blind to the remaining -isms that keep others from opportunities to pursue happiness. It's quite another to create a whole generation of people who see themselves as victims by their membership in some group, whether that group is designated by sex or race or poverty.

The unrelenting message — *you are a victim, you are a victim, you are a victim* — is psychologically destructive. Imagine paying $20,000 a year to write that message repeatedly in exchange for a degree. Victimology thus writes a false meaning for millions of individuals without much input from those individuals at all. It kills practiced virtues like personal responsibility, toleration, and striving. It attenuates the content of character. And it subordinates individuals to the brute fact of privilege, which, according to victimology, is the lopsided ability to oppress.

> *Nothing is your fault. You are a victim. Who shall forgive your student loan debt?*

None of this meant to diminish the suffering of racism's victims, much less deny racism exists. But when one uses race as a lens to see everything, it distorts a more complete, higher resolution picture of power in America. It requires that we close our eyes to victims of government violence who are not black. It tells us we have to deny the consequences of human choices. It distracts us from unpleasant and complex truths that are the root causes of specific disparities. And it confines millions to a plantation of the mind in which they can only see themselves as victims to get ahead in life. Perhaps the victimology narrative is so destructive precisely because it has a grain of truth to it. Then again, to acknowledge a grain is not to infer an entire silo.

THE DEATH OF DISCOURSE: REACTION

Newton's Third Law says that every action has an equal and opposite reaction. Likewise, cultural forces of sufficient potency will cause a response. Enter the Reactionaries. This merry band of basement dwellers, trolls, white nationalists, angry boomers, Karens, and burn-it-all-down adolescents are united by one force: oppose the victimologists.

The philosopher Richard Rorty, a man of the left, warned about victimologists and the Reactionaries in his 1998 book *Achieving Our Country: Leftist Thought in Twentieth-Century America*. First, he warned of the illiberal excesses of critical theory. Then he warned of a "strongman" who would give working-class people an "outlet" in response:

> One thing that is very likely to happen is that the gains made in the past forty years by black and brown Americans, and by homosexuals, will be wiped out. Jocular contempt for women will come back into fashion. The words 'nigger' and 'kike' will once again be heard in the workplace. All the sadism which the academic Left has tried to make unacceptable to its students will come flooding back. All the resentment which badly educated Americans feel about having their manners dictated to them by

college graduates will find an outlet.[260]

In 1998, Rorty's warning would fall mainly on deaf ears, and it would take a couple of decades to be rediscovered. Perhaps the only thing he didn't anticipate was the degree to which the Internet would be a place where people could say hurtful things with relative impunity.

Political correctness had dialed down to a simmer in the naughts, overshadowed by the events of 9/11, not to mention a couple of wars in its wake. Then the financial crisis grabbed most of the attention. But as the quagmires dragged on and the economy recovered, people eventually turned their attention back to the culture wars. Of course, those making the long march through the institutions never stopped marching during those two decades. Americans were distracted as higher education, and other 'institutions' were being utterly transformed. The idea that all issues should be viewed through the lens of race and gender began to leak out again — into the workplace, into entertainment, and into the media.

But by the end of President Obama's second term, much of the American electorate had had quite enough of being lectured to by coastal elites. Obsession with race and gender issues seemed so alien and, frankly, tone-deaf to the concerns of Rust Belt workers of all races. But it wasn't just the working class, although that is what anti-Trump navel-gazers like to tell themselves. It was also highly educated people, and it crossed racial lines. According to a 2018 study, 52 percent of blacks thought the U.S. should become less politically correct, compared with only 36 percent agreeing the country should become more politically correct.[261]

Reactionaries are an indicator of what amounts to a rightwing populist digital insurgency that exists as of this writing. As Jordan Hall reminds us,[262] a "blue" digital counterinsurgency has arrived. Some are looking for blood. Both sides are looking for power. The fragile detente that restricted ideological warfare to the Web has begun to spill into the streets.

But in all of this warfare, discourse dies. Instead of pointing out the excesses of victim culture, reactionaries wear the ring of pseudonymity and find all the various ways of telling the victimologists to fuck off. Since its peak in the rise of Trump, the memetics of Kek have all but disappeared. The reactionary nature of the counter movement has not. One unhealthy culture begets another in a clash of incivilities. The very forces of darkness that the victimologists had hoped to eliminate with their righteous zeal have come back stronger. To razz victimologists, trolls masqueraded as racists for so long that they eventually turned. In this way, victimology fueled the flames of everything it loathes. White nationalism is on the rise again as of this writing, and has been since the rise of Trump. *How many ways can we find to insult coastal elites? Become what they hate.* Those who oppose the excesses of identity politics are neither extremists nor racists, except in the victimologist's mind. Dare to disagree, and they will come after you with pitchforks. Back and forth it goes.

What's so strange about this phenomenon is that each 'side,' far from being entirely at the fringe, represents a cultural vanguard that threatens what remains of social coherence in America. It's not just that partisans fight over tax rates. A new culture war pervades nearly every conversation. Each fights harder to mock, to accuse, or eventually to destroy the other. Underlying all of this struggle, these culture warriors perceive a high-stakes game of winner take all.

And that is why it is important not to let reactionaries off the hook. The reactionary mind is one which can take delight in being contrarian. But this is not smart Devil's advocacy. It is an unreflective commitment to whatever position appears to oppose the victimologist. In its unhealthiest incarnations, the reaction is a mental disease linked to one's degraded self-concept, or what Francis Fukuyama called the *thymic urge*. In this condition, one cannot find one's self-worth in ordinary ways, so one seeks recognition in the empty categories of race, religion, or nationality. Take, for example, Rust Belt workers looking for a scapegoat among immigrants. It's crude collectivism, a wraith that should never have been re-summoned. But it was.

The very existence of crude contrarian collectivism makes victimology a self-fulfilling prophecy, and it offers fodder to those like humanities professor of antiracism Ibram X. Kendi, who writes:

"Trump held up a mirror to American society, and it reflected back a grotesque image that many had refused to see."[263]

"Antiracists" like Kendi believe they bear no responsibility for racial animus in America. To their minds, reactionaries aren't a reaction at all, nor are they fodder for availability cascades. They represent the tip of that white racist iceberg, a pervasive majority secretly if not unconsciously committed to supremacy. That iceberg has been there from the start.

Kendi shows his true colors in a social media post in response to the idea of whites adopting children from the developing world:

> Some White colonizers "adopted" Black children. They "civilized" these "savage" children in the "superior" ways of White people, while using them as props in their lifelong pictures of denial, while cutting the biological parents of these children out of the picture of humanity.[264]

In an ironic twist, the infamous white nationalist Richard Spencer replies "not wrong." A frightening number of victimologists leapt to Kendi's defense. But posts like this are indefensible. They not only reveal the bizarre pathology of antiracism, but feed reactionary zeal.

Reactionaries are not an entirely homogeneous bloc, though. It is instead a more varied coalition, but one that we can carve into five basic subtypes, overlapping in the manner of a Venn Diagram.

Trolls. The most visible due to their online activism, this group's goal is to foment contempt for victimologists and, where possible, to offend them for kicks. Predictably, victimologists use trolls' online activity as evidence of widespread and irredeemable isms.

Nationalists. Many people think that American institutions ought to be by and for Americans. These nationalists probably make up the largest group. They see economic and social relationships not as between two parties who choose one another, but arrangements that ought to benefit citizens. An 'America First' mentality has grown primarily out of the concerns of working-class whites who have lost economic standing in some areas. They are quick to blame foreigners and corporations for their plight.

Gullibles. This group of conspiracy theorists generates false narratives, distorts truths, and propagates falsehoods. Gullibles have no more respect for truth and good discourse than victimologists. In some respects, they're worse. Still, gullibles are eerily similar to critical theorists in that the narrative is more important than reality. The difference is, this group doesn't believe *x* because they imagine it to be good or moral. They believe *x* because they'll believe anything, or because leaders in their in-group believe *x*.

Racists. So much of the fuss is about this group. Though they are a relatively small minority in America, their very existence horrifies us. Sadly, whether as a reaction to victimology or due to different working-class victimhood narratives, racists live among us. Their ranks are growing.

Theocrats. This group feels beset from all sides. Due to the rapid advance of secularization in America, they have come to feel marginalized. Bizarrely, they have devised their own 'intersectionality' and teamed up with many of the groups above. Because they think secularism has ruined America, they are willing to scrap the liberal institutions that have protected them for so long. To do so, they either deny America's secular founding, or they seek to institute a theocracy.

Whether the internet's relative pseudonymity has emboldened a nation of secret troglodytes or reactionaries are truly a reaction to the excesses of victim culture, it's hard to say. I suspect that the truth lies somewhere in between. We can say that neither victimologists nor reactionaries bring much of any value to a peaceful liberal order. Instead, each camp is functioning as a rival gang that could become violent at any moment. Or, worse still, either side could completely take over the machinery of coercion we call the state as the rest of us watch from the bleachers. Because neither has a shred of cosmopolitan liberalism, both are just as dangerous.

As we have shown elsewhere, the real privilege is granted by that protection racket in Washington, one fed by seemingly limitless debt, patronage, and votes from a pliant electorate. When we couple these realities with the fact that the center has not held, we must prepare for the possibility of living in a world where rival groups start a civil war.

In her left ear, the true liberal of peace, freedom and the content of one's character is being told that color-blindness is old fashioned, that privilege is Original Sin, and that the only path to redemption is to abandon the search for truth. In her right ear, the true liberal is being told that racism doesn't really exist anymore, that we must cling to tradition and stasis, and that there was once an American Golden Age to which we must return.

Perhaps the greatest casualty in this new civil war is truth itself. Collective intelligence, or at least some measure of social coherence, has fractured into competing falsehoods. Our civil order is dying. Between victimologists and reactionaries, you get a set of pincers that threaten to squeeze the last bits of rationality, normalcy, and liberal humanism out of American life.

PART

II

AFTER
COLLAPSE

7

THE BREAKDOWN OF THE FEDERAL GOVERNMENT

'My name is Ozymandias, king of kings:
Look on my works, ye Mighty, and despair!'
Nothing beside remains. Round the decay
Of that colossal wreck, boundless and bare
The lone and level sands stretch far away.
Percy Shelley, from *"Ozymandias"*

In 1990, the tiny country of Estonia was under the occupation of the Soviets. Several years prior, Estonians, including the young historian Mart Laar, had engaged in nonviolent resistance, reviving songs of Estonian identity that predated the occupation. The "Singing Revolution" lasted four years, until 1991, which marked the collapse of the Soviet Union, of which Estonia was an unwilling satellite. With the Soviet downsizing, the Baltic States had to find their own way.

When Mart Laar took the reins of power of the newly independent country in 1992, he was thirty-two years old. As the Soviets had left them, Estonia was rudderless, poor, and only beginning to heal from nearly fifty years under the heels of Russian boots. Laar intuitively thought that the way to ensure Estonia's success was to cultivate freedom and self-determination — but of course, he was no expert.

After only two years in office and with no diplomatic experience, Laar negotiated Russian troops' complete withdrawal. Despite being no expert on monetary theory, he introduced Estonia's currency, the kroon, which is one of the world's stablest currencies today. He instituted a flat tax rate, removed price controls, discarded unnecessary regulations, and presided over Estonia's growth into the highest real per capita income of any of the former Communist states.

But again — as Laar himself admits — he was no expert.

> I had read only one book on economics — Milton Friedman's *Free to Choose*. I was so ignorant at the time that I thought that what Friedman wrote about the benefits of privatization, the flat tax and the abolition of all customs rights, was the result of economic reforms that had been put into practice in the West. It seemed common sense to me and, as I thought it had already been done everywhere, I simply introduced it in Estonia, despite warnings from Estonian economists that it could not be done. They said it was as impossible as walking on water.[265]

And yet there was Estonia, walking on the Baltic Sea on its way to prosperity. The High Minds shook their heads and went back to their drawing boards as Estonia became a Baltic Tiger.

What else can we say about this proud little Baltic population?

First, their rebirth as a nation occurred through nonviolent resistance. What a beautiful testament to the power of a people longing for freedom: Estonians used song to maintain solidarity, but otherwise answered oppression with ahimsa. The Russian bear looms next door to this day, but Estonia outperforms its former oppressor on almost every metric of wellbeing.

Second, Estonia's debt to GDP is 8.4 percent. The

U.S. debt ratio is almost 108 percent, as of this writing. Estonia practiced austerity during the 2008 financial crisis and was among the first to emerge from Eastern Europe's Great Recession. The percentage of people living in poverty is among the lowest in that region. And on indices of economic freedom, Estonia consistently ranks in the top fifteen.

Third, Estonia has introduced governance innovations such as e-citizenship, which allow people from all over the world to enjoy the benefits of being an Estonian without living in Estonia. With a population of roughly 1.4 million people, they have chosen the way of Eros Feminine by opening themselves to the world. They had no choice. And yet it works.

Maybe there's something to the idea that small is beautiful, that small is manageable. Maybe nothing is too big to fail. Among the top twenty wealthiest countries in the world, only three have more than 30 million people. We should pause to consider whether and to what degree size matters.

Per Capita GDP (USD) by Country[266]

	Country	Per Capita GDP
1	Luxembourg	$113,196
2	Switzerland	$83,716
—	Macau	$81,151
3	Norway	$77,975
4	Ireland	$77,771
5	Qatar	$69,687
6	Iceland	$67,037
7	United States	$65,111
8	Singapore	$63,987
9	Denmark	$59,795

	Country	Per Capita GDP
10	Australia	$53,825
11	Netherlands	$52,367
12	Sweden	$51,241
13	Austria	$50,022
—	Hong Kong	$49,334
14	Finland	$48,868
15	San Marino	$47,279
16	Germany	$46,563
17	Canada	$46,212
18	Belgium	$45,175
19	Israel	$42,823
20	France	$41,760

On Transactions and Transfers

When it comes to goods, services, and experiences, most valuable things have to be produced by someone. How they get made is another conversation entirely, so let's assume for now that people — perhaps with the aid of computers, machines, and other people — are busy producing things of value. Once these things of value get produced, let's stipulate that the producing parties *own the things*. In this condition, there are two primary ways things can change hands: *transfer* or *transaction*.

In the two scenarios to follow, we've taken out currency as a medium of exchange for the sake of simplicity, but we could add it back in.

In the case of a charitable act — a form of transfer — one person gives something she has to another. Say the giver has two units of the item at first, but after the gift, the second person now has two units, and the giver has none. The recipient is better off thanks to the gift. Maybe the giver feels good that they gave away the item, but only marginally. They'll have to work harder (produce) to get back to having two units of the item.

In a transaction, both give away a thing of value, but get a thing of value in return. Each one values the item he or she gained more than the item he or she gave up; otherwise, there would be no exchange. Each started with two units they preferred less, and each ends up with two units they preferred more. Both parties are happier.

One might wonder which of these two scenarios is the most morally praiseworthy. The answer might depend on the context in which the question is asked: If the charitable act keeps someone from starving, for example, because the thing of value is food, most people would say that act is morally praiseworthy. A food exchange between two people, neither of whom is starving, seems less laudable somehow, though maybe each gets to enjoy more variety. And yet if a starving person traded water for food with a dehydrated person, that seems intuitively right.

Now, let's suppose the food transfer wasn't an act of charity by the giver at all. Instead, a powerful third party took the food from her. Some would argue that this forced transfer is justified. And yet in another context, if the thing of value is not food but sex, we'd be hard-pressed to say that either charity sex or a forced transfer of sex is morally praiseworthy. Perhaps a general discussion of moral praiseworthiness won't get us very far without more details about the circumstances.

Fair enough, then. Another more meaningful question might be: Which of these two scenarios is the most sustainable over time? Or put slightly differently, which method — transfer or transaction — ought to predominate in society?

Well, we know that, as stipulated, both parties to the transaction are better off by *their* lights. We also know that, through exchange, each party is relatively better off. In this way, transactions are positive-sum. In the case of a transfer, though, the arrangement is zero-sum. Apart from any feeling of magnanimity one might have after giving a gift, the net benefit to both parties is greater in the case of a transaction. Even ignoring the fact that forced transfers almost always reduce the satisfaction of those coerced, transactions are more sustainable. I'll let you decide whether there is any moral praiseworthiness in this fact.

If the difference between transfers and transactions is that stark, which would we want to be the predominant way things of value change hands? The paradox is that transactions create more aggregate value than transfers, even if we consider some transfers more *morally* praiseworthy. What we have learned through the bitter experiences of history, whether in ancient Rome's bread and circuses or modern Venezuela's petro-state socialism, is that when the ratio of net transfers to net transactions tips too far towards a predominance of transfers, collapse looms.

"Transferism is a system in which one group of people forces a second group to pay for things that the people believe they, or some third group, should have,"[267] write economists Jim Harrigan and Antony Davies. "Transferism isn't about controlling the means of production. It is about the forced redistribution of what's produced." [268]

One might think that transferism is a type of socialism, but socialism usually involves nationalizing industries, as postwar Britain did with coal. So when some politicians say that they are "democratic socialist," what they probably mean is that they are democratic transferist.

The United States government has fully embraced transferism. And so, it seems, has a consistent voting majority.

RATIONAL STATISM

As we have suggested, voting for social programs is a lot less costly and involved than participating in a community of mutual aid or effective charity. Following economist Bryan Caplan, we might call this *rational statism*. Rational statism simply means that people are willing to accept higher degrees of transferism because they don't feel any immediate costs of doing so. Indeed, 'rationality' in economic jargon means that people tend to act based on what benefits them. In the near term, such a payoff might be an immediate sense of rectitude, or virtue, or in-group identification. By contrast, the negative consequences of transferism are easily obscured and can play out over very long timescales. Thus, rational statism is not a 'rational' argument for statism. It is a form of rational irrationality.

TRANSFERISM AND DEBT

Federal transfers are resources the U.S. government gives directly to people or state and local governments. These are not transactions. As we pointed out above, the money is given in exchange for nothing. Federal transfers to individuals have gone from 11 percent of federal spending in 1953 to 53 percent today.[269] That means that more than half of what the government spends goes from one group of people to another group. When you add in state and local governments, 69 percent of funds are transfer payments. That means that almost 70 percent of what the government does involves taking resources from one group and giving them to another, skimming some off the top in the process. According to Harrigan and Davies, "Less than one-third of the money Washington spends is spent in the name of actual governance."

Partisan affiliation doesn't matter, either; politicians love transfers. Most Americans can't imagine the country without the major entitlement programs, including Medicare, Medicaid, Social Security, and various others. Because politicians and policy wonks never run out of ideas for ways to spend other people's money, most are defined by just how creative they can get. Technocracy becomes the handmaiden to transferism. A cynical person might start to think of these as vote-buying schemes. Recent ideas include a universal basic income (UBI), Medicare for All, and student loan debt forgiveness.

"L'État, c'est la grande fiction à travers laquelle Tout Le Monde s'efforce de vivre aux dépens de Tout Le Monde,"[270] wrote the inimitable Bastiat in 1848.

When anyone asks politicians how the government will pay for it, creativity stalls. And therein lies the problem: Neither Congress nor any president wants to be the one known for taking away the goodies. Instead, they use debt. But this short-term political calculation eventually comes at a terrible long-term cost. Whatever you think about the breakdown of hierarchy as a driver of collapse, perhaps the clearest and most sobering assessment of matters, especially if you are an American, is this: We've run out of money.

Not only is the U.S. government in debt, but the debt is unprecedented. U.S. taxpayers now owe more than the annual revenues collected by all of the world's governments combined, and more than the output of the U.S. economy.[271] Let that sink in. As of this writing, the U.S. federal government owes more than $24 trillion — with a T. The only way to erase that debt in a stroke would be to confiscate all of the assets of all of the rich people in America, with the rich defined as the top quintile. Never mind the economic catastrophe that would follow. Confiscation would only erase the current debt; that is, what the government already owes, *not* what the government *has promised into the future*. And that, too, is a significant number, as the U.S. government has *promised to pay* for Medicaid, Medicare, and Social Security programs anywhere from ten to twenty times the current debt. It's an unimaginable sum, which continues to balloon as we move out into the future. By the time you read these words, collapse will be that much closer.

"The perilous state of our fiscal future is not in doubt,"

warns Rudolf G. Penner of the Urban Institute. "Our problems are driven by the aging of the population and the rate of aging is easy to forecast. Gross spending on Social Security, Medicare, and Medicaid constitutes slightly more than one half of total spending and these programs will be under intense pressure as large numbers of baby boomers enroll in coming years."[272]

If the population wasn't getting older, Medicare and Medicaid programs face the problem that spending per capita on healthcare will be growing faster than income. Combined, aging boomers plus rising costs means total spending will grow more quickly than the economy, and thus, faster than tax revenues. With deficits and debt ballooning this way, debt service will be a growing part of the annual budget. That means that more and more money going to paying creditors instead of, well, anything else the federal government does.

THE HOLE

If you're not afraid, it's because you're bored. And all of this *is* boring, mainly because most of us just can't feel the pain of an abstraction such as *scores* or *hundreds of trillions*. "Counting unfunded liabilities," write economists Davies and Harrigan, "the federal government actually owes somewhere between $100 trillion and $200 trillion. The numbers are so ridiculously large that even the uncertainty in the figures exceeds the annual economic output of the entire planet."[273]

By this point, if you're able to grok the enormity of these numbers, you might be left feeling as if the federal government has become somewhat like a cancer growing upon society. And yet that feeling might be slightly at odds with the idea that only the government can assist people when they get cancer. After all, that is what Medicaid, Medicare, and the rest of the technocratic healthcare system was set up to do. Can these feelings be reconciled?

We should not just pick on so-called 'entitlement' programs. Much of the debt growth has also come from defense spending, also known as the Military-Industrial Complex. Despite all the poor-mouthing from the Pentagon, it is not only a massive consumer of taxpayer resources, but an enormous generator of waste, both in fiscal and environmental terms.

Whatever your partisan outlook, we can make our sober assessment an ironclad mathematical surety: The government spends too much, and it cannot go on. The war in Afghanistan alone cost U.S. taxpayers $2 trillion, also with a T. To put that into perspective, that amount of money would have funded the state budget of Texas for a decade. It would have paid off half the personal debts Americans currently carry. Or if you like, the Afghan War cost every man, woman, and child in America $6,666.66 as of this writing.

We can only imagine how our creditors would respond to such debt levels. So who loaned the federal government all this money? Four groups: foreigners, Americans, the Federal Reserve, and government trust funds. But in the last ten years or so, three of these have wisely cut their lending back. Foreign investors have reduced their lending from about 20 percent per year at the turn of the century to 3 percent today. Domestic investors have cut back by an average of 2 percent each year, when you take out the Great Recession years. So, according to Davies and Harrigan, the Fed "is the only game left in town."[274]

We didn't forget about government trust funds. The biggest one that ever existed, Social Security, is gone. The federal government borrowed all the past eighty years' surpluses and, assuming it will return the money borrowed, has to start paying it back. But from where?

The federal government is borrowing more and more each year by 6 percent. Since 2001, the Federal Reserve has increased its lending to the government by more than 11 percent per year on average. The Fed only has between $4-5 trillion in assets. So when will it stop lending?

Now, if we are to believe economists like Davies and Harrigan, when the Federal Reserve acts as the lender of last resort, it's going to hurt. If the Fed simply prints the money it loans, that causes inflation. At some point, the United States will be the equivalent of a banana republic in which you'll have to push a wheelbarrow full of cash to buy a cup of coffee. Every Federal Reserve loan thus devalues every dollar you have, from what's in your savings account to those stuffed under your mattress. In this way, the spend-happy U.S. government essentially taxes any remaining frugality among U.S. savers as they try to pay down their personal debt.

If the Federal Reserve starts printing money, the U.S. will look like Greece or, worse, Venezuela. Venezuela is an excellent example of what collapse could look like, though it's difficult to predict the magnitude of such a collapse in America. Considering that the U.S. doesn't have a large benefactor, as Greece did in the EU after the Great Recession, we could end up relatively worse off, pulling down other economies with us. Too much of the global economy is tangled up with the U.S. The layers of dependency at home and abroad, from welfare recipients to government contractors, artists to airmen, seniors to salaried bureaucrats. Anyone dependent on federal largesse, directly or indirectly, will be affected.

THE LARGEST EMPLOYER

When you ask people who they think is the largest employer in America, most people will say Walmart. The company does employ 1.5 million people. Yet this is small compared to the number of people who rely on the federal government to butter their bread. The federal government employs 9.1 million people, or 6 percent of U.S. jobs. This figure can be broken down further into 2.1 million federal employees, 4.1 million contract employees, 1.2 million grant employees, 1.3 million military personnel, and a half million postal workers.[275]

And yet this 6 percent of the workforce is shielded from economic downturns. When the U.S. economy experiences a contraction, most companies have to make painful cuts. The government has very different incentives, though, because it can use virtually unlimited taxation and debt. Furthermore, government employees receive 17 percent higher compensation than a comparable private sector employee, yet the private sector counterpart is 45 times more likely to be laid off.[276]

THE NEW DEAL AND THE WELFARE-WARFARE STATE

I spent some time picking on NASA and Space X as exemplars of the technocratic-industrial complex. I chose these examples *because* they have always been dazzling, and our dazzlement tends to obscure true costs. I personally am fascinated by the idea of a Mars colony. Therein lies a story of possibility, wonder, and human expansion so powerful that even this old skeptic can get misty-eyed. Suppose we could get away with the fallacy of hypostatization. That means a 'society' can act and make choices. We might argue that there is great value in knowing that 'we' are exploring the great beyond, together, as a species. 'We' might also decide that anything related to space is a drop in the bucket. And it is. For example, NASA only takes up about .5 percent of the federal budget, as of this writing.

But if we overlook the costs of all the things that have the potential to dazzle us (or appeal to some other emotion that causes us to look away from underlying truths), we'll eventually find a straw that breaks the nation's back.

Whether it's space, farmers, green energy, high-speed rail, cutter ships, high art, education grants, or dubious research, there is always something that someone, somewhere, finds dazzling. It all adds up. But nothing adds up in America quite like the welfare-warfare state.

The welfare-warfare state is a term for the simultaneous development of two classes of expenditure. It goes back quite a long way in the United States. In America, its first stirrings were probably most noticeable with Woodrow Wilson, but became most pronounced with Franklin Roosevelt. Arguably, it was with FDR that technocracy found its footing. Whatever one thinks of FDR, he had to fight the Great Depression and the Second Great War. He fought both with technocracy, though with mixed results.

One of the greatest frauds perpetrated against generations of children has been the New Deal's story in the United States. In civics and social studies classes, it has been orthodoxy. The High Minds were able to disseminate the false idea that FDR 'got us out of the depression' with the New Deal. That myth persists to this day. Under the title "Putting People Back to Work," USHistory.org authors write:

> Out of work Americans needed jobs. To the unemployed, many of whom had no money left in the banks, a decent job that put food on the dinner table was a matter of survival.
>
> Unlike Herbert Hoover, who refused to offer direct assistance to individuals, Franklin Roosevelt knew that the nation's unemployed could last only so long. Like his banking legislation, aid would be immediate. Roosevelt adopted a strategy known as "priming the pump." To start a dry pump, a farmer often has to pour a little into the pump to generate a heavy flow. Likewise, Roosevelt believed the national government could jump-start a dry economy by pouring in a little federal money.[277]

A little federal money? Per capita spending for the New Deal was $5,231.[278] By comparison, the American Recovery and Reinvestment Act was about half that, with both measured in 2009 dollars.

What does it mean to get out of a depression? One indicator on everyone's mind is unemployment, so let's start there. The New Deal hurt the U.S. economy and prolonged the Great Depression. One key table assembled by economist Robert Murphy puts this into perspective, comparing the U.S. and Canada.[279] The former had a New Deal, while the latter had a far milder response.

Roosevelt was elected in late 1932, and was inaugurated in early 1933. (Presidents were sworn in on March 4 back then.) The table shows that absolute unemployment remained abysmal for the next eight years. It wasn't until 1941 that the yearly average unemployment rate got back into the single digits — and only just, at 9.9%. Many critics will try to lay all of this on Herbert Hoover, who was the original architect of the New Deal in many ways.

In 1933, U.S. unemployment was 5.6 percent higher than Canada's. But the following year, the gap widened to a 7.2 percent difference. If we move forward in time to 1938, a full five years after FDR is sworn in, the U.S./Canada difference is even starker, at 7.6 percent.

If the economic indicators above are accurate, why in the world would anyone say that FDR got the U.S. out of the Great Depression? Or, as Murphy asks, what would the unemployment data have to look like for social studies books to say that FDR's policies *kept the US mired* in the Great Depression? There are many reasons for this myth, but a couple stick out.

First, it's human to focus on perceived effort and apparent benefits. FDR's government was highly activist. In troubled times people will turn to leaders, ascribe them with godly powers, and require them to *do something.* FDR and his technocratic 'Brain Trust' *did something.* But so often, it's the centralized way of doing something that can drown decentralized efforts. When it comes to America's national mythology, people will say that it had been any number of alphabet soup agency efforts, such as the TVA, that should get the credit. You probably read that in your civics textbooks in eighth grade.

But some, those with local memory, are more fully aware of the costs. Folk-rock songwriter Mike Cooley channels that memory:

> They powered up the city with hydro-electric juice.
> Now we got more electricity than we can ever use.
> They flooded out the hollow and all the folks down
> there moved out, but they
> Got paid so there ain't nothin' else to think about.
> Some of them made their living cutting the timber
> down, snaking it one log at
> A time up the hill and into town. T.V.A. had a way to
> clear it off real fast.
> Lots of men and machinery, build a dam and drown
> the rest.[280]

When national mythology such as 'FDR got us out of the Depression' gets maintained by powerful government officials, published and republished by intellectuals, and lauded by direct beneficiaries of past goodies, it's harder to transmit a reality closer to the truth in story and song. The national mythology functions more to preserve social coherence around the modus operandi of the welfare-warfare state.

Few are willing to sing the songs of investors and entrepreneurs who must make decisions in a condition of "regime uncertainty," a term coined by the economist Robert Higgs.[281] Regime uncertainty occurs when an activist managerial state attempts to address some crisis or another. But in its lurching centralized actions, the true engines of creation lose stability and predictability in the socio-economic order. Unless they directly connect to the state's make-work programs, entrepreneurs and innovators withdraw and wait, which compounds economic malaise. At worst, cascades of failure take marginal firms first then spread like falling dominos through sectors. There is a return to normal activities only after the technocrats settle down, and entrepreneurs can see some measure of predictability in the patterns.

Since the New Deal, a series of crises have contributed to technocracy's growth and created the illusion that big plans and big projects must pave the road to progress. This illusion was complete when the United States entered World War II, and the illusion was cemented by the apparent success of battle plans, tanks, and bombs. The Depression was finally starting to abate by 1941. Unemployment dropped below 10 percent. But this is also the year that the Japanese attacked Pearl Harbor, which pushed the U.S. into war. By the end of 1942, defense spending had tripled. The unemployment rate was under 5 percent that year as nearly every able-bodied man in America was *conscripted*. By the following year, the U.S. was fighting a war on multiple continents, and a lot of its manufacturing base was growing to back the war effort, which is a most destructive form of technocracy. And yet most Keynesian economists consider World War II to be a slam dunk case for debt and fiscal stimulus.

First, it should be obvious that conscripting people into war is an unideal and unsustainable form of employment. And that is why one shouldn't look at the unemployment rate in isolation. Instead, we have to look at quality of life. Of course, it is also problematic to think that living standards are improved by razing cities, much less nation-building far away, as economists Steven Horwitz and Michael McPhillips discover in their research.[282] We must remember that macroeconomic indicators are only as good as the living standards with which they correlate.

In response to contemporary arguments that the expenditures associated with World War II were a major factor in ending the Great Depression and should therefore be imitated today, we offer historical evidence to suggest that the wartime economy was hardly a model of success in the eyes of most Americans. Expanding on Robert Higgs' criticisms of the ability of conventional macroeconomic data to tell the real story, we examine newspapers, diaries, and other primary source material to reveal the retrogression in living standards in the U.S. during the war. Our investigation suggests that wartime prosperity is largely a myth, and hardly a model for recovery from the Great Recession.[283]

Another way of putting all of this might be that if war stimulus is such a great idea, then more recent wars like those in Iraq and Afghanistan, starting in 2003 and peaking with the 2007 surge in Iraq, should have moved Americans towards heaven on earth in 2008-09. But precisely the opposite happened. Nevertheless, controversy surrounding the origins of the Great Recession remains. Well-intentioned housing and banking policies lead to banks playing a game of *hide the toxic assets.* The housing market crashed. Nearly everything else followed. Bad fiscal policy slowed the recovery for years. Despite a spate of technocratic responses, including the de facto war stimulus, banking, and auto bailouts, the American Recovery and Investment Act of 2009, and early monetary stimulus from the Federal Reserve, the U.S. endured the most protracted economic recovery in its history.

You might remember news commenter Rachel Maddow standing in front of the Hoover Dam after the Great Recession, trying to convince her viewers that the state (which she calls "the country") must tax and build some major make-work projects to revive the economy. Maddow was using moonshot thinking when what the U.S. needed during that time was mycelial thinking. What will send the U.S. and much of the world headlong into collapse is another perceived crisis. Because in times of crisis, politicians appeal to the national mythology of the New Deal and marry it with magical theories of debt and deficit spending.

Of course, the seeds of 'crisis' have already been sown as of this writing. Politicians and pundits fret about what they perceive as the destructive nature of automation and AI, which they argue will eventually render human laborers redundant. To rescue an army of unemployed workers, they think they will have to figure out how to pay for a Universal Basic Income (UBI) or a similar scheme. And that requires magical thinking. More recently, pandemic panic has set off quantitative easing and fiscal stimulus. And the clock ticks.

Before we turn to today's magical thinking, we should return to another set of crises that expanded transferism and the welfare-warfare state. In 1964 and 1965, two events come to mind: The first had been the announcement that the percentage of people living below the poverty line had increased. The second had been the Gulf of Tonkin affair. President Lyndon Baines Johnson (LBJ) declared war on poverty at home and 'police action' on the North Vietnamese in Southeast Asia. Both ended in quagmires. By the time LBJ's programs took effect, the U.S. poverty rate sat at around 15 percent. Bizarrely, despite a massive increase in welfare spending, the US poverty rate has hovered between 12 and 15 percent between the Great Society and the election of Donald Trump — 50 years. So much for "the power to eliminate poverty from an entire continental nation."[284]

MAGIC MONEY THEORY

When politicians rationalize all the transfer programs they dream up to get elected, they need intellectual support. Many politicians have found aid and comfort in a formerly obscure group of economists who adhere to Modern Monetary Theory (MMT).

MMT economists have become visible promoters of

deficit spending as the motor for economic growth. Boosters of unlimited debt and spending are welcomed with open arms by those who seek to grow the welfare-warfare state. Specifically, MMT adherents argue that there is a causal relationship between deficits in the public sector to a savings surplus in the private sector. The idea is of a balanced external account. MMT uses a macro equation, which means public sector deficits *imply* a savings surplus in the private sector.

Critics of MMT argue that this is a sleight of hand because none of the mathematics indicates any arrows of caution. Only economic analysis, not simple equations, determine the levels of private-sector economic activity. Specifically, the MMT equation says that when debt spending has finally weakened the economy, the private sector will have a savings surplus. But if this surplus happens at all, it would result from a decline in private investment; a decrease in private investment means entrepreneurial decline and economic stagnation.

This criticism tracks closely with our overall concerns about technocracy and transferism, namely that when the state controls an ever-growing slice of global resources, it abandons more and more of the nation's dispersed knowledge and decentralized skin in the game.

WHEN THE GOVERNMENT REACHES ITS CREDIT LIMIT

U.S. debt levels are untenable, so much so that one wonders if the government will have already defaulted by the time this volume is published. If not, we can offer some speculation as to what is likely to happen.

First, raising taxes now simply won't work, even if the government implemented confiscatory double taxation measures like wealth taxes. Most of the tax increases would go toward interest on the debt, leaving nothing for all of the ballooning transfer programs and military spending that got the U.S. into this. Never mind that higher taxes would slow the economy down as businesses found fewer profits to invest in growth. In less than thirty years, the government will spend more on debt service than all the entitlement programs and national defense combined.

If there had ever been a time to cut back on any of these programs, that time has passed. So what if the government simply refuses to pay its debts? A global economic meltdown would follow; a financial collapse. For example, the Japanese own the equivalent of about 20 percent of its GDP in U.S. debt, which takes the form of dollar-denominated treasuries and federal reserve notes. China owns more than a quarter of U.S. debt. Between these two economic giants, each holds more than $2 trillion of U.S. debt.

The U.S. government will have no choice but to reduce transfer payments radically. Pensioners will receive meager Social Security checks, if they receive anything at all. Medicare, far from being for all, will be for no one. The U.S. military will have to figure out a triage system for its priorities and suspend all non-essential activities from its de facto empire, activities which officials claim are essential today. All of the supplicant companies, such as Boeing and automakers like Fiat-Chrysler, will no longer have a sugar daddy in Uncle Sam. Owners of treasury bonds will be disappointed as these holdings will become valueless. One can go on and on.

I wish there were a crystal ball that would allow us to see the magnitude of financial collapse and its human aftershocks. What percentage of the population will roam the streets to beg, to loot, or to agitate for government aid that can never come? When will stewards of capital be able to release the death grip on investment monies at a time of severe regime uncertainty? Will enemies of the U.S. feel the pain of the collapse or remain solvent enough to take advantage of the vacuum that a bankrupt Pentagon will leave around the world?

Something's got to give. And it's gonna hurt.

THE INTERSECTIONALITY OF GRIEVANCE

James Dale Davidson and Lord William Rees-Mogg were particularly prescient in their 1997 book, *The Sovereign Individual*:

> In its twilight, with a faltering capacity to redeem something for nothing from an empty pocket, the welfare state found it expedient to foster new myths of discrimination. Many categories of 'oppressed' people were designated, especially in North America. Individuals in groups with designated status as 'victims' were informed that they were not responsible for shortcomings in their own lives. Rather, the fault was said to lie with 'dead white males' of European descent, and the oppressive power structure allegedly rigged to the disadvantage of the excluded groups. To be black, female, homosexual, Latino, francophone, disabled, etc. was to be entitled to recompense for past [or current] repression and discrimination.[285]

The duo argues that technologically advanced, connected societies in their "senile state" will see this sort of mythology emerge.

I am loath to agree that the intersectionality of grievance is made up entirely of "myths"; there are problems of racism and discrimination in North America along various dimensions. But these problems are generally overblown. The narrative of white supremacy in America, for example, is challenged simply by looking at income data for various ethnic groups. As of 2018, the highest income-earning group was made up of a vaguely drawn but highly diverse group known as "Asian," according to U.S. Census data. Of course, this group is made up of ethnically and racially diverse people. Those who originate from the Indian subcontinent, not to mention ethnic Chinese, all land in this group.[286]

- Asian — $87,194
- White/Caucasian — $70,642
- Hispanic — $51,450
- Black — $41, 361

If the American power structure is currently white supremacist, whites are not doing a very good job of white supremacy, at least when it comes to money matters. Regarding the purported systematic exclusion of people of color from opportunity, Asians, whether from the Indian subcontinent or China, are outperforming everyone. Of course, issues of income and ethnicity are complicated and dense. But at the very least, data such as these should leave one with questions about whether there could be sociological or anthropological reasons that help explain income disparities among different ethnic groups, even if those explanations challenge the narrative of white racism.

Davidson and Rees-Mogg are right to be suspicious insofar as the intersectionality of grievance becomes the intersectionality of 'gimme.' They were correct then (and are correct now) to argue that the outrage machine serves as a moral high ground from which to make further demands of an already depleted welfare state. And if, as they warn, the grievance bloc accelerates its hectoring, the government will go even deeper into debt.

LOSING OUR RELIGION

Before closing Part One, Dear Reader, know that we have arrived in an America about which Alexis de Tocqueville warned.

> After taking each individual one by one into its
> powerful hands, and having molded them as it pleas-
> es, the sovereign power extends its arms over the
> entire society; it covers the surface of society with a
> network of small, complicated, minute, and uniform
> rules, which the most original minds and the most
> vigorous souls cannot break through to go beyond
> the crowd; it does not break wills, but it softens
> them, bends them, and directs them; it rarely forces
> action, but it constantly opposes your acting; it does
> not destroy, it prevents birth; it does not tyrannize,
> it hinders, it represses, it enervates, it extinguishes, it
> stupefies, and finally it reduces each nation to being
> nothing more than a flock of timid and industrious
> animals, of which the government is the shepherd.[287]

How did we get here? We voted. Americans worship
false gods in a revival tent that comes around every four
years. That vote they're sticking in the ballot box? It is
as good as a crumpled up fiver in the collection plate of
a sick religion. I'm not just talking about the candidates,
whether slick or boorish, well-meaning or doctrinaire, venal
or stupid. They can be all of these, of course. I'm talking
about the system itself.

There is no salvation in any of this. Elections cannot
nourish our spirits. After the great wheel of power makes
another grinding turn, we must remind ourselves and our
loved ones that none of this has made any of us any better.
Indeed, we might be worse for it.

You see, democracy, as such, makes people desperate
to believe lies. It makes us spiteful towards our neighbors.
It gives us the illusion that we are somehow smarter, better,
more upright people than we are. And it gives people the
idea that it's okay, first, to outsource their idea of charity
and the right and the good, and then worse, have people in
Washington shove it down our throats.

We have to use intellectual gymnastics to rationalize
such a system. From the social contract to the angels of

politics, we operate in comfortable mythology. Deep down, we have to know that all of this is designed for rival gangs and rival mobs to exploit each other, and legally. But just think of what that must do to our souls over time.

Do you want to help your neighbor? Go help your neighbor. Do you want to solve a social problem? Get to building, or coding, or serving, or innovating. Because when people work together, *really together*, like ants or bees, we can do amazing things.

But this — this state apparatus we imagine is good — only permits us to outsource our civic and moral responsibilities to the soulless functionaries who teem in distant capitals, feeding on largesse that should be going to better causes. They operate the Circumlocution Office. They crusade to raid. And they are not our friends.

Behind the spectacle — pick your metaphor: circus tent or revival tent — there is violence. We can legitimize it with terms like 'democracy' and 'justice' and 'public good.' But it is not good. For this whole thing to operate, well-paid officials must be in charge of jails and men with guns. And they are not here to *serve* you or me. They serve *power*.

We timid, industrious animals have arrived on the brink of collapse. And everywhere you look, the proposed solution is to *go out and vote this next election. The right person will save us.* If we still can't see by now that this is all one big spectacle designed to put team sports out in front of an immense system of graft, then we are the fools. And we deserve to be laughed at.

"Democracy is the art and science of running the circus from the monkey cage,"said H.L. Mencken.[288] If we don't laugh, we'll surely cry. The circus tent is getting bigger. As I write, partisan monkeys are howling and hurling feces like never before.

There was a time when I wanted to see it all burn down, though not out of some adolescent rage or romantic fantasy. Rather, I have found a way to stare into this thing

— to see it down to its rotten bowels. But if we stare too long, Dear Reader, we might start to see ourselves.

Now, a little grayer in my temples, I don't want to see it all burn down. But the fire was started long ago. Modern Neros fiddle, making promises they can't keep. The hierarchies burn. The government burns. Our communities burn. Maybe it's enough simply to stand by and watch. And dream. And wonder.

What can we build in the ashes?

INTERREGNUM

*If the injustice is part of the necessary
friction of the machine of government, let it
go, let it go: perchance it will wear smooth
— certainly the machine will wear out...
but if it is of such a nature that it requires
you to be the agent of injustice to another,
then I say, break the law. Let your life be a
counter-friction to stop the machine. What I
have to do is to see, at any rate, that I do not
lend myself to the wrong which I condemn.*
Henry D. Thoreau, from *Civil Disobedience*

In June 1963, a car turned up at an intersection in
Saigon's streets, a few blocks away from the Presidential
Palace. A man named Quảng Đức emerged from the car
along with two other men, all in saffron robes. One monk
placed a cushion on the pavement while the second monk
opened the trunk and took out a five-gallon gasoline can.
Quảng Đức sat down on the cushion and formed his body
into the traditional lotus position. He calmly began to medi-
tate as marchers encircled him. One of the monks poured
the contents of the can over Quảng Đức's head as Đức
rotated a string of beads.

"Nam mô A Di Đà Phật," he repeated before striking a
match and dropping it on himself. As black oily smoke and
flames engulfed his robes and body, he sat completely still.

"His body was slowly withering and shriveling up, his

head blackening and charring, writes journalist David
Halberstam who watched from the crowd.

> In the air was the smell of burning human flesh;
> human beings burn surprisingly quickly. Behind me I
> could hear the sobbing of the Vietnamese who were
> now gathering. I was too shocked to cry, too confused
> to take notes or ask questions, too bewildered to
> even think... As he burned he never moved a muscle,
> never uttered a sound, his outward composure in
> sharp contrast to the wailing people around him.[289]

Quảng Đức's act of self-immolation is disturbing. But
it should prompt us to ask: For what are we willing to die?
(Considering all that happened in Vietnam in the interven-
ing years, we also want to ask for what we are willing to kill.)
It turns out Quảng Đức had chosen to die in the service of
his religion and for the Buddhists of Vietnam who, at the
time, were being oppressed by a Catholic leadership.

Here's what Quảng Đức said in his own words, which
he left on a note:

> Before closing my eyes and moving towards the
> vision of the Buddha, I respectfully plead to Presi-
> dent Ngô Đình Diệm to take a mind of compassion
> towards the people of the nation and implement
> religious equality to maintain the strength of the
> homeland eternally. I call the venerables, reverends,
> members of the sangha and the lay Buddhists to
> organize in solidarity to make sacrifices to protect
> Buddhism.[290]

Such is the power of Thanatos, leveled and aimed right
at the heart of injustice.

Maybe you have heard the story of the burning monk.
Maybe you think it's zealous or crazy. I admit that there
are so many things that are hard for me to grok, steeped as
I am in my comfortable Western life and habits of mind.
But behind the sensation and shock of the event there was

a man with a commitment and an enormous presence
of mind. He was willing to *end it now* and *let things go*. Like
Quảng Đức, we must believe that after the end there can be
a beautiful new beginning.

It Won't Always Be This Way

When you close your eyes, you can feel that you are
alive. You are warm. Feel your pulse. Your arteries carry
oxygen-rich blood to all the cells in your body. Open your
eyes again. The chatter in your mind as you read these
words corresponds with the excitation of neurons. Notice
ambient sounds. Even the slightest noises impinge on your
consciousness. Attend now to the whole, including the heat,
the pulse, the vibrations. You are alive.

It won't always be this way.

Maybe you'll die peacefully, in your sleep. Maybe you'll
be in a violent car crash. Try not to think too much about
what comes after in either case, because what remains is not
you at all. You will have been that heat, pulse, and vibration.
Your animated body, energetic, biological, self-organization, has a miraculous window on the world, for a limited
time only. Or maybe it's that the universe has a window on
itself? Never mind. When it comes to being dead, there's no
you at all. It's easy to think of ourselves as having a spirit,
because our minds and bodies seem like separate entities.
When it comes to being alive, though, you can't have one
without the other. A living body without a mind would be
an automaton. A living mind without a body would be a
ghost.

Something similar can be said about human systems
like the one we call America. When the system stops working, it's dead, and some culture dies with it. If what is left,
the remnant, can reconstitute itself, it will enjoy a renaissance. Even if we call that America, it will have become
something else. You and I will have become someone else.

LET IT GO

In Chapter One, we discussed four human forces that affect our behaviors, and which in turn give rise to our human systems. In other words, these forces get instantiated in our cultural outlook and political institutions. Here's each, with its relevant mantra.

- **Eros Masculine** — *Exert control.*
- **Thanatos Masculine** — *End it now.*
- **Eros Feminine** — *Let it flow.*
- **Thanatos Feminine** — *Let it go.*

Throughout Part One, we discussed the excesses of Eros Masculine in America, especially how it tends to suppress the flow systems of Eros Feminine. As we prepare for the collapse, we must also start to embrace Thanatos Feminine.

I should be clear that each quadrant in this matrix of human drives has healthy and unhealthy expressions. So it's not merely that imbalances can occur, but that unhealthy aspects of each can be manifested.

Four Human Energies

Eros Masculine
- Unhealthy: An overbearing boss who barks orders or micromanages.
- Healthy: An inspiring coach who leads a team to victory.

Thanatos Masculine
- Unhealthy: A dictator who assassinates his political rivals.
- Healthy: A person who quickly breaks off a dangerous relationship.

Eros Feminine
- Unhealthy: A person who indulges to excess or irresponsibility.
- Healthy: A parent who lets his child try things and learn from mistakes.

Thanatos Feminine
- Unhealthy: An entrepreneur who gives up on her venture before it can scale.
- Healthy: A grandparent who leaves a do not resuscitate order in hospice.

Even apparently healthy manifestations of Eros Masculine can be out of balance, or suppress, Eros Feminine. When Eros Feminine is suppressed, that means it has not yet reached its fullest expression. Any of the four forces can manifest unhealthy aspects, and healthy aspects of the four forces can suppress or get out of balance with any other force.

Thanatos Masculine's bellicosity, when in excess, should be obvious, as should be the dreary torpor of Thanatos Feminine. In thinking about Eros, which we have said is the generative aspect of life, we want both healthy expressions as well as appropriate balance with Thanatos.

But remember that Thanatos has healthy expressions, too, in both its Masculine and Feminine variants. Death. Ending. Absence. In polite company, it's taboo to suggest such things. There are plenty of people like my friend Michael, though, who have a healthy view of death even though most people in America do not. Michael's father has been hospitalized four times in the last year, having taken falls associated with severe Alzheimer's. The man who had once been his father is long gone, but according to American society and laws, the family is obliged to keep the father's body alive at all costs. One wonders whether there is any dignity in this.

The fetishization of life in the Terri Schiavo case

meant that a young woman's family kept her in a persistent vegetative state for seven years. Just as America is a society that is overcome with an urge to control, Americans are also preoccupied with youth. In some places, people have so much plastic surgery they appear to be wearing masks. Some find this macabre, but others see it as a status symbol. At some level, it reflects America's unhealthy relationship with aging and death. We don't accept these as facts of life as much as we hide them, warehouse them, or sublimate them. Thanatos gets expressed not in solemn rites and reason but in movies and games. Even our Memorial Days are more about potato salad and forgetting. When it comes to the end of life, we expect heroic measures.

When it comes to America, we still expect national greatness. Our status as a world power is an unquestioned faith, which too often stands in for our own feelings of inadequacy and loss of close community. So it's not just that masculine is out of balance relative to feminine in America, it's that we have forgotten how to let people die, and die well.

But there can be good endings. Think about leaving a company to which you are loyal but whose work no longer fulfills you. Think about living with a terminal illness in great pain compared to its absence upon death; or the sense of relief you might feel knowing that a loved one is no longer living in pain. Even the most ambitious among us have had to learn to accept failure. Accepting failure is healthy. Sometimes we cling to systems, relationships, or other arrangements well beyond their expiration date, usually out of obligation. Maybe you can think of a time when one of those arrangements came to a healthy end. Whatever new story came afterward was not possible without that chapter coming to a close.

Though Thanatos is a drive, too, we often seek to suppress or avoid it. The very thought of the *end* is depressing; the very thought of ending ourselves is morbid. But not all death is to be avoided. Not all endings are bad. There is certainly no contradiction between raging against the dying of the light while accepting the end. Christians accept that Jesus had to die in order for subsequent generations to experience the living Christ and to be saved. In the Bhagavad Gita, Vishnu appears to Arjuna and offers a vision of the end, which is just the start of another cycle.

Sometimes we have to find the courage actively to end something, even a life. It's brave and good to have a sick pet put down. That courage originates in Thanatos Masculine. But sometimes we also have to find the wisdom to *let go*. When a conscious decoupling is better for the children than staying together, such wisdom originates in Thanatos Feminine.

In the moments just before letting go, we can feel conflicted, which shows up as guilt, anxiety or inner turmoil. But once we let go, relief can flow over us, signify a healthy close. Letting go isn't always passive. To accept changing circumstances and adapt can be a conscious process.

Thanatos Masculine speaks to us in words like *revolution!* The tree of liberty, said Jefferson, must be "refreshed" with the "blood of patriots and tyrants."[291] As a man and a liberal, I certainly identify with that revolutionary fire. But we are living in different times. Thanatos Feminine says *let things go*. What America has become is not something Jefferson would recognize. What is needed, then, is not violent resistance or overthrow, but for a people to hold hands as we step into the black waters of the river at night. Let it envelop us, cleanse us, and shed us of all this rage for order and will to power. Tomorrow we will be new.

Call this underthrow.

THE GHOSTS OF AMERICA

Some of us feel the first stirrings of that inner turmoil as we reckon with the possibility of America's end, at least of America as we know it. Ghosts of history tell us to keep it together at all costs. It. This. The Republic. We the People. The Exceptional State. We have long labored under the idea that without a national father figure presiding over armies and functionaries, we would cease to be a people. Abraham Lincoln, despite being a melancholic, fought through bouts of unhealthy Thanatos Feminine. Why? To keep himself intact. To keep the union together. That he was murdered in Ford's Theater is an irony that will always haunt us. "Sic semper tyrannis!" cried John Wilkes Booth as Thanatos Masculine ravaged his disordered mind. There is a sense that if we let the Republic fall we are turning our backs on the sacrifices not only of figures like Lincoln, but of all of those who died under his command.

What about the Founders who, despite their sins, gave the world the first liberal order? What about the men who stormed the beaches at Normandy or battled at Iwo Jima? What about those who marched on Washington, suffered in Selma, or were otherwise set upon by attack dogs and fire hoses and humiliation at the hands of bigots in the Jim Crow South? Won't all those rights, so long fought for, be washed away as America 1.0 disintegrates? What unimaginable theocracies, retrograde regimes, and back-water factions await, ready to rise up from the hinterlands to seize power? Without the welfare state, won't an army of the penniless storm our gated communities or comfort-able universities ready to kill for a tin of fish? Without the warfare state, won't some rogue nation destabilize the world?

Maybe America can be something more than the welfare-warfare state.

Fear and history sit on either shoulder, whispering

warnings: *We have to keep it together.* But keeping the nation state together at all costs is a directive from Eros Masculine. The dam is holding back the forces of change, but the dam can't hold forever. In other words, we are on a death watch. And that means that we might not have a choice but to let this all play out, however it's going to play out. Because unlike Lincoln, we won't be in control.

When the dam breaks we can be more or less radical in our response. I will begin with the least extreme measures I believe will be necessary, though these will surely seem radical to anyone who has sat pickling too long in the status quo. As we go on, chapter by chapter, you may find our ideas will get more radical by degree. What seems radical to you might seem commonsensical to me. In a time of transformation, what becomes is what becomes. I can only speculate.

But I hope to persuade you that some of the possible worlds we're going to explore are not improbable. They are far preferable to unthinkable totalitarian power or fractured warlordism. The kinds of things you'll read about in Part Two might seem strange, but they are hopeful. Just in case there is a chance to keep the Republic, I'll spend some time talking about measures that could save it. You might call these the remaining options. Whether one considers these emergency measures a way to avoid collapse or just a symptom of it, we can offer them due consideration, for our foremothers and fathers.

One might assume from reading up to this point that I'm writing pre-collapse. I think it's difficult to deny, though, that we are already collapsing. This is a process, and we're in it. The interregnum, as such, is a collective reflection on this state of affairs. In the interregnum, the human system becomes conscious of its own collapse. We are waking up to it.

SINKING, FAST AND SLOW

Collapse is not always sudden, like a soufflé falling. Nor is it followed immediately by the sound of a firing squad, as with the execution of Nicolae and Elena Ceaușescu, which signaled the end of the Eastern Bloc. Sometimes the process is more drawn out, as with the fall of Rome. How on earth did people live with the fact of an Eastern and Western Empire? How did they make due without the system that built the aqueducts and roads? Just fine, apparently.

If America's collapse parallels that of Rome, we're probably in the bread and circuses stage, empire and entitlements. Our governance systems are somewhere between malaise and paralysis, occasionally lurching to manage a crisis, or 'project power' in some imperial backwater. Only a small minority is starting to question whether any of it is sustainable.

Looking forward, we have set the stage for what writer James Fallows thinks of as a coming era similar to late antiquity in Europe, in which "duchies and monasteries" experimented with different forms of governance and civil association. "Yet for our own era's counterparts to duchies and monasteries," writes Fallows, "for state and local governments, and for certain large private organizations, including universities and some companies — the country is still mainly functional, in exactly the areas where national governance has failed."[292]

Fallows seems vaguely plaintive, though, as if he assumes all of this centralized governance had been necessary, but that we'll somehow make due with a suboptimal system. Despite quibbling about the optimal loci of power, his point stands: We will do okay without Washington. Maybe all this time it's been just a weight on our backs and an illusion, like a rucksack full of rocks we were told was full of gold.

It might not seem like much in the interregnum, but I believe that our twenty-first century duchies and monasteries are going to be beautiful and bountiful. I aim to spend the rest of this book persuading you of that fact. But just know that before we enjoy that beauty and bounty, we will have to get our spiritual and moral houses in order. I say this not as a moralist, but as a realist. Because the rules we write and the culture we build all begin in the deepest places in the heart.

8

REIMAGINE LIBERALISM

In the presence of one firmly established in
nonviolence, all hostilities cease.
Patanjali, from *the Yoga Sutras*

All over the world, Shaolin monks are known for their superhuman abilities[293] — crouched atop wooden posts, they can balance for hours. To develop palm strength and bone density in combat, they repeatedly strike hard objects such as vessels of water or pieces of wood. Eventually, they learn to crash through those objects in a single blow. A few have learned to break a piece of glass with a sewing pin; one monk, Zhao Rui, has trained his skin to withstand sharp objects. And in the Chinese provinces of Qinghai and Sichuan, you can find a unique sect of Tibetan monks called the *tummo* meditators, who can use their minds to control their breaths and bodies. They do this to raise their body temperatures, which allows them to dry wet sheets wrapped around them. What is significant about all of these extraordinary gifts is not that Shaolin monks are genetically modified humans. It's that they *practice*. Most spend their days honing their skills, which takes cycles of patience, discipline, and focus.

The problem with the liberalism of the past is that it was incomplete. The abstract, legalistic orientation of liberalism was not enough. What has been missing is practice. Even the moral ideals of Enlightenment thinkers, as presented in textbooks and tomes, is insufficient to animate a people. Not only must we give liberalism life again, but we must live it so that we can bring it into the iteration cycles of daily life. In other words, we have to exercise liberal values as daily practices. Such might seem like a strange thing to say.

But bare rules are like the walls of the Shaolin monastery, cold and inert. Of course, you have to follow the rules as you travel a hallway, but the monastery's walls have a purpose beyond the functional. They are intended to be animated by people, by warrior monks. And the monks are there to practice, every day, to stay on the path to enlightenment, to pass their wisdom onto others with each generation. So it is with liberalism.

INTEGRAL LIBERALISM

Life on the other side of collapse will not be tolerable without liberalism, but the liberalism of the past had been anemic, kept together with bromides and old social studies books. Americans today need improved liberalism, a new secular religion complete with a new cultural outlook and spiritual configuration. Vestiges of that former liberalism are timeless and necessary for the renaissance. Still, our reimagined liberalism must transcend and include Enlightenment maxims like liberty, equality, and fraternity, not to mention the fundamental commitment to understanding grounding in truth.

In what follows, we will explore facets of this new liberalism. These won't be exhaustive. I hope that more spiritually developed beings continue to improve upon what is only here a sketch. Americans need a humanistic life philosophy that leaves room for people of all dispositions and moral languages to express themselves. They need space to build their utopias and to collaborate with others to do the same. Ours should be a system that weaves people together in peace, despite our various life plans. However, it cannot be a mere legal latticework, as it has been in the past; it must be a moral and spiritual path, too. That is why we borrow from the East's Vedic practices, to hybridize them with our Western values in brazen acts of cultural appropriation.

I'm reminded of this passage by liberal writer Leonard Read, wherein he calls for humility:

> For any person to become aware of how little he knows — not very difficult an attainment — is a sure way to reduce the number of authoritarians by one. Who knows? The awareness might even catch on. And if it did? Millions of us would forsake society's most corrosive pastime — meddling in the affairs of others — meddling not only through the political apparatus, but personally. Millions of us could then concentrate on the wholly rewarding venture of freeing ourselves from our own fears, our own super-stitions, our own imperfections, our own ignorance. The individual human spirit, neglected while we play the futile and authoritarian game of imposing our wills on others, cries out for its freedom.[294]

We can build integral liberalism on this simple insight.

High Minds will seek to obstruct the renaissance. To be a High Mind is to be fundamentally at odds with liberalism. We have claimed that High Modernism is an unhealthy intellectual expression of the Eros Masculine, occasion-ally referred to as the urge to control. High Minds are its priest class; the Blue Church, its propaganda arm. The welfare-warfare state is its apotheosis, and the very exis-tence of all of it depends on compulsion. High Minds will never be able to escape this brute fact: Behind every plan, every policy, every political power play are armed men and prisons waiting for those who refuse. Their future is the one Orwell saw, of a boot stamping down on a human face —

forever.

In my view, which includes healthier doses of Eros Feminine, coercion is not the prime mover, it is the last resort. Liberalism differs from all other ideologies in that it is the only worldview that accommodates and integrates competing conceptions. That makes it both cosmopolitan and sustainable; it also makes it *integral*. A new liberalism, call it *integral liberalism*, invites other ideologies to find a home. Integral liberalism's superstructure of peace and pluralism makes each ideological home possible. *No other doctrine can say that*. This fundamental asymmetry makes me wonder if integral liberalism is an ideology at all. After all, most ideologies require compliance — *or else*. Liberalism only requires consent, that is, that we abstain from threatening violence or initiating harm when we set about building our communities.

And yet that is a price many will find too steep.

SACRALIZE SELVES

We must not only have basic respect for others; we must go further. We have to practice seeing them as sacred. We have suggested that others are just apertures into some greater unified self to which we all belong. If we are not *literally* a part of an animating Allmind, then it might be useful to think of ourselves this way. To love oneself is more straightforward than loving a stranger, but to think of a stranger as yourself moves her and you towards the Golden Rule's ancient wisdom. The more we practice sacralizing others, the more others are likely to sacralize us this way, loving you as they love themselves, treating you as they might a temple. At the very least, we are interdependent and interconnected as never before.

Continuous practice won't be easy, but it will pay enormous dividends. I am reminded of a story by Sri Swami Satchidananda, an interpreter of the Yoga Sutras, about the myths of sages who lived in the forest.[295] They developed vibratory patterns of harmonious coexistence so powerful that even the forest animals were affected, only killing when they were hungry. If the old liberalism required only indifference, integral liberalism requires we practice *ahimsa*. It is in such practice that we will start to recreate the meditation forest in our lives and our world.

MIND CONTROL

It is when we are most fraught that the opportunity to practice is most important. Moments of fear, for example, cause us to retreat into the urge to control that itself can take on the veneer of courage. But at the scale of society, there is almost always a disconnect between those who approve the use of force and those who are recruited to use it. And it is in this disconnect between the aggressor and the aggressor's proxy, that wisdom gets lost. To cheer the exercise of police power, for example, is rarely the same as being the one to break into someone's home and throw them to the ground — or worse.

Before acting with aggression, much less enacting a law that requires the threat of violence to enforce, there is a moment to pause. Only those with self-mastery can see that moment when it arrives, often when passions are most inflamed. It is at that moment that we must find inner calm. We have to hold back the fires of our primal selves and regard the situation, not just in the moment, but in how our responses will take on a life of their own. Transitioning to a less violent world will require an inner discipline that acknowledges how sentiment can cascade through a people to the powerful, and then to their proxies. It requires finding out where you are in that nexus of power to become a force of nonviolence.

Of course, in war, there is discipline, too. Sun Tzu could never have devised his stratagems in a white-hot rage. And yet it takes discipline greater than that of the most victorious generals to appreciate the fact that the most significant victories are those we never have to fight, and for which there will never be glory. "Trying to overcome evil with evil is not the way to peace,"[296] writes monk Thich Nhat Hanh.

Indeed, the most significant change agents practice nonviolence, a practice that is a discipline unto itself. The Dalai Lama teaches peace and nonviolence in exile despite having fled Tibet, which came under occupation and subjection by the Chinese government in 1959. He still struggles against injustice, and may continue until his death. But we are familiar with nonviolent struggles that have borne fruit. Mahatma Gandhi and Martin Luther King, Jr. helped to liberate millions of people through these practices. We might also learn a lot from Hongkongers trying to stay out from under the Chinese mainland's thumb.

The paradox of practicing ahimsa is that it makes us stronger. In certain ways, it means not only abstaining from harming others but also taking some emotional punches. Ahimsa is not the way of victimology; it is the way out of it. Before Gandhi became the "mahatma," he had been a lawyer practicing in South Africa. White authorities kicked him out of a train car for "whites only." Before Nelson Mandala helped do away with apartheid, he suffered many indignities, including twenty-seven years in prison. Gandhi and Mandela were each entitled to righteous anger. Yet I can't imagine either of them in paroxysms over the content of a book or a tweet.

THE AHIMSA HYPOTHESIS

Let's return for a moment to the idea of the meditation forest mentioned above. Hindu mythology includes the story of a tiger who drinks next to a cow. Both animals had been among the sages of the forest practicing ahimsa; the sages' peaceful radiance had a calming effect on all life in the forest. Who knows whether this is true, but surely there is truth to the idea that the practice of ahimsa is infectious. Not only can it change those of us who practice it, but those who practice it can change others by degree.

We hypothesize that if we make the practice of ahimsa conscious and continuous, we will expand the patterns of peacefulness upon which so many other practices can rest and become manifest. The idea, more or less, is that we can extend the radius of the meditation forest outward, indefinitely.

Perhaps what is missing in the West's liberal tradition is meditation, and those ideas that we can learn in meditation. *Kamma*, or as we say, karma, is one such idea. We can reconcile *kamma* with the Western metaphysics of causation. When the skeptical intellectual Śāriputra first came upon one of the earliest Buddhist monks, he asked the monk about Buddha's teaching, who replied that Buddha's teachings could be summed up quite simply: *If there is some effect in this world, there must have been a cause. If you don't like the effect, take away the cause.* It's no wonder, then, that ahimsa extends to the Buddhist tradition, too. The monks have always known that life involves suffering, and that human beings are frequently the source of their suffering. It is through our practice that we 'evolve' out of our evolutionary defaults.

Consider the Ahimsa Hypothesis, which has a positive and a normative formulation:

- *The Law of Himsa/Ahimsa.* Whenever we threaten or harm others, whether in their person or their property, sorrow always follows; but to the extent that we actively practice nonviolence, happiness and harmony will be in greater abundance.[297]

- *The Ahimsa Principle.* To the extent that we seek happiness, harmony, and abundance for ourselves and others, we ought to abstain from threatening or initiating harm; then, we should actively, consciously, and continuously practice ahimsa.[298]

In our formulation, we bundle in *asteya*, which means non-stealing. Both ahimsa and asteya are two of the Yamas of the Yoga Sutras. It's simple to overlook these crucial practices because it's easy to say *I don't harm people or steal their stuff*. But there are subtler ways we are violent or steal. For example, we might take credit for someone's hard work, or speak cruelly, or joke to the point that it causes someone's suffering.

And yet the active, conscious, and continuous practice of ahimsa (along with asteya) can be the most potent force for change on earth. That is quite a bold hypothesis in an era of technological transformation. The sages — the yogis, the monks, and the rabbis — have been telling us this for thousands of years. It is time to listen, and then to expand the circle.

At the same time, then, practice is ascending to a mastery that requires not only the self-control we described but a conscious and continuous commitment to peace in all spheres. When our commitment is active, conscious, and continuous, we will start to experience realizations. The culture we live in, and many of our institutions, don't accord with our commitments. In seeing this reality, we will start to engage in nonviolent resistance. We might even engage in subversion — as long as it accords with ahimsa.

PRACTICE NONVIOLENCE

The practice of ahimsa is not for the weak. Not only does it require strength that comes in control and self-discipline, but that control also begins in the mind. Harmful words and acts begin as negative thoughts. So practice starts in rephrasing and reframing the internal chatter that keeps you company from moment to moment. In some respects, controlling one's innermost thoughts is the most challenging part of the practice because we imagine these thoughts are private. And many are: Because one's thoughts are also immediate and can simply arise out of our control, it's easier for harmful thoughts to leach into or words and deeds. Mastery of one's thoughts takes training.

The easiest way to begin practicing ahimsa is, perhaps surprisingly, to log onto social media. People on these fora behave differently to how they behave in person. You'll see all manner of different opinions, many of which you will find irritating. Remember that the practice begins in your thoughts, maybe before you read a single post.

> *Today I'm going to have an open mind about what I see. I will observe with the mirror of empathy and be patient and circumspect in my response. If, that is, it's meaningful for me to respond at all.*

The practice is most important for those with whom we share our time. Yet it's often in being around those we love that we allow ourselves to fall into old habits. It's for the ones we love that we should carry out the practice first. Maybe an ambitious goal for a parent is to create a certain culture of peace in the home. Such starts by setting an example. But as spiritual teacher Thich Nhat Hahn writes, "When you practice with others, it is much easier to obtain stability, joy, and freedom."[299]

Hahn advises us to retreat to a monastery, when we can. Otherwise, we must take the practice wherever we go. "This kind of life can be described as monastic culture."[300] Most of us don't live near beautiful and contemplative places where monks can guide us. Some of us live with children, who can be barbarians. That is why we have to remember that everywhere there is nature, there is a monastery. Taking walks among trees or grasses is enough to reset in contemplation. Otherwise, practice begins at home, and the circle expands.

A related suggestion here is, just as we begin to practice ahimsa, we must also take on a mind-frame of nonviolent resistance against those who would harm or subject us.

That includes agents of a state whose threat is comprehensive and systematic. Remember that when we get beyond the smiles, the elections, and the parades, politics terminate in the institutionalized threat of violence. Because integral liberalism puts ahimsa at the center of all questions involving human relations, all of our ideas about politics — how it works, what it's for, and who should run it — are open to revision.

Just as ahimsa is the first of the Yamas among the yogis, ahimsa must become the presumption in resolving disputes and making laws. Ahimsa thus calls into question the legitimacy of the whole edifice of what we currently call America.

I write in the wake of the George Floyd incident, in which Floyd lay dying under the knee of a police officer for several minutes until he could no longer draw breath. Protestors took to the streets. Marches turned to madness. Violence and property crimes burned out of control in most major cities. Thanatos Masculine killed Floyd, and Thanatos Masculine among the demonstrators clouded all the messages that mattered. And the response by most authorities — of rubber bullets, tear gas, and riot shields — was just more Thanatos Masculine. This whole idea that we must solve problems with force is not uniquely American, but it is destroying America.

Marches as a form of nonviolent resistance were effective in the twentieth century. These days, picket signs and chanting can get lost in conflicting agendas or obscured by saboteurs. Too frequently, protesters are their own worst enemies, and create their own worst optics. Circumstances can go from marching to mobbing in seconds. Peaceful demonstrations get co-opted by looters and professional activists seeking to foment social unrest, or who get their jollies from destruction. Afterward, the narratives end up being about the nature of the protest, i.e., which factions were to blame and who started what. The intended message can't get oxygen. So for the twenty-first century, we should ask: How can nonviolent resistance be productive? Or more keenly: How can innovation work toward subversion?

Though it seems contradictory, we need civility and civil disobedience at the same time. Through such practice, we make what the late Congressman and civil rights activist John Lewis called 'good trouble.' Ahimsa first, then *satyagraha* (truth-force), animated Gandhi in his struggles against the British Empire in India. It animated James Morris Lawson, Jr. and Martin Luther King, Jr. during the Civil Rights era. And it can animate every coder, legal scholar, and organizational innovator who dares to compete with the state by offering new forms of self-government.

Think back on the first time you ever got into an Uber. If your first trip was in 2014, there was probably a legal gray area associated with that ride. But in your bones, didn't you think that what you were doing was right, even if it wasn't yet clearly legal? Today, ridesharing apps operate in most major cities around the world. It's been normalized. But it wasn't always normal, nor always legal. Municipalities had to play catch-up because the people built massive constituencies around these services. It was a flood of Eros Feminine. Just as with ridesharing, after collapse the most important elections will happen outside the voting booth.

"One need not have an actual conspiracy to achieve the practical effects of a conspiracy," writes political scientist James C. Scott. "More regimes have been brought, piecemeal, to their knees by what was once called 'Irish Democracy,' the silent, dogged resistance, withdrawal, and truculence of millions of ordinary people, than by revolutionary vanguards or rioting mobs."[301]

With Irish Democracy, people simply stop paying attention to some rule (or ruler) because it has outlived its usefulness. But, let's be clear: the right rules are good things. Laws are like our social operating system, and we need them. But we don't need all of them — much less all of them to stick around forever. Every law presents opportunities for frictions between police with qualified immunity and citizens who have little recourse.

Like our device operating systems, our laws need updating, too. These updates should proceed with greater frequency, but we shouldn't have to wait around on authorities to have the rules we want and need.

But Max, you might be thinking, w*hat about the rule of law? You have to change the law through legitimate processes.* That's reasonable. After all, we don't want mob rule, and we don't want just anyone to be able to change the law willy-nilly — especially those laws which grow out of the Ahimsa Principle and its legal Presumption. There is an important distinction, however, between justice and law, one that's never easy to untangle.

But untangle it we must. Or so thought Henry David Thoreau.

> Unjust laws exist; shall we be content to obey them, or shall we endeavor to amend them, and follow them until we have succeeded, or shall we transgress them at once? Men generally, under such a government as this, think that they ought to wait until they have persuaded the majority to alter them. They think that, if they should resist, the remedy would be worse than the evil. But it is the fault of the government itself that the remedy is worse than the evil. It makes it worse. Why is it not more apt to anticipate and provide for reform? Why does it not cherish its wise minority? Why does it cry and resist before it is hurt? Why does it not encourage its citizens to be on the alert to point out its faults, and do better than it would have them?[302]

Today's peer-to-peer civil disobedience is tomorrow's emergent law.

Indeed, the best law comes about not through a few wise rulers getting together and writing up statutes; instead, it emerges among people interacting with each other, seeking to avoid conflict. When people engage in a peaceful activity like trade, they generally want to keep it that way. When people find new and creative ways to interact peacefully, old laws can be obstructions.

So as we engage in subversive innovation, we are making choices that lead to the emergence of new laws, however slowly or clumsily those laws come online. This process doesn't need the permission of authorities, but rather the assent of peer communities, which is the nature of customary law. The *lex mercatoria*, or Law Merchant, is an ancient form of law that emerged from traders stretching from Europe to the Middle East. Law Merchant evolves whenever commerce happens. Law that facilitates commercial exchange, whether in India, Indiana, or on the Internet, will develop without planning. Emergent law can even support underground markets.[303]

It could be quite a spell before we fully evolve away from our outmoded system of sending politicians to capitals to make statutes. Lawmakers will continue having to play catch-up with emergent systems, which could make matters awkward in the interim. But the emergent arrangements (feminine and consensual) will continue to push up through the cracks in the monoliths of the old order (masculine and imposed). When we think that the purpose of law is to help people interact peacefully, peer-to-peer civil disobedience will accelerate. New rules will sprout up in the humus of the dissolved order.

But none of this is possible without conscious, continuous practice, with more and more practitioners gathering with enthusiasm, ready to weave together the new liberal order. Our hope is, if enough of us become active practitioners of peace, we will create new channels of human interaction. Healthy Eros Feminine will balance out the excess of the Masculine. The Law of Flow will work to our flourishing.

PRACTICE INTEGRITY

If nonviolence — *ahimsa* — is the prime directive for the integral liberal order, the second is integrity. In other words: First, do no harm. Then, be of your word.

People use the term integrity in different ways, but in this context, it means honoring your agreements to yourself and others, committing to doing what you say you are going to do. I could have spent an entire chapter in Part One talking about the breakdown of contemporary society's integrity, which is certainly as important as the others when we think about the cultural conditions of collapse. Competing ephemera tempt too many people. Too many people seem to think having a smart device absolves them of their responsibility to keep their word, for example to be on time. But the wholesale transformation of society from a masculine control paradigm to a more balanced paradigm will only come about if people can be trusted to keep their word. Society, after all, operates on people being able to rely on others.

Harvard Business School professor Michael Jensen thinks that integrity is rather like gravity:

> Integrity is a necessary condition for maximum performance.... The proposition is that if you violate the Law of Integrity, the opportunity-set for your performance will shrink and therefore your actual performance is likely to suffer. As with the gravity analogy, this is just a plain fact: if you attempt to violate the Law of Gravity without a parachute, you will suffer severe consequences. We argue that if you respect the Law of Integrity you will experience enormous increases in performance, both in your organization and in your life.[304]

Jensen's formulation implies that a failure to respect the Law of Integrity will mean that some part of the whole is not operating according to expectations. Functionally, this amounts to inefficiency and breakdown. Of course, bad feelings follow.

Jensen is referring specifically to integrity within organizations, but we can scale the Law of Integrity right up to society. We already have expectations of others we take for granted: We expect there to be half-and-half at the supermarket, but that depends on the production, packaging, logistics, and deliveries which came before. We hope that there will be kind people to watch over our children while we work; we expect that if we have a deadline that depends on another colleague's work input, the colleague will do the work on time. And so on. The interdependent society operates almost entirely on people keeping their word. To the extent they do not, we start to see dissolution.

The yogis call this kind of integrity *satya*. Before you speak, ask yourself, 'Is this true? Is this necessary?' Satya includes not just being of your word but also one who listens closely and with discernment in seeking truth. To be in integrity means that you are always speaking the truth and tracking the truth, so that your words and deeds are in alignment. Such alignment includes taking care not to think one thing and say another, and extends to the simulacra of self you might put on social media. And of course, it includes the commitments you make to your friends and family.

Integrity starts with being honest with yourself, a commitment to the sphere of integrity. The foundation of being a person of integrity comes in the recognition, first, that you're only as good as your word, and then, that you commit to being a person of integrity. This outlook requires conscious, continuous practice.

PRACTICE PLURALISM

The practice of ahimsa and integrity are fundamental to integral liberalism. Though it might be necessary to move

these from passive values to active practices, it is not sufficient. Some, at least, must go deeper, into *pluralism*. It would
seem that there is nothing new under the sun. After all,
isn't pluralism already a liberal value? Here again, liberals
have been too passive, and liberalism has historically been
a rather bloodless and rules-based worldview. In our view,
pluralism is not just the recognition of diversity in society,
but rather an active practice. It will take true mastery to
ascend to this practice level because it requires new habits
of mind.

So what does the practice of pluralism look like?

First, we can say it doesn't look like a diversity agenda
based on victimology. Any such agenda is antithetical to
pluralism because diversity, under the victimologist conception, obliges people to become mindless drones in an ideological monoculture. I once heard Matt Ridley cheekily ask:
"What is the opposite of diversity? A university." Tenured
radicals and High Minds having made their long march
through the institutions. Diversity is *obeisance to victim narratives*. The integral liberal is after real pluralism. Pluralism, in
practice, comes in *seeking understanding and synthesis*.

The first instinct for most ideologues is to dig in their
heels and cling to a checklist of group-identity criteria.
Identification with one's group comes before sound thinking. If someone else proposes an idea that is not on the
checklist — or that someone belongs to an out-group —
the ideologue is biased to look for what's wrong with that
person's position. But what if we started looking for what's
right?

One who practices pluralism will have an open heart
and mind. They will not be so quick to retreat into tribal
allegiances. Instead, they will be disciplined, looking for
the best ideas and healthiest expressions. They'll borrow
from many different perspectives. And then they will *seek to
synthesize the ideas*.

Take the example of poverty alleviation, and consider

that in America, three different groups have strong opinions on the matter:

- Progressives think that people ought to emphasize care as one of society's highest values, and that entrepreneurship and markets are not enough to help society's least advantaged.

- Conservatives think there are right and wrong ways to help the least advantaged, and that blanket welfare policies can create dependency cycles which destroy communities.

- Libertarians think that entrepreneurship and markets do most of society's work in terms of poverty alleviation, and the rest can be done through charity and civil society.

Many of us would look at these three claims and try to figure out which one is at the top of our checklist. But the integral liberal looks for what is valuable in each and weaves the strands together. In doing so, we borrow liberally from the Integral practitioners' transcend-and-include approach of thinkers such as Clare Graves, Don Beck, and Ken Wilber.

And yet this is not without paradox. Eastern traditions speak of non-duality, *advaita*, which can be realized both in contemplation and meditation. We have suggested that it is important to resist thinking of others as separate, yet liberal pluralism acknowledges each person's separateness. Pluralism must be reconciled with the oneness of the universe, which is non-duality.

Non-duality is challenging to articulate in cumbersome Western prose. Perhaps it is better to refer to the inner struggle Arjuna faced before going into battle in *The Bhagavad Gita*. The hundred who Arjuna is to slay are his cousins, which symbolizes all those lower-order temptations and distractions that are the sum of our embodied humanity. Of course, these hundred are under the command of the

Blind King, who is Ego. Krishna's vision requires that
Arjuna overcome these lower-order aspects of himself on
the battlefield of his inner world so that he can understand
his place in the cosmos. And with Krishna driving the chariot, Arjuna can access just a little of that understanding,
which will allow him to see that higher-order understanding is a triumph over Ego, but that everything that exists
extends backward into the same cosmic source. Maybe the
Gita is a kind of source code for recognizing one's singular
place in the cosmology, but one interpreted as a unique
manifestation of space-time's fabric. Krishna, Vishnu,
and all of the other manifestations are aspects of the same
mystery, partially revealed, unifying us all.

> O Arjuna, in this world, all beings are born in utter
> ignorance due to the delusion of dualities (pairs of
> opposites, likes and dislikes), arising from desire and
> aversion.[305]

The paradox of pluralism is that understanding difference and diversity is a path to understanding a whole
underlying truth. It connects all things. It *is* all things. So,
for example, when we explore dualities like Eros/Thanatos
and Masculine/Feminine, we regard forces of the universe,
of which we are part, which are expressed *through* us.

The practice of pluralism is about seeking a synthesis
of perspectives, but it is also about seeking *unity*. In reconciling the paradox, philosopher Robert Nozick invites us to
consider organic unity. The idea is that within any system,
there is value in the balance of diversity and unity. Whether
we're talking about art, science, or society, Nozick saw a
pattern: *One can find value where unity and diversity are in balance.*
In society, too much conformity means oppressed people,
marching soldiers, and brutalist architecture as far as the
eye can see. Too many stark differences and you get faction
and unrest. According to Nozick, diversity and unity are
mutually constraining; such mutual constraint yields a sweet

spot between rigid order and unruly chaos.

"Can we draw a curve of degree of organic unity with the two axes being degree of diversity and degree of unifiedness?"[306] asked Nozick in *Philosophical Explanations.* The diversity axis will constrain the unity axis and vice versa to achieve a kind of stasis. The beauty of Nozick's graph, apart from its simplicity, is its appeal to some intuitive notion of balance.

The dollar's dictum *e pluribus unum* (out of many, one) is good, but so also is *ex uno plures* (out of one, many). Integral thinkers are comfortable with the synthesis view of pluralism: On the one hand, each person is unique and deserving of respect, but each is a manifestation of the same cosmic unity. Or as tantric philosopher Sally Kempton says of the Hindu gods, "These deity energies are both internal forces and external, subtle presences. From an ultimate point of view, however, they are simply waves in the ocean of one cosmic mind."[307]

Why is pluralism in unity essential to our idea of society? When we are unified, we are at peace; but when we are at peace, we set about pursuing happiness, which comes in different flavors. Pluralism means that people with different conceptions of the good life can coexist in their pursuits. The practice of pluralism means not only that we balance our diversity with unity, but that we attempt to cross the empathic divide to weave together our perspectives into a new tapestry of truth. Getting a glimpse of that truth helps one see that monocultures are not always healthy, that experimentation is needed, and that reconciliation is possible.

Organizing society is, therefore, not about finding a singular ideal to be crafted by masterminds; rather, it is about acknowledging our differences, accepting them, and unleashing the creative forces that arise in the overlaps. Becoming a practitioner of pluralism does not come easy, and it starts with good old-fashioned toleration. In mastery, though, the practice means holding multiple values and perspectives in cognitive and affective juxtaposition. That takes discipline, and suppressing our reflex responses. It means seeking to understand and empathize with points of view that might go against the grain.

The hardest part comes in weaving together various perspectives into coherence while avoiding contradictions. To achieve coherence, we might have to shed fragments of those perspectives. These fragments can sometimes be pieces of our identities, insofar as our ideology or in-group identification shapes who we are. But no matter. That's what makes it hard. If we fail to achieve coherence, what we end up with is not a greater truth at all, but a muddle. And if we fail to seek greater truths, we will cling to fragments and remain in a state of disharmony.

PRACTICE COMPASSION

Despite the gothic histories of the South, tenant farmers once shared rugged communitarianism that defies stereotypes of rugged individualism. In North Carolina, where my family is from, poor folks roamed the red clay as much together as apart. In the days before people lined up at the Department of Social Services, they had to depend on each other — and they did. Before my great grandmother died, she recounted a story involving her husband, my great grandfather, Garland. Since that telling, the story has prompted me to ask myself what it means to be compassionate.

One night, a neighbor came over and asked Garland for help in something you and I might find unthinkable: to help him with his son. The boy had been bitten, and was rabid. The disease had progressed beyond the medicine of that time and place. So the two men would have to put the boy between two corn-shuck tick mattresses and suffocate him. It may be hard for us to understand the ethic of that time, but these two men, separated pretty much only by a fence, were united that day in a gruesome rite of mercy killing. Had it been Garland's son — my grandfather — who had been afflicted, the neighbor would have done the same. That's just the way things were.

When we think of compassion as a practice and not a bright moral rule, we can understand that my great grandfather knew to channel Thanatos Masculine. His circumstances must have helped him be more attuned to that kind of compassion. And that is rather the point; that we practice within some set of circumstances. Compassion is not an abstract rule that can be applied. It is a way of seeing and a mode of being, which result in actions that *order reality. Tikkun Olam.*

If you have ever had a small child, compassion comes a little more naturally. The little ones need us, and nurturing them is more comfortable than caring for a grown stranger. It can be harder to have compassion for adults who, as my mother used to say, "ought to know better." But we can follow the Sufis Muslims who see the light of the divine in everyone. Compassion starts with looking for that light. Whether or not you believe that Allah, or God, or some animating Atman is present in others, the practice of compassion works because we see value in others.

But compassion is also the act of being attuned to suffering. The Sikhs practice *daya*, which is a form of compassion that involves *taking on the suffering of others.* It is deeper even than sympathy. Sikh compassion observes the stranger's pain and becomes touched by it, then responds to the sufferer. It moves us to act with mercy and kindness. But it does not require unreflective self-sacrifice, nor does it require the machinations of politics, which are in almost every case an excuse for one to remove oneself from the responsibilities of compassion's conscious and continuous practice.

The practice of compassion can then be broken into the

affective, the deliberative, and the active. That means that practice starts with being attuned to the suffering of others, and then one must ask oneself whether it is in one's power to relieve someone else's suffering, and then ask how best to go about it. Finally, after deliberating, one takes action. The action could be a gift of assistance, money, advice, or emotional support. The point is that there are myriad ways compassion manifests itself in action, but the deliberation and action parts are the most important and tend to be the parts people neglect.

PRACTICE STEWARDSHIP

The final sphere we will call stewardship. Like the other practices, it too involves several dimensions, which might be broken out and practiced in isolation. It's useful to think of stewardship as a cluster, mainly because it's easier to remember a word when getting started.

In thinking about old liberalism as a facet of integral liberalism, we have suggested that we owe the relative plenty of the modern world to the liberalism of the past. That relative plenty means that wealth has been created. It doesn't mean that wealth was created in a perfect world, nor does it mean that the sum of the world's material wealth is automatically distributed according to anyone's ideals. It simply means that any given person alive today is likely to be wealthier than any given person at any time in human history. We begin by honoring that fact.

Once we honor the fact of relative wealth, we should forget about all ideologies of envy and violence and focus then on stewardship of resources — whether we own a little or a lot of it. There is great dignity in stewardship. You might recall that old liberal value was a rule of private property. And it's a good rule; but like many rules, it is not enough. Owning property comes with responsibilities and expectations, and ownership should also be seen as a practice.

Stewardship involves moderation. Whether in the Aristotelian tradition or in the Yamas, it's good to adjust your consumption habits or behavior to a reasonable level, avoiding extremes. Just because you have a lot of ice cream, for example, doesn't mean you need to eat it all today. Just because you earned a lot of money doesn't mean you need to spend it all or live a life of ostentation. Moderation helps one protect the seed corn. It helps one appreciate scarcity before it arrives while taking a healthy attitude towards plenty — especially when one is tempted by it at every turn.

Stewardship involves non-attachment. Whether in the Yamas, in Buddhism, or the traditions of Christian asceticism, non-attachment is a vital habit of mind. One develops non-attachment to avoid privileging the destination over the journey, the salary over the effort, or the praise over the achievement. Goal-directed action is sufficient as far as it goes, but the very nature of practice means losing yourself in habituated thought and action. Stewardship means honoring the fact that resources are in your care, and that when you die they will be in another's care. We declutter our homes, declutter our diets, and declutter our minds.

Stewardship involves leaving the world better than you found it. Any resources in your charge should be improved, or improve the lives of others when they pass from your care. If you're not a good investor, your poor stewardship will be obvious in time. Investors who get wealthier from their investments are good stewards, as long as the resources are going to real value creation. If you own a lot of possessions, then keep them in good condition. If you own a modest plot of land, care for the lawn and gardens. If you own a business, remain profitable and grow.

Ownership is mere possession. Stewardship is a practice of continuous improvement and growth of the resources in your care. Once we start to reframe ownership as stewardship, we will see an immediate improvement in ourselves and in the world, material, and spiritual.

The Integral Liberal

Thus, the integral liberal adopts five spheres of practice, which we have already set out:

1. *Nonviolence*, or ahimsa, is the practice of abstaining from harm in thought, word, and deed. In our formulation, it extends to both persons and their property. Such can include nonviolent resistance against harmful institutions and individuals who would harm.

2. *Integrity* is the practice of truthfulness and fidelity to one's word. Being a person of your word means that others can count on you. Your reliability is infectious.

3. *Pluralism* is the practice not just of tolerating differences among people, but of actively seeking to understand and synthesize multiple perspectives to maintain peace and glimpse a greater truth.

4. *Compassion* is the practice of being concerned for others' suffering and, when appropriate, actively and directly seeking to mitigate their suffering or improve their wellbeing.

5. *Stewardship* is the practice of taking care of something, whether resources or property, while actively seeking to improve that which is in your care, leaving circumstances better than when you found them.

Recall that liberalism was born, more or less, in the Enlightenment. The Enlightenment's major exponents were enamored of reason, and so are we. But reason is not enough. If you go too far in stripping your doctrine of what it means to be human, to *feel* human, people will not readily adopt it. None of this is to argue that integral liberalism should be irrational, nor should it be about sharing our feelings from one moment to the next. Taking on a pre-birth perspective or applying a game-theoretical algorithm is useful, to a point. But employing reason shouldn't be so bloodless. Practice requires more than just adopting an abstract political philosophy; it requires embodied wisdom, attention to feedback, and being completely attuned to your inner life.

Because people live in a society, their philosophy must be more than a legal doctrine. It must also be a life philosophy. In other words, it's not enough to hope that some enlightened legislators will make our laws. We have to *live our liberalism*. In this way, It takes discipline to practice our values. Unrestrained passion pushes us into making poor decisions and causes us not to see other perspectives. But the integral liberal must think and feel and practice, too. In taking on other perspectives, they can *think* what others are thinking, and *feel* what they are feeling. By weaving together multiple, partial truths into a greater transcendent truth, reason and empathy operate in tandem.

Therefore, integral liberals practice liberalism in the same way one practices a religion. Or, their liberalism is an active moral and psychological practice, as one is always listening and open to the perspectives of others. They remain attuned to opportunities to synthesize rather than contradict. At the highest levels of mastery, they can recommend a way forward based on a synthesized truth that they have appreciated. The rarest integral liberal will be able to communicate or build something upon her insights to make them useful.

Synthesis can be 'meta,' but not always. Unfortunately, smart people can be *more meta than thou*. That's not to say that we shouldn't all try to click out our minds another order of magnitude, from time to time. It's healthy to take a different perspective. Thinking 'meta' can be healthy. But it is unhelpful when few, or one alone, can appreciate their insights. In this, one achieves self-satisfaction. Smug solipsism. The integral liberal has to watch out for lapsing into immoderate meta-ness. The point of synthesizing perspectives is to discover a deeper truth and share it with people at different development stages.

Realizing the irony here, we must take a step back from our own meta-ness. We should ask what rules, guides, or heuristics can help ordinary people along the path to change. The truth is, most of us just aren't that smart or spiritually developed, which is another reason why we need practice. To lead, one has to not only to speak with reason and restraint. One has also to relate one's ideas to allow others; to understand and integrate the change. If one's cognitive scaffolding is so far above the ground that everyone looks like ants, no one will be able to hear.

The integral liberal will build fewer towers of intellectual solipsism, and their thinking will be advanced and nonlinear. Otherwise, at their best, they will speak clearly. They will build new tools and write new rules that reconcile multiple perspectives. And, most importantly, they will live by example, engaging their practice, always moving towards mastery. Of course, not all integral liberals will achieve proficiency in all five spheres. Very few will. We must hope there will be enough. We must hope, at the very least, more people embrace ahimsa. As my mentor, entrepreneur Chris Rufer says, our best protection comes when more people adopt the social values of peace.

Finally, the integral liberal is neither a collectivist nor an individualist. Collectivism subordinates the individual to the group, especially the power structures of groups. Individualism puts the right emphasis on autonomy, but some variants neglect the reality of interdependence and community. The integral liberal sees no contradiction in the integration of concern for self and concern for the whole. Individual and group cohere in balance.

NONVIOLENCE IS NOT PACIFISM

Before moving away from the integral liberal practices, we should point out a couple of things: first, ahimsa is a habit of mind; second, ahimsa is not pacifism. Nonviolence is the conscious and continuous practice of creating peaceful conditions, whether in oneself or in one's immediate sphere. But that does not mean the practitioner should fail to defend oneself from harm. Though there are always risks in meeting force with force, psychiatrist and Buddhist teacher Paul Fleischman believes that protectors and peacekeepers must ask themselves the following:

> Can you do this task as an upholder of safety and justice, focused on love of those you protect rather than on hate for those you must kill? If you are acting with vengeance or delight in destruction, then you are not at all a student of Dhamma. But if your hard job can be done with a base of pure mind, while you are clearly not living the life of an enlightened person, you are still able to begin walking the path towards harmony and compassion.[308]

On the path to liberation, dhamma, for which the Buddha was perhaps the ultimate spokesman, ahimsa is a mode of conduct; a way of life. Liberalism has missed understanding itself as a mode of conduct, which is why it has broken down. Our effort to borrow from traditions East and West lies in service of harnessing powers we have in our immediate control. In this way, Buddhism, for example, releases practitioners from ideology. By deepening one's understanding of oneself and one's place in the universe, one comes to embody the moral teachings, rather than imposing them or paying lip service. Through cultivated, gradually deepened experiences, the Buddha led his followers to autonomy from one-dimensional dogmas and doctrines. Many Buddhists don't even call themselves Buddhists, because it implies allegiances at odds with the

Buddha's teachings.

Suppose we are to transmute liberalism from ideology to practice. In that case, we will have to take care not to make too many unreasonable litmus tests. Pacifism is *not* the practice of bringing the Thanatos Masculine into balance with the other forces; pacifism, ironically, is about killing Thanatos Masculine. But we need Thanatos Masculine. We just don't need as much of it as we currently have in our society today.

SHAPED BY RULES, SHAPERS OF RULES

In my last book, *The Social Singularity*, I tried to show that humanity would evolve according to technological change that introduces new rules and new tools. I lean heavily on an errant quote, credited to social theorist Marshall McLuhan, which he didn't actually say: *We shape our tools and then our tools shape us.* I presented my parallel formulation, which is apt here, too: *We shape our rules and then our rules shape us.* The basic idea here is that new culture and new values emerge with the mass adoption of any technology. Humanity evolves. And in the combination of new rules and new tools, such as communities formed using digital ledgers, we will be able to lateralize our relationships and decentralize power.

But in exploring the reconfiguration of rules, I see now how important it is to begin with the innermost circle: self. This time around, I want to emphasize that we each have the power to 'shape us,' that is, our very humanity. Directly. Right now. Otherwise, those who shape the new rules will have been shaped too much by the old rules' incentives. Because our cultural values and rules work in vacillating tandem, it is necessary to practice the spheres of integral liberalism. As we are ascendant in our practice, we will be more likely to create new tools and new rules that allow us to be even better practitioners in a virtuous, reinforcing circle.

This new commitment to integral liberalism might be the only way to escape the cycle of destruction we're currently in. I say this with a note of caution: this cycle may have to play itself out before a more generative one can begin. Thanatos Feminine ascends? We simply don't know. We can therefore be happy warriors from this point forward. We can *let things go*, *let things flow*, and start our practice. We must suppress our urge to control those things which ought to be outside of our control. And most importantly, we must never allow ourselves to submit to authorities who never gained our consent. Our integral liberalism must not only be a conscious, continuous practice but a lodestar for nonviolent resistance.

THE CONSENSUAL SOCIETY

One of the fundamental questions of law is whether people actually follow it. If the laws within a system are good, the more likely people are going to migrate to that system and follow that set of laws. In this way, it really doesn't matter what High Minds think of as justice. We're entering an age of experiments that can be carried out on smaller scales than the revolutions of the past. Suddenly, systems of justice and law can compete. This new reality is another reason to think of the coming era as the *post-ideological age*: If a system is unable to attract people or keep them from leaving, that system is no different from a bad restaurant.

"It turns out there's only one thing that guarantees production of good laws," writes hedge fund manager and philosopher Michael P. Gibson.

> The people bound by the laws have to agree to be bound by them. Not hypothetically or tacitly, as in some imaginary will of the people or behind a veil of ignorance. Consent must be real, transparent, and

continuous. No law can bind a single person only
when and because that person consents to be bound
by that law. All laws must be strictly opt in. Lawmakers could be saints, devils or monkeys on typewriters
— doesn't matter. The opt out-opt in system lets
only good laws survive. Bad laws are driven out of
production.[309]

Bad governance can only inflict harm up to the costs of
exiting. And that is why Gibson thinks we can "underthrow
the state one contract at a time."

When governance systems compete, ideology takes a
back seat to real human choices. If you think you've got a
better system, you'll have to start it. Authorities we never
chose architecting our way to utopia by threat of force is no
longer viable. *Governance will function more like a market*, whispers Eros Feminine. *People will start to exit failing systems*, adds
Thanatos Feminine, *and let them go*. Indeed, if there is real
competition among systems of governance, corruption will
start to evaporate. After all, corruption drives people away.

Some people won't feel comfortable with the ascen-
dance of Eros Feminine, because they will still be under
the sway of that masculine urge to control. Governance
markets, which are just the product of real people making
real choices, they imagine, will be too unpredictable.
And yet these self-same detractors will use terms like 'the
social contract' in every sense but the literal one. Integral
liberalism will be unapologetically literal when it comes to
consent. And where there is an absence of monitoring or
enforcement, consent-based systems require the cultivation
of the spheres.

We liberals have always made the mistake of thinking
that society can and should only operate according to
abstract, objective rules. Here we argue that rules, though
absolutely essential, are not enough. A vital synthesis
between rules and practice is not only possible, but necessary to human flourishing.

9

RESTORE THE LOST CONSTITUTION[310]

Deliberate, therefore, on this new national government with coolness; analize it with criticism; and reflect on it with candor: if you find that the influence of a powerful few, or the exercise of a standing army, will always be directed and exerted for your welfare alone, and not to the aggrandizement of themselves, and that it will secure to you and your posterity happiness at home, and national dignity and respect from abroad, adopt it; if it will not, reject it with indignation-better to be where you are for the present, than insecure forever afterwards.

Cato I, *Anti-Federalist*

In the throes of collapse, people will want to turn to something familiar, something that feels timeless. Though the U.S. Constitution was designed by mortals, the document was once imbued with a sense of the eternal. Some argue that it's out of date. Others argue that there is much to be found in the penumbra, and that what can be found can save the republic. I don't consider it my job to say whether there ought to be a Constitution after collapse. My job is to consider the best possibilities for human flourishing in light of change to our human systems, which may or may not include the Constitution.

Over the years, though, High Minds have argued that the Constitution is outdated. *We don't need protection from unreasonable searches and seizures*, they said from the right. To keep us safe. *We don't need guns and militias anymore*, they said from the left. To keep us safe. In what remained, the Constitution became a document of political opportunism used to block one's opposition, but was never respected in its totality by the political class.

Packed courts and activist judges twisted the original meaning out of all proportions. The political class ignored whole amendments, and continues to do so. Legislators raced to pass bills that would cause the Framers to scoff, tut, and turn in their graves. *Who cares what a bunch of old powdered wigs thought? We have to evolve with the times*, they said. Emergency after emergency awakened the urge to control, even though some past intervention caused most of the emergencies.

Nevertheless, these emergencies became pretexts for actions that left the document in tatters and sowed the seeds of collapse. In this way, it was a mindset that undermined the Constitution. And an undermined Constitution makes for a vulnerable Republic.

History professor Margaret O'Mara captures the essence of the High Mind:

> The battle against [insert crisis] already has made government — federal, state and local — far more visible to Americans than it normally has been. As we tune in to daily briefings from… officials, listen for guidance from our governors, and seek help and hope from our national leaders, we are seeing the critical role that "big government" plays in our lives and our health. We also see the deadly consequences of four decades of disinvestment in public infrastructure and dismissal of public expertise. Not only will

America need a massive dose of big government to get out of this crisis — as Washington's swift passage of a giant economic bailout package reflects — but we will need big, and wise, government more than ever in its aftermath.[311]

Big. Central. Wise. This might as well be inscribed in gold lettering over the Blue Church.

Time and again the High Minds have agitated for more. Crisis after crisis. Fear grips the mind and locks it down. The irony is that the intellectual elites, more than anyone, seem to wallow in this perennial failure of imagination, looking to the state to be Mommy, Daddy, and God. The Blue Church's public 'expertise' is presented as a rare form of intelligence or magical insight. Private expertise — *whatever that might be* — should be suppressed or ignored.

Such is not to argue that government experts are always wrong; instead, it is to say that if public expertise is a hammer, everything looks like a nail. That hammer should smash, smash, smash its way to a solution. They'll need bigger budgets. They'll need more comprehensive plans. The Constitution? *How can anyone worry about the Constitution when [insert crisis].*

As we stare down collapse, it is tempting to join the High Minds and suggest we simply scrap the Constitution and start over completely. But even those drowning in a storm will look around for what remains in the wreckage to cling to it. So I imagine what is needed is rather like what philosopher Otto Neurath described:

> We are like sailors who on the open sea must reconstruct their ship but are never able to start afresh from the bottom. Where a beam is taken away a new one must at once be put there, and for this the rest of the ship is used as support. In this way, by using the old beams and driftwood the ship can be shaped entirely anew, but only by gradual reconstruction.[312]

And indeed, you will find a lot more speculative thinking in the remainder of this book. Maybe the Constitution will become completely irrelevant in the wake of collapse. And if so, there is plenty ahead that satisfies a prescription for simply starting over. However, my hope is that the Constitution is a mechanism through which we can evolve our institutions, rather than a failed experiment to be discarded as what had once been America descends into chaos, warlordism, or authoritarian dictatorship. I can't help but think there is still something vital about the Constitution, even if it is only a stepping stone to a healthier regime that no longer requires it. It still has the effect of being secular scripture, a connection to our origins, and a source of unity as a people. It is both timeless and amendable, so it can be a path to our renaissance. It will all depend on what Eros and Thanatos Feminine have in mind for the future.

When we think of the Constitution, it's mostly as a static thing that exists as an artifact from the past. In our highly polarized times, it's hard to imagine changing it. And yet it *has* been changed, seventeen times since the Bill of Rights was written. Surely, in the face of cataclysm, we can at least enforce what is vital to our reorganization, even if we make no Amendments. Some sort of latticework will be necessary, one imbued with the timeless gifts of the enlightenment. Like pluralism.

Recall that philosopher Robert Nozick believed that we can find value in things that exhibit organic unity, which, put quite simply, is the balance of unity and diversity. One might say that this conception of value maps nicely atop our idea of the Law of Flow. After all, flow systems have both diverse elements and unified-ness. So, for example, the world is biodiverse in its flora and fauna, but all living things share an underlying code. Most life on earth participates in the oxygen cycle of respiration and photosynthesis, even though we share that cycle with Venus flytraps, Siberian tigers, and psychedelic cuttlefish.

Americans, too, are united in our self-concept as Americans. *E pluribus unum.* Likewise, a binding set of basic laws gives rise to many different lifestyles, religions, and conceptions of the good. *Ex uno plures.* When we can maintain our diversity and yet remain unified in peace, that's valuable. For about two hundred and fifty years, the constitutional order has helped Americans be more organically unified. Though there had been some lurches away from the ideals expressed in those founding documents, from the ill-treatment of Native peoples to Jim Crow laws, pluralism and unity found some balance.

It's tempting to abandon the Constitution, especially in times of crisis. Activist courts, hellbent legislators, pliant voters and presidents with Great Man complexes have all turned against the rule of law. But in this chapter, we will discuss ways to restore the lost Constitution, realizing that this might turn out to be a lost cause. Though it is not perfect, the Constitution is a familiar social operating system that has the benefit of evolving. Because it is customary and manages somehow still to be part of our collective consciousness, I cannot conclude that it should simply be discarded. Still, later we will think about how to be prepared for that eventuality. Perhaps someday, the Constitution will outlive its usefulness. Perhaps it will be replaced by some other, superior social operating system. Maybe it will crash with the system.

Or maybe it can be useful again. Maybe we can restore it. If so, we must upgrade it.

ENFORCE THE NINTH AND TENTH AMENDMENTS

The most pragmatic, immediate, and obvious measure that must be taken *as soon as possible* is to enforce the Ninth and Tenth Amendments. That means shaking ourselves from our collective amnesia and agnosia.

If your civics are rusty, here are Amendments Nine and Ten as a reminder:

> *Amendment 9:* The enumeration in the Constitution, of certain rights, shall not be construed to deny or disparage others retained by the people.

> *Amendment 10:* The powers not delegated to the United States by the Constitution, nor prohibited by it to the States, are reserved to the States respectively, or to the people.

One would do well to commit these to memory. If they do not stick in the mind, or if one is reading from some other country, I suggest the people of all nations emulate these amendments or advocate for something similar, such as a principle of subsidiarity. Switzerland, with its canton system, is one to emulate. Tiny Liechtenstein too. But the idea is that power should be devolved.

I follow the old progressive Justice Louis Brandeis, who said a "state may, if its citizens choose, serve as a laboratory; and try novel social and economic experiments without risk to the rest of the country."[313] Ironically, Brandeis spent much of his career risking the rest of the country. He helped to create a series of monstrous (and probably unconstitutional) federal agencies. And his most dubious achievement might be his assisting the creation of the Federal Reserve Bank. While one shudders to think what else Brandeis might have dreamt up in some state's laboratory, that rather proves his original point.

Reining in the High Minds with their unconstrained visions is precisely the point of having fifty laboratories. To wit: if one experiment fails, there are forty-nine that might succeed. If two experiments fail, there are forty-eight that might not. And so on. Other states can avoid failures and replicate successes. One wouldn't want to argue that state legislatures aren't prone to jumping on bandwagons. But at least not every state will be California, where politicians fancy that they can suspend reality by the force of law. (Statewide rent controls are just one example.)

The United States government, with its bloated federal register and one-size-fits-all statutory regime, has become a megalith on stilts that were never meant to bear such a load. Still, it's not just that too many laws and regulations weigh heavily upon the states and the people who, according to the Constitution, anyway, have unenumerated rights. It is that if the grand experiments of Congress fail, that failure is catastrophic. Fifty guaranteed failures.

So, in the interests of merely cutting losses, it might be time to accept that some of the highest High Minds will infest the state capitals — even if they've just scurried away from what they wrought. If their grand plans are sustainable, they will survive. If not, they will fail. But the High Minds must be run out of Washington. Let them go to Springfield, to Albany, and to Sacramento and bring those states to ruin. Of course, the hawks of endless war and business 'incentives' and corporate welfare will infest the state capitals, too. Will they flock to Phoenix, to Austin, or Tallahassee? Who can say? But let them be dispersed and not concentrated in that red light district known as K Street. For they have made collapse all but assured.

How one goes about enforcing federalism is another question. In a time of impending disaster, it might well be a combination of factors:

- A barrage of lawsuits based on Ninth and Tenth Amendment grounds, brought by individuals and the states.

- Threat of secession by individual states.

- A federal statute detailing enforcement.

- Refusal by states to comply once Washington no longer has the power of the purse.

The idea of federalism is that the tasks of governance

should be handled as locally as possible. If no one has plans to enforce the Ninth and Tenth Amendments, then maybe it's time for a Subsidiarity Amendment: "Reasonable people will disagree about the exact boundary of public goods, even when a rigorous definition of public good limits the range of possibilities," writes political scientist Charles Murray. "The mechanism for coping with such disagreements is embodied in the principle of subsidiarity. *The legitimate functions of government should be performed at the most local feasible level.*"[314] (Emphasis mine.)

If Congress were to pass such an amendment, it would probably be redundant, making one wonder whether our nation's great charter will *ever* be enforced if it is not being enforced today. Maybe a court case will emerge that catalyzes changes to case law. Maybe something will change once everyone realizes that the federal government does too much, and that it has broken the bank. Again, a Subsidiarity Amendment is probably unnecessary, because we have amendments Nine and Ten, and they are close enough. But if we can't enforce the Constitution we have, maybe a desperate Congress will see fit to pass something plainer. I can't imagine how much clearer one can be than what we have now. One gets the feeling a Subsidiarity Amendment would be a refresher of sorts, perhaps one that gives courts more teeth in striking down unconstitutional laws. Honestly, it isn't easy to imagine Congress sacrificing its power. Matters would have to be grave indeed. But we can dream.

RIGHT THE UPSIDE-DOWN CONSTITUTION

Today we see a lot of unnecessary social fracturing, as political factions rage to make the rules and control the federal purse's power. State governments must submit to all manner of overreach due to the federal government's ability to tax the people, then make the states dependent on that

very same largesse. "The federal government has been able
to exceed the enumerated limits on its powers by bribing or
coercing the states with their own citizens' money," writes
legal scholar Randy Barnett. "Indeed, under this system,
states have become major supplicants and lobbyists under
federal laws."[315]

From harmonized drinking ages to force-feeding the
states a monolithic healthcare policy, what we have today,
according to Barnett, is "cooperative federalism." But what
we need is "competitive federalism."[316] Search cooperative
federalism online, and you'll see any number of benign
treatments of the concept. In reality, the federal government's idea of cooperation is more akin to something one
would read in a Mario Puzo novel.

Legal scholar Michael Grieve thinks this outsized power
yields an "upside-down Constitution," in which the states
can neither innovate nor truly express their inhabitants'
cultural values. That means there are vast disagreements
among the states and the people. Instead of trying on different forms of governance, as with Switzerland, their only
choice is to engage in a political "war of all against all,"
which, of course, refers to the darker passages of Hobbes's
Leviathan.[317]

Under these conditions, the states cannot become
laboratories. States that try something new, or otherwise get
out of line, will usually get threats from Uncle Sam. But this
creates no release valves for policymakers trying either to
reflect their constituents' conceptions of the good or otherwise tailor their own laws.

"Arguably, this violates Article I, Section 8," writes
Barnett, "which requires that taxes only be raised only
'to pay the debts and provide for the common defense
and *general* welfare of the United States.' According to
this objection, money taken from a state cannot go to
any program that wholly withholds benefits from a state,
because such a provision would not be 'general' but would

be partial." (Emphasis Barnett's.)

I'll pass over the irony that, for once, the General Welfare Clause is not being used for political chicanery. Any spending program that does not benefit every state equally, but instead leverages tax money for the state's "cooperation," is unconstitutional. States must be left to craft policies that might do better than what the High Minds have planned for every single one of us 350 million citizens. If there is a Constitutional order after collapse, the federal government must not be allowed to bribe or threaten states into acquiescence.

CREATE THE CONDITIONS FOR PROTECTED SECESSION

I'll go one further: As a radical for rules, I recommend a Secession Amendment. Under such a rule, a state must be allowed to secede from the union, but only if it meets the following conditions:

- Majority referendum
- Two-thirds vote by the state legislature

Then, if the secession passes, conditions placed on the seceding state are that it:

- Retain the U.S. Constitution, including all amendments, as its own.
- Repeal any past amendments by an amendment process.
- Make any changes to the Constitution by amendment.
- Trigger a peace treaty with the remaining United States.
- Continue all trading relationships with the remaining United States.

- Allow free movement of people between the seceding state and the United States.

The U.S. federal government must abide by the following conditions:

- Trigger a peace treaty with the seceding state.
- Continue all existing trade relationships with the seceding state.
- Allow free movement of people between the seceding state and the United States.

Such is, of course, a sketch. The spirit of such a proposed Amendment would be to create a more vigorous check on the authority of the federal government. Secession would be a kind of 'nuclear option' that the states would possess, but which would prohibit punitive or retaliatory measures by the federal government — all while ensuring some measure of harmony and a quasi-union.

KILL THE LIVING CONSTITUTION

For more than a hundred years, High Minds have been trying to get around the Constitution. If we're charitable, maybe it's that they believe, like legal scholar Peter Strauss, that we must commit to the idea of a "living Constitution." A living Constitution is one that evolves, changes over time, and adapts to new circumstances, without being formally amended. On the one hand, the answer has to be yes: there's no realistic alternative to a living Constitution. Our written Constitution, the document under glass in the National Archives, was adopted two hundred and twenty years ago. It can be amended, but the amendment process is arduous.[318]

It's so tough to change the Constitution, goes the argument. It's too rigid. To adapt, Strauss suggests, we have to undertake intellectual gymnastics and abandon the *original meaning*, which is to say, *its meaning*.

> Meanwhile, the world has changed in incalculable ways. The nation has grown in its territory, and its population has multiplied several times over. Technology has changed, the international situation has changed, the economy has changed, social mores have changed, all in ways that no one could have foreseen when the Constitution was drafted. And it is just not realistic to expect the cumbersome amendment process to keep up with these changes.[319]

As we have devoted a good chunk of this volume to ideas like emergence and evolution, Strauss's case seems plausible. Still, I don't think Strauss fully appreciates federalism's power in helping to resolve issues surrounding the supposed rigidity of the Constitution. The Framers designed it to be rigid primarily in its constraint of *federal power*, though not in its constraint of the states or the people. The operating assumption is that the federal government needs to be able to evolve with the times. We've shown that if the federal government does considerably less, it's the states that can evolve with the times. So can regions and counties and wards.

We can probably attribute the idea of the living Constitution to President Woodrow Wilson, who, during his presidency, was the principal architect of so many destructive policies, both constitutional and unconstitutional. According to Randy Barnett, Wilson used to join clubs but immediately set about seizing on emergency provisions that "could be wielded to make the system more efficient, hierarchical, and subject to its own wishes."[320] If that didn't work, he'd simply rewrite those charters. Very early on, Wilson never let a document get in the way of his High Modernism.

In fairness to Peter Strauss, though, even if we don't find agreement in the idea that the Constitution ought to be a "living" document, we agree with this from Strauss: "The good news is that we have mostly escaped [the predicament of federal power], albeit unselfconsciously. Our constitutional system, without our fully realizing it, has tapped into an ancient source of law, one that antedates the Constitution itself by several centuries. That ancient kind of law is the common law."[321]

As regards the Common Law, my only quibble with Professor Strauss is the idea that we have escaped this predicament; from where I sit, we're sitting squarely within it. And I fear only the threat of collapse can dislodge us from it. We have only just begun to realize the real power of the Common Law.

UNCHAIN THE COMMON LAW

The best form of law we have is the one that has been utterly suppressed and limited: The Common Law. In the English-speaking world, the Common Law has survived for more than a thousand years. It's a form of law that is not so much about building utopias with guns, but rather about settling disputes and enforcing agreements.

Legal scholar and computer scientist Nick Szabo has written extensively about how Statute Law and the Common Law have conflicted. In particular, he reminds us that the Romans built roads to manage their empire in all directions, but in doing so, the empire paved over more flexible and adaptive forms of law:

> The Anglo-Norman legal idea of jurisdiction as property and peer-to-peer government clashed with ideas derived from the Roman Empire, via Justinian's legal code and its elaboration in European universities, of sovereignty and totalitarian rule via a master-servant or delegation hierarchy. By the 20th century, the Roman idea of hierarchical jurisdiction had won mainly, especially in political science, wherein government is usually defined in terms such as "sovereign" and "a monopoly of force."[322]

One can't help but think about how far back the
worship of power by High Minds extends. One can't help
but wonder if collapse is the only opportunity to forever
change our institutions' structure to inoculate us from High
Modernism. We need not emphasize this point because
Szabo does it for us:

"Totalitarianism in the nineteenth and twentieth
centuries was "inspired and enabled by the Roman-derived
procedural law, according to Szabo. He continues:

> The accompanying political structures — encom-
> passing Napoleon, the Csars, the Kaisers, Commu-
> nist despots, the Fascists, the National Socialists,
> not to mention the vast bureaucracies of 'demo-
> cratic' countries — should cause us to reconsider
> our commitment to Justinian government. The
> master-servant dominance hierarchy, says Szabo,
> has been better suited to military organization than
> to legal organization. But even that is starting to
> change.[323]

If I might be so bold, Szabo is suggesting that it's the
very form of law we prefer that has done the most damage
to our society.

The alternative, as we've said, is the Common Law.
This form minimizes frictions among people and uses
resulting case law to create a more highly localized, relevant, and proven body of law in the context of real human
interaction. It is not, like many statutes, contrived in the
vapors of imagination. At root, though, *frictions* are ultimately disputes based on alleged injuries or violations of
another's person or property. So, law that emerges from
settling disputes creates precedents or customary laws. As
legal scholar John Hasnas explains,

"[T]o avoid running headlong into Hume's is-ought
problem — one must show that spontaneous orders
advance a legitimate moral value more effectively than do
constructed orders. They do. That value is peaceful cooper-

ation."[324]

Spontaneous order, also referred to as emergent order, can be contrasted with planned orders in that the former arises through voluntary self-organization. Customary or Common Law comes out of the frictions that invariably arise as people self-organize. Planned orders almost always require a design for group behavior, predetermined by an individual or small group of individuals. Hasnas points out that planned orders frequently require violations of the people's unenumerated rights, especially in that peaceful cooperation rarely flows from Statute Law, that residue of Rome.

Note also that a robust, rigorous Common Law is potentially better at protecting the environment than Statute Law. It's so much easier for a few legislators to be captured and their statutes frozen in amber by special interests. For example, a polluter might meet some statutory minimum and still pollute. With the Common Law, all one has to do is prove nuisance or injury based on a preponderance of the evidence, which is determined not by a blanket policy, but on a case-by-case basis.

The same can be said for regulation. Certain kinds of regulation can grow out of Common Law legal precedents, while others can grow out of the need to guard against liability. Such is 'bottom-up' regulation, which is highly relevant to circumstances of time and place. Bottom-up regulation gives both progressives and conservatives what they want without a heaping helping of authoritarian power.

One of the most pragmatic things we can do, therefore, is restore the Common Law as the most basic form of American law.

BALANCE THE BUDGET

Future generations ought to be protected from debts accrued by earlier generations. "I say, the earth belongs to each of these generations during its course, fully and in its own right, wrote Thomas Jefferson to James Madison in 1789. "The second generation receives it clear of the debts and incumbrances of the first, the third of the second, and so on. For if the first could charge it with a debt, then the earth would belong to the dead and not to the living generation. Then, no generation can contract debts greater than may be paid during the course of its own existence."[325]

Because Congress is unwilling or unable to reduce the debt through ordinary means, it might be that only a constitutional amendment will do. Besides rigorous federalism, what else will be strong enough to rein in lawmakers' tendency to act in fiscally irresponsible ways? By now, everyone should know that members of Congress, and Presidents too, have every incentive to be fiscally irresponsible. They are in the business of buying votes through transfers. They are not in the business of taking away constituents' goodies. To fail on either count would mean the death of their political careers. And yet, this calculation is a trap.

As blogger Scott Alexander suggests:

> Only 9% of Americans like [Congress], suggesting a lower approval rating than cockroaches, head lice, or traffic jams. However, 62% of people who know who their own Congressional representative is [and] approve of them. In theory, it should be really hard to have a democratically elected body that maintains a 9% approval rating for more than one election cycle. In practice, every representative's incentive is to appeal to his or her constituency while throwing the rest of the country under the bus – something at which they apparently succeed.[326]

From a god's-eye view, every Congressperson ought to think only of the good of the nation. From within the system, you do what gets you elected.

We've seen legislatures escape this kind of thinking, but only rarely and only on the verge. It almost always takes a crisis of epic proportions. Examples include: New Zealand, which liberalized and cut back in the early 1980s under a democratic socialist Labor government; and Sweden, which liberalized and cut back after years of democratic socialism in both the 1970s and 1990s.

In short, if the U.S. experiences a sovereign debt crisis, the federal government will almost surely have to live within its means, if it can reconstitute itself. Who in their right mind would lend it anything after default? More importantly, a Balanced Budget Amendment is simply the right thing to do.

RESTRAIN THE WELFARE-WARFARE STATE

Two of the main Constitutional culprits are the vaunted General Welfare Clause and the Common Defense clause, both of which have allowed the federal government to grow beyond all reasonable proportions. Suppose the Constitution is to remain the law of the land. In that case, it will be vital to amend it such that these two clauses are clarified and limited, which would thereby limit the powers of the federal government. How these two clauses are defined will no doubt require enormous debate, but it is a debate that needs to happen if the republic is to go on.

My humble suggestion would be something along the following lines:

1. General Welfare is to be interpreted as those functions that simply cannot be dealt with by the states, or other smaller jurisdictions for specific functional reasons. Any spending justified under the General Welfare only applies to other federal functions enumerated in the Constitution.

2. Common Defense is to be interpreted only as what is required for states to organize cooperatively to

assist any other state in the event of a clear threat or imminent attack. The language would preclude global imperial ambitions, create a citizen 'peace dividend,' and make America more like Switzerland in fierce 'armed neutrality.'

These changes would have two primary effects: The first would be to push the question of state welfare down to the states, which would allow for competing systems. The second would be to make U.S. military power leaner and incentivized to maintain peace as opposed to the perpetuation of war.

Before turning away from the vain hope of restoring the Constitution, I should urge that what I have suggested above might not go far enough for New America's needs. As we will see, the first time around, there had been a titanic series of debates known as the Federalist Papers.

The winners got the America they wanted. But it appears the losers might have been right.

ET TU, BRUTE?

The winners write history, goes the saying. And though the words of the Antifederalists like Robert Yates (Brutus) are still with us, the Blue Church educational apparatus treats them as footnotes; at best honorable mentions. But Brutus's foresight is breathtaking.

Every one of his "Brutus I" concerns has hatched and grown into the monster he warned about.[327] If there is to be a next time around, a free people will do well to heed the words of this powdered wig from New York.

> A free republic cannot succeed over a country of such immense extent, containing such a number of inhabitants, and these increasing in such rapid progression as that of the whole United States.[328]

Brutus was worried about the fact of pluralism. He

knew that people of different cultural outlooks would struggle to have their ways of life respected and represented.

Therefore, for New America, stronger subsidiarity rules are a minimum requirement.

> Both [Greece and Rome], it is true, in process of time, extended their conquests over large territories of country; and the consequence was, that their governments were changed from that of free governments to those of the most tyrannical that ever existed in the world.

Brutus thought the United States would become an imperial power. The more it sought influence over territories beyond its borders, the more it would consume itself internally. Today there are nearly eight-hundred U.S. military bases around the world. Not only does the executive routinely exercise unconstitutional war powers, but the military-industrial complex also consumes resources that feed America's war machine.

Therefore, New America must, as we have suggested, declare its neutrality and resist entanglements abroad.

> [A republican form] must be confined to a single city, or at least limited to such bounds as that the people can conveniently assemble, be able to debate, understand the subject submitted to them, and declare their opinion concerning it.[329]

All politics is local, thought Brutus, or at least it ought to be. Too large a republic would mean that America's far-flung peoples would be distracted by faraway matters and pulled away from deliberating about matters affecting them most. Presidential elections are a spectacle. Hot button issues in another state pull our attention away. In the meantime, few can name their Congressman; fewer can name their State Senator. Less than 20 percent turns out for municipal elections. National politics distort our perceptions by minimizing that which affects us daily, but over which we have more control.

Therefore, New America must devise rules and processes that change the dynamics such that politics is more decentralized, and at the local level, more participatory.

> In every free government, the people must give their assent to the laws by which they are governed.[330]

If most of Walla Walla's relevant laws are made in Washington, D.C. then representative government is a mirage. It would be nigh impossible for the former to have any influence whatsoever over the latter. This is not merely a problem of distance versus localism, it is that there is no actual social contract, which is to say no real consent.

Therefore, institute consent-based systems within far smaller, more participatory jurisdictions, or cloud jurisdictions, as relevant.

> The territory of the United States is of vast extent; it now contains near three millions of souls, and is capable of containing much more than ten times that number.[331]

Today the territory of the United States contains more than ten times that number. Soon it will contain more. Since Brutus's time, the territorial United States grew and eventually annexed territory from Kentucky to California. Later it included Alaska and Hawaii. And yet the people of Fairbanks and Maui live under the thumb of people clustered in the Beltway.

Therefore, let three million be the maximum population for any territorial jurisdiction called a state. Any jurisdiction that exceeds that number must divide into two jurisdictions, in a process we'll call calving. All laws that apply to more than three million people must be specifically enumerated in the Constitution and comport with the doctrine of equality before the law.

- *Region — 30 million*
- *State — 3 million*

- *County — 300,000*
- *District — 30,000*
- *Ward — 3,000*

Whether or not the Constitution exists, let three million be the limit to the size of the most powerful jurisdiction. Superordinate regional authorities will be accountable for far less, and have specific powers. Subordinate jurisdictions, such as counties, will have less control than the state's authority, and it will be restricted to specific domains. Only dispute resolution will go to a superordinate authority, whose decisions are final.

> Now, in a large extended country, it is impossible
> to have a representation, possessing the sentiments,
> and of integrity, to declare the minds of the people,
> without having it so numerous and unwieldy, as to be
> subject in great measure to the inconveniency of a
> democratic government.[332]

In discussing the people's sentiments, Brutus is talking about their sovereignty as individuals and communities, not just popular sovereignty in the form of elections. This allergy to democratic government is a warning about the attenuation of community and individual sovereignty.

Therefore, majoritarian democracy should only be used at the most local feasible level and only when other more robust consensus mechanisms are inadequate.

> In a republic, the manners, sentiments, and interests
> of the people should be similar. If this be not the
> case, there will be a constant clashing of opinions;
> and the representatives of one part will be continual-
> ly striving against those of the other.

The idea here is that people can and should cluster according to their values and culture, and they are likely to do so according to proximity. Brutus foresaw titanic election cycles where politicians sought to bring radically diverse peoples under a single statutory monolith. Interestingly, not only was Brutus correct that there would be major clashes, he saw that these would tear the country apart.

Therefore, let people not only self-organize by geography and proximity, let them self-organize by culture and through technological means.

> In despotic government... standing armies are kept up to execute the commands of the prince or the magistrate, and are employed for this purpose when occasion requires: But they have always proved the destruction of liberty, and [are] abhorrent to the spirit of a free republic.[333]

Arguably, it is the apparatus of violence — both in standing armies and police working at the behest of politicians (magistrates) — that has turned America into an empire. We have even militarized our police to the point that we incarcerate more of our people and have more instances of police brutality than any of our peers. Brutus saw it coming a mile away.

Therefore, reorient our national defense and domestic police forces around peace and security. Make them directly accountable to citizens through partial or wholesale privatization.

> In so extensive a republic, the great officers of government would soon become above the control of the people, and abuse their power to the purpose of aggrandizing themselves, and oppressing them.[334]

Self-aggrandizement and abuse of power are as American as apple pie. Brutus saw that the special interest state would obscure the machinations of the powerful, to the point that it would become exceedingly difficult to 'throw the bums out.' Most people don't have a clue what the bums are up to most of the time; said bums are certainly not in our control. Our democracy creates the *illusion* of control, which keeps the people obedient in between elections.

Therefore, when it comes to the monied and the powerful, make their meetings and machinations completely transparent to the public.

> They will use the power, when they have acquired it,
> to the purposes of gratifying their own interest and
> ambition, and it is scarcely possible, in a very large
> republic, to call them to account for their miscon-
> duct, or to prevent their abuse of power.[335]

Brutus believed that centralization of authority would
cause too much power to be concentrated in the hands of
the few. The less power is concentrated in the hands of the
few, the less power there will be on auction.

Therefore, limit the power officials can put on auction.

Legal scholar Trevor Burrus believes that not only
were the antifederalists correct in their dire predictions,
but that their concerns could be combined into a single
pressing question: "Will a remote and distant government
that wields a large amount of power over a vast land and a
diverse people increasingly be seen as not representing the
people, and, in the process, sow discord between them?"[336]

Welcome to America.

And though the antifederalists have come to be known
as those who would stand in the way of progress — that
is, in the way of a document many revere — they are not
"knuckle-dragging philistines who allowed their parochial
concerns about states' powers to trump the good of the
nation."[337] No. They were wise. Now they are being vindicated, even as their voices are still being drowned out by the
sound of *Hamilton*:

> I practiced the law, I practic'ly perfected it
> I've seen injustice in the world and I've corrected it
> Now for a strong central democracy
> If not, then I'll be Socrates
> Throwing verbal rocks
> At these mediocrities[338]

And throw verbal rocks Hamilton did. Written ones too.
Of all the American Founders, we can conclude that,

although Madison made efforts to constrain the new republic's central power, Hamilton was the greatest exponent of centralized authority. He actively opposed the Bill of Rights. He was the High Mind of the Constitutional Convention. To the extent Hamilton got his way is the extent to which the republic has transmogrified into a creature that horrified the antifederalists: empire. With or without the Constitution, we'll need to tone down the Lin Miranda songs after collapse. And someone, somewhere will need to write some new songs about another New York sage almost nobody has heard of: a sage named Robert Yates.

10

PREPARE FOR THE POWER SHIFT

*Anarchy comes from the greek "an", mean-
ing without, plus "arkhos", meaning rulers.
Anarchy doesn't mean without rules, but
without rulers.*
  Brian Robertson, author of *Holacracy*

Morning Star Packing Company is a vast commercial empire of fruit. But not just any fruit: Tomatoes. Last time I counted, there were five Morning Star factories dotted around California's Central Valley. Telescope in upon any given plant, and you'll find caravans of trucks queueing up to deposit ripe red tomatoes at the top of a mound. That innovation, clean and straightforward, uses gravity to send the tomatoes down a flume into the guts of the processing facility. To and fro the trucks go, feeding a series of mechanized sorters, boilers, ph meters, and sundry computerized processing machines that ensure the quality and consistency of outputs: tomato sauce. Any time you buy spaghetti sauce, ketchup, or barbecue sauce in America, chances are you're getting products from Morning Star Packing Company.

It's difficult to describe the scale of these operations. But if the country had a vascular system of tomato products, the beating heart would be Morning Star. Depending on the season, there might be two thousand or more 'colleagues' teaming around the facilities. Up close, one will find people wearing either hard hats or hair nets and coverings. From far away, they all look like ants; the industrial might and ingenuity of these factories are impressive enough. But something more significant stands out about these operations.

They run entirely without bosses. In this way, cliché references to ants are warranted, because Morning Star operates like a super-organism: through simple rules and evolved algorithms, signaled in ants' case by pheromone trails. Of course, the analogy is imperfect insofar as ant brains aren't as sophisticated as human brains, which have 86 billion neurons compared to an ant's 250,000. So we are capable of processing far more information than ants. It's the combination of ant brains working according to good rules and roles that make super-organisms so interesting. Suppose we extend the analogy to the collective intelligence of human brains. When we do, we see interesting things materialize from the combined thoughts and efforts of autonomous colleagues swarming in teams to serve a mission.

None of this is meant to diminish the contributions of the founder, Chris Rufer. Despite training as an agricultural economist, the seventy-ish-year-old founder is something of a polymath. Rufer was the first to *show* me how the world can run on rules without rulers. As regards so many of the innovations around Morning Star, Rufer deserves credit. From the plants' design to the rules that govern them, you can find Rufer's influence. But he doesn't manage. He doesn't bark orders. He persuades. And with this persuasive leadership style, he has moved mountains. Of course, though he is a one-man information and innovation hub, he is not the only leader at Morning Star. Rufer, like everyone else, subordinates himself to the corporate operating system, the kernel of which is just two rules:

1. Never threaten anyone; and
2. Honor your agreements.

All of the other processes and protocols for decision making, role assignment, and disputing resolution are built on these two principles. And these sound a lot like ahimsa and satya.

If an industrial-scale company can create such abundance without a single boss assigning tasks or barking orders, further questions about the limits of democracy and hierarchy should shake us to our very cores.

SHIFT POWER

Imagine turning on your smartphone one morning to find only two apps: Red and Blue. It's bad enough that these are the only two choices. Usually only one works at a time — and not very well. This is more or less the social operating system upon which much of the developed world runs, certainly America. The democratic republic was a great innovation, but it was built atop a DOS (Democratic Operating System), which is two thousands years old. "It has been said that democracy is the worst form of government," Winston Churchill famously remarked, "except all those other forms that have been tried from time to time."[339] Is this the best that we can do?

Most people share Churchill's fatalistic view; it excuses the two-party status quo and its attendant popularity contests. Deep inside, we know that we can do better. The trouble is, dislodging ourselves from the old order will take a mass movement, an enormous crisis, or both. In any case, it's time to rethink governance.

Brian Robertson is the founder of Holacracy One, a consulting firm dedicated to helping companies transform using different internal operating systems to *change their relationship to power.* If you've never heard of holacracy, it's a style that differs rather dramatically from other forms of management. Instead of managers issuing orders and employees taking them, workers self-organize and self-manage. Those who adopt holacracy have to *dismantle* their management hierarchies. Most people are so inured to the firm's manager/managed model that many can find the transition difficult. But in time, the transformation allows the organization to scale and colleagues within the organization to thrive.

Brian Robertson is a friend. I've had the pleasure of talking with him deep into the night on many occasions. He once shared with me a chapter that editors had cut from his successful book, *Holacracy*, before its publication. I want to share some of those ideas with you, because they're too important to have been cut. We're going to crib a lot of the ideas from that very chapter, even as I put things in my distinct way. Still, you can think of this as something of a tribute to Robertson's cut chapter. First, though, a brief detour.

GROK THE NATURE OF SYSTEMS

The universe is full of systems. They're so prevalent, in fact, that most of us probably think we know them when we see them. But a rough and ready definition can't hurt. We can start simple and build outward. To wit: *a system is a collection of elements related in ways that work together.* For example, a solar system is a collection of planets around the sun. The Internet is a collection of computers connected by a set of protocols. A cell is a collection of smaller elements that do work in the organs of the human body. We could go on, but things don't get interesting until we start to see the differences *between* systems.

Distinguishing between different types of systems can get confusing, if not boring, so I'll sacrifice subtlety and get to the point. Consider a three-part distinction: *simple, complicated, and complex* systems.

- *Simple.* There is little or no change, variability, or interconnection among the elements of a simple system. Cause and effect are clear. *Builder, meet hammer and nail.*

- *Complicated.* There are multiple, interconnected elements, but these are tightly coupled and work in a predictable, mostly linear fashion. *Mechanic, meet the 747 aircraft.*

- *Complex.* As with complicated systems, complex systems have multiple interconnected elements, but the interconnections are difficult if not impossible to understand in their totality. These systems are marked by non-linear relationships. *Mayor, meet Manhattan.*

Some examples are more intuitive than others.

The question of whether a system is *complicated* or *complex* is one we should consider carefully. For most people, the two words are more or less synonymous. For others, complex is just the degree of complication. But not here. We know one system can *seem* complex, while the other will *really be* complex.

A 747 is not complex in the sense we stipulated. That's because, despite the myriad parts and electronics, the 747 really only does a few things that boil down to this: fly people around safely. Yes, it has many different interconnecting parts, valves, wires, and gears — probably more than we could ever memorize. It is certainly a complicated system. But each part relates to any given other part in a predictable sequence of cause and effect.

We need something more to achieve complexity. In a living brain, the relationships among elements are dynamic. A staggering array of neurons fire in patterns, such that behaviors at one level of description somehow give rise to different phenomena at another. In other words, excitations in gooey gray matter give rise to a person's conscious, waking life. The patterns of interaction among the neurons are mostly unpredictable. 85 billion neurons can fire in any number of ways, with varying degrees of strength, affecting any number of other neurons. They self-organize. *That's* complexity.

Simple systems can appear complicated, too. Think of three long strings of Christmas tree lights. Pretend the lights are nodes and the three strings's power originates at one end connected to a live power strip. All three strings have several bulbs along the line and terminate in a bulb. If you were to drop all three strings at once into a tangle on the floor, they would seem complicated to a child that happens by. But you can untangle the strings and show that they are not complicated at all. In this case, we might consider the power source the super-ordinate node, and the bulbs all obeyed a simple command from the power source: "light up."

While three strings of tangled lights might look complicated, they are actually quite simple.

DIFFERENTIATE BETWEEN COMPLICATED AND COMPLEX

What, if anything, does this have to do with human systems? Let's start with a simple system that comprises only two periods as its elements (yes, like the end of this sentence). In this case, it's an organization with only two people. We can represent these two people as *nodes*.

.   .

Now, a line indicates interaction between the nodes. Arrows will tell us something about the nature of that interaction. Arrows that point at another node means "potential command." If there are no arrows, it means "potential collaboration or exchange."

If one of the nodes has a super-ordinate role in the system, the other will have a subordinate role. That means that one node issues commands while the other node carries them out (and perhaps reports relevant information back to the super-ordinate node). Such a relationship would look like this:

Pictured immediately above is a basic hierarchy.

On the other hand, if both nodes are autonomous, then the interaction between them may be one of exchange and/or cooperation. We call this a network:

The most significant difference between hierarchies and networks is the degree of autonomy possessed by any given node to interact or communicate with any other node in the system. The more comprehensive the interaction among nodes, the more "networked" the system is.

The number of possible actions in a hierarchy is limited to those actions permitted by the superordinate nodes. In other words, you can only do what the person upstairs allows you to do. But in a networked organization, your actions are unlimited — unless, of course, your actions fail to serve the mission. That means with networked organizations, such as holarchies, there is a far higher degree of autonomy among the nodes.

Because networks can handle a level of complexity greater than what the busiest node (smartest person) can handle, holarchies can scale beyond hierarchies. When you combine self-organization with scale, you get an organization that has undergone a transition from hierarchy to hive-mind.

SCALE HOLACRACY UP

Holacracy provides a *holonic* governance framework, where holonic means, roughly, *systems within systems*. In this way, a holacratic organization approximates a living organism instead of a machine to be 'run' in the Taylorite management style.

Practitioners aren't arranged by managers as cogs within a traditional org chart, but rather define their own functional roles within wider spheres of activity, or 'circles.' Just as cells make up organs within organisms, people have roles within teams within organizations. And though certain cells in the body (or roles in the organization) might arrange themselves into an 'executive function,' both the organism's and holacratic organization's brains are self-organizing.

At the risk of oversimplifying, let's briefly sketch out holacracy:

- *Mission.* This is why the organization exists at all and the end that all roles serve.

- *Holacracy Constitution.* This meta-charter sets out the relatively fixed protocols and fundamental rules that establish holacracy's open-source 'operating system.'

- *Tactical Meetings.* These are group processes for addressing one-off, operational issues in a formalized way, relevant to some functional sphere of activity.

- *Governance Meetings.* These are group processes for creating roles, making policies, or assigning ownership of responsibilities.

- *Transparent Data.* The inputs and output of governance meetings get recorded so that anyone can see the rules, roles, policies, and system interconnections at any time.

With holacracy, you take the hierarchy of titles and commands and reconfigure it into a heterarchy of work. Again, the work is clustered in circles, which are defined by their function. Maybe a circle has to do with marketing the organization. Within that circle, there are 'roles' for which individuals are accountable.

To whoever fills the role, accountability means authority — but not the authority of one colleague over another. It's the control of ownership over one's manner and mode of serving the mission. In this form of organization, nobody can tell you what to do. There are neither bosses nor managers, so you have to make your own decisions. It's up to you to figure out how best to serve in your roles, take action, and create value.

In governance meetings, a neutral facilitator invites each member of a circle to make proposals; for example, about how to update the organization's policies. This process makes every meeting radically participatory, relevant to one's role, and ensures that partners apply local knowledge. Practitioners iterate to solve problems. This evolutionary algorithm encodes continual adaptation into the organizational DNA. Over years of trial and error, the rules, roles, policies, and accountabilities get shaped and reshaped, even though the fundamental 'source code' is the Holacracy Constitution. The Holacracy Constitution is, of course, also open to revision and is available open source, but it changes more slowly than any given organization's policies. When an organization adopts holacracy, the current power holder (such as a CEO) cedes their authority to the process and gives up the right to be above the constitution.

Today, more than one thousand companies worldwide have adopted holacracy, which means they got rid of the traditional firm structure. They fired the managers. They dismantled the hierarchy. And instead of that hierarchy, holacracy turned these organizations into complex adaptive systems. Unlike hierarchies, complex adaptive organizations respond with relative autonomy to stimuli that are — for lack of a better way of putting things — *not quite right.* Practitioners call these "tensions." So, every part of the organization wants to get things flowing. To resolve tensions is to respect the law of flow — but also to realize the mission.

And that is a real power shift for which not everybody is ready. And yet most holacracy adopters love how liberated they feel, how empowered their colleagues are, and how much the culture of the organization is transformed. In time, partners become habituated in new patterns of interaction, notably different from the patterns one finds in traditional firms. The devil is, of course, in the proverbial details. Learning the system is rather like learning a team sport: You can't understand the game just by reading the rulebook, you have to get out there and practice. In doing so, practitioners can become real holacracy pros — increasing organization efficiency while helping the organization scale. But how far up can holacracy scale?

Outside of organizations and a couple of small municipalities, no one has tried holacracy. But arguably, the strongest candidate for a large-scale social operating system is holacracy, or something like it. Some are skeptical that holacracy can replace hierarchy. And it's no wonder: Command-and-control systems have been working for blue-chip companies and standing armies alike for centuries. But recall that in Part One, we took considerable pains to articulate the limits of hierarchy, especially in our discussion of Hayek's knowledge problem and Bar-Yam's complexity transition: "It begins with widespread individual action that transforms society," writes Yaneer Bar-Yam, "a metamorphosis of social organization in which leadership no longer serves the role it has over millennia. A different type of existence will emerge, affecting all of us as individuals and enabling us to live in a complex world."[340]

In a word: *teamwork.*

"To be successful in high complexity challenges requires

teamwork. Each team member performs one part of what needs to be done, contributing to the complexity and scale of what the team does while limiting the complexity each individual faces."[341]

Holacracy — or something similar to it — is a human organization system that can deal with complexity by applying superior team dynamics. Indeed, if we are to believe Brian Robertson, it might be possible for Holacracy to scale beyond the for-purpose organization. Robertson draws influence not only from his computer science background but from integral theorist Ken Wilber. In his philosophical work, Wilber expands on Arthur Koestler's holarchy; that is, the idea that systems can give rise to systems (that can give rise to systems) at different levels of description.

And with that, we come full holon. Robertson puts it best:

> If you have the right rules, the absence of top-down rulers doesn't remove order — it merely enables order to emerge dynamically from peer-to-peer interactions distributed throughout a system, one tension at a time. So by this definition, you could describe Holacracy as a rule system for humans working together in anarchy — with rules, but without rulers.[342]

Turns out that anarchy isn't all punk rock and Molotov cocktails. But keep in mind that as society becomes more complex, hierarchical governments running on DOS will have difficulty keeping up with the information processing demands. Meanwhile, practitioners of holacracy will be running their distributed organizations and changing their relationship to power. Maybe some in some variant lies the source code for a new era of rules without rulers.

DESIGN FOR EVOLUTION

It seems like something of a contradiction, but holacracy is a design for *evolution*, a process that creates its own designs. Evolution is thus a discovery algorithm.

"Evolution creates designs, or more appropriately, discovers designs, through a process of trial and error," writes economist Eric Beinhocker. "Evolution is a method for searching enormous, almost infinitely large spaces of possible designs for the almost infinitesimally small fraction of designs that are 'fit' according to their particular purpose and environment."[343]

One can only be a 'market fundamentalist' to the extent that one is a Darwinian. Guilty as charged. Not only is life or death a binary proposition for organisms, so also is the success and failure of some mission-based unit we call an organization. Either revenues exceed costs, or they do not. The critical insight here is that no person or group should ever try to run society like a single organization (or organism), but that the organization should exist within clusters of interdependent organizations. The 'holonic' feature of holacracy — systems within systems — might allow for a scalable solution to accelerating evolution inside and outside organizations. That means, even if it's impossible to intelligently design New America, intelligent protocols like Holacracy can unleash evolution's discovery algorithm.

UNDERSTAND EVOLUTION FROM THE INSIDE

Before we begin our exploration of evolution at society's scale, let's revisit how evolution works. Evolutionary theory identifies four aspects necessary for the discovery algorithm to work its design wonders:

- *Encoding*. How some designs and features get recorded for reuse through time.

- *Expression.* How designs and features appear in their environments.

- *Variation.* How designs get altered, say, through mutation or changes to code.

- *Testing.* How or whether designs and features persist in time, thanks to environmental factors

These aspects show up in the biological domain and determine an organism's characteristics. Almost always, the ecosystem helps shape those characteristics.

So, DNA is responsible for coding the design specs. Then, our cells decode the DNA and express the design in the wider environment. But as the environment presents various challenges to the organism's existence, it must find a way to vary the code, such that the species can adapt, or else it will die and potentially go extinct. (In mammals, that's sexual reproduction and random mutation.) Finally, designs are tested to some degree or other by factors in the environment. This process determines the organism's 'fitness.' Fitness-friendly designs continue or become amplified, while unfit designs get culled or left behind. We know this process as *natural selection.*

When these four aspects start to function together within a fitness landscape, they unleash an enormously creative set of processes. This process of design without a designer has given rise to all the diversity of life on this planet. But it doesn't always have to do with biology. The same process occurs within the economy and society, too. To repeat: Evolution takes some code, expresses it, tests the results to amplify fit designs, culls the rest, and varies the code to find even better designs. This process continues iteratively through ever more significant refinements to achieve creative emergence. And as long as the environment continues to change, the process never stops.

We know that this process occurs within organizations that use holacracy. When Robertson says that holacracy is evolution-powered, this is not just a metaphor. For example, colleagues sometimes process 'tensions' by changing the rules. These governance meeting outputs mean the organization is encoding a new design — its policies, roles, accountabilities, domains, and so on. Because these changes are carried out continually relative to tensions — and not master plans — the organization evolves.

In a company that uses holacracy, the workers who fill some organizational role decipher that code and express it in the world. The results get tested either internally or in the market. Fit designs are selected and kept. To the extent that some design is less than ideal for some purpose, tensions will surface. Our human capacity to sense and process these tensions gives us a way to vary the code.

Some might think that in human systems, the process isn't so Darwinian. That is to say, people making decisions isn't analogous to random mutation and mating dances. But in meaningful ways, it is, because every change to the code will either succeed or fail. The question of success or failure, therefore, lies at the heart of the algorithm. So, each successive iteration through governance gives us a new variation on our organization's code, and each variation gets further expressed and tested in an ongoing process of development. Evolutionary innovation either carries the organization forward to the mission, or it doesn't.

"With Holacracy, no single person designs the organization, and no single group sits down and designs the organization," says Robertson. "Rather, an organization's design is an emergent result of an evolutionary algorithm — and that's a good thing because when it comes to finding fit designs, evolution is much smarter."[344]

RECODE THE CORPORATION

Most people don't realize it, but the fundamental problems of hierarchy originate in the corporate structure itself. If you look at the typical C Corp, it has hierarchy baked into it. The legal structure itself creates it. You have an executive board, executive team, and sometimes shareholders. To move away from the problems endemic to hierarchy, you have to recode the organization right down to its legal structure.

Tom Thomison, an early co-founder of Holacracy One, is an innovator in this space. Thomison has devoted much of his career to what he calls a 'power shift.' There is no board of directors in a power shifted organization, no CEO, no C-Suite executives, no bosses, no managers. Everything is self-organizing. And after Tom helped found Holacracy One, he went on to found Encode, an organization dedicated to helping found for-purpose organizations.

Encode helps transform organizations from traditional non-profit and for-profit structures into power shifted organizations. Once these organizations are power shifted, they self-organize. Such includes:

- New legal rules shift the framework from workers as 'employees' to workers as 'stakeholders,' operating in a structure that fosters engagement and entrepreneurial opportunities for everyone. These new models facilitate changes in the ever-changing dynamics of risks and rewards for each individual as they contribute to the corporate purpose.

- Novel agreements encode the distribution of decision-making authority and make equity profit sharing proportional to each colleague, so far as they can add value. In this way, power shifted organizations are *not* egalitarian. They build in proportionality: *From each according to the value he receives, to each according to her contribution to realizing that value.*

- New relational models and cultural tools such as authentic relating allow for the organization to integrate diverse individuals in an environment of complexity and pluralism.

These models, which function more like meritocratic cooperatives, align the incentives, and bring out the best in people. Legacy models, including democratic organizations, suffer from the same problems that democracy does. Power-shifting organizations allows us to realize the aspirations of democracy without all of the pathologies.

The beauty of all of this is that we can start transitioning *now*. The only problem is that these models are not the current default, either in the eye of the law or the average person. They're mostly unknown, which can be scary to startup founding teams and to investors, and not really on the radar of regulatory agencies responsible for approving or taxing corporations.

In this way, the tax code privileges the hierarchical corporation. Some default models such as the limited liability corporation can be adapted to create power shifted organizations. We will all do well to find ways to raise awareness of these models and reduce the legal cost of adoption. Because there is no single point of ownership or locus of power, neither executives nor founders are given undue power or a disproportionate share. In some cases, executives simply don't exist. Everyone serves the organization's purpose.

"No longer are we dependent on inspired, progressive leaders," says Thomison, "we can be inspired by something else, something greater than ourselves."[345]

With Encode's alternative corporate structure, self-organization is coded in from the start, which is a completely different way to conceive and grow businesses. Even the employee, as such, goes away under this model. Partners, equal before the rules, are rewarded according to their contribution, and each is empowered to serve the mission in her own way. Such makes it possible for one person to be a fractional partner in multiple enterprises.

For-purpose enterprises will be healthier for society,

too, since there isn't likely to be a significant concentra-
tion of shares among any single partner in the enterprise.
You're more likely to see a distribution that balances the
two paleolithic senses of 'fairness' that might otherwise be
at odds, where one sense is *fairness as equal outcomes* and the
other is *fairness as proportionality*. The first sense means that
one has an emotional reaction to the idea that someone gets
too much of the firms' revenues, when someone else has
too little. The second is an emotional reaction to knowing
that someone carried a larger share of the work (or risk,
or innovation) but isn't being rewarded accordingly. Power
shifted enterprises have a bias for proportionality. Founders
don't get some fixed portion of the pie that they get to keep
when the company has been grown, years later, by others'
efforts. And those who work hard and have good ideas that
result in the company's growth are rewarded according to
their contribution. It's an omni-win set of cooperative rules.

People with a traditional 'conservative' outlook might
not like power shifted organizations at first because they
have an old-school idea about how rewards should flow to
investors and founders. People with a more socialist ideological outlook might not like private corporations at all, but to
the extent that they tolerate them, will prefer that rewards
flow to 'need' as opposed to value creation. It doesn't
matter. People across the political spectrum can experiment
with different models for pay and dividing shares. If they
were to adopt an integral liberal mindset, most would find
that the default power shift model strikes a healthy balance,
whether your moral dispositions skew in the direction of
equal outcomes or proportional contributions.

Indeed, I suspect that if power shifted for-purpose organizations predominated, we'd see not just a bigger middle
class, but one that pushes our concept of middle class life
into higher standards. Income inequality would still be with
us, of course, but it would look much more like the scaling
laws we see in the natural world, because these models work

with the Law of Flow. As we have said, whether its information, energy, or economic flows, the distribution of every
living system is determined by vascular patterns, like those
of tree branches or river tributaries. They calve and change
to create new flows. Naturally, these branches and arms
are not, and can never be, equal. Within a self-organizing
organization, the same processes can be unleashed, unstop-
pered, and un-dammed by c-suite executives who once had
multi-year plans.

Another exciting aspect of power shifted organizations
is that stakeholders can commit to different amounts of
time. Someone might work 100 percent of her time for a
single organization; another might spend 20 percent. Both
contribute differential value per unit of time, and each
contributes a different amount of time on net. Assuming
100 percent of one's time is forty hours, we can imagine the
20 percent contributor working for three or four different
organizations as a stakeholder if they choose. And as digital
ledgers begin to track the focused work outputs, compensation can be adjusted each pay period dynamically.

Go Teal and Scale

Holacracy is just one example of a bigger trend in organizational change, and this trend can and should extend to
legacy models of governance. Frederic Laloux, in his book
Reinventing Organizations, borrows the term 'teal' from philosopher Ken Wilber's Integral Theory.[346] Teal designates a
point of psycho-social development in which persons or
groups are attuned to complexity and understand how to
lead amid the flows of evolution and change. The teal organization movement is guided by three notable principles,
which Laloux has reverse-engineered and distilled from his
research findings: *self-organization*, *evolutionary purpose*, and
wholeness.[347]

Self-organization means that power and control are

embedded throughout the organization, and are no longer tied to a few top leaders' positions. We can think of *evolutionary purpose* as a mission, but the mission can't be random. We must tune the mission to the 'fitness landscape,' which is composed of human desires. But human desires don't just lie in the hearts of customers. In these power shifted models, partners can reclaim their *whole selves*, including their ideas and hopes for the future. People feel free to express themselves more fully, bringing positivity, energy, and creativity to work.

Companies such as Morning Star Packing Company, Valve Software, and G. L. Gore forged unique ways of expressing these principles. But the general idea is that all are enormously successful and none is organized as a dominance hierarchy.

In truth, governments are just another kind of organization. And if this is true, then there are good reasons to think that if organizations can make a peaceful transition from hierarchies to self-organizing entities, so too can governments. In this respect, it's time for the power shift. The more people learn how to function in self-organized environments, the more prepared they will be to transition out of the conditions of dominance hierarchies, whether corporate or government.

MAKE MONEY THE RIGHT WAY

In the early 1900s, the German sociologist Franz Oppenheimer introduced an under-appreciated distinction which is highly relevant today. Oppenheimer described two approaches to acquiring wealth, which he called the "economic means" and the "political means."[348] I call those who employ these approaches Makers and Takers.

Through the economic means, you generate value through your labor or exchange your labor's fruits for another's. The political means is more or less the forced appropriation of the fruits of others' work. To steal, to raid, or to commit fraud are all obvious ways in which you can take the fruits of another's labor. But there are subtler acts, too, such as externalizing costs, which is to say foisting them on others without their consent. When a polluter legally puts gunk in the river you live on, he's a Taker, because if a company saves money by dumping this way, others pay the cost in the form of smell, dying fish, or cleanup. Another neighbor, a farmer, might have lower yields from poisoned fields. When a bank executive lobbies for a bailout or an interest group bellies up to the subsidy trough, that's political means, too. Ordinary taxpayers not only pick up the tab but have to function in a less competitive landscape. The Takers live at the expense of the Makers.

Society starts to unravel when the political means outpace the economic means, i.e. when the Takers take too much. And in keeping with our biological metaphor, we know that too much parasitism can lead to imbalances in an ecosystem. Indeed, we've explored the mechanisms of evolution within an organization using holacracy. Now we can broaden the exploration to society and the market. How do evolutionary processes show up there, at the level of the ecosystem?

As I have said, organizations have internal rules, strategies, and processes, which we refer to as their DNA. The organization expresses this DNA via staff members' and colleagues' actions as it goes about its business each day. In the marketplace, these organizations live or die by their capacity — sustainably — to take in more energy (revenue) than they expend in the process (cost). Those that generate revenue over costs grow and spread. Those that don't wither and die. Yet those who cry out against 'profits' are trying to suspend evolution itself.

It's tempting to dust off our hands and end the analysis there: *The market is an evolutionary environment in which organizations (people working together) create value or die.* But to understand the situation with any subtlety, we have to go back to our discussion of Makers and Takers. In other words, to get a grip on the sort of selection at play in pre-collapse America, we have to understand how some firms generate profit. In short: Too many use political means, so human systems in New America will have to reduce opportunities for exploiting them.

Those using political means improve their lot by taking from others, almost always in collusion with authorities. I pointed this out in Part One, but it bears repeating: Firms that generate a profit by economic means don't shift costs; they satisfy customer desires. They create wealth. Firms that generate a profit by political means displace costs and collude with the state to put a regulatory boot on upstarts and competitors, or otherwise take corporate welfare. They destroy wealth. The former improves our lives and move our economy forward. The latter creates little or no net value and exists at the expense of other firms and taxpayers.

The beauty of free and voluntary exchange between two parties — without coercion — is that they have, by definition, to leave *both* parties better off. If either party doesn't see value in the transaction, *it won't happen.* In exchange, we are creating value for each other. One might question another's judgment or challenge their values in some cases, but the transaction is worth it *to them.* That means that Maker organizations are leaving everyone they touch better off. As long as they conduct *all* of their business transactions strictly in this manner — with customers, vendors, employees, and all other stakeholders happy — they are operating through economic means, and their profits are justified. Their existence is prosocial.

MAKE POLITICS AS WE KNOW IT OBSOLETE

Generating value through production and peaceful inter-action is hard. That's why so much of human history has involved political means. Just think of the lords who served royalty while the serfs worked the land and created the value. It wasn't until the dawn of the 19th century that entrepreneurs began to tinker and toil. Eventually, they got out from the yoke of the parasite classes, claiming a Divine Right. After millennia of modest progress, world-wide economic growth exploded upward around 1800 and never stopped, which gave us what economic historian Dierdre McCloskey calls "The Great Enrichment."[349] In other words, growth turned exponential. And so did living standards.

Relative to the medieval baronies and feudal societies, there has been tremendous improvement in the institutions that protect private property, entrepreneurial capital, and resources of those who work to create value. Along with the Great Enrichment, we have seen some mechanisms to protect the Makers, but we have also seen the political process become co-opted by Takers. From the perspective of shorter time horizons, the ebb and flow between the economic and political means is more pronounced.

And yet shifting power from parasitism to prosocial behavior is possible. We should note that evolution doesn't weigh in except on the question of success or failure. Lampreys, eye-infesting worms, and feminizing barnacles are all "successful" species. But we can imagine a shift in the selection function for organizations. In other words, through better rules, tools, and culture, we can make the economic means more accessible; and make the political means more costly. The more that selection function shifts to favor those people and firms who generate value through voluntary transactions, the greater abundance there will be for any given person.

But we have a long way to go. In America, as around the world, there are two kinds of wealthy people: those who get rich through making our lives better, and those who get rich by using the political process to transfer wealth from others. You'll find Takers anywhere officials have the power to pick winners and losers in the economy — whether through regulations, subsidies, or favors. Likewise, you'll discover Makers anywhere people are free enough to get an honest enterprise off the ground. Trouble is, the rules don't always favor the Makers.

"The organizations that come into existence will reflect the opportunities provided by the institutional matrix," said Douglass North, in his 1993 prize lecture. "That is, if the institutional framework rewards piracy then piratical organizations will come into existence; and if the institutional framework rewards productive activities then organizations — firms — will come into existence to engage in productive activities."[350]

Great civilizations emerge where Makers can flourish. Once-great civilizations declined as the Takers started to outnumber the Makers. Greece. Rome. Britain. America will soon follow. In these prosperous centers, the firewall between business and the state had been dismantled. All lost ground because they succumbed to the influence of Takers — also known as special interests. While many believe that authorities should wield government power for the greater good, most of what gets done in the public's name is *politics without romance.*

To make obsolete the political means, we have to make politics as we know it obsolete, and that prospect might make some readers feel uncomfortable. But as long as we feel uncomfortable confronting the political means — the lobbyists, the backroom deals, the unholy alliance between power and money to create exclusionary cartels — the more we will continue to blame 'capitalism' for all our woes when the problems lay with politics itself all along. The beneficiaries of the status quo will fight tooth and nail to keep it. One silver lining in collapse is that the Takers will no longer have access to any transfer regime. But what if the collapse is not severe enough to shake the Takers from the institutions?

Invert the Perverse Logic of Collective Action

Political scientist Mancur Olson nailed it when he argued that our republic — most any republic — will turn into a corporate state due to the problem of special interests. If you can pass a regulation or subsidy, some small group is going to win. The small group that stands to benefit most from a policy also has the greatest incentive and lowest cost to organize. The benefits are concentrated (on the interest group), but the costs are diffuse (we all pay marginally higher taxes and marginally higher prices). We The People have neither the incentive to, nor can we afford to, organize against every group behind this little legislative tweak or that. But the tweaks add up. The costs mount but go mostly unseen. Special interest groups almost always win. The result is tremendous deadweight loss. Representative democracy ends up serving the Takers.

What if we could invert the perverse logic of concentrated benefits and dispersed costs? Olsen might have been delighted to see Uber and AirBnB. They showed us how things can change. These entrepreneurs found legal gray areas to exploit, and by exploiting those gray areas, they broke the politically-created cartels of the taxi and hotel industries. Ridesharing and couchsurfing are here to stay. But these examples of Makers prevailing over Takers are rare. Are they rare because there are too few legal gray areas, or because there are too few subversive innovators? I cannot say. I hope we can all become subversive innovators, especially if collapse is in the offing.

In my 2018 book, *The Social Singularity*, I wrote that "every innovation is an act of subversion."

> Just before Satoshi Nakamoto published his 2008 white paper on the rudiments of Bitcoin, it must have been a bit like holding a lit match over dry forest underbrush. Did he linger for a moment before hitting enter?
>
> Maybe in that moment he closed his eyes and saw flashes from the future: of a thousand pimply geeks becoming millionaires overnight. Of Ross Ulbricht, Silk Road's Dread Pirate Roberts, being led away in handcuffs. Of mutant strains, copycats, forks, and tokens competing in an entire ecosystem of crypto-currencies as in a digital coral reef. Of booms and busts and troughs of disillusionment.
>
> We don't know. But we do know one thing about Satoshi Nakamoto: he hit enter.
>
> A coder strings together lines of instruction. Once he publishes his code, there is a potential butterfly effect. Technological change, happening moment to moment around us, adds up quickly. Before you know it, people everywhere are taking rides with strangers. Bangladeshi women ply their produce trade on smartphones. Every wingbeat is a potential gale of creative destruction. A billion lines of code, created by millions of coders, represent innumerable wingbeats. Some are amusements. Others are bold experiments in social transformation.[351]

As we've suggested, the government sees cryptocur-rency as a threat to its monopoly on money. Government officials guard this power because it enables them to pay for anything they desire while passing the true costs onto citizens. Whether indirectly through inflation or directly through taxation, we pick up the tab. Increased spending (concentrated benefits) and diffuse costs (inflation, which reduces the value of savings) are hallmarks of the current money monopoly.

But as the authorities fight against cryptocurrencies, they might eventually find the tables turned: The beneficiaries of these diffuse systems are legion, and spread throughout the world. The costs of enforcing prohibitions on cryptocurrency are borne primarily by authorities, and this will get more and more expensive as more and more people adopt these technologies. This problem will be compounded as the value of the dollar goes down and down. As the enforcers go deeper into debt, enforcement will become nigh impossible.

Such developments turn the logic of political action on its head. Thanks to technological progress that introduces new rules and new tools, along with the distributed nature of networks, we may no longer be beholden to this regime that thrives at the intersection of power and money. We will see a power shift as the Eros Feminine crashes against the beachhead as the tide comes in. The old order chokes in the swells and gets pulled away in the undertow.

KEEP COERCION CAGED

I have said that the Masculine force is coercive. I have also said that it is essential to bring it into balance with the Feminine. This doesn't mean we have to jettison the Masculine entirely, nor does it mean we have to get rid of coercion, either. Our hypothesis is that we can cease to *initiate* violence against the innocent. And we should.

Society and open markets sometimes require the occasional use of self-defense or violence to exact just compensation. But by now, it should be easy to see how placing such power with a central monopoly provider is problematic. The Leviathan Formulation and the Great Temptation required that we depend on benevolent authorities, which we have shown live in the land of unicorns, faeries, and angels.

Decentralization's lessons will become more salient as we understand the limits of centralization and appreciate the benefits of decentralization. When we're talking about the authority to lawfully coerce others through the threat of violence, at the very least, it's a question to be taken seriously.

"The modern state is a compulsory association which organizes domination,"[352] wrote Max Weber. Such an association ought to get a great deal more scrutiny than it does, whatever we conclude about the need for it. We have to figure out how to keep coercion in its place.

DISTRIBUTE ULTIMATE AUTHORITY

About those angels: When thinking about how best to improve government, most people's first instinct is to argue that we need better authorities. These authorities would then craft better laws, because they would be either morally upright, public-spirited, or wise. Few consider that what we need is to question such fundamental assumptions. "When I hear a call for better government," warns Brian Robertson, "it sounds much like the call to improve organizations by hiring a better CEO, or better managers, or installing better leadership development programs."[353]

The same fundamental assumptions are operating in each of these perspectives: the current underlying operating system — hierarchy — should be taken as given. But maybe we don't need a single point of authority. If we distribute decision making authority and unleash emergent order, then top-down hierarchy with its attendant pathologies will go away. "Can our societies benefit from that same shift," asks Roberston, "or do we just need 'better managers'?"[354]

The power to threaten violence is centralized in government as we know it; that power will be purchased by those with the means to purchase it. And that is what we are seeing in America today: Well-funded financial institutions and corporations don't want to face failure due to bad business practices, or failure to create real customer value.

Recall that, along with James C. Scott, I argued that the state started as a protection racket. Is it any different now? If anyone else extracted resources by force from people to shower them on favored groups, we would call that a mafia. But when the government does it, legitimacy confers a veneer of justice. And yet intuitively, we know that something is wrong with crony capitalism. Corporations buy power on the auction block. Politicians trade favors and buy votes using corporate-sponsored war chests, precisely because the power is there to be bought. *It's legal, so it must be right* — just as it was legal for the patricians to do what they wanted with the plebs, the royals to do what they wanted with the serfs, and the aristocrats to do what they want with the peasants. *But we have democracy!* So the political class can do what it wants with taxpayers. We tend to hope the right leader, the right law, or the right movement will stop it. So far, it hasn't. *We have to get money out of politics* they cry, hoping that the ring will pass from the hands of the corrupt to be worn by an ideologue. Heaven help us. That might actually be worse.

The Ring tempts Gandalf and the good little hobbits in *The Lord of the Rings* from time to time. They are good, right? So the power to "rule them all" could be used for good, as well. Most people feel something like this when they seek to deploy the power of the state. But, of course, one of the critical lessons of Tolkien's story is that no matter one's intentions, no good comes from wielding that much power. If you can handle the spoiler, recall that the wizard Gandalf rejects the Ring's power. The only thing to do with that kind of power is to cast it back into the fires whence it came.

Tolkien is a great one — but like many greats, he cribbed the idea; in this case, from Plato. Even though Plato is perhaps the original High Mind, his channeling

Gyges' story and his invisibility ring started one of history's most fascinating philosophical conversations. In one of the dialogues in Plato's *Republic*, the central question is whether it is better to *be* just or to *seem* just. Glaucon makes a convincing case that the power to act with impunity rewards our deepest desires, which are frequently at odds with justice. That's because 'justice' is something like an agreement we come to, a kind of concord. The concord is valuable because it keeps a certain order and security; we tend to accept it because we don't want to be the victim. Our justice systems exist because we want to keep people from breaking the agreement or abusing the rules. It's a cooperation game, with the occasional defector. The ring invites defection.

Socrates might argue that what is true, beautiful, and good about humanity doesn't involve indulging our basest desires. And there's something to that, to be sure, something decidedly human about our ability to reach for the sublime. Yet there's something human about our baser desires, too. The Vedics understood this. One of the reasons we have set about expanding liberalism into active practice is to create a learning, changing culture. Moving from our lower natures to our higher spirits means we are also more likely to develop better tools and better rules. The reverse is also generally true. "It is, rather, an intuitive discernment that transforms," writes scholar of religions Huston Smith, "turning the knower eventually into that which she knows."

But even if Glaucon's view of humanity is wrong — that is, that everyone would have sex with your spouse or take your stuff if they could — what we might imagine is that people fall along a continuum from Mother Teresa to Mussolini. We might even grant that the longer someone wears the ring of power, they will feel the gravity, continually being pulled *away* from Mother Teresa and *toward* Mussolini. And so we should. The political process is more likely to select for those who operate closer to the Mussolini end. But even if politics biased choosing, we would still have a situation in which the national voting lottery hits from time to time on a sociopath. Alas, the system selects for sociopathy. Thus, every election cycle is an opportunity to pick a Stalin or a Mussolini or a Mao. And they don't give a shit about your version of justice.

It's time to allow the centralized power of current governments to dissolve. Collapse might just be the opportunity, the liminal event that lets something more beautiful and more humane rise from the ashes of empire. In the transition, we can allow new methods of achieving order to emerge, as well. These methods won't involve purchasing legislators, and might just include all peaceful relations between consenting adults, bringing Eros Feminine into balance. Still, everything will be subject to the design algorithm of evolution. As long as the selection mechanism is value creation and not legal predation, humanity is going to be alright.

11

BUILD A FRAMEWORK OF UTOPIAS

*More decadences, more burgeonings have
followed one another in Clarice. Populations
and customs have changed several times;
the name, the site, and the objects hardest to
break remain. Each new Clarice, compact
as a living body with its smells and its
breath, shows off, like a gem, what remains
of the ancient Clarices, fragmentary and
dead.*

Italo Calvino, from *Invisible Cities*

Whitecaps and sea foam greet us in the foreground. As
we approach, silver shafts rise over blue-green waters, creating an impossible cityscape. Skyscrapers cast a distorted
mirror image of themselves on the water. Their spires glint
in the sun, but they appear to terminate in great hexagonal platforms down around their bases. It's as if Poseidon
plucked structures from Dubai or Singapore and set them
down upon the platforms, arranged in logical, interlocking
patterns.

These configurations reveal the city's contingent nature,
as each great hexagon can itself float away or be broken
down into smaller units. The power of exit is built into the

city; what holds the floating city together, then, are network effects. Value is drawn to value. If not? Here today, gone tomorrow. All one has to do is vote with his boat. This city is an evolving ecosystem, morphing under continuous revisions. As with any city, that which is profitable persists — only now agreements tie everything together.

On the outer rim, glassy fullerenes, clustered like barnacles, collect light for the greenhouses, fish farms, and algae processing facilities they contain. From afar, they float together in such a way that mimics the ridge of some coral reef, or perhaps fungi and lichen in a primeval forest. People of all races teem and bustle in the waterways between structures. One can see grass and trees planted among staggered architectural shelves, designed to offer a little bit of what those denizens may miss about wherever they came from. And if you look closely enough, you can see temples, shrines, and areas of contemplation.

The outermost reaches are populated by the Rimdwellers, who might as well be cousins of the Bajau Laut, and who function as hunter-gatherers of the sea. They are poor by our standards but well adapted to the sea, and enormously resourceful. And like everyone else who comes, they are drawn to Clarice's generative nature. The Rimdwellers array their sea shanties and elaborate floating structures in clever patterns, which allow vessels to pass and reefs to form along the bottom of their houseboat clusters. They use flotsam and jetsam as their construction materials, yet somehow manage to create versatile structures which not only have a recognizable style, but they also remind those who work in the ivory towers and research centers what it means to thrive in survival.

Unleash Markets in Governance

The description above is of a world that exists only in possibility. But the vision of seasteading, of floating cities, persists in our imagination. If a man on the moon is the ultimate technocratic vision, a city on the sea is a vision of the integral liberal. Seasteading is an idealized form not merely because it would be a technical feat to build a modularized city upon the sea, but also because it captures our intuitions about markets in governance.

But markets in governance can happen in New America, too, from sea to shining sea. Imagine what had been fifty states becoming a new set of jurisdictions, perhaps held together by some compact, such as that of the Hanseatic League. This compact would avoid federal power growing like a cancer. Instead, it would be established to facilitate interstate trade, passage, and dispute resolution. Otherwise, each of the fifty states has its own peculiar laws and norms. Within each state, each county would have its own laws and norms — much as they do now, only fully self-determined and secure.

Now, what if those laws and norms were administered and enforced in entirely different ways? Remember that in Part One we discussed Strong's Law, which states that "properly structured free enterprise always results over time in higher quality, lower cost, and more customized products and services."[355] It's time we think of how Strong's Law can be applied to the most important aspect of society: governance. I can already hear the howls of the High Minds whose dreams of becoming philosopher kings would be dashed by competitive governance. Some will stay trapped in the mental model of *corporations evil*, with its attendant notions of exploitation. They will say that we are just market fundamentalists and that we are evil, greedy, or otherwise benighted, perhaps scions of the Dark Enlightenment. Then, they will prostrate themselves before the biggest corporation of all.

The lure of the Dark Enlightenment is strong, as the pull of a black hole. But we are integral liberals prepared to stare directly into the dark and retain far much more of the light — perhaps from the safe side of the event horizon. Still, philosopher Nick Land's words are powerful: "His awakening into neo-reaction comes with the (Hobbesian) recognition that sovereignty cannot be eliminated, caged, or controlled."

We have expended effort to deal with Hobbes. We have not yet reckoned with this recognition, which Land sees more as a blind, unstoppable process of power accretion, which we are otherwise doomed to repeat. Land might even grant us our collapse thesis. But he says the Leviathan will return anyway, in time: "The state isn't going anywhere because — to those who run it — it's worth far too much to give up, and as the concentrated instantiation of sovereignty in society, nobody can make it do anything."[356]

Whether this outlook requires a healthy or unhealthy dose of Thanatos Feminine, it is the most important concern we have to face. The way we will face it differs, but only enough to make our position a cousin to the Dark Enlightenment. Writer and software developer Curtis Yarvin (aka Mencius Moldbug) presents a solution that is not altogether different from our own:

> To a neocameralist, a state is a business which owns a country. A state should be managed, like any other large business, by dividing logical ownership into negotiable shares, each of which yields a precise fraction of the state's profit. (A well-run state is *very* profitable.) Each share has one vote, and the shareholders elect a board, which hires and fires managers.[357]

The customers are residents. Like any business, such a state will serve its customers better or go out of business.

Although it is undoubtedly an improvement, the problem with the neocameralist formulation is that it continues to rely on certain unneeded assumptions about the firm's nature. We have already pointed the way to improvements in how firms self-govern. Though continuing our discussion of power shift takes us into a different zone of inquiry, let's keep it in the back of our minds. Our conception is less dark by shades: A Grey Enlightenment.

The idea of the government as a corporation might not sit well with many people. Still, we can no more deny the fact of the Eros Masculine as we can deny the fact that power can reconstitute itself after collapse. Just look at the difference between Germany in 1919 and 1939. World war should not have to be the only check on empires; formalizing the state as a kind of power-shifted corporate entity represents a peaceful way to check political power and hold authorities accountable. After all, democracy is a myth. In this way, we agree with Land.

"It is essential to squash the democratic myth that a state 'belongs' to the citizenry. The point of neo-cameralism is to buy out the real stakeholders in sovereign power, not to perpetuate sentimental lies about mass enfranchisement."[358]

In a sense, we also suggest that one way to deal with power is to create *formal* mechanisms for some aspect of the government to go out of business. Currently, there are only informal processes, like collapse, which are far more devastating. We seek to light a way through some of the shadows of corporate sovereignty. We think that transformations after collapse can pull reality towards something a little more ideal than The United States of Google.

EMBRACE THE GREY ENLIGHTENMENT

And yet we take quite seriously the idea of markets in governance, where the alternative is monopoly government. People want and need governance. The question, old as humanity, is: how can we have governance that puts coercion in its place? We grudgingly go along with those versed in the Dark Enlightenment in suggesting that might making right will always be with us in some form. Only the most brilliant and spiritually enlightened beings can imagine, much less instantiate, a society of angels. The question for any self-respecting liberal then is not whether power ought be restrained; it is how we hope to restrain it. An 'ought' uttered to power is no different from a child's wish, a coin thrown in a well.

The integral liberal's experimental program assumes that we are humans, and that humans are a mix of sinners and saints. So, ultimate authority should be reserved for neither. Never mind that your idea of a sinner or a saint might not resemble mine; a saint will turn into a sinner just as readily as a white hat will turn black when they get hold of the Ring.

Those unfamiliar with this way of thinking are probably wondering how it is that corporations are not necessarily evil and that governments are not necessarily good. I hope any reader who has made it this far has let go of such foolish notions. Anyone prepared to shed Ms. Crabapple's social studies lesson is now invited to open their mind a little. There is a lot that is counterintuitive about this direction, so bear with me. Hope for humanity after collapse lies in getting over any residual notions of seraphocracy. Instead, let's work on re-illuminating the world beyond the Dark Enlightenment so that we can at least enjoy a moment of twilight.

Melt the Ring

One of the most vexing questions for the integral liberal is how humanity can melt the Ring of power. Despite their sins and shortcomings, perhaps no better group of thinkers has ever been assembled to answer this question than those who came to Philadelphia to ratify the Constitution. Yet some of them left the convention feeling as if they had not done enough to rein in the excesses of tyranny, which, as we have suggested, is to tamp down the excesses of Eros Masculine, and to put fetters on Leviathan. Franklin's answer to the question of what was going on in Constitution Hall still stands: "A republic, if we can keep it."

But if we can't, so be it; as long as we can figure out how to melt the Ring.

So how do we do that? It's a hard problem. Remember that Constitutions are statutes, and statutes tend to suffer from legal sclerosis in some circumstances; and in others, are vulnerable to corruption by interpretation. We need law by agreement. We need to adopt the code, fork the code, and exit the code entirely in some instances. Code is law, after all. The difference is that the code should depend far more on value's network effects than the prospect of violent enforcement. That means that the new liberal order will have to be fashioned by sovereign individuals coalescing in new systems of agreement that are neither legislated nor managed by angels. What remains in those covenants' in-between spaces should be fair means to resolve disputes and protocols for good laws to emerge.

Maybe the answer is not to destroy the Ring at all. Maybe the answer, following philosopher/fund manager Michael Gibson, is to see to it that everyone has a Ring:

> The diffusion of the smartphone, strong cryptography, and peer-to-peer decentralized public ledgers will weld individuals, networks and voluntary hierarchies into single units of sovereign power capable of opt-out and opt-in governance without precedent. Today about half the world's adults own a smartphone. By 2020 80 percent of adults will have a supercomputer in their pockets.[359]

Up to this point the Westphalian nation state has expressed its power within borders, which delineate the extent of its use of legal violence. That means that the old power structures envelop citizens within geographies. In this order, you're mostly hemmed in or locked out. Immigration restrictions make it difficult and costly for you to choose Texas's institutions over that of Mexico if you're born south of the Rio Grande. But we're racing headlong into an age where legal entrepreneurs will figure out how to decouple many governance functions from territory. We will opt in or opt out without leaving our bedroom slippers. A new kind of citizen will come into being.

And all of this, by the way, leaves little room for democracy as we currently think of it. Most of the American Founders saw democracy as a form of national suicide — and they should have. Majority rule needs to be kept in its place; that is, kept as a last resort when no other option for consensus is available. Given what we know now, I suspect such instances would be exceedingly rare. Before going back towards the light, take a look at one more observation by Nick Land:

> Given a population deeply infected by the zombie virus and shambling into cannibalistic social collapse, the preferred option is quarantine. It is not communicative isolation that is essential, but a functional dis-solidarization of society that tightens feedback loops and exposes people with maximum intensity to the consequences of their own actions. Social solidarity, in precise contrast, is the parasite's friend. By cropping out all high-frequency feedback mechanisms (such as market signals), and replacing them with sluggish, infra-red loops that pass through a centralized forum of 'general will', a radically democratized society insulates parasitism from what it does, transforming local, painfully dysfunctional, intolerable, and thus urgently corrected behavior patterns into global, numbed, and chronic socio-political pathologies.[360]

Just think about the last ten bumper stickers you saw, or perhaps the last fifteen social media posts. Are these really the thoughts that form the demos?

Whether it's a formalized mob that shows up to cry its teardrops into the ocean demanding the tide turn (elections), or a spontaneous mob that runs through city streets tearing down every bit of what it had no hand in creating (riots), mob rule has no place in New America.

Try Cellular Democracy

Our resistance to democratic governance won't sit well with some readers. I want to clarify that there are indeed some interesting forms of majority voting out there, such as ranked-choice voting[361], the Janacek Method[362], or liquid democracy.[363] They might even improve matters. I worry they won't go far enough, though, when it comes to decentralizing power. Majoritarian democracy is deeply problematic in that it is fundamentally agnostic about normative questions of central authority. But one form of democracy might yet have a life in New America.

Political economist Fred Foldvary has suggested one such system, which he calls "cellular democracy." Cellular democracy is a radical alternative to imposed mass democracy. It begins and ends as a form of voluntary, small-group voting, making the smallest jurisdiction the most powerful unit.

Think about the human body, which is composed of small cells. The body politic would likewise be divided into neighborhood 'cells,' the population of which should be small enough for the participants to know all of the candidates and meet personally to discuss the issues. (Earlier, I suggested that the maximum size of a ward, following Thomas Jefferson's Ward Republic conception. Foldvary suggests one thousand. Maybe it's Dunbar's Number, which is 150. Whatever it is: keep it small.) Voters in the cell would only elect a neighborhood council.

Then, a group of councils would elect representatives to the next level, or broader council. In turn, the second-level council elects the third-level council, and so on — up to the highest superordinate body. That body could then elect an executive, but only for cases where a swift, unitary decision is needed.

Cellular democracy could replace the imposed mass democracy of the form we're used to seeing. Because voting for superordinate representatives happens entirely through subordinate bodies, the subordinate bodies have the ultimate right to exit, and can withdraw from any superordinate council at any time. Cellular democracy could represent a major improvement in representative democracy, at least when it comes to *getting money out of politics* and *keeping most decisions proximate.* As with many of the other proposals you'll find in this volume, it too requires another change: the right of exit. That means replacing imposed democracy with voluntary democracy; coercion with persuasion. But how?

All the power would be local. The most localized cells might be organizations made up entirely of agreements; that is, of contracts. Imagine something like homeowners' associations, except that the homeowner's associations would send delegates to represent it in the council at the next level. This form of democracy would completely invert the current imposed power structure, as superordinate organs would always feel the threat of defection, or otherwise being undermined by subordinate cells. That's why the terms 'subordinate' and 'superordinate' refer only to the structure of stacking councils within some geography and do not refer to the relationships of power between levels. The only powers likely granted to the highest levels would be *those appropriate to that level.* Subsidiarity by default.

Some will see cellular democracy as something closer to Murray Bookchin's communalism.[364] Bookchin's form seeks to jettison any production and trade the primary civic unit understands as working at odds with environmental stewardship or egalitarian sharing. Others will see cellular democracy as a way to keep power out of elites' hands, which keeps interlopers from meddling in decidedly local matters. More or less 'capitalist' arrangements are both possible. Because such a system is simple to implement, it might become a transitional form, as communalism has become for the Kurds under the leadership of Abdullah Öcalan. I view it as one approach among many, but at least one that would rein in democratic forms that work in serivice of centralized power.

Whether via cellular democracy or some other more robust decentralized system, the feedback loops become much tighter. Accountability means less force and more integrity; less *himsa* and more *satya*. In this way, the institutions demand more disciplined spheres of practice from all stakeholders, instead creating incentives to scrap them. The rules and practices start to align. Profound transformation takes hold as people are rewarded for practicing the Spheres of Integral Liberalism while contributing to shared abundance. In this way, the system disciplines us and we discipline the system. The consequence is an upgraded humanity that unfolds stronger and wiser from the ashes of the old republic. Despite still being power, local power ensures diverse islands of consensus and freedom of movement among those islands. Strong incentives to settle disputes between local jurisdictions ensure something stronger than any peace imposed under the Eye of Sauron. The forces of Eros and Thanatos, masculine and feminine, would be more likely to come into mutual constraint, which we have called balance.

START A STARTUP CITY

Not only are we suggesting that there should be little-or-no national jurisdiction in America, but we might also suggest that there should be many such jurisdictions, and that competing firms offer governance services. One suspects objections to a private city will be motivated by the idea that it might work. Therefore, most authorities will not be receptive, especially if such a city's success means that the jig is up for the legacy model. But, as we have suggested, there is more to life than the public-private binary, which we'll dissolve later. The idea of private governance need not terminate in the concept of corporate governance, although we ought to explore that idea, too. For now, we can say that there is no better way to ensure that people have a say in how they are governed than to let people sign a real, enforceable contract with whoever would govern them. That contract marks the difference between public and private under our conception.

In his 2018 book *Free Private Cities*, entrepreneur jurist Titus Gebel modifies Paul Romer's Charter City concept, which amounts to the idea of importing existing laws into some area suffering under corrupt or failed institutions. Gebel's version is more radical. But despite its radicalism, it is likely a superior option because it doesn't require importing bugs from a legacy system.

Under Gebel's conception, in what he calls a "free private city," a private company offers residents protection of life, liberty, and property in some limited territory as a "government service provider."[365] The offer might include a bundle of security and rescue services, a legal and regulatory framework, and independent dispute resolution. Those residing in the jurisdiction would pay a contractually fixed amount for these services every year. The operator, say Gebel's company, would not be able to change the contract unilaterally.[366]

Resident consumers of these governance and security services would have a legal claim to adequate service provision. Otherwise, if the private city performed poorly, the resident would be entitled to damages. Disputes between residents and the provider would be brought before an independent arbitration tribunal, a custom which is already well established in international commercial law. Then, of course, if the operator ignores the arbitration award or misuses its power in some other way, its customers go away.

The city's reputation is tarnished. Eventually, the operator goes bankrupt.

Of course, privatization means the end of sovereign immunity, the doctrine that means governments can do no legal wrong.

Private cities of the form Gebel envisions are created with a real social contract. That means the relationship is not quite as Molbug (Curtis Yarvin) imagines, that of a private monarchy. Instead, if the operator wants to make a profit, they must do so by fulfilling their obligations set out in the agreement. In this way, the contract is the boss. There is no legislative funny business or kingly caprice. There are only the promises the entity makes to We the Customers.

Note, Gebel and Yarvin agree that offering shares in the governing entity might be a good idea. Shares represent a different sort of check on the authority of the operator. We touched on this in the idea of power shifting, but used a different conception of the corporation, one that is more dynamic and decentralized. The question before us is how far these or related ideas can extend.

EXPAND POLYCENTRISM

It's a pretty amazing thing: When people have choices, they can better find a choice that suits their idea of a happy life. They can find others who share their conceptions of the good. When you think about going out to dinner, would you like for there to be just one choice or many different options? If you had Thai food last night, you might want to have Mexican food tonight. If there were only one restaurant chain operated by a monopoly, you'd probably find much to disagree with about its operation and its products. Otherwise, you would have to learn to cook or eat the same thing tomorrow.

Polycentric law — or a condition in which legal authority is broken up into different 'centers' — extends the observation about restaurants to governance. Just as competition makes life better for those who seek good food, good beer, and a nice atmosphere, it can benefit those seeking a fairer and more efficient legal system. Competition among systems ensures citizens get a better deal if they want it. You might think this is a radical claim, but it's already happening. U.S. citizens can already select from among fifty different governance options, just as many Europeans can move freely and settle among E.U. states. People living in New Hampshire enjoy a lower overall tax burden than people living in Vermont. People are fleeing California for Texas. After collapse, removing the federal monopoly will only improve these competitive dynamics.

The services traditional governments provide — defining rules, policing their application, and settling disputes — are areas that desperately need market competition. When a state claims a monopoly on the law, as the federal government has done, it tends to neglect citizens' needs. But in a polycentric state of affairs, providers are competing for customers. That's one reason that I made an adamant case for subsidiarity. Another is that every option is an exit option when a jurisdiction becomes insufferable.

Unleash Polyarchy

Polycentrism is a simple and powerful idea, but polyarchy improves upon it — because polyarchy extends the idea of polycentrism beyond terra firma. The polyarchist, therefore, asks: *What is inherently important about territories and borders that bind them to law?* The answer, in many cases, is nothing. Just because the law is an artifact of conquest over some jurisdiction doesn't mean that the law ought to be binding within that territory. It is, as ever, a question of might making right. But the polyarchist wants to know why they can't select from among different legal systems wherever they live, as long as the law doesn't relate specifically to a relevant territory. It's a system that suggests secession might just have an upside.

The events of 1860 America overshadow the genius of polyarchy. In December of that year, South Carolina seceded from the Union, which made the secession crisis very real for the newly elected President Abraham Lincoln. The legacy of racism and the Civil War's bloodshed make all talk of secession taboo to this day. But it is time to take the idea out from under the shadow of racism, because we need it. Like the Basques, the Scottish, the Catalans, the Quebecois, and the Hongkongers, secession is self-determination. And polyarchy is self-determination on steroids.

Note that in the very same year as the Civil War, 1860, a Belgian liberal named Paul Emily du Puydt offered humanity a brilliant challenge:

Question: What form of government would you desire?

Quite freely you would answer, monarchy, or democracy, or any other.

> Anyway, whatever your reply, your answer would be entered in a register arranged for this purpose; and once registered, unless you withdrew your declaration, observing due legal form and process, you would thereby become either a royal subject or citizen of the republic [or a Democrat, or Republican]. Thereafter you would in no way be involved with anyone else's government. You would obey your own leaders, your own laws, and your own regulations. You would pay neither more nor less, but morally it would be a completely different situation.
>
> Ultimately, everyone would live in his own individual political community, quite as if there were not another, nay, ten other, political communities nearby, each having its own contributors too.[367]

That, folks, is polycentrism on steroids. It means that you could freely join or exit a particular civil association with its attendant responsibilities and benefits. And of course, thanks to modern communications networks, you would never have to leave the comfort of home.

Join a Civil Association

Imagine, then, a future in which, instead of joining a political party, you will join a civil association. Instead of political parties competing for votes to gain power and make the rules for 350 million people, these civil associations will compete for members. Who knows? Maybe it would look something like this:

The Society of Virtue
- 17% income
- Health
- Unemployment
- 4 out of 5 stars
- Requires abstaining from tobacco, drugs, and alcohol

Progressive Alliance
- Tiered income, average 25%
- Health
- Unemployment
- Basic income assistance
- 3.7 out of 5 stars

Free Builders
- 10% income
- Mutual aid assistance
- Legal assistance
- 4.5 out of 5 stars
- Pledge requirement

Basic Income Alliance
- 25% income
- Basic income on sliding scale, according to income
- 4.1 out of 5 stars

Friends of Hillel
- 20% income
- Health
- Mutual aid
- 4.7 out of 5 stars
- No Judaism requirement, pledge requirement

St. Mary's Society
- 15% income
- Health
- Mutual aid
- Unemployment
- 4.4 out of 5 stars
- Catholic requirement

Order of the Leaf
- 25% of income
- Health
- Unemployment
- 4.5 out of 5 stars
- Veganism requirement

The Freethinkers
- 15% of income
- Mutual aid
- 4.8 out of 5 stars
- Atheism requirement, pledge requirement

Union of Working People
- 20% of income
- Health
- Mutual aid
- Basic income assistance
- 4.7 out of 5 stars
- Pledge requirement

Peace Communists
- 70% of income
- Basic income assistance
- Two-year minimum commitment
- 4 out of 5 stars

We can imagine each of these civil associations having unique content, programming, and opportunities for prosocial member interaction. I made these all up, of course. What would other creative people create together?

Suppose this sort of civil association replaces much of politics in the future. In that case, some will want to know how a majority of people will be able to oblige non-members to pay their 'fair share' or otherwise live by their conception of the good. Beyond the power of persuasion, they won't. The whole point of membership is that a moral-political community shares similar commitments. If that community is able to help its membership thrive sustainably, they will gain more adherents. If one believes that there is some objective percentage one should set aside to help others, they will have to find others who feel the same. Otherwise, those outside your community may have different commitments and seek to belong to another civil association. But at least that civil association cannot bind you to its rules, either. You have a choice.

Some will not be comfortable with this idea. But people in Texas are no more able to require those living in Thailand or Tahiti or Tijuana to conform to Texas laws or norms, much less those of the U.S. Again: Why should the history of conquest over great expanses of soil bind one to the same laws or monolithic taxation and debt regime? In polyarchy, the only questions anyone needs to worry about are whether or not their civil association delivers on its commitments to members and stays solvent.

But why shouldn't there be one justice for everyone? Why can't there be a philosopher king who has absolute knowledge of the right and the good? Because, as biologist E.O. Wilson says, "Like everyone else, philosophers measure their personal emotional responses to various alternatives as though consulting a hidden oracle." He continues:

> That oracle resides in the deep emotional centers of the brain, most probably within the limbic system, a complex array of neurons and hormone-secreting cells located just beneath the "thinking" portion of the cerebral cortex. Human emotional responses and the more general ethical practices based on them have been programmed to a substantial degree by natural selection over thousands of generations.[368]

Because our hidden oracles don't always say the same things, there is wild variation. Our ethical practices will be diverse, too.

This is just cultural relativism, some might argue, but I don't think so. Instead, it is an acknowledgement that each of us has different moral proclivities. Instead of trying to force everyone to share one's proclivities, we allow different systems to self-organize. What binds us together are the meta-moral values of integral liberalism.

One of the benefits of polyarchy is that it dismantles any central levers of authority over which parties clamber. In this way it dismantles monopolistic claims to moral authority. Politics is a perverse, cyclical tug o' war that locks the people in conflict. The two American political parties have formed a cartel of bitter rivalry, but it is a cartel never-theless. The only thing they agree on is that they, Democrat and Republic, are the only combatants in the war.

The partisan duopoly conscripts most Americans into that war. Social media tends to make things worse, because airing one's views is an inexpensive proposition, one that is even cheaper than voting. Those who neither argue nor vote might be blissfully ignorant, but they are just as power-less. Everyone lives with the acrimony around them and waits for whatever changes are to be handed down. Such a system creates enmity. And it's no wonder.

With the dissolution of the federal apparatus of power, people will self-organize. They will have to adopt sweet talk to gain more market share for their ideas. Agitation and anger will start to dissipate as people transition from competition to collaboration. None of this is to say that conflict will go away entirely; people are people. It's to say that people will have stronger incentives to be kind to each other, honor their word, and generally do the right thing when they are active participants in civil association.

Seed Cloud Governance

Civil Associations in a condition of polyarchy are but one dimension to a general trend in decentralized governance likely to emerge after collapse. Let's call this category *cloud governance*. Such a phrase captures the idea that a jurisdic-tion needn't be attached to territory, and that civil associa-tion can happen across boundaries that once belonged to nation-states.

Cloud governance, therefore, extends to areas such as security and legal protection. One might object on the grounds that different legal associations will make for a patchwork quilt of incommensurable legal systems. This is where the Common Law can help. Customary law is organically unified and has a few crucial features:

- In general, everything is permitted that isn't expressly prohibited.

- Focus remains on torts, or wrongs and injuries by one party against another.

- Focus remains on court precedents, which can be overturned.

- Focus remains on agreements and the enforcement of agreements.

Such will represent a great inversion as the Common Law becomes ascendant. Statute Law will be restricted to the charters of civil associations and apply to members only. Matters external to civil associations will fall under the Common Law, and protective associations (similar to civil associations but responsible for security and legal defense) will have strong incentives to adopt open source law. Legal scholar Tom W. Bell has already developed an online Common Law database called Ulex, written on a digital ledger.[369]

Parse Territorial and Extraterritorial Rules

Some laws and municipal codes are designed explicitly for territories. Subsidiarity rules and the Common Law should cover these functions, including any covenants and ordinances within a given territory. Here again, statutes are circumscribed by smaller jurisdictions, which are established according to subsidiarity rules.

Extraterritorial rules are determined by members of some association who have signed an agreement. Almost any that are worthwhile will include a dispute resolution provision and deference to the Common Law. If there is no higher-level governing function that requires evoking subsidiarity, then a charter or covenant suffices for that territory.

Territorial law is that form of law essential to questions of territory and real estate, such as environmental torts, the governance of thoroughfares, roadways, conservation trusts, and other areas managed as commons. Territorial law *excludes* matters involving healthcare, income support, or education, for example. Because the world is strange, people will stumble on edge cases that seem to have territorial and non-territorial aspects. Such cases can be resolved in courts.

JOIN PROTECTIVE ASSOCIATIONS

I have argued that nonviolence should form the basis of morality and law. I have also said that the Ahimsa Presumption extends equally to those who administer the law, as it does to those who live under the law. But that doesn't mean that people won't commit immoral or illegal acts.

Protective associations can provide security or legal protections separately or in a bundle. Far from being a monopoly on the initiation of violence in a jurisdiction, these protective associations would instead compete to serve customers. Legacy policing has fewer incentives to treat citizens as customers, much less to protect and serve. As the name suggests, protective associations would have stronger incentives to protect their customers against criminal acts. Protective associations working on behalf of the accused would have stronger incentives to fight for the accused's legal rights. The accused would have legal recourse to sue any protective association in court, say, for excessive force, false arrest, or some other violation. Far from the conditions of immunity currently enjoyed by police and officials, paid protective associations would have far more alignment with the customers they serve. In a marketplace where firms profit for supplying truth and justice, you're likely to get more truth and justice.

Because people will belong to competing protective

associations, disputes between associations, whether legal or procedural, will also have to be resolved. Protective associations will sometimes pay arbitration firms to settle disputes between members of different protective associations, or within the associations themselves. The extent to which associations adopt incommensurable forms of law, arbitration firms will also have to decide which set of laws apply. Mechanisms for introducing new laws or overturning laws will proceed according to the negotiations among arbitration firms keen to reduce their costs and work according to established, customary legal standards.

Some will be concerned that the rise of civil and protective associations that replace the welfare-warfare state will exclude those in poverty. Many will object that the poor will remain ungoverned or under-protected. While there is currently no status quo of protective associations to evaluate right now, we always have to ask: *As compared to what?*

When it comes to criminal justice, the poor already get a bad deal in America. First, poor people are already more frequently victims of crime than wealthier people. Getting caught up with a traffic ticket can be an expensive proposition, as fines and court costs mount. Avoiding these costs further criminalizes the poor person, which compounds their problems. If a poor person is accused of committing a more serious crime, not only are public defenders generally inadequate, the court systems are overloaded.

Under-provision of justice by governments results in prosecutors heaping on charges against suspects, both in order to guarantee a prosecutorial win but to push people to accept plea deals. The perverse result is poor people accept plea deals to avoid the overloaded system and to mitigate risks of longer sentences — *even when they are innocent.* Most simply cannot afford protracted legal battles with little chance of success.

We hypothesize that we would see marked improvements over the current system, even if certain inequities remained. Note that many of the inequities in the current system arise out of its monopoly privilege. Public provision of resources to the criminal justice system is neither competitive nor tracks necessarily with rises in demand for justice services. Bureaucracies administer flat budgets. Consequently, functionaries underproduce in certain areas (such as protecting the innocent), and overproduce in others (such as making drug arrests). In a condition where firms compete to provide protective services, the poor might avail themselves of mutual aid arrangements, charity associations, or relatively low-cost providers. Many protective associations might also be structured as mutuals. Because markets give us a better idea about supply and demand, excesses and shortages in the justice system would become far more evident. Far from undersupplying security and justice, the civil society sector can make up for service shortages among the poor.

Think also of large, competing protective associations: we can imagine firms that bring their prices down by merely serving more people, with some economies of scale. Even though fewer poor people shop at Dean and Deluca than they do at Target, the latter is bigger and more dominant.

CREATE A UTOPIA OF UTOPIAS

There is no single utopia. Just as you like chocolate ice cream and I like vanilla, you might have greater toleration for risk than I do. You might prefer to share all of your possessions. I might prefer to share only a percentage. And while all this talk of preferences seems to leave us in a more relativistic universe, we acknowledge that people are different, one to the next. To some extent, that's okay.

We follow the late philosopher Robert Nozick in recommending a "Framework for Utopia."[370] The idea is that sustainable communities are experiments in living. Some succeed. Some fail. But the failure of any given system should not be catastrophic. People can try things out locally while respecting other's consent. Instead of encouraging civic participation in electoral politics, which is cheap and meaningless, more people would be encouraged to be actively compassionate.

We should see our new liberalism as a blanket of protection for those who hustle together peacefully to create a better life according to their shared commitments. By virtue of our relationships, we can discover all manner of beautiful and serendipitous community features, many of which we seek to preserve in traditions. Or we might find that, upon joining any such community, it wasn't all it was cracked up to be. And in that disappointment, we will be happy to discover a right of exit. Perhaps another, more tailored community lies waiting. Maybe we'll start one of our own. None will be perfect, but none will be a monolith, either. Some will be based on shared interests, others on ideology. Some will be based on proximity, others will be virtual. But we can imagine more of our lives will be taken up by our movement in and out of our various associations, contributing where we can, participating in a life beyond the internet's hall of mirrors.

People self-organize into communities to enhance their wellbeing. But wellbeing is a state that is achieved through different means, depending on the individual. Discovering the right community will be life-changing for many. And the proliferation of markets in these communities will be profound relative to what is currently governed by distant monopoly schemes.

Many will value their community not merely because it helps them enhance their wellbeing, but also because it allows them to improve others' wellbeing. Nozick's framework creates an ongoing discovery process. Under the robust, decentralized umbrella of the Common Law, people will experiment with and modify the various experiments in living together. They will recruit and support their kindred souls. They will work to sustain this entity from which they give and take so much. But like any living organism, it must take in more energy than it consumes; that is, it must be profitable. That doesn't mean organizations have to be 'for-profit' entities. Revenues to the organization must exceed costs, or it will eventually die.

Not all communities will survive in this marketplace of communities. Some will fail to retain members. Others will spend too generously, be poorly managed, or fail due to extravagance. But these communitarian utopias, if they are to exist, must be established in *ahimsa*. Any community that only exists through the threat of violence is probably not a community at all; rather, it is an institution that sows seeds of despair. Anyone seeking to fashion community by force doesn't understand what community is, including communitarian philosophers. Community coalesces and persists when people work together to build it from the bottom up.

Such is both good news and bad news for the High Mind, particularly those of a socialist bent. The good news is that anyone can build a socialist system within the broader framework of voluntary association and systematic pluralism. The bad news is that you can't use coercion to preserve it. Taxes are out; fees are in. If the socialist objects by arguing that they would not find enough members to sustain the commune, they make our argument for us. In that case, too few people will be interested in your masculine form of imposed justice, which means it is both undemocratic and untenable. If enough people see fit to join your commune, then you don't have to tear down the rest of society — in all its diverse splendor — to realize your conception of the good. Remember: integral liberals are committed to nonviolence, but we are not committed to pacifism.

Happily, though, under a system of integral liberalism, people will create all manner of agreements and legal frameworks. Some of them are cooperatives, syndicalist communes, and intentional communities. There is power in pluralism. Given the enormous diversity among individuals, I have no idea what sort of community might be best for you, nor do you have any idea about my ideal community beyond what I've written here. And it might change as I get older. We cannot, therefore, design a single, inclusive utopian society. We have to let people gravitate to various experiments.

Two of the most important aspects of localized living experiments come first in scalability and then in preference. To give an example, the kibbutz movement in Israel has shrunk over the years. *Kibbutznikim* — people who live and work in a kibbutz — now make up less than 5 percent of the population, which is down from more than 7 percent decades ago. And yet the *kibbutznikim* are reinventing themselves to attract new members and overcome issues of mismanagement. "We have some kind of economic sharing," says Israeli kibbutznik Michal Gomel, quoted at NPR. "We celebrate holidays together. We also have a lot of ideological sharing, which means we learn a lot from each other."[371]

That's how you do it. Whether there are institutional impediments to joining a kibbutz, I cannot say. I hope that non-*kibbutznikim* reduce those barriers. What many members have learned the hard way is that most kibbutzim have scaling limits, which are probably close to Dunbar's Limit; so, there are multiple reasons not to institutionalize this particular form of socialism for all Israelis. The first might be that scaling problems infect all versions of collective ownership and administration. The second is that if more Israelis wanted to live in a kibbutz, they could start one or move to one, so there is no sense in abandoning *ahimsa*. In any case, most Israelis choose a decidedly more bourgeois life. There is no sense in imposing the ideals of the 5 percent on the 95 percent. And yet that is what Marxist revolutionaries everywhere have always wanted. The integral liberal says: If your system doesn't work without the threat of violence, it's the wrong system. You might think of governance systems rooted in preferences as being ideological. One might grant that it's meta-ideological in that it leaves room for diverse experiments. But it's just as important to think of these experiments as being pragmatic.

DEAL WITH DEALBREAKERS

As we have suggested when it comes to integral liberalism, the ultimate trade-off is that, in order to have your ideal system, you must forego imposing your ideals onto others. It means sweet talk. The practice of pluralism means that we'll have to learn to tolerate more about others in the way they organize and live their lives. Still, are there dealbreakers? Of course.

Perhaps you have never encountered the slang term dealbreaker: It's that one thing that keeps us from agreeing to something, the *one thing* that is important enough to cause you to stop short.

For the sake of exploration, let's assume that a mile up the road from you, there is a compound, a node in a networked Civil Association we'll call The Cult. That makes The Cult both proximate and also part of a more extensive network of organizations of its kind. Within this group, an adult priest class practices ritual sex with their young acolytes. This coming-of-age rite happens when an acolyte turns thirteen. The young members, perhaps born into the community, never got to choose their membership. In whatever way you slice it, people will have serious questions about ritual sex with thirteen year olds. This is one of those instances we might call a 'dealbreaker.'

In our formulations up to this point, we have said that a subsidiarity rule only applies to territorial goods and services. That is, governance should more or less apply to the features of some territory. Think of a rule governing riparian rights, or a law that states, *Here, we drive on the right.* Is the age of consent a territorial or extraterritorial rule?

Again, enter the Common Law. Even if parallel bodies of law compete to answer the age of consent question, people will have incentives (and moral imperatives) to settle and harmonize the law. No doubt someone will haul Cult members into court. Some protective associations might even evoke their police powers and arrest Cult members. After all, individuals or associations would have a strong case that having intercourse with psychologically underdeveloped teens *injures* them, even if this is a relatively new idea in human history.

The problem with the very idea of dealbreakers is that one person's taboo is another's totem. Polygamy is just one example. Some people are mortified by the idea of polygamy in Utah, but don't think much about polygamy in Senegal. One might call this jurisdictional bias; that is, if one quite literally can't make a federal case out of behaviors of which he disapproves, then he worries about it less. When there are a more significant number of self-determining communities, there will be more emergent norms that others find taboo.

Still, if we can be united by the Common Law, one that rests fundamentally on proving injury (*himsa*), most of the issues involving dealbreakers evaporate in court. Those for whom a dealbreaker involves no injury are welcome to associate with those who feel the same. In the case of ritual sex with young teens, all one would have to do is demonstrate in court that the practice harms teens.

Sometimes competing sets of emergent law will be harmonized, sometimes not, so we can't predict exactly what would happen in the case of the Cult. But if it isn't clear by now, integral liberalism is allergic to statute law. Collapse is an opportunity to abandon Justinian Codes, including state statutes, in favor of emergent law. After all,

High Minds make statutes, but Common Law courts care far less about High Minds. Even if the Leviathan Formulation is a representative form, representatives are routinely captured and corrupted. Ideally, the Common Law with professional judges and juries can do the work of legislators, but with greater flexibility.

It's time for Roman Law to fall.

Extend Ahimsa to Fundamental Law

Academic arguments about the extent to which government as such goes away are just that; what plays out in the real world remains to be seen. Still, the discovery processes of competitive governance ensure the right balance of the practical and the idealistic. That doesn't mean that we shouldn't make our case for a powerful animating assumption for all law.

Call it the Ahimsa Presumption, which one derives from our commitments as integral liberals. It goes something like this:

All human institutions should be established with the Ahimsa Presumption at their cores and should extend to every sphere and scale. This presumption is that the Ahimsa Principle must be applied to all law and to each legal steward, whether public or private.

Recall that Ahimsa Principle is a moral commitment to nonviolence, that is: "To the extent that you seek happiness, harmony and abundance for yourself and others, you ought to abstain from threatening or initiating harm; then you should actively, consciously and continuously practice *ahimsa.*" One should, of course, apply such a principle in one's day to day life. But the idea here is only that the Ahimsa Principles provides a presumption in the formation and adjudication of all law.

Such a bold proposition challenges not only much of the political philosophy in the Western tradition but also the justification for every political institution dominating the planet. In short, most all politics boils down to *who gets to initiate violence* and *by what means*. Our formulation assumes that every human being should abstain from initiating harm, and any justifiable violence will be a response to harm another initiated, which is illegitimate by definition. In this way, all courts would have to wrestle ultimately with the Ahimsa Presumption, and all decisions would have to conform to it.

At this point, one might object that applying *ahimsa* to questions of politics are somewhat at odds with Buddhism or Jainism. After all, the Buddha was not all that interested in politics, and Buddhism was never intended to be a political philosophy. Buddhists simply expect their adherents to bring their practices to all life spheres, and so do we. Still, as Buddhists weigh in on matters of politics all the time, we might upset the apple cart by suggesting that a commitment to *ahimsa* should be about *ratcheting towards anarchy*. Put more baldly: To practice ahimsa is to renounce power politics to the fullest possible extent. After all, politics is about who gets to wield the state's violent apparatus and to what ends he or she should wield that apparatus. And that sounds nothing like nonviolence in thought, word, or deed.

Before we set about challenging all those coercive institutions, we should define what we mean by 'sphere and scale.'

- *Sphere.* Questions of whether there are *special conditions* for non-adherence to the presumption.

- *Scale.* Questions about the *extent* of *ahimsa* as a governing principle in society.

Most failures of imagination in applying the Ahimsa Presumption will turn on specifics of one of these two. In other words, nonviolence can be counterintuitive to most people, accustomed as they are to those dominance hierarchies that depend on the threat of violence for their existence. *Sphere* issues usually involve exceptions, edge cases, or competing conceptions of the good. *Scale* issues usually involve generalizations about aggregates, such as the purported common good, positive rights, or group rights. (Of course, sphere and scale get conflated.)

We can look at how the Ahimsa Presumption can be applied at different spheres and scales, as someone arguing in a court proceeding would. Think of it as being similar to the presumption of innocence. In criminal law, the presumption of innocence comes with a strict evidentiary standard: *beyond a reasonable doubt.* The Ahimsa Presumption should track with our intuitions about the criminal law, which is that the burden is on the accuser to prove guilt. Likewise, it is the actor's burden, including state actors, to justify initiating violence.

But the Ahimsa Presumption should also track with our understanding of torts in civil disputes, which requires evidence of *injury.* These parallels are important for two reasons: Frictions and edge cases should be resolved in courts and not in legislatures; and because The Ahimsa Presumption will be *the very basis of law.* Simply put, any person, group, or institution must meet an extremely high bar when seeking to justify initiating violence or coercion.

Our broad objective is, of course, to reduce violence in all of its variants and increase cooperation. Harm — even 'legitimate' harm — reduces happiness, harmony, and prosperity. Institutionalized threat of violence creates social frictions, even when such threats are intended to reduce social friction. Indeed, institutional harms introduce *institutional* frictions as groups compete for state transfers or favors. As we have said, most of what the American government does is take resources away from one group and give it to another group.

If most politics amounts to the promise of discriminatory wealth transfers, as we learned from political economists James Buchanan and Gordon Tullock, most policy is transfer policy.[372] However radical it might seem, we claim the vast majority of what the government does violates the Ahimsa Principle. In the form of imposed electoral majorities, politics is an invitation to vote on which individuals to harm and which individuals to 'help.' Voters rarely ever get what they vote for, anyway. Still, when they do, they regularly acknowledge that most of their preferences are rooted in inter-group violence.

If applied, it could be that this principle eats through the very existence of the state. We don't know. But we do think the Ahimsa Presumption will have a definite ratcheting effect. For now, we can say at the very least that we have a moral obligation to take greater care in proposing actions or policies that harm those who have made no injury. But to the extent that anyone does cause injury, the institutional framework should require them to make victims whole.

The Ahimsa Presumption means that all of us, including authorities, have to take the utmost care. As law professor Stephen L. Carter reminds us:

> Law professors and lawyers instinctively shy away from considering the problem of law's violence. Every law is violent. We try not to think about this, but we should. On the first day of law school, I tell my Contracts students never to argue for invoking the power of law except in a cause for which they are willing to kill. They are suitably astonished, and often annoyed. But I point out that even a breach of contract requires a judicial remedy; and if the breacher will not pay damages, the sheriff will sequester his house and goods; and if he resists the forced sale of his property, the sheriff might have to shoot him.[373]

American society, as it happens, is a mix. Politics is a coercive apparatus that sits atop spheres of relatively peaceful collaboration — institutional Eros/Thanatos Masculine atop Eros/Thanatos Feminine.

Some would respond to Carter's warning that things aren't so bad. They worry that non-state violence might burn out of control with the Ahimsa Presumption. We should always remember that it's state-sponsored violence that is the largest killer of humans by humans in recorded history — which dwarfs those killed in war. R. J. Rummel defines the mass-killing of a population by its own government as "democide."[374]

In the twentieth century alone, we saw the following democides:

- 61,911,000 Murdered: The Soviet Gulag State
- 35,236,000 Murdered: The Communist Chinese Ant Hill
- 20,946,000 Murdered: The Nazi Genocide State
- 10,214,000 Murdered: The Depraved Nationalist Regime
- 5,964,000 Murdered: Japan's Savage Military
- 2,035,000 Murdered: The Khmer Rouge Hell State
- 1,883,000 Murdered: Turkey's Genocidal Purges
- 1,670,000 Murdered: The Vietnamese War State
- 1,585,000 Murdered: Poland's Ethnic Cleansing
- 1,503,000 Murdered: The Pakistani Cutthroat State
- 1,072,000 Murdered: Tito's Slaughterhouse

It appears violence monopolies are responsible for most of humanity's suffering at the hands of other humans. We should never forget that.

RESIST LEVIATHAN

One potential line of argument against the Ahimsa Presumption might be that the coercive apparatus of politics is the main reason that relatively peaceful collaboration is possible at all. Without that coercive apparatus, the U.S. would descend into chaos marked by gross violations of the Ahimsa Principle. *At a minimum*, the argument goes, *the government must function as a powerful nightwatchman and final adjudicator.* You might recall this line of thinking. We called it The Leviathan Formulation.

We have to challenge that assumption. Putting nonviolence at the center of our institutions is more likely to reduce harm and increase the likelihood that any given person will flourish. The great game of groups jockeying to violate other groups in the name of the 'greater good' is responsible for so many problems throughout history. In short, Hobbes's Leviathan has become Engineer, Fixer, Godfather, Redistributer, Father, Mother and Old Testament God.[375]

It's no wonder politics have become so acrimonious. You can't have that much power and largesse to fight over and expect people not to fight; a negative-sum system engenders negative-sum thinking. From the standpoint of an individual's moral behavior, people will agree to have agents do things in the service of their political ideals that *they might never do to another person one-on-one.* Such is why Stephen L. Carter reminds his students to consider only those laws for which *you would be willing to kill.*

GOVERN IN ANARCHY

So what could this society look like? What systems would replace our current systems? We don't know exactly, but we have a clue. One might or might not have predicted the emergence of bitcoin, but James Dale Davidson and William Rees-Mogg predict "cybercash," (e.g. *The Sovereign Individual* 1997) just as Orson Scott Card anticipates email (e.g. *Ender's Game* 1985) and Neal Stephenson foresees virtual reality (e.g. *Snow Crash* 1992). It seems to go like this:

"As cybercommerce begins," write Davidson and Rees-

Mogg, "it will lead inevitably to cybermoney. This new form of money will reset the odds… A crucial part of this change will come about because of the effect of information technology in liberating the holders of wealth from expropriation through inflation." Quite ominously, they add: "It will consist of encrypted sequences of multi-hundred-digit prime numbers."[376]

Unique, anonymous, and verifiable, this money will accommodate the largest transactions. Remarkable predictions such as this show a pattern: sci-fi speculations become entrepreneurial solutions to address needs. And as the force monopoly service providers collapse, innovations of Eros Feminine will flow peacefully into the vacuums.

Likewise, we won't be able to predict just what can emerge as entrepreneurs rethink how to serve up governance functions. But as people become more dissatisfied with the current regime, those entrepreneurs will be waiting to serve them. Coercive taxation will become a relic.

There are myriad examples of purpose-driven organizations providing traditional governmental services, including schools, roads, policing organizations, and dispute resolution services. The end of forced monopolies doesn't end the need for the services they provide, it just creates space for purpose-driven organizations to develop novel means of providing them. If some government's way of providing some good or service is superior, it will compete if the selection mechanism is customer value, rather than force or subsidy. The key difference is competition, collaboration, and choice.

High Minds will probably be horrified by these ideas. In their cramped rationalism, all social order has to be decided not by individuals according to their needs and desires, but by the fever dreams of philosopher-kings who impose systems and hand you the bill. That means that those committed to the status quo have to admit that they are unwilling to give up on the threat of coercion to maintain their institutions. Those who want to build New America will be committed to competition, collaboration, and choice within a condition of peace. They will solve collective action problems locally and resolve disputes in creative ways. Those who do not want to build New America will retreat into the sclerotic, linear thinking that led to collapse in the first place. Anyone who wants to build cities of peace and prosperity will keep an open mind; those who are uncomfortable with the idea of companies administering security and justice should stay tuned. The corporation is about to become power shifted, too.

When it comes to the current criminal justice system, there too many examples of its failures to list, which include:

- Police abuse and violence.
- Police shakedowns and hassling.
- Police used for revenue collection.
- Police not held to account and immune to liability.
- Prosecutions that heap impossible odds upon the poor.
- Prosecutions that ruin lives, punishing non-violent crimes.
- Prosecutors who force plea deals, punishing the innocent.
- Statutes that curb the discretion of judges.
- Frivolous lawsuits that clog the courts.
- Activist lawsuits that clog the courts.
- Minor infractions that clog the courts.
- Mass incarceration, especially of minorities.
- Victims not made whole, because the debt is 'to society'.

When a monopoly provides anything, you are more

likely to get both underproduction and overproduction. Such distortions are far less likely to happen in competitive market systems because it's easier to align incentives as providers tailor to different customer demands.

Even law courts for dispute resolution and criminal justice may not require a monopoly provider. In the absence of a monopoly, that is, in the presence of choice among competing providers, it might be easier to keep power in its place as a more restorative form of force, carefully and reasonably applied. We already see examples of justice being provided in the world today without a monopoly provider, such as instances where disputes happen across national boundaries. International business law is just one such example. It's not uncommon to see court cases where each party is in a separate jurisdiction, where each uses either the same system of arbitration or each party uses its own court system and legal code. They don't need bloodshed to come to an agreement because they have established processes for reconciling their legal codes, and they have strong incentives to abide by their decisions. They have replaced paternalism with process. As most of us prefer resolving disputes without bloodshed, we would see more of this sort of thing.

If you and I were free to choose our preferred governance systems, their respective associations would have strong incentives to work out differences; any two associations would not want to stay in conflict forever, and it would be less costly to defer to a predetermined third-party court of appeals. Likewise, mission-driven enforcement organizations would have strong incentives to ensure all reputable courts had reached clear, integrated decisions before carrying out enforcement measures. Enforcement organizations would otherwise be subject to costly lawsuits. So why should we expect to find systems harmonizing to some degree?

One answer lies, again, with organic unity: Too much diversity in legal systems becomes too costly. Too much unity in law fails to reflect the diversity of preferences. My hope — and admittedly it is a hope — is that an open market in legal systems will create incentives that bring about an equilibrium. There will be organic unity in that equilibrium, which is to say a relatively high degree of diversity and a relatively high degree of unity.

In other words, if a company wants to do business in one thousand different jurisdictions, corresponding to one hundred different court systems, that might be unworkable. But if commercial law has harmonized to a degree such that the regulatory environment is predictable, then compliance costs will go down accordingly. On the other hand, if there is too much monolithic law, there will be far less jurisdictional arbitrage, which is a fancy term for voting with your feet. In other words: there will be nowhere to run. Ventures that can't exit, whether civil associations or firms, will wither on the vine. In any case, a high degree of system interoperability depends on deference to the Ahimsa Presumption, which is currently absent in American law.

The same, of course, can be said for issues of personal freedom and cultural expression. To the degree that there is diversity among jurisdictions, people will gravitate to jurisdictions that serve them. In this way, they will be able to organize themselves into communities of culture most suited to their conceptions of the good. To the degree that there is unity in peace, collaboration and exchange will flower.

12

REPLACE MONOPOLIES OF WELFARE AND WAR

You want my property? You can't have it.
But I did you a big favor. I've successfully
privatized world peace.

Tony Stark, *Iron Man*

Most of us grownups don't believe in magic anymore. Sometimes, though, it can be helpful to imagine. In J.R.R. Tolkien's *The Lord of the Rings*, a ring of power turns the wearer invisible. That power means the wearer can act with impunity.

We, too, can imagine characters with superhuman abilities and consider the implications. These thought experiments help us to put ourselves and our society into perspective. In Tolkien's world, we wrestle with questions on the nature of power. In our scenario, though, let's imagine not only that wizards exist but that one supremely powerful wizard has cast a spell over the realm.

The wizard's spell is of nonviolence. Call it 'The Spell of Ahimsa.' Under this spell, no one can threaten or commit any act of harm against another person or their property. When a brigand tries to attack a caravan on the road, his fingers weaken, and his dagger simply falls from his grasp. When a tax collector tries to arrest a merchant in the town, the handcuffs slip from his fingers. When a bully tries to push another girl, she pushes against an invisible wall of protection. It doesn't matter whether you think violence is being used in the service of good or evil. The fact is, the spell ensures a condition of complete nonviolence in society.

What should we make of this? Would the realm be better off under the wizard's spell?

People will have different answers, depending on where they find themselves on some ideological matrix. Intuitively, though, I think most people agree that things *would* be better if there were no violence. Nearly every society has laws against theft, fraud, and injury — and for good reason. Strangely, as soon as we get into questions about the nature and justification for the state, answers start to diverge. Differences are starkest when we think of the spell affecting government officials. Consider the Spell of Ahimsa as it relates to issues of government welfare. In other words, if everyone is compelled by magic to abstain from violence, how will government authorities implement their plans? More specifically, how would authorities tax the rich to redistribute to the poor? If we are consistent in our commitments and practices, we need to confront this question.

ACKNOWLEDGE THE VIOLENCE OF REDISTRIBUTION

The modern redistributive state is relatively recent in history. What made the welfare state affordable at all was a rapid advance of industry and enterprise. After about 1800, this advance helped create opportunities for people to create more value for each other. For probably the first time in history, there were more people trading than raiding, and people living in this Great Enrichment rocketed out of poverty. According to economic historian Dierdre McCloskey:

Earlier prosperities had intermittently increased real income per head by double or even triple, 100 or 200 percent or so, only for it to fall back to the miserable $3 a day typical of humans since the caves. But the Great Enrichment increased real income per head, despite a rising number of heads, by a factor of seven — anywhere from 2,500 to 5,000 percent.[377]

A few entrepreneurs got amazingly wealthy in the Great Enrichment, but a massive middle class emerged, too, as people figured out how to organize themselves into productive firms. These firms weren't perfect, but they were responsible for unprecedented improvements in living standards. But with such growth came wealth inequality. And wealth inequality expresses the envy gene.

In the late nineteenth and early twentieth centuries, wealthier governments began instituting welfare programs and other centralized forms of social insurance. The idea was to see that the least fortunate in society could meet their basic needs. But these systems brought along a set of problems. Among them was that, as these compulsory systems began to predominate, civil society's existing voluntary systems disappeared. Important features of voluntary systems, such as the practice of compassion and the development of personal character, disappeared along with them.

The Spell of Ahimsa helps us see more clearly a feature of the redistributive welfare state that is frequently overlooked: *its very existence depends on the threat of violence.* In other words, how would the system operate if authorities couldn't threaten to imprison those who refused to pay for the system? Most people don't think about matters this way, accustomed as they are to the welfare state being a permanent fixture of life after more than a century. As we will see, it hasn't always been this way.

CONSIDER SAVINGS CLUBS

In some of the poorest parts of the world, there is little in the way of government welfare or modern banking. So in places like sub-Saharan Africa, people contribute a modest monthly allotment to a *su su* (or sou-sou). Those who aren't very good at saving money by themselves are encouraged to use a *su su* because club members hold each other accountable.

Here's how it works, according to South African writer Lihle Z. Mtshali, describing the Afro-Caribbean variant in America:

> The group elects a treasurer who will collect the members' contributions. She will also create a payout roster, or members can request to receive their hand at any given date during the cycle. Everyone agrees on how much and how often they want to contribute. If ten members contribute $100 a week, each week a member will receive a $1,000 hand or cash lump sum. The cycle begins again after ten weeks. Any member who can afford it can also double their contribution and get paid two hands in one cycle.[378]

Because there is no interest to be collected, members always get out the exact amount they put in. The recipient changes each period in a rotating fashion, such that every member of the group is eventually a recipient. Africa and the Caribbean are not alone in this regard. Quite curiously, this type of arrangement has sprung up in various forms worldwide throughout history.

Tanomoshi is a locally organized system of mutual aid. These community resource pools have existed in Japan at least since the middle Kamakura period of 1185 to 1333 BCE.[379] Under this system, each member would contribute a small sum at regular intervals and receive a single lump payment whenever there was a significant life event.

In medieval Japan, per capita GDP is estimated to

have been between 500 and 800 dollars in 2011 dollars.[380] (Compare this with today's U.S. poverty level of $12,760 for a single person and Japan's per capita GDP of about $40,000.) Every month, people would travel to the *tanomoshiko* to leave a little bit of money. A trusted party there would accept their contribution with a bow. *Tanomoshiko* is translated as 'reliable group,' so the community selects someone of wisdom and integrity. Though most medieval Japanese earned very little, they were committed. One family might have arranged for a daughter to be married. Another might have found a parent has become gravely ill. Each would be able to go directly to the *tanomoshiko* for support.

A similar system called *kye* in Korea is still around today, even among Korean immigrants to the U.S. Similar rotational systems include *tandas* (Latin America), *cundinas* (Mexico), *partnerhand* (Carribean/UK), *hui* (Asia), *Game' ya* (Middle East), *pandeiros* (Brazil), and *arisan* (Indonesia). These systems facilitate personal savings, investment in property and enterprise, insurance, and personal loans, as well as assistance to poor people. In developed countries, people can use these systems to build credit.

REMEMBER MUTUAL AID IN AMERICA

We explored the decline of mutual aid in America in Part One, so we'll keep this section brief. But let's turn to what ought to be an unlikely source of agreement in *Jacobin Magazine*, an unapologetically socialist outlet. Writer Maya Adereth makes a startling admission, which I present with emphasis:

> *Ultimately, a socialist society can't be commanded from above, it must be built from below.* In the midst of this dramatic shift, thousands of volunteers have managed to organize hundreds of mutual aid networks for groceries, healthcare, and other needs.

> This isn't the first time that mutual aid networks have proliferated across the United States. Between the mid-nineteenth and mid-twentieth centuries, thousands of "fraternal societies" provided access to healthcare, paid leave, and life insurance to workers in nearly every major city.... As we build solidarity today, we can look to this past to help pave a path forward.[381]

Of course, Adereth's passage is open to interpretation. I suspect there is a difference between the system she sees as her ideal and the one that is a necessary evil. I also suspect that Adereth is more comfortable with violent revolutionary change and top-down control of society than I am. But I take heart in the fact that there is some overlap in our perspectives, because it is in these overlaps that facets of a more complex truth can be found, and in which great things can be built.

For now, that overlap is mutual aid. Most human beings care for others, and this care can extend to strangers. Only misanthropes relish the idea that anyone should suffer in poverty. So at some level, we all want to know that the least advantaged can get help when they need it. Most of us want to know that those who seek our help *really need our help* and that any form of assistance doesn't create dependency.

Unlike state redistribution, mutual aid societies serve this function because members can keep an eye on other members. State welfare policymakers views successful people primarily as human ATMs and the poor as statistical plot points. In this way, there can be no discernment. By contrast, mutual aid arrangements keep us from outsourcing our compassion. They preserve our humanity. And they can be much more effective at helping people rise up out of poverty with real support.

BECOME THE SOCIAL SAFETY NET

If you have ever heard of a distributed ledger, such as a blockchain, then you might have heard of a DAO, or 'distributed autonomous organization.'[382] In these forms of virtual governance, the ledger keeps people honest and uses digital escrow features in lieu of trusted third parties. People in DAOs sometimes have to make decisions *as a group*, despite members being scattered around the world. So, they experiment with different consensus mechanisms to make decisions as a group without resorting to crude majoritarian rule.

If a DAO is a decentralized way of coordinating activities to create value, which upgrades the traditional organization, then a DISC is a decentralized way of coordinating community assistance, which upgrades mutual aid. DISC stands for 'distributed income support cooperative.'[383] DISCs, like DAOs, will be voluntary, permission-less, and most likely ambivalent to questions of national origin. These cosmopolitan entities will bind people based on the desire to create better social safety nets instead of having support accrue based on some accident of birth (like citizenship eligibility). Of course, such is not to argue that only female Guatemalan weavers can't or shouldn't form their own DISC. It is rather to say that these restrictions are not inherent to the concept of a DISC.

One of the next big advances for these technologies will be to enable what I refer to as "human fractals." The idea here is in contrast to *disintermediation*, which is to take out middlemen. And that is one of the virtues of the blockchain. In some cases, we will need *hypermediation*, which efficiently introduces *more* middlemen.

I quote liberally once again from *The Social Singularity:*

> To sketch hypermediation, imagine that technology enables a system of numerous checkers. Those checkers use their minds to do the checking on the

activities of others, but they themselves are checked
in a kind of fractal. Each checker builds and guards
a reputation so as to be considered and rewarded for
future work as a checker. It's not disintermediation,
but rather virtuous recursion with associated good
incentives. There is no perfect human fractal, but it
would still be virtuous when compared against the
status quo ante.

Such is not to argue that the original blockchain,
with its logic fixed at the level of the network, isn't
profoundly useful for a host of use cases. Rather,
there will be circumstances in which people will
want to self-organize in ways that take into account
their particular strengths, aptitudes, perspectives and
context. As I write, blockchain-inspired alternatives
are being developed along these lines. There will
be distributed ledgers for identity, reputation, and
improved trust networks. And sometimes hypermediation will be required.[384]

If human fractals work, they are likely to make decentralization even more potent, not less.

DISC developers might want to avail themselves of
both hypermediation technologies and disintermediation
technologies. I am no technical expert, but DISCs will
probably always involve human 'checkers' to operate,
at least at the outset. Just as with the original mutual aid
societies, communities are formed by people who check up
on each other, check in with each other, and check to see
whether they're doing the right things.

The DISC framework differs considerably from a
universal basic income (UBI) in that it's designed primarily
as a system of mutual aid instead of a system of redistribution. Such is important because DISCs:

- Are emergency measures, as in, they are quasi-insur-
  ance that kicks in when needed, reducing perverse
  incentives;

- Are decentralized such that they can't be used as a

massive lever of central authority;

- Don't require politics, so they can be voluntary and self-organizing;
- Are affordable because they target specific needs;
- Are supportive of community because they operate embedded in human fractals and reputation systems;
- Can be relativized to various regional and individual economic circumstances;
- Can be built in tandem with DAOs, so that people can get income support between jobs, for example, in the fluid labor marketplaces of the future;
- Can be configured as a mutual-aid system in which the community surrounding a person validates the need and stakes reputation capital on such validation;
- Use reputation as a currency of trust;
- Scale with displacement and poverty without being monolithic.

While we are only at the genesis of the decentralization and polycentrism revolutions, the world is moving away from monolithic social systems. Instead of thinking about how we can outsource our sense of responsibility for each other to distant capitals, let us think about how we can create and join systems that, eventually, allow us to *become the social safety net*.

MOVE BEYOND CENTRALIZED WELFARE

One of the major problems with traditional welfare and central systems of government largesse is that they don't generally take into account particular circumstances of time and place. After coercive taxation, welfare payments are dispensed from a central bureaucracy, according to bureaucratic rules and processes. But as we have suggested, this removes the vital element of community:

- Who knows you?

- What is your reputation?

- How can you improve it?

- Do you have skin in the game?

These are questions that appear nowhere in redistributive welfare or UBIs, but will be vital to DISCS.

DISCs, therefore, might have peer pools and peer juries. These mechanisms mean that people can join communities of contributors, but each community member is accountable to every other member. That you're accountable to the other members means that you always have incentives to do what's right to keep your membership privileges intact and enjoy the DISC's future potential benefits.

Peer pools are the internal mechanism of DISCs' mutual aid support systems. Pools collect dues periodically as a membership condition, although the dues might be as low as pennies a month. People can be members of multiple DISCs, which means that you might be a member of a pool associated with healthcare and another pool associated with unemployment. In any case, maybe members contribute based on their ability to contribute. I realize this sounds vaguely Marxist, which is fine. I prefer to think of it as a form of distributed social insurance that includes some members who are more likely to be net contributors and some more likely to be net beneficiaries. We assume that enough higher-income people will become members. In this way, pools are neither purely transactional nor purely charitable, but rather a hybrid.

Peer juries will be responsible for making determinations about the validity of claims to peer pools. Perhaps each member of a DISC will have, say, a mix of members they know and others they don't know to serve as their peer jury. DISCs can experiment with ways to make juries fairer and more game-proof. Still, the idea is to use reputation as a strong incentive to get things right — both with respect to disbursement of support and strong incentives to apply for pool benefits based on genuine need. Aligning the incentives this way balances individual members' needs against the health of the DISC as a whole. This balance will be critical to the long-term success of these entities. Peer juries serve a vital feedback function that UBIs and legacy welfare do not, as the latter treat some population as a black box into which largess must flow. We can imagine all manner of governance functions and consensus mechanisms within peer juries, including liquid democracy, dominant assurance contracts, and prediction markets.

Can DISCs be tokenized using cryptocurrencies? They almost certainly can and ought to be. We can imagine a token in which people are invited to participate initially. Still, instead of expecting some return, membership fees in the DISC are discounted in exchange for their advanced contribution. We can also imagine larger token holders having the option for a more robust presence on peer juries, or a stake in establishing early terms and conditions as charter members. We can imagine DACs, DAOs, high-net-worth individuals, or legacy firms contributing large sponsorships in exchange for marketing visibility or naming rights. We can even imagine tokens being used not just for initial capital raises but also for "programmable incentives" inside the DISC.[385] Tokens can serve as incentives for good health, loyalty rewards, or any other rewards that contribute to the DISC's overall health — including bonuses for attracting new members.

DISCs need not always disburse monies with no expectation of a return. Some DISCs could contrive micro-loans systems and other access to capital for helping members build small businesses, for example. In these hybrid DISCs, people will be required to pay loans back at certain intervals, and their reputation in the DISC will be affected if they fail to meet their obligations. In this way, jury members might decide to be more or less rigid with respect to the criteria they establish. People can discover just the right rulesets as they choose among DISCs competing in the mutual aid market.

Pools of resources have the potential to grow if adequately stewarded, which means that DISCs can create differential rates of dividends to members of the community based on different criteria. Similar to a UBI, this potential feature might be worth trying — especially if it helps align all the members' incentives in service of a DISC's mission. And mature DISCs with lots of members may discover that membership dues are reduced thanks to surpluses being stewarded in a fashion similar to mutual funds. With some caveats, the most exciting model might be that 'dividends' or surpluses could accrue in an emergency fund that protected members in the event of some protracted economic recession. Or surpluses might enable DISCs to attract more high-risk, low-contribution individuals.

What's so interesting about DISCs is that they will be diverse and experimental. No DISC is a single, monolithic scheme unless one happens to find the absolute best rule structure and health measures, drawing in more and more members. This evolutionary aspect to DISCs means that they will continuously evolve relative to changing circumstances and new information. Such cannot be said of legacy welfare or a UBI, of course, because these are generally thought of as products of statute, not of innovation. DISCs will take on different forms and evolve like genomes, mainly as DISCs offer a right of exit — which means that the threat of member defection is a built-in accountability mechanism.

We should accept any cautionary notes about potential problems that might crop up in some DISCS, particularly as they're getting started, and they're in early experimentation phases. There might even be a pretty sizable die-off of poorly conceived or executed DISCs. Why?

There will be participants who try to game DISCs by hacking, creating rules, loopholes, or coalitions that allow members to take advantage of other members. As this part of the evolution of DISCs plays out, we are likely to see what many perceive to be a 'race to the bottom' as stronger, more solvent DISCs emerge in the fitness landscape.

As with ICOs and cryptocurrencies, this macro process is likely to play out here, too. But when the dust settles and the vulnerable DISCs die off, strong, secure DISCs will emerge to attract new members. However, it will behoove any DISC designer to construct criteria and/or secure templates that start with fidelity to mission and a view to the benefit of all members, even if certain members end up volunteering to be net contributors to the DISC.

RECOGNIZE WEALTH'S LAW OF FLOW

A lot of people think that wealth inequality is a problem. Some argue that inequality would be mitigated if certain institutions, government and corporate, didn't create a rigged game that benefits those at the top. Others think that, however one arrives at the inequality, it is always inherently bad. For this discussion, I want to put aside those debates and think of inequality as a given.

Recall our discussion of the Law of Flow in Part One. If the Law of Flow is true, we know that natural systems organize according to scaling laws, which reveal vascularization in all aspects of life. Physicist Adrian Bejan has formulated the constructal law to show this in trees, river systems, circulatory systems, animal forms, and the design of highways and roads. Here's a summary from politics reporter Ephrat Livni:

> Bejan illustrates that [vascular] hierarchy is unavoidable using Horton's law of stream numbers, which says that three to five tributaries emerge over the lifetime of a mother stream. As the mother streams calve and then the next generation of tributaries in turn calves again, uniformity disappears. When Horton's law's multiplier is applied to the movement of wealth in a society, Bejan says, even modest complexity — five families in a tiny village, for example — leads to a non-uniform distribution of wealth.[386]

In other words, differential contributions of labor, risk, or capital will result in differential wealth outcomes, which creates some measure of inequality in every case. Therefore, any system we contrive will be concerned with reducing poverty or closing the wealth gap through coercive redistribution. My argument is that poverty reduction should always be the goal. Inequality, so long as it is a natural consequence of the Law of Flow, will always be with us.

When creating DISCs, one is concerned with reducing poverty. We assume that some inequality is a natural feature of life, integral to any complex system in which economic flows are involved. There are many reasons to prefer poverty alleviation to coercive distribution, but I have tried here to restrict mine to the pragmatic. In short, we need each other to create wealth so that whatever system of civil association we contrive respects the generative aspects of the broader economic ecosystem on which it will depend.

INVITE MORALITY-BASED MEMBERSHIP

I suspect that for DISCs to work well, they will have to mirror the scaling-law vascularization of the wider society. In other words, DISC designs should be prepared to have members with differential contributions and differential relative benefits. High net worth individuals, for example, might be aware that their participation in a DISC is mostly charitable, and indeed it might be possible to structure DISCs so that people can contribute dues/fees with no expectation of future benefit.

You might be wondering: Why in the world would rich people be members of DISCs? What incentives do they have to participate if they have little expectation of ever using benefits? To that, I would respond:

- Why do wealthy donors give to charity?

- Why do wealthy congregants in churches tithe?

- Why do wealthy people build research centers at universities?

- Why do wealthy companies sponsor things?

- Why do wealthy patrons support arts and letters?

- Why do wealthy magnates like Warren Buffett support higher taxes on the wealthy if they wouldn't support powerful mutual aid organizations like DISCs?

Wealthy people are generally also in a good position to have greater stewardship privileges than the rest of us, which is to say they might have more powerful voting privileges in exchange for their proportionally greater contribution. Such might function as trustee boards for nonprofits.

If your response to any such DISC proposal is, 'We simply can't count on rich people to support others,' then you'll likely return to the project of trying to figure out how to make a UBI viable in a post-collapse world. And that's fine. In the meantime, the rest of us will criticize by creating.

ASK THE FUNDAMENTAL QUESTIONS

We must ask a series of important questions in an age of rapid technological advance and material abundance.

1. If you could choose nonviolent means of achieving some social goal such as poverty relief, wouldn't you? After all, the threat of violence causes suffering. Causing unnecessary suffering against innocent people is wrong.

One might respond to this question by saying that nonviolent forms of poverty relief are impossible; therefore, the suffering is necessary. But if you combine the fact of mutual aid with modern technological sophistication, it's much easier to dispel skepticism of voluntary arrangements.

2. If one can demonstrate that mutual aid and charity could be robust enough to help the least advantaged, wouldn't that mean that the violent redistributive state causes unnecessary suffering?

It would seem so. Some might argue that society's wealthiest members don't suffer all that much when they are coerced through taxation, especially when they comply. It's hard for most people to give a shit about rich people, but most people would want to avoid causing unnecessary suffering. A practitioner of ahimsa certainly would. But if we agree that the goal is to help the poor rather than to punish the rich, then we should always seek to uplift the least advantaged.

The vast majority of the superrich's assets don't go to consumption at all, but are capital that fuels other endeavors such as business investments that employ people and launch a thousand experiments in effective altruism. Capital is seldom idle.

3. If it's possible to help the poor (or for the poor to help each other) without doing harm, isn't this something we ought to do? Doesn't that also mean

we ought to transition away from the violent welfare state to a nonviolent condition of community support, charity, and mutual aid?

We have demonstrated that mutual aid is not only possible but also more effective even among the poorest people. Even if there is a subset who cannot afford to participate in mutual aid, the least advantaged would be able to rely more on families, churches, charities, and communities — all of which can receive more generous support. As we said, people are more likely to find these options without a vast government monopoly on welfare. Net contributors will be happier, as we argued in Part One.

Mutual aid arrangements are not just superior because they are voluntary. These systems build in mechanisms of accountability and integrity for members. By contrast, government welfare is impersonal and treats everyone the same, which reduces incentives to work and engenders an unhealthy sense of entitlement.

As radical as it may sound, charity and mutual aid systems actually create *more* trust, engender *more* integrity, and offer *more* accountability. With all of the abundance available today, we think that the mutual aid sector is due for a renaissance. But if the system of compulsory redistribution continues to grow, there will be fewer opportunities for mutual aid experimentation.

CAST THE SPELL

Of course, there is no Spell of Ahimsa; it is impossible to cast such a spell on everyone. But one thing is possible: You and I can cast this spell on ourselves.

In so doing, we can form a moral community of people who refuse to support institutions that threaten violence to operate. I'd be willing to bet that where there is more peace, there is also more compassion. As more people cast this spell upon themselves, we will start to see the shoots of human flourishing grow in the detritus of political power.

The world is a violent place. That means that violence is a part of life. Even if more peaceful societies begin to dot the world map, there will probably be hostile powers, waiting like wolves. Enemies are not just abroad; people with violent intentions live among us, too. Some of them are opportunists and sociopaths. Others seek to dominate and to suppress.

So what does that mean for the integral liberal?

AVOID WEAKNESS

While integral liberals are committed to nonviolence, we are also committed to free expression and free association. I am under no illusions that there will be authoritarian hostility to our ideas among High Minds, victimologists and reactionaries. And if they get traction, enemies — whether through frothing, whining, or violence — will do everything in their power to tear down the nascent structures of New America.

Practice *ahimsa*, and be strong for as long as you can in nonviolence. But also understand that *ahimsa* is never an invitation to be weak or to fail to defend yourself and those you love. "'There are three things that are beyond my control," said the twelfth-century Japanese emperor Go Shirakawa-In, "the rapids on the Kamo river, the dice at gambling, and the monks of the mountain." The monks, or Sohei, were both Buddhist monks and fierce warriors. In feudal Japan, even the monks had to be prepared to defend their way of life.

We understand that building a Framework for Utopia requires us to confront the decidedly unideal likelihood that certain groups will want to organize according to structures that traditional liberals would find offensive. External foes will threaten people living in proximity to one another. The Framework itself, therefore, represents the extent of our extended olive branch. When authoritarians go out of bounds, we must be prepared to defend ourselves on all fronts. For once we have tasted true freedom, we will be prepared to live and die for it.

*　　*　　*

Reimagine Defense

"War is the health of the state," wrote intellectual Randolph Bourne after living through the First World War. We might add that the health of the warfare state is the disease of peace. If the welfare state is the state's left leg, then the warfare state is the right leg. Together, the welfare-warfare legs are running headlong into a sea of debt. Bourne understood that the state is just an abstraction that in reality is an apparatus of violence run by "common and unsanctified men."[387] The idea of society, which Bourne called "country," gets conflated with the idea of the state, especially during times of war. Bourne writes:

> Country is a concept of peace, tolerance, of living, and letting live. But State is essentially a concept of power, of competition; it signifies a group in its aggressive aspects. And we have the misfortune of being born not only into a country but into a State, and as we grow up we learn to mingle the two feelings into a hopeless confusion.[388]

Of course, one ought to acknowledge that the unsteady peace after World War II was made possible in great measure by the American state acting as a kind of global constable. But *projecting power*, which is more or less colonizing the world with bases equipped with industrial-scale killing machines, is neither sustainable nor particularly effective anymore. Because we can't see the possible world that isn't there, a world without the eighty year American supremacy might actually have been worse. And yet there is a perverse, self-reinforcing aspect to the American psychological default to Thanatos Masculine. Having the world's most powerful military is now a central part of the American story, which offers people a largely unearned sense of national pride. The default position seems to be to expand the military empire indefinitely.

What we'll argue will no doubt challenge the pervasive psychology in America. I realize that's no way to sell books. Still, I'll mount an offensive against The Leviathan Formulation's last article of faith. I also recognize that, in collapse, a mighty military will be the last thing to go; it is fear's organized religion. But the warfare state is shot through with problems. The least we can say is that, like everything else, it has become unaffordable. But what about all the bad guys around the world?

My late father always said that he'd happily go to prison defending his family. If he ended up behind bars, he said: "I'd just walk right up to the biggest, meanest sumbitch I could find and call him darlin'." There is some logic in his rationale, just as there is logic to the idea that maybe there has to be the biggest, meanest bully in the world to keep all the smaller bullies in line. If you're American, the biggest, meanest bully doesn't seem like such a bully at all if he's on your side. In a world after collapse, though, it's not clear what this vast military bureaucracy looks like. Does it run on the fumes of patriotism and dwindled debt spending? Does it break up? Does it fall into disrepair and disorganization? It's hard to say. But to imagine a central military bureaucracy broken up or broken down, it becomes easier to question some of its fundamental assumptions.

The problems that infect the military-industrial complex are more or less the same problems we touched on elsewhere. Bureaucratic allocation makes everything more expensive and less efficient. There is no connection between the value anyone places on national security and how much gets spent. A shadow army of special interests and rent-seekers parallels the real army; the military's deep state and complex of contractors is real, and it is powerful. None of it gets subjected to the ordinary rules of competition, value creation, or profit and loss. So it grows based on the unmoored incentives of functionaries, politicians, and contractors. It feasts on the sentiments of a people who have so little connection to its cost, extent, or efficacy — much less any concept of mission. Chants of *we're number one* do not suffice.

For at least twenty years, the Department of Defense explicitly defined its mission as providing "the military forces needed to deter war and to protect the security of our country." But according to the U.K.'s *Independent*, in 2018, the Pentagon quietly changed the mission: "The mission of the Department of Defense is to provide a lethal Joint Force to defend the security of our country and sustain American influence abroad."[389]

When someone discovered the change, there was media blowback, but at least the new mission was truthful. It's as if the critics were hoping that the Pentagon would go back to lying to them. As of this writing, there is no clearly stated mission on the main pages, though there is still an archived version of the former mission statement available via web search.

The point of this is not to pick nits with the Pentagon's website editors, but to point out that this language probably reflects a fundamental change to the purpose of America's war bureaucracy, from defense to empire, but one that happened long, long ago. When we couple this mission creep with the fact of the Pentagon's unchecked bureaucratic growth and unrestrained budgets, we can see that the institution that fought the Nazis and Imperial Japanese has metastasized into something less recognizable and more corrupted.

As the war bureaucracy will be a driver of collapse, we can take some measure of comfort in the idea that if collapse comes, there will be an opportunity to reset the warfare state.

CHANGE THE RELEVANT UNIT OF PROTECTION

The default unit of protection is the nation, and there are two main reasons for this. The first comes in the Leviathan Formulation, with its attendant logic of peace through hegemony. The second comes in the now-classic understanding of national security as a so-called "public good," which is a definition that comes from economics textbooks and is presented most famously in the work of economist Paul Samuelson.[390] But the idea is, the extent to which a given person in some geographic area is defended from foreign attack or invasion, other people in that same area are similarly defended. That makes it hard to charge people for defense. Such is supposedly a classic free-rider problem. Indeed, most economists think that the only way to provide a sufficient level of defense is to have the government fund such with taxes.

Interestingly, though, maybe it's time to question this *defense-as-public-good* orthodoxy. Recall that the economist's definition of public good is *non-rivalrous* and *non-excludable*. Unless we get into specifics, it seems plausible that national defense fits this description. But when we get into the particulars of defense resources, the idea starts to break down slightly. For example, if an anti-ballistic missile (ABM) protects Seattle, then it cannot protect Los Angeles. That means any given ABM is rivalrous.

Likewise, if a terrorist cell was hoping to launch an attack, then the most likely way they would try is to get into a major event center to detonate some sort of bomb. Metal detectors and similar devices protecting Madison Square Garden cannot be used elsewhere. Therefore, these kinds of resources are not public goods in the economic sense, although, in their totality, they work towards 'national security' in a vague and metaphorical sense. But even in cases where the public goods rationale seems more clear cut, as in cases where security forces guard some geographical area, those public-good benefits quickly disappear the further away you get from that area.

Nathan P. Goodman and Christopher Coyne think that this sort of analysis breaks apart the Samuelsonian conception:

> Appreciating geographic context matters because the orthodox view of defense assumes that national security involves externalities at the scale of the entire nation-state and, therefore, must be provided at the national level. However, this presumption requires homogenizing defense into a single public good with a single scale — "the nation." In practice, however, defense is not a single good. Defending a marathon from a terrorist attack is distinct from defending a city from a missile attack. Both are distinct from defending a nation-state from a ground invasion by soldiers or from citizens defending themselves against an authoritarian despot. Each one involves different scales of externalities.[391]

If they are correct in their analysis, then a decidedly different kind of economic analysis can be brought to bear. Indeed, Goodman and Coyne think a polycentric alternative to the public goods idea of defense recommends itself.

DECENTRALIZE DEFENSE

The polycentric alternative to national defense is *not* the same as network-centric warfare. You might have heard the latter phrase starting in the 1990s and up through the Iraq War. At the risk of oversimplification, network-centric warfare was just getting the bureaucracies to talk more and use networking technologies to push some kinds of decisions to the 'edge,' not to mention having the edges gather more intelligence. But with this type of military, taxes still flow into the Department of Defense. Decisions are still primarily made at the top. And there is still a single bureaucratic center of authority that is immune from market forces.

The polycentric alternative involves multiple, separate decision makers and completely different budgets within distinct organizations. These forces might engage in a loose confederation so that they can align or coordinate when necessary. For now, we don't need to decide whether these separate defense organizations cover smaller geographic monopolies, cover overlapping jurisdictions in competition, or function more like benevolent private military companies such as Academi (formerly Blackwater). Rather, the point is that polycentric defense is likely to be more responsive to local circumstances, as local actors apply their local knowledge. Moreover, just as private or Ostrom-style commons management is superior to bureaucratic management, polycentric defense will be better, too.

Let's take a real-world example: Imagine if, instead of having competing firms and white hat individuals operating in different aspects of the entire industry, the federal government was entirely responsible for all aspects of cybersecurity, from protection against breeches to antivirus. Should we imagine that this Department of Cybersecurity would fare as well?

Per dollar spent, one could argue that the Taliban is more effective and more polycentric. Though they share some central authority in decision making, their military activities are almost entirely decentralized. We can say something similar about al-Qaeda, which continues to operate in Afghanistan with little friction from the Taliban. "As a result, al-Qaeda today maintains a presence in different pockets of Afghanistan," write analysts Javid Ahmad and Husain Haqqani. "It relies on the Taliban for sanctuary, protection, supply networks and facilitation routes.[392]

No doubt, the United States fighting forces in Afghanistan have been formidable occupiers since 2001, but they have been there almost two decades as of this writing. The Taliban and Al Qaeda continue to operate in the war-torn country. The irony is that Afghanistan has a de facto polycentric form of defense. It's a crude form and not always unified in its objectives, but it has managed to hold up despite incursions by two occupying superpowers. And though different factions have come to the negotiating table in recent times, it's hard for anyone to claim victory after twenty years. Occupation has brought modest returns, including symbolic wins such as the killing of Osama bin Laden. But despite U.S. military might, the U.S. government's successes in nation-building have been mixed at best.

Let's imagine the emergent defense capabilities of the local Afghans — including the Taliban — as being applied in the U.S. with comparatively more resources. Orders of magnitude more resources. It's not hard to imagine that Americans would be able to defend themselves, even if the polycentric regime couldn't maintain a global empire for a time.

Some might worry that a big monocentric force like China might step into any vacuum left by the United States. The main benefit of hegemony has been the United States' protection of trade routes and the various channels of globalization; that means that there are deep interests in ensuring that these channels remain open, and that includes China's interests as it continues to pursue export-led growth. Interestingly, China is on a collapse trajectory, too, for reasons that might fill another book. But if the U.S. collapses and China does not, other countries will have to decide whether they want to work together to check China's military might. Perhaps a New American polycentric defense would be leaner but still capable of protecting the interests of allies who want stability.

We don't know how things will look post-collapse, but our job is to figure out plausible paths in an uncertain world. In writing this, of course, I'm motivated by my own answers to specific normative questions: What sort of foreign policy ought the United States have? What is the role of a monocentric or polycentric military in the world? And how should either be funded when we seek to extend ahimsa to every sphere and scale? I realize we must balance normativity against pragmatism. But there is nothing more pragmatic than people having to think about defending themselves in a world where the federal budget has dried up, and Washington is no longer in charge. If all anyone can think of is *I can't imagine otherwise*, that's not good enough. Failures of imagination can kill.

In 476 CE, the Roman Emperor should have known that Rome's cash flow problems couldn't be helped by further incursions into Africa or east into Arabia's deserts. The returns on imperialism had dried up. Couple its fiscal woes with the difficulty of bringing the Germanic tribes to heel, and Rome was in a situation where, after 476, its decline could only accelerate. Historians agree that if you could put a date on Rome's fall, it was the day Odoacer staged a revolt and deposed the Emperor Romulus Augustulus. Otherwise, there was no pivotal event, only a confluence of events that had led up to this fateful year. Could it be that 2020 was America's 476 CE?

Something similar can be said about the British Empire; its welfare-warfare state would mean its undoing. Two World Wars and industry nationalizations had brought Britain to financial ruin, and though scarcely anyone would argue Britain's fight against the Nazis was indispensable to the Allied victory, virtually no one would argue against the idea that the war helped break the empire and that the Suez crisis was the straw that broke Britannia's back.

Alternatively, *die Hanse*, or the Hanseatic League (1356-1862), was a group of separate, wealthy city-states that combined efforts to form a polycentric military to protect its collaborative and commercial interests. This polycentric form of governance lasted for just over five centuries, and included military cooperation. Specifically, *die Hanse* managed to fight off commercial raiding by the English in a maritime war that lasted some years. There was not always unanimity, and there were some coordination problems among the Hanseatic city-states. But peace and commercial relationships were restored, and *die Hanse's* polycentric military was ultimately a success.

Today, technology and robust markets make it much easier to solve coordination problems. Failures of imagination only keep us from dreaming up less expensive coordinated defense among smaller jurisdictions.

13

UPGRADE COLLECTIVE INTELLIGENCE

*In an imperfect world, the best insurance we
have against truth's being politicized is to
put no one in particular in charge of it.*
Jonathan Rauch

*The Humean condition is also the Human
condition.*
W. V. O. Quine

Philosophers have struggled for millennia with questions about the nature of truth and our ability, as humans, to know it. Some are just puzzles that don't seem to have any relevance to modern life; others are central to who we are. The more we explore these questions, the harder it gets to tell the difference between what's practical and what's merely puzzling.

If we're going to bring about a renaissance in the post-collapse era, we will have to improve our collective intelligence. That means that we not only have to improve our epistemology, i.e. our ways of knowing, but we are also going to have to improve our ability to store, access, and share what we know *together*.

When I think about what we know together, I'm not

talking about any attempt to stand outside of my skinsuit to verify some mind-independent reality. Last I checked — as of this book going off to print — I can't do that. Instead, I'm willing to settle for what we have termed *intersubjective agreement,* which, for all I know, could be a language game inside a Matrix-like simulation. Again, these are the sorts of puzzles that preoccupy philosophers. Right now, I'm willing to settle for enlarging the class of things we can usefully say we know, and from that derive measures of progress along certain dimensions.

If our ideas about collective intelligence include forging intersubjective agreements, we'd better make sure such agreements aren't groupthink. So how do we do that?

First, we have to make reason and evidence great again. That doesn't mean that we have to go so far as to apotheosize Reason and Evidence, capitalizing them out of some genuflect to the Enlightenment. It is instead to step back from the postmodern precipice. Some postmodernists would have us deny reason and evidence entirely; critical theorists would have us replace reason and evidence with radical political assertions and contrived narratives. But that approach is dangerous, primarily because humanity will invariably run up against reality's icebergs.

What we can find useful in postmodernism, though, is the idea of intersubjective agreement, or what neo-pragmatist Richard Rorty called "solidarity"[393] in discourse. Intersubjective agreement is necessary for truth tracking under our conception, but it's not sufficient. Still, we can acknowledge that part of what we do when we track truth is share a common vocabulary. What is left is somehow to test that vocabulary and its referents in the onrushing flux of experience.

Okay, so let's figure out how to get on with the business of tracking truth without either falling back into Enlightenment dogmas or stepping off into a postmodern void. We seek a synthesis, or at least a way of integrating the best in each tradition, allowing us to become a more cooperative species. But before we do, let's take a detour into the hall of mirrors.

MOVE BEYOND THE HARRIS HYPOTHESIS

Tristan Harris became famous for defecting from a large internet media company and then crusading for social media reform. Because social media is the primary way most of us get our information these days, we should touch briefly on what we'll call the Harris Hypothesis. This hypothesis has elements of truth, so it's important to acknowledge it while also dispelling the attendant hype and hyperbole. The summary is my own, so discerning readers might want to give Harris an independent hearing, for example, in the 2020 documentary, *The Social Dilemma*.

1. Social media companies are profit-driven.

2. Social media companies use sophisticated algorithms and supercomputers to monitor our activity online and develop sophisticated psychographs that predict our wants and behaviors.

3. Social media companies use these psychographs to serve up content we want, so they can get more and more of our attention to paying advertisers.

4. Users are 'forced' to use social media due to powerful network effects.

5. Users get lots of media that conform to their biases; advertisers get access to users' attention; social media companies make more money.

6. Social media companies inadvertently reinforce people's biases, which causes political polarization, social fracturing, and disconnects from reality.

7. Users are pretty helpless, as these systems hijack their dopamine and limbic systems, creating a perfect method of both positive and negative reinforcement.

8. Reality-based civic engagement required by a healthy democracy is lost as more and more people descend into a self-reinforcing downward spiral.

9. Democratic institutions are at risk; populist nationalism is on the rise due to social media.

10. Government must regulate social media companies; and government must tweak social media algorithms.

The forgoing is a plausible-sounding hypothesis, which makes it dangerous.

Let's pass over just how the Harris Hypothesis focuses on social media's perceived downside while virtually ignoring the tremendous upside. The hypothesis assumes that people are more like tropistic creatures than thinking, choosing agents. The narrative is that we're all addicted to social media content like grannies are to slot machines. Of course, there is a mildly addicting property to media, just as there was to television media forty years ago. But we are neither living in a massive Skinner Box, nor are we utterly helpless to all the highly-paid engineers' algorithms or the supercomputers that power them.

Tristan Harris is one in a string of social media whistleblowers who won accolades because it appeared he courageously went up against powerful social media companies. But the whistleblower trope assumes that people are clueless about how social media companies work. It also assumes those self-same clueless people *ought* to be able to publish information on the internet and expect no one to scrape it, analyze it, or use it to offer them things they want. The idea is that it's *your data*, just as a chair or a toothbrush is your property. But information is a non-scarce good. You can't expect to give it freely to the world and keep it, too.

Remember Cambridge Analytica? The Trump campaign retained the company in the lead up to the 2016 presidential election. Whistleblowers with guilt complexes were greeted with fawning adoration and instant halos when they bravely came out. Cambridge Analytica's CEO stepped down. Congress convened hearings. Mark Zuckerberg folded like a Dixie cup, then apologized and reinforced the narrative of manipulation-by-psychograph. Trump got elected, and suddenly the other team was interested in the ethics of using big data in elections. Before that, everyone had been blissfully unaware of micro-targeting practices that had been called brilliant and innovative after President Obama's 2008 and 2012 victories. The yearning for integrity seemed to be motivated more by partisan team sports and horror at Trump's election than by any categorical imperative. The Harris Hypothesis runs adjacent to the Cambridge Analytica guilt complex.

The most troubling part of the Harris Hypothesis, though, is that there is one Master conception of the true, the beautiful, and the good that a cadre of Silicon Valley Philosopher Kings happens to possess. Implicit in all of this is that Tristan Harris will ride in astride a white horse and help benevolent angels in the government create just the right algorithms. That way, we can all be well-informed and civically engaged *in just the right way*. Then we'll all be upright voters.

The problem, with all due respect to the Founders, is that there is no such thing as a voter who is knowledgeable and civically engaged enough to make decisions on behalf of 325 million people. Each of us operates in a complex adaptive system we call society, and no algorithm on earth will ever change that fact. The problem, therefore, lies with the very idea of democracy.

Social media might have helped illiberal regimes such as Trump's or Bolsonaro's (or, arguably, Obama's). Still, algorithms didn't magically tap into the worst in people. For better or worse, people were dissatisfied with some prior regime. Populism has been around a lot longer than YouTube.

Never mind. Let's go deeper. Because if social media targeting the masses during elections is of concern to anyone, maybe we're looking at the wrong problem. Maybe we should reconsider our very system of government.

Forget Democracy as We Know It

Putting aside the notion that partisans are moralists, I think the concern is that no one wants to be governed by anyone who is so susceptible to targeting. At best, they're pliant jellyfish; at worst, they're wrong about everything. Call them rubes. (Let's define a rube as anyone you disagree with and think you're smarter than.)

There have always been rubes. There have always been demagogues. There have always been election arms races between marketers like Richard Viguerie, Frank Luntz, or Edward Bernays. For those who believe democracy is the best hope of humanity, our system of government is supposed to be "by" and "for" everyone — including the rubes. If rubes are a majority, however, you get rubocracy.

What's wrong with our system, then, is not that rubes exist or that there are cynical marketers out there who have every incentive to exploit them. What's wrong with our system is majoritarian rule. Currently, that's manifest as a great tug o' war between the Red rubes and the Blue rubes. Cynical elites try to corral them to their respective polling stations. The whole thing is pathetic and outdated when you think about it. So let's do so for a moment.

The following is an all-too-brief critique of democracy:

1. The chance that any given person's vote will affect the outcome of a national election is remote. You're

more likely to be struck by lightning on the way to the voting booth. If anyone has the tie-breaking vote, it will probably be a rube.

2. Rubes are everywhere. We should no more have millions of rubes picking our leaders than having one prominent rube leader to make decisions on behalf of so many people. Often we get both.

3. Society is too complex to have 300 million people vote for a single executive to make such titanic decisions, even if the executive is not a rube, or chosen by rubes.

4. Representative government means that leaders represent those who elected them. If they are faithful to their campaign promises, it's honoring commitments to rubes. If they are not faithful, then they are keeping deals with special interests.

5. Whatever the national government does is monolithic. That means whatever gets decided gets decided for everyone. But monolithic law does account for particular circumstances and contexts, as we have suggested.

Whizbang tech like liquid democracy can't do much to fix the above, though matters might be marginally better. Democracy had a good run. We need a different system.

The idea that tech wizards or social media saboteurs could come along and sway an election is tough for many people to swallow. But let's be honest: The real reason people freak out about Big Data is that there is too much at stake in a given election, which is to say, too much power to be grabbed. Those freaking out about it *love* the idea of all that power when they fancy that their angels will be installed. But when villains replace those angels, suddenly they're worried about the *ethics* and *integrity* of elections.

"Ethics" means *I worry my team might lose the upper hand.*

"Integrity" means *figure out how to keep the rubes from turning out.*

This two-step between integrity and expedience is bipartisan. For the winners, the ends justify the means. For the losers, integrity is conveniently front and center. But if the whole thing weren't such a spectacle, we wouldn't worry so much about the process. Beneath the surface, it legitimizes granting power to the few over so many. It's time to unleash the power of decentralization. Then the rubes won't be able to monkey with our utopias.

In this volume, we've spent buckets of ink on alternatives to democratic governance. What remains, then, is to begin to explore the question of how we might improve our collective intelligence while acknowledging that most of us are rubes, and more of us are not omniscient. Even though we will never have the kind of knowledge or intelligence required to run or fix a complex system with a dominance hierarchy, we need to improve our collective intelligence.

IMPROVE COLLECTIVE INTELLIGENCE

In the interest of brevity, my short formulation for upgrading our collective intelligence is:

1. Practice discernment;

2. Rely on reason and evidence;

3. Gain intersubjective agreement;

4. Seek evidence for competing claims;

5. Adjudicate among claims;

6. Ensure the adjudication mechanism imposes a cost for being wrong;

7. Ask whether the claim in question is proximate to the claimant;

8. Ask whether a single mind can know the claim.

It used to be that our collective intelligence ran mostly on what worked. In other words, what kind of result do we get out of holding a certain kind of belief? I'm not going full-tilt pragmatist, but, generally speaking, one couldn't make an internal combustion engine without getting some things right about air, heat, and properties of metal. Extending this logic to the many, we had to coordinate our human actions through mechanisms that were, well, tracking truth. Again, I'm fully aware of all the philosophical puzzles. I'm just assuming that the more we know, individually or collectively, the easier it is to make progress and improve lives.

Now, criteria 7 and 8 above might seem weird on their faces. But another way to understand collective intelligence is to acknowledge that there are things that can only be known by a *group* of minds (collective intelligence) and that any given mind might have only part of the puzzle (local knowledge). Remember Thwaites' toaster? His know-how did not extend to making a toaster from scratch. We can say the same for economic journalist Leonard Reed's pencil, who says:

> There isn't a single person in all these millions, including the president of the pencil company, who contributes more than a tiny, infinitesimal bit of know-how [to making me]. From the standpoint of know-how the only difference between the miner of graphite in Ceylon and the logger in Oregon is in the type of know-how. Neither the miner nor the logger can be dispensed with, any more than can the chemist at the factory or the worker in the oil field — paraffin being a by-product of petroleum.[394]

The pencil reminds us of a more astounding fact about his creation. He adds that in his creation there is "the absence of a mastermind, of anyone dictating or forcibly directing these countless actions which bring me into being. No trace of such a person can be found."[395]

This type of self-organization, whether for pencils, toasters, or any other phenomenon in nature, is indeed astounding. But what we can learn from this overall lesson is that some phenomena just can't be known by a single mind. Even though toasters and pencils are relatively simple items, maybe even the simplest things require multiple knowers within complex systems, as each contributes a little to collective intelligence.

THE AGE OF COMPLEXITY

So, welcome to the age of complexity. Like other intellectual movements, the age of complexity is characterized by a unique aesthetic. Where the Moderns made foundational structures the beginning or the end of inquiry, the Postmoderns thought structure was just another form of dogma.

Faith in the fixedness of things — truth, progress, order, and the universal laws of nature — came at the expense of that which is random, ironic, and mysterious about the world. Postmodernism offered something playful; at times, an intellectual movement that could celebrate irony and disabuse us of old habits. Some postmodernists seemed to delight in the paradoxes of language. Others played language games. Somewhere in the play, though, the world got lost.

Though postmodernism as a movement seemed destined to stick around, there was a sense in which it could move little earth. Once research programs had been reduced to either critical theory or discovering irony in all things, criticism and narrative became one of the only remaining tools. The critical theorists tossed aside the tools of the thinker as a creative force — a builder. And they abandoned the faculties of exploration, observation, and discovery.

If reason, truth, and liberal inquiry were tools of the oppressor, what could replace them? If structure was just the dogma of a bygone era, or blueprints of the Master's House, how would we know that we live in the same world? The postmodern aesthetic, while occasionally strange and wonderful, operates in a vacuum. But in vacuums, human beings will begin to look for Archimedean Points to reckon with the world around them.

Perhaps the postmodernist can appreciate one final irony: structure has returned from the pyre's ashes. But the age of complexity isn't built on Enlightenment absolutes, traditionalist dogmas, or folk superstitions. It borrows a little irony from its postmodern predecessor. It preserves the Moderns' rationality and skepticism. And it integrates the wisdom of the ancient traditions before combining the best of these into a framework for world-making. But this is not the world-making of fantasy or science fiction. It is the world-making of creativity within constraints.

So now we're in a new age — one that is after postmodernism.

Because we have never built much of anything with weapons (criticism) or toys (play), postmodernism left us sitting in a smoldering intellectual wasteland. We have to take up the tools of construction again; we could never wholly do without structure in our intellectual lives. While structure is still, in part, an aesthetic commitment, something has changed. Structure is now a feature of self-organizing complexity. It demands coherence, even tensegrity, as a geodesic dome.[396] In this way, the structure of our knowledge is indispensable to us, whether in building our theories, constructing our reality, or establishing common rules for playing more prosocial language games.

By the way, the universe doesn't care. It will exert itself whether we like it or not. We either start to understand and approximate its flux and flow, or we try to go against them and suffer.

The lessons we have to learn in the age of complexity lie between what philosopher Catherine Z. Elgin calls "the absolute and the arbitrary."[397] Because we must now operate in areas devoid of many Enlightenment assumptions, we must look to structure *itself* for answers; that is, to the form and function of our claims within different fitness landscapes. We might therefore ask how some way of thinking about the world works in our lives.

Operating in the chaos of uncertainty, we engage in construction, destruction, and reconstruction. Such is the end and means of inquiry. We will always have to work within our intellectual traditions — limited by language, culture, and human nature. As we enter another aesthetic, cultural, and intellectual paradigm, we must be able to recognize its indicators.

If we're in a new paradigm, how can we articulate its properties, its character, and its aesthetic more fully? And once our thinking gets infused with this aesthetic, what lessons will we take with us into the world?

Two Cheers for Motivated Reasoning

To my knowledge, there is no membership card to be in the Rationality Community; as far as I can tell, you only have to be generally committed to what I have called truth tracking. While truth tracking requires acknowledging one's limitations, it's a general commitment to using one's cognitive powers to the ends of discovery. I agree that we should overcome certain kinds of cognitive biases to better understand the world around us. And it's true that sometimes our baggage, whether in our ideological priors or our inborn biases, can get in the way of understanding. We use embodied cognition.

In the process of arguing that expertise is breaking down, I want to make two cheers for motivated reasoning. I realize that some in the Rationality Community might not like that, though I hope to persuade them. If you've never heard of it, motivated reasoning is, in isolation, a kind of fallacious reasoning in which people form beliefs, make arguments, or investigate some claims because the investigator is hoping to reach a certain conclusion. This kind of reasoning would seem to run counter to the pursuit of truth; moral psychologist Jonathan Haidt calls it *post hoc rationalization*. That means that you start with what your intuition says is right or what you wish to be true, and then you get better at arguing for that wish. But rationality requires us to be less biased. And in this sense, the Rationality Community is right: We should never let wishes father lies. We should never let our biases blind us from feedback from the world.

But if we're honest with ourselves, that is, meta-rational, we must also admit that we'll never completely rid ourselves of our human baggage. Our biases, ideological priors, and inborn proclivities are part of the psychosocial furniture of our species. And while thinkers in the Enlightenment pushed us philosophically headlong towards the elegant and value-free methodologies of pure reason, we can no more deny the 'elephant' (emotional and intuitive centers) that our 'rider' (or logical and reasoning faculties) sits on.

Let me be clear: I am not arguing that the Rationality Community is filled with elephant deniers. I suspect that other community members are more *neuro-atypical* than you or I, which is to say they're a hell of a lot smarter. But it could be that you and I are a little more in touch with our inner elephants, which confer gifts beyond those restricted to the tips of our prefrontal cortices.

Another way of looking at motivated reasoning has to do with the idea of a whole hive of truth trackers. Yes, we want them to be rational in their pursuits. But, frankly, what sort of hive would we want to unleash upon the most important questions? Would we want them to be utterly devoid of motivated reasoning? I say no. We need motivation in small doses.

Michael Polanyi was a polymath philosopher of science who defected to Britain from Hungary in the middle of the twentieth century. He'd seen the centralization of science under illiberal regimes and did not like what he saw. He saw scientists as seekers, and he considered their independent activities sacrosanct. Thus the idea of the Republic of Science was born.

Polanyi thought that scientists, in following their curiosity and judgments about what problems to investigate, were cooperating as a kind of greater human community. Each scientist is engaged in seeking his or her answers. But each must adjust frequently, based on the results of the others' findings in that community. Coordination by mutual adjustment within the same overall system brings about an overall result, which is neither premeditated nor planned. Scientists, driven by their thirst for understanding, are participating in the enterprise. Polanyi called this the Republic of Science.

Wouldn't we want each truth tracker to shed as much of their baggage as possible before launching their investigations? To some degree, of course. But a little motivated reasoning in the Republic of Science can be healthy within limits. When we follow our curiosity and judgments about what problems to investigate, we are impelled to look in different places and in different ways. As long as the resulting methodological diversity has a mechanism for achieving consilience, we might well track the truth.

For example, let's suppose one — call them 'the skeptic' — is suspicious about some healthcare policy's predicted outcomes. Let's also assume that the policy is fundamentally at odds with their ideological priors. The trouble with motivated reasoning can be that the skeptic will overlook data that conforms to their opposition's narrative on the policy's effects. They will be motivated only to look for data that fits their counter-narrative. While it's true that there is a certain mix of self-delusion and intellectual dishonesty in seeking only that data which gives their position more firepower, they might also be hellbent in turning over rocks and looking for truths that their opponents are unmotivated to find. It might be that they make a critical discovery about the policy *because* they are hellbent. It just hasn't occurred to anyone to investigate in the mode and manner that they do.

In an important sense, all investigation is both value-laden and theory-laden. Of course, we must discipline ourselves not to look away from whatever feedback the world gives us. But when a million truth trackers are loosed in the Republic of Science, we might want to tolerate some motivated reasoning. On aggregate, it offers us an overall pluralism of perspectives, diversity of locations to look, and paths others might think are not worth considering. In accepting our humanity, we are embracing pluralism. Yes, we want to keep our biases in check to minimize contributing fictions or falsehoods in the Republic. But we don't want to turn ourselves into soulless automata, either. Otherwise, we'll miss the curiosity, passion, and instinct that impels us to set off on a particular journey of discovery.

What's missing is not a system that mutes motivated reasoning entirely, but a mechanism for adjudicating among rival claims. Without a mechanism to adjudicate, many remain in a condition of epistemic tribalism, which is made worse by social media's incentives.

EXPAND THE REPUBLIC OF SCIENCE

In his prescient *Kindly Inquisitors* (1995), Jonathan Rauch warns against the first wave of victimology, which came largely in the political correctness movement of the 1990s. Rauch believed that illiberal attacks on reason and evidence would undermine the very mechanisms of human progress.

In the system Rauch calls "liberal science," which we have referred to as the Republic of Science, it is through the exchange of ideas and competing viewpoints that beliefs and observations are turned into knowledge. But that means the domain of knowledge is restrictive: some things are true and others are not. The only way to find out what is true is by putting forth claims and subjecting them to challenge. Hypotheses are considered until they can be toppled by discounting evidence or superior hypotheses (usually both).

Because all claims get subjected to challenge and new evidence, there is no certainty, only a constant jockeying to corner the market on the best available evidence. This is the process upon which nearly all knowledge depends. And without freedom of speech, thought, and open inquiry, Rauch thinks the Republic of Science will fall. Fact and fiction will be indistinguishable. Progress will be retarded, and humanity will fail to thrive.

The Republic of Science cannot withstand too many attacks from fundamentalism. It doesn't matter what kind. It could be the Church's unkind inquisitors who imprisoned Galileo or the kindly inquisitors that now control what's left of the Blue Church and the insurgent victimology. Rauch sees fundamentalism as the "search for certainty rather than for errors." We must always discipline ourselves to be receptive to skepticism, especially when it invites countervailing evidence. Luddism, conspiracy theory, and politicization are all dangers to collective intelligence, too. Still, the Republic of Science can be inoculated from these dangers, as long as there is neither a *de facto* nor *de jure* monopoly on claims to truth. As long as there's a clear distinction between *is* and *ought*.

The Republic of Science is supposed to be a decentralized system. Even better, it should be a disintermediated system. But we're not there yet. There are still too many High Minds claiming monopolies. There are too few costs to those who make false claims in the service of their oughts.

Balance Conjecture and Refutation

Philosopher Karl Popper taught us that the process of science is evolutionary. Popper inspired Rauch by teaching us that our knowledge domain is ever-changing, imperfect, and undergoing constant revision.

> It is easy to obtain confirmations, or verifications, for nearly every theory — if we look for confirmations… [but] a theory which is not refutable by any conceivable event is non-scientific. Irrefutability is not a virtue of a theory [as people often think] but a vice. Every genuine test of a theory is an attempt to falsify it, or refute it.[398]

Too many people fall in love with their conjectures, and in so doing they forget that their highest responsibility is to try to refute them. As we alluded to, though, most people are not truth-tracking automata. We seek to confirm our biases. Happily, we can tolerate some amount of motivated reasoning in the Republic of Science if the system is set up so that more checkers are allowed to participate. And most importantly, we can improve these open networks if no one is in charge, and each participant has something to lose when they're wrong.

Put Skin in the Games

The less skin in the game one has on the question of, well, anything, the more one ought to keep his opinions to himself. In other words, when it comes to truth tracking, it's *put up or shut up*. And if the question is of utmost importance, then there should be mechanisms that allow people to put skin in the game. "If you give an opinion, and someone follows it," writes Nicolas Nassim Taleb in *Skin in the Game*, "you are morally obligated to be, yourself, exposed to its consequences."[399]

Whether we're talking about bankers handling other people's money or bureaucrats deciding to bomb other countries, the more distance there is between a person and the consequences of their decisions, the more likely we are to see poor choices and catastrophic results.

Rational irrationality typically drives decisions in the absence of skin in the game. And American life is infected with rational irrationality, from our politics to our personal opinions. Recall that this term describes a situation in which one's preferred opinion confers some benefit to them, but the consequences of holding that opinion are negligible. Whether it comes in group affinity or the self-anointing of virtue, that benefit frequently causes them to hold a false or irrational belief. Such usually happens in situations where people have *belief preferences*. Some beliefs are more appealing than others, and the marginal cost to an individual of holding an erroneous (or irrational) belief is therefore too low.

Here are a few examples:

- Those suspicious of vaccines don't vaccinate themselves or their children because they attribute nefarious motives or bad secondary effects. Because enough people around them do vaccinate, the costs of holding this belief are low.

- Mansueto Ventures, the corporation that owns *Fast Company* magazine, routinely publishes articles in which its authors malign corporations and profits. Customers pay for these articles. Without some kind of corporate structure and the ability to make revenues in excess of costs, the company could not run such articles. Bizarrely, Mansueto Ventures makes money writing articles to this effect.

- Voters in crowded cities frequently support rent control, believing that it is for the common good.

Very few economists support rent contol, however, due to the deleterious effects such policies have on the production of additional housing units that would bring prices down for everyone.

Having rationally ignorant and rationally irrational views is legal, of course. The problem is, we live in a system in which people are not only insulated from the direct consequences of their false beliefs, but the costs of those false beliefs are borne by everyone else. To the extent that New America's institutions and cultural norms force people to confront their false beliefs more directly, fewer people will hold such beliefs.

So how might we put skin in the proverbial game?

VOTE VALUES, BET BELIEFS

Let's assume that post-collapse America looks more or less like what we have now, only with one modest upgrade. Economist Robin Hanson has proposed we "vote on values, but bet on beliefs."[400] He calls this system Futarchy, which includes a prediction market with some legal force. Hanson does not intend Futarchy to be ideological, nor even idealistic. Instead, he seeks to eliminate policies rooted in rational irrationality by increasing the payoff for getting things right.

In Part One, we demonstrated that expertise can easily break down. Hanson argues that far fewer dumb policies would get adopted if there were more reasons to anticipate unintended consequences. Currently, we rely on policymakers' good faith and the idea that experts inform them. Officials cluster in their ideological tribes and ignore experts who aren't members, but outsiders have the relevant perspicacity to call bullshit on many occasions. The Great Temptation whispers *we just need to get better experts in positions of influence* — but getting these experts into those positions changes their incentives, that is, not to track truth so much as to play politics. Such changes experts' behavior and blunts their expertise. In other words, it's not clear what reshuffling the experts to find the 'best ones' would do, whatever their values.

With Futarchy, democratically elected officials would continue to let people express their values in the voting booth, just as they do today. But betting markets would determine *whether those values would be expressed.* "That is," writes Hanson, "elected representatives would formally define and manage an after-the-fact measurement of national welfare, while market speculators would say which policies they expect to raise national welfare. The basic rule of government would be: When a betting market clearly estimates that a proposed policy would increase expected national welfare, that proposal becomes law."[401]

I'm admittedly troubled by the feature that elected representatives would define and manage national welfare measures, even if those measures were not tied to any given policy over time. Perhaps an independent group could be charged with the responsibility of setting up such definitions. The system would need to guard against any political legerdemain.

Still, according to Hanson, Futarchy is designed to be "ideologically neutral" under his conception. And in time, the outcome might be anything from extreme socialism to extreme minarchism, depending on what voters say they want and what the speculators think the policy would get for them.

Despite my deference to Foxes, the modest Hedgehog in me thinks that policies designed to create long-term improvements in social welfare will have to respect the Law of Flow and leave room for experimentation and self-organization. So even if all we got after collapse was an upgrade of this form, I suspect Futarchy's discovery process would start to select out un-pragmatic ideological positions over time. Over what timescale? That's hard to say. And there would still be problems. But these problems could be worked out through careful attention to local experiments and a meta-science of engineering the markets to eliminate distortion. Even after experiments help the markets develop better methods, Futarchy will never be perfect. There's no such thing as perfect. We're always looking for better than the next best alternative. And in that regard, Futarchy would probably be a significant improvement over the status quo.

In this way, it would still be better to have some skin in the policy game than no skin. Even if we stopped short of Futarchy, legalizing prediction markets would go a long way toward improving collective intelligence. These ideas are worthy of consideration, not because they confer omniscience or yield perfection, but because they're better than living in a hall of mirrors. In asking the all-important question *as compared to what*, the 'what' in this case is a system that is driving us towards collapse.

And I'm willing to bet on that.

DESIGN PERCEPTION MARKETS

In all likelihood, though, politicians are not going to give up being capricious and High Minds are not going to give up advising them from Mt. Hedgehog. So how might we better equip ourselves in this Hall of Mirrors?

Entrepreneur Andrew Moore once introduced me to the concept of 'truth assets.' In the interest of full disclosure, I agreed to advise on his project, Themisia, which is an effort to create a digital marketplace for truth in journalism. The idea is to tokenize facts to eliminate fake news. I remain both skeptical and intrigued by Moore's project, but for purposes of this discussion, I am most interested in Moore's concept of a "truth asset."[402]

Specifically, might it be possible to treat journalistic or scientific claims as propositions on a prediction market? Bettors would invest for or against whether some proposition is likely to be accurate, based on the weight of the evidence. Could this market allow for the introduction of related claims, particularly those that involve new evidence? Would such a system provide the appropriate incentives for tracking truth?

As with Futarchy, the system would require careful design and testing. And of course, not all claims are clear cut, or rather, vagueness is a feature of the world. For example, the claim *John is bald* is not going to be settled as true or false by drawing an arbitrary line between 10,000 hairs and 10,002 hairs. This is why people use 'bald' and 'balding' interchangeably, depending on the person in question. Indeed, some truths really are relative truths, while other truths seem to change character depending on their contexts.

Another way to drive up the value of a truth asset is to get people to place a bet on one or many pieces of evidence. In time, such would give the community a *weight of evidence,* by showing what supporting evidence assets work for or against the claim. As currently conceived, the problem with perception markets is that they would have to involve some independent committee or judge to conclude in light of the evidence. On one hand, such a committee rather defeats the purpose; on the other, it's not clear how these markets would work in the absence of a conclusion. It might then be that the purveyors of claims get the valuation, rather than just claims.

Still, it should be possible to present certain kinds of claims to bettors with skin in the game. We can imagine these media markets outperforming traditional journalism and providing a useful corrective. We can also tell more about what media outlets are serious about tracking truth and what outlets have some other agenda. Skeptics might argue that no outlet has an incentive to track truth; the Media is, after all, set up to confirm readers' biases. But wouldn't the existence of a 'truth market' ensure those incentives come into existence? Might certain outlets then report on their own claims' performance, say to corner the perception market? Might certain outlets even become investors in their own claims, to gain more visibility? To gain credibility? To make money? The fact is, finding out what outlets or journalists are *less wrong* is inherently interesting. Eyeballs will follow, even if those who earn the market's trust aren't bettors.

Furthermore, what if it were possible to set up the system such that those most confident in their claims would have to stake to submit? Those holding the claims the market determines to have best tracked the truth will have bragging rights, improved reputation, and higher returns.

WEAVE SHARED REALITY

The problem with evaluating discrete propositions and claims is that such a system can atomize and isolate claims in ways that rather divorce them from larger truth tapestries. For example, suppose a journalist claims *the senator said x*, but it appears that they and only one other person heard the senator say x. Sometimes, what we want to know is *not* what the senator said, but what the senator *meant*. In the case of x, suppose that later, a recording of the senator saying x surfaces, but the recording has been edited so that everything the senator said immediately after x is missing. Suppose also that the missing portion clarifies x and provides more information about what the senator meant. With a prediction market, it might be simple to propose a straightforward claim, benefit from taking the senator's message out of context, and win a bet about the claim's literal truth. That's fine as far as it goes. But it only goes so far.

For perception markets to work, it might be useful to have adjacent mechanisms for what relational consultant Michael Porcelli calls "weaving shared reality."[403] According to Porcelli, such is a communication process that allows people to establish a common vocabulary and mutual understanding. Shared reality can include interpersonal dimensions in the context of specific environments like work or community, but it need not always. He writes:

> There is your reality, what *you* experience as true. This includes your perceptions, your thoughts, your feelings, your perspectives, your beliefs, your hunches, and so on. And there's also their reality, what *they* experience as true — including *their* perspectives, beliefs, perceptions, hunches, and so forth.
>
> Shared reality is where we discover an overlap between the two. Weaving shared reality is an exchange of communication where you both come to understand that there are some things that are true for you *and* true for them, *and you both know that's the case.*[404]

Therefore, weaving shared reality is a more intimate way of relating, according to Porcelli. My question is: Can this communicative process be scaled? And can it include evidence from the world as it is rather than the world as we would like it to be? As it applies to truth tracking and truth assets, few claims can be reduced to proposition statements devoid of context. I bet that once perception markets emerge, systems of weaving shared reality will coevolve with them. After all, incorporating shared reality is one of the all-too-human ways we construct our models of reality. It's going to take yarn with the threads of affection, openness, and truth.

OPERATE WITH HUMILITY

In undertaking any such project as I've outlined above, we have to be humble. Truth tracking is hard because truth can be elusive. Any system that aims to track truth is going to have to face all manner of problems.

1. No one in existence can be the final arbiter. The best we can do is deal in probabilities and find inter-subjective agreement.

2. Uncertainty and skepticism, paradoxically, drive the pursuit of truth as the search prompts people continuously to look for errors.

3. 'Facts' are metaphors that people construct, isolate, and remove from the fabric of a larger reality, usually to make a cognitive shortcut.

And that's just for starters.

Writer and coder Mike Elias, echoing Jonathan Rauch, reminds us that truth tracking is always tentative and uncertain: "While people tend to accept this in theory, the metaphor of Facts connotes certainty and permanence, and inspires a fervor often indistinguishable from religious fundamentalism. The metaphor of Facts thus creates a countercurrent to the spirit of science in public discourse and everyday life."

Recall our discussion of the 'science says' trope, the preponderance of so-called fact-checking websites, not to mention accusations involving alternative facts launched as a term of derision rather than the acknowledgment of a competing claim. But even if we assumed these fact-checkers held some definitive god's-eye perspective, most people are not all that persuaded by 'facts.' "The verdict is clear," adds Elias. "Research on numeracy, cult behavior, science denial, and scientific suppression shows that people tend to be far more concerned with the social-psychological and identity implications of a proposition than with its truth value."[405]

If we're going to survive the collapse and thrive afterward, we're going to have to get better at truth tracking. But if truth tracking relies solely on obliging people to be more rational, we're probably doomed. Evolution has made other plans, which include rationally irrational allegiance to our in-groups.

Ironically, it's irrational to think that enough people can overcome their biases to in-group affiliation to be more like Vulcans. Indeed, *just give them the facts — slower, harder, and with mustard* is unlikely to get you very far. But if you can architect a system of truth assets in a perception market — that is, a system of evidence plus skin in the game — suddenly there are more blind men's hands on the proverbial elephant.

DISCERN WITH A DOSE OF SKEPTICISM

Like any other big change in the world, tracking truth depends on the maxims:

> *We shape our tools, and then our tools shape us.*
> *We shape our rules, and then our rules shape us.*

In *The Social Singularity,* I focused on some ideas about how we could reshape our rules and tools for the sake of human flourishing. In this book, I try to focus just as much on how we can reshape ourselves, so that we can shape better rules and tools so that those rules and tools can, in turn, shape us in a prosocial way. Hopefully, this dance of culture, rules, and tools continues far into the future, improving humanity with every successive generation.

We discussed the Spheres of Practice for integral liberalism. Recall that *satya,* which is the practice of integrity, requires us to speak the truth and track the truth so that our words and deeds are all in alignment. It might seem strange to leave a place for skepticism in *satya,* but we must. How else are we to open our minds?

14

CONJURE MEANING

Arjuna saw in that universal form unlim-
ited mouths and unlimited eyes. It was all
wondrous.

The Bhagavad Gita[406]

Imagine you were offered two stark choices: You could be
the first to implant a chip in your brain that puts you in
a state of total bliss until you died; or, you could be among
the first to settle a Mars Colony. In the first case, serotonin,
dopamine, and oxytocin would keep you feeling good.
Really good. But that feeling would attach to little in your
real-world circumstances. In the second case your life would
be challenging. You would have to train for months, if not
years, before you launched. Upon arrival, you would have a
lot of work to do to survive in an environment in which you
did not evolve.

Which would you choose?

I'm not here to argue that none among us would choose
bliss over Mars. But I am here to say that a significant
number of people would choose Mars over bliss. The
simple fact is we're made for challenges, and we want to be
remembered for rising to them. Bliss? Yeah, it feels good.
But will you be remembered for it?

Now, suppose we added a third choice. You get to live
a bucolic life in some of the most beautiful mountains on

earth, to tend goats, make art, and be there for your children and grandchildren. There's work involved, but you're surrounded by people you love.

Now, which would you choose?

MEET MY MOTHER

I know someone who has chosen to live option three: my mom, Ann. Of course, she never got to choose between that or perma-bliss or Mars. But if anyone pressed her, I bet she wouldn't give up on the life she has. She is not only happy, she has found what the Greeks called *eudaimonia*; that is, fulfillment, or happiness with meaning. Anyone who knows her can see it.

Interestingly, Ann's days include some measure of bliss and some measure of, well, unpleasantness. First, the good stuff: she experiences psychological flow when she weaves or makes her dolls. When she weaves, her warp and weft connects her to the past, and handling them connects her to the present. She relishes the ritual of tending to the garden and goats. Her vegetables are lush, and her flowers are lovely. She always imagined her grandchildren running among the fruits of her labors.

But they are labors. All of these carefully cultivated delights require attention and care. There have been weeks when Ann had to bottle feed the kids because the nanny (goat) got mastitis. She wakes at dawn on winter days when the frozen grass crunches underfoot to tend to some animal or other. The thing is, Mom wouldn't be as happy if she paid someone else to do everything. *Eudaimonia* requires creativity and sweat.

It's a bit unfair. My mother and her wife Trish live in a remodeled, reimagined bead-board farmhouse with a panoramic view of the mountains. Wild turkeys roam the land. The goats nestle between the hen houses and garden. Old tractors and farm implements, though rusty, somehow look curated. And they enjoy four distinct, crisp seasons. True to the name, vistas of the Blue Ridge overlap in various shades of blue until one's eye settles on the verdant foreground. When the leaves turn — red, orange, burgundy, or yellow — they explode. If you took a photo, you wouldn't need to use saturation effects.

Maybe now you can see why Ann would forgo Mars and MDMA without end. But what does it have to do with meaning?

CENTER IN THE HEXAGRAM

Up to this point, we have merely alluded to some of the ways we can derive meaning. With the help of Aristotle, we can categorize them: Aristotle offers us a heuristic called the *Septem Circumstantiae*. Journalists will be familiar with these because any column will answer most if not all the questions: Who? What? Where? When? Why? How? These are necessary for reporting the news. When it comes to making meaning, we have to go deeper.

Imagine each of the *Septem Circumstantiae* represented as points. Together, they create the vertices of a hexagon, or maybe a lotus. If we were to connect all of these points with lines, we would get something that looks vaguely like sacred geometry. I hope the symbolism helps you remember the six questions, since the Modes of Meaning might be among the most important things to take away from this book.

As we go through these in serial, imagine that they are arranged in that hexagonal pattern *with you at the center.* And as we discuss each mode of meaning, see if you can use yourself as an example.

The six Modes of Meaning:

1. *Contextual.* (What?) This mode is derived from our functional role in a community. This context makes up part of our identities. Such was particularly

important in ancient times because everyone in the community had a vital role to play for every other person. For example, John is the blacksmith of our village, Dwight is a church deacon, or Yoshi is a samurai in the Shogunate. *I derive meaning from how others understand my function in the community.* Meaning-making of this sort is mostly *external*. That means that others perceive you as such and such based on how you operate within the group. Today, of course, contextual meaning can be a lot fuzzier.

2. *Authored.* (Who?) This mode is derived as one moves toward their aspirational self. We call this *authored meaning* because it is *internal*, or originates primarily from within the subject. Authored meaning is perhaps the most Western of the modes because it's the most individualistic: *I derive meaning from what I want to become.* During the Enlightenment, people began to understand themselves as individuated. In other words, they began to see themselves as independent of their function within the collective, though contextual meaning never went away. We start to get a lot more ideas about rights, such as those by Mary Wollstonecraft in *A Vindication of the Rights of Woman.*

3. *Mission.* (Why?) This mode is derived from the pursuit of a mission, whether implicit or explicit. We can call this *mission meaning.* If we set out on some mission with others, we find a sense of place, which overlaps with contextual meaning. But with mission meaning, the goal is a kind of guide star that answers the *why* questions of our identity. *I derive meaning from what I want to achieve.* If a physician wants to cure a particular disease, they will find meaning in that pursuit.

4. *Situational.* (Where?) This mode is derived from

identifying with others who share your values, are proximate, or are culturally similar. We can also call this *situational meaning*. Because we rarely carry things out in isolation, we tend to bind together as a group. Group identification offers a sense of place, which comes from our affiliations, or our nearness to one another. Situational meaning animates us in subtle ways. It gives the Inuits multiple words for 'snow.' It means that Tar Heels have a taste for vinegar on pulled pork. It's identifying with the fecund soil upon which one takes root.

5. *Qualitative.* (How?) This mode is derived from striving for excellence in one's pursuits, roles, or personal development. We call this *qualitative meaning* because one asks whether one is doing the best they can. *You're doing x. But how? And how well? Have you done your ten thousand hours?* Such questions refer to putting in time for mastery. The *how* is not just the amount of effort you put in, though; it is also how carefully and skillfully you've worked.

6. *Temporal.* (When?) This mode is derived from different ways of orienting ourselves in time. We call this *temporal meaning* because it deals with where we are situated historically, and in shared circumstances. We will be able to find meaning in surviving a global pandemic. Living in a connected age has meaning. And it means something to be situated as we are in time, relative to the wisdom and experience we gain with age.

I doubt these are exhaustive, but they are certainly a start. Even within these six modes, meaning compounds as the modes overlap in powerful ways. Contemplate the myriad ways they overlap for you and you get a combinatorial effect. For those who have found balance, that effect can be profound. Life, far from feeling empty, can generate more meaning than one could ever hope to process. You might want to think of it as a ritual.

I suggest you start by gathering six pretty pebbles, one representing each mode. Arrange the pebbles around you, encircling yourself. Go from one to the next and ask yourself the appropriate question for each mode. Then contemplate answers. The exercise should at least help you shed any nihilism from thinking about your place in the Milky Way. Once you start to overlap the modes of meaning, you might discover a mandala.

Pray Among the Pebbles

Most of us continue to understand ourselves as members of communities. To some extent, we try to make sense of the world using a common reference frame. It turns out that community and collective sense-making are closely entwined phenomena, and, more deeply, vital aspects of our human systems. Amid all this change, though, we have to look more carefully at our Modes of Meaning and try to restore balance.

With modernity, life has become far more dynamic. Our Modes of Meaning are in disarray. And this comes at a cost, psychologically and spiritually. The rate of change, whether life changes or generational turns, has sped up. Our relationships with our communities and to nature have become out of balance. That can be disorienting. Not for everyone, but for many. You might say that we live in a condition wherein the order of things and our place in it scarcely has time to culture before things change again.

"Now, here, you see, it takes all the running you can do, to keep in the same place." So said Lewis Carroll's Red Queen in *Through the Looking Glass and What Alice Found There*. "If you want to get somewhere else, you must run at least twice as fast as that!"[407] As you try to keep up with all the change, your Modes of Meaning can quickly get out of balance. The *what* shifts. The *where* gets scattered among the ephemera of modern life. The *who* is contingent as we shift to become an online avatar. The *why* gets confused in the blur of tribal groupthink, memetic warfare, and the general outsourcing of our *mission meaning* to political spectacles.

It might be time to stop, take a breath, and pray awhile among the pebbles.

REMEMBER THE LAW OF FLOW

Okay, so why have we devoted the last chapter to meaning? If it's not yet obvious, I want to make it clear: When people create human systems, they are sometimes channeling energy flows. At least we should be. But into what is all this energy flowing? Well… *us*: into what the energy flows, where meaning lives.

As we said, the Law of Flow expresses life's vascular nature. We don't just find energy in moving river systems or the wires that power our devices. Energy animates every living system, from our bodies to the agglomerations of us we call society. We are not inert meat; we are thinking, feeling beings. We are the culmination of a generative process that started with the Big Bang and ended with you pondering these words. But at some level, we are still energy. However strange it is to say, the meaning we make is the end of energy flowing.

"When we look at the ocean, we see that each wave has a beginning and an end," says Buddhist monk Thich Naht Hhan. But, he says,

> A wave can be compared with other waves, and we can call it more or less beautiful, higher or lower, longer lasting or less long lasting. But if we look more deeply, we see that a wave is made of water. While living the life of a wave, the wave also lives the life of water. It would be sad if the wave did not know that it is water. It would think, 'Some day I will

have to die. This period of time is my life span, and when I arrive at the shore, I will return to nonbeing.'[408]

We are as waves, and the universe is as water.

Only an emerging locus of spacetime regards itself and asks: Who? What? Why? Where? How? When? No one else can do that for us. No matter how strong, successful, or wise anyone else is, each makes their own meaning. The Modes of Meaning are our unique vectors into which energy flows and becomes an identity — an endless source of wonder.

Before we close, let's acknowledge a philosophical point: Meaning is a human construction. A derivation. A contrivance. Our socially constructed realities keep us from receding too quickly into the dark water. Still, there is no meaning *in the world* waiting for us to discover it as one might a black hole, quark, or neutrino. Meaning doesn't live in the universe's fabric. The universe is a powerful self-referential loop. And it has questions.

As part of the universe, we are physical beings, but we have a subjective view. Meaning is, therefore, subjective. That doesn't make the experience of meaning less real. Quite the contrary, in our eagerness to share our modes with others, perhaps to weave a shared reality, we invite others into solidarity. We weave our modes together intersubjectively. When we do, we're at our best. And we are not alone. But these filaments are so unique and so subtle, they have to be woven by each of us. Solidarity is intimate. It cannot be forced, and it cannot be centralized; any purported meaning that is forced or centralized is not meaning at all. It is a uniform that causes us to lose ourselves in the aspirations of the powerful. No, we must integrate our values with those of others, carefully, little by little, making room for transformation.

And then we pass away.

All along, life was energy unfolding in time, towards something meaningful. And it will do so again.

AFTERWORD

My daughter Sophia was born on August 17th of that awful year, 2020. Three weeks later, my father died. When I set out to write this book, I did not anticipate that my explorations of life and death or masculine and feminine would be so salient. My daughter symbolized the world to come. My dad's urn contains the past. America might be breaking down, but the world is in the process of becoming something else. You and I are looking for meaning in all of it, but we are trapped here as the chrysalis. Our hearts are filled with a yearning for recognition. And yet we are so busy making demands, we miss the opportunity to give it to each other through simple acts of love and respect.

When Minneapolis police officer Derek Chauvin put his knee on George Floyd's neck and killed him, fear and rage pent up by virus lockdown, erupted. Protestors across America spilled into the streets. The vast majority was young and white.[409] I was angry, too, and yet I could not identify with the protestors. Maybe it is a subconscious matrix of privileges that bias me, but I hope I have demonstrated that illiberal impulses won't cure what ails society.

The sad truth is that some just wanted to break things with impunity. The ouroboros feasted. And liberalism died a little more. Consider those, like author Vicky Osterweil, who would justify the chaos. In an NPR interview, Osterweil said:

> [Looting] attacks the very way in which food and things are distributed. It attacks the idea of property, and it attacks the idea that in order for someone to

have a roof over their head or have a meal ticket, they have to work for a boss, in order to buy things that people just like them somewhere else in the world had to make under the same conditions. It points to the way in which that's unjust. And the reason that the world is organized that way, obviously, is for the profit of the people who own the stores and the factories. So you get to the heart of that property relation, and demonstrate that without police and without state oppression, we can have things for free.

We can have things for free. Combine the unrestrained rage of a mob with the idea that all of life's good things could just fall from the sky, and you get the makings of a dangerous cult. Unhealthy Thanatos Masculine burns the cities down. Unhealthy Thanatos Feminine invites the looters' apologist to offer a "controversial" interview on NPR.

Osterweil continues:

Looting strikes at the heart of property, of whiteness and of the police. It gets to the very root of the way those three things are interconnected. And also it provides people with an imaginative sense of freedom and pleasure and helps them imagine a world that could be. And I think that's a part of it that doesn't really get talked about — that riots and looting are experienced as sort of *joyous* and *liberatory.* (Emphasis mine.)

Violence as joyous. Looting is the opposite of *ahimsa*, of *Satyagraha.* Gandhi and MLK inspired us to vanquish the demons of racism, division, and dominance hierarchy that live within, which set us on a path to peace. Abram X. Kendi and Vicky Osterweil invite us, respectively, to loathe ourselves and to let homes and businesses burn. For many whites, these are perverse purification rituals; a means to atone for American Original Sin. For blacks, according to Osterweil anyway, it's meant to be "joyous" in the same way one might find joy at a festival of revenge. *It doesn't matter if the get-back is gotten from the innocent. No one is innocent in white supremacist America.*

Violence as liberatory. The idea that violence can be a force of liberation is not without precedent in history. It's hard to argue, for example, against the occupation of Iraq when the same military stormed the beaches at Normandy. But in Minneapolis or Portland, we would have to understand the looters as righteous soldiers; innocents as enemies. Is the twenty-year-old white 'anarchist' really a liberator? Is a Black looter liberating the Black small business owner when he breaks her windows and takes her wares?

Even Martin Luther King once said riots were "the rumblings of discontent from the 'have nots' within the midst of an affluent society."[410] Strange then that in 2020 the majority of rioters were white and affluent. I choose to believe that King's nonviolent actions speak louder and represent his true Legacy. Today, destruction is justified by *getting to imagine a world that could be.* A world without have-nots? A world like the Red Guard must have imagined, like post-purge Russia or Cambodia or Cuba. Perhaps the world that could be is an egalitarian utopia like North Korea where everyone is truly free.

This book is an antidote to violence.

My hope for this book is that it is viewed not as a statement of ideology, but as a call to reflect and to practice. The cow and tiger drank from the lake together because the yogis practiced ahimsa in the meditation forest. If there is a place that is the opposite of the meditation forest, it is pre-collapse America.

When I heard George Floyd call out for his mama or Kelly Thomas crying out for his dad, I felt the rioters' rage. Then came the urge to control. When I saw mindless youth act like the Taliban destroying Buddhas, I felt the riot policeman's rage. Then came the urge to control. And so it goes. Both the violent protestors and violent cops are symptoms of the same underlying pathology. But at some point, despite all the rage, we must consult an inner oracle that is not in our limbic systems.

One of the hardest lessons I have had to learn in my life is that fear and rage are the real enemies. They are tricksters. I remember feeling the white-hot fire after 9/11. I lived in France with an English girl, so I never really got to feel the closeness Americans felt after that sad day. For a couple of months, Americans were unified in the patriotism of anger and grieving. By the time I returned to the U.S., the unity had waned. All I or anyone felt was a wave of rage that would soon find expression in political division. *You're either with us or against us.* Axis of evil? WMDs? Good enough. I transmuted my anger into a justification for what would become the wars in Afghanistan and Iraq.

The Hobbesian rationale had persuaded me that the United States ought to use its global hegemony to bring terrorist-friendly regimes to heel. The rest would be the details. I became a cheerleader for those wars, and to this day, I can retrace the arguments in my mind. After watching decades of quagmire unfold, year after year, I realized I was wrong. All that time, I had been acting as a stooge for empire builders and military contractors. Too many innocents died. Now I know that in some small way, I helped create collateral damage.

Once you learn a lesson like this and eat a three-course meal of crow, you have to spend years figuring out what to do with it. Honestly, I didn't know how to *do* peace. My father taught me to pull the 'crazy card' if anyone ever bullied me at school. Being raised in the American South, the idea was that bullies would leave you alone if they thought you would fight. It was just residual honor culture, I guess. I'd used intellectual gymnastics to rewrite what had amounted to redneck justice mixed with the searing logic of Leviathan. Deep down, it all originated in rage, fear, and the urge to control, all of which had control of me. It's a powerful force, programmed in us by evolution. But by the time the pandemic (or the protests or the Presidential Election) rolled around, I recognized those feelings and saw them for what they were. I would not let them turn me into Hyde again, as 9/11 had.

At the risk of sounding cliché, adversity has something to teach us. In this case, I had to figure out a way to warn the world. *It's not the crisis that will do us in. It's us.* We have to focus, using reason, calm, and self-possession when the time arrives. We must keep what is good about us and strive to become better all the same. Our disposition should not be to look to power to solve our social problems, but to look inward first, then criticize by creating.

I'm under no illusions. This is America, where humility has been out of fashion for some time. Reason, calm, and self-possession don't get as many clicks or likes. The return of wisdom and reflection won't come from people reading a book. But we have to try. We'll have to learn the hard way and reorganize ourselves accordingly.

Author Charles Eisenstein put matters well when he wrote:

> There is an alternative to the paradise of perfect control that our civilization has so long pursued, and that recedes as fast as our progress, like a mirage on the horizon. Yes, we can proceed as before down the path toward greater insulation, isolation, domination, and separation. We can normalize heightened levels of separation and control, believe that they are necessary to keep us safe, and accept a world in which we are afraid to be near each other. Or we can take advantage of this pause, this break in normal, to turn onto a path of reunion, of holism, of the restoring of lost connections, of the repair of community and the rejoining of the web of life.[411]

He could have been talking about the novel coronavirus. He could have been talking about the riots. He could have been talking about the election.

I remember what it felt like in 2002 to look upon cooler heads like Eisenstein with contempt. Like they were weak. No doubt others will look upon me this way if I offer circumspection about power during a time of crises. If you say the urge to control yields nothing good, you might be the first they seek to control. Greying temples and a father's heart will show that people like Eisenstein aren't weak at all. To live and die well, we cannot afford to fetishize life or ignore death. We have to seek the sacred balance our ancestors knew in their bones. It takes strength to be wise; to look death in the eyes and keep living.

Maybe Sophia and my boys will be okay after all. It took a little time, but eventually, I went from a hand-wringing father at the start of the pandemic to reclaiming my agency in a bewildering set of circumstances. There are lessons to be learned in the chaos and confusion, measures to be taken, and traces for posterity. Most lessons don't have to do with one's opinions about masks, or lockdowns, or big white statues of big white historical figures. They have more to do with knowing how to live well, die well, and look out for each other.

Even as crises like those in 2020 prompted us to confront the inevitability of death and the cycle of endings, we have cause to celebrate life and consider new possibilities. At the very least, we ought to reflect on what we're prepared to leave our children.

To this point, I have not spoken much about the 2020 presidential election. I'd have little to add but odium. Elections in general, and this one in particular, deserve to be ignored until they go away. They create needless animus. They create brainless, soulless partisans. We don't have to pick a team. When groups on either side of an issue are getting it all wrong, you say, 'A pox on both your houses!' This time, the pox had already come.

As we continued to watch the death toll together, like

some macabre weather report, the first vaccines were trickling out. Another storm is gathering on the horizon. The hell of it is, we have to start wrestling with the idea that maybe, just maybe, we'll all be better for it.

Acknowledgements

This book would not have been possible without an anonymous benefactor who supported this work without conditions.

Other supporters include my love, Jenny Clary, whose patience through the process at home has been invaluable. Jenny is the muse behind so many of the ideas in this book. She also painstakingly typeset the first print edition.

Justin Arman has sat on the other end of a phone line at critical times to offer advice and support. Justin has also offered assistance in helping me market the book and, truth be told, he is a master marketer.

Michael Porcelli deserves plenty of thanks for reading critical passages and helping me get unstuck in key places.

My children have lent me hours of time to write when I should have been wrestling, playing games, or helping them with homework. I hope they grow up as proud of me as I am of them.

I want to extend special thanks to Brian Robertson, Jim Rutt, Andrew Ross Powell, Trevor Burrus, Paul Forrest, Adam Bellow, and Jenny Clary, whose conversations improved the work. My dad, Rick Borders, also spent valuable time talking through the ideas with me. May he rest in peace.

Appreciation goes to my editor, Jon Darga, for taking the time to make the prose professional, neat, and in line with the latest conventions, some of which I fought him on. Jon was also willing to interrogate my claims and point out flaws, which caused me to temper my positions. The book is stronger for it.

Thank yous to Sheryl Williams and Gabriel Mitchell for their assistance in getting my footnotes in order.

Thanks also to Matthew Balter, Aaron Ross Powell, Hannah Frankman, Brittany Hunter, Daniel Bier, and Gene Kusmiak for generously donating their time to proofread.

REVIEW AND SUPPORT

The best way you can support me and my work is to go immediately to Amazon or Goodreads and say how much you loved the book and why. If you hated it, well then, I'd obviously prefer you kept it to yourself. My kids have to eat.

Buy a copy for a friend or family member. And if you'd like to support our little indie publishing operation, you can go to social-evolution.com/

ENDNOTES

1   Peter Zeihan, "Coronavirus: The Finance and Banking Guide," *Zeihan on Geopolitics* (Zeihan on Geopolitics, March 31, 2020), https://zeihan.com/coronavirus-the-finance-and-banking-guide/.

2   Peter Zeihan, "Coronavirus: The Finance and Banking Guide," *Zeihan on Geopolitics* (Zeihan on Geopolitics, March 31, 2020), https://zeihan.com/coronavirus-the-finance-and-banking-guide/.

3   Jonathan Franzen and Rachel Riederer, "What If We Stopped Pretending the Climate Apocalypse Can Be Stopped?," *The New Yorker*, September 8, 2019, https://www.newyorker.com/culture/cultural-comment/what-if-we-stopped-pretending.

4   "Gated Institutional Narrative," *The Portal Wiki*, accessed January 6, 2021, https://theportal.wiki/wiki?title=Gated_Institutional_Narrative&mobileaction=toggle_view_desktop. Note that this entry refers to Eric Weinstein's podcast from Episode 18 of The Portal: https://tinyurl.com/GatedNarrative

5   Daniel Schmactenberger, "Mitigating Existential Risks," *Neurohacker Collective*, accessed December 11, 2020, https://neurohacker.com/mitigating-existential-risks.

6   Steven Pinker, *Enlightenment Now: the Case for Reason, Science, Humanism, and Progress* (London: Penguin Books, 2019), 291.

7   Nick Bostrom, "Existential Risks," Existential Risks: Analyzing Human Extinction Scenarios, accessed December 11, 2020, https://nickbostrom.com/existential/risks.html.

8   Nick Bostrom, "Existential Risks," Existential Risks: Analyzing Human Extinction Scenarios, accessed December 11, 2020, https://nickbostrom.com/existential/risks.html.

9   Steven Pinker, *Enlightenment Now: the Case for Reason, Science, Humanism, and Progress* (London: Penguin Books, 2019), 28.

10   Sylvie Lorente and Adrian Bejan, "Few Large, Many Small: Hierarchy in Movement on Earth," *International Journal of Design & Nature and*

Ecodynamics, Volume 5 (2010), Issue 3, 254-267.

11   Lacey Simon, Randall Stilla, and Krish Sathian, "Metaphorically feeling: comprehending textural metaphors activates somatosensory cortex," *Brain and language* 120, no. 3 (2012), 416-421.

12   Steven Pinker, "Block That Metaphor!," The New Republic, October 9, 2006, https://newrepublic.com/article/77730/block-metaphor-steven-pinker-whose-freedom-george-lakoff.

13   Max Borders, "The Economy: Metaphors we (shouldn't) live by," *Library of Economics and Liberty,* August 1, 2011, https://www.econlib.org/library/Columns/y2011/Borderseconomy.html.

14   James C. Scott, *Seeing Like a State: How Certain Schemes to Improve the Human Condition Have Failed* (New Haven, CT: Yale University Press, 2020), 88.

15   James C. Scott, *Seeing Like a State,* 88.

16   James C. Scott, *Seeing Like a State,* 88.

17   Walter Lippmann, *The Good Society* (New Brunswick, NJ: Transaction Publishers, 1937, 2005), 30.

18   Evan Thomas, "Attack From the Left: Paul Krugman's Poison Pen," *Newsweek,* September 14, 2010, https://www.newsweek.com/attack-left-paul-krugmans-poison-pen-76063.

19   "How to Fix the Economy: An Expert Panel," *Bloomberg,* September 16, 2010, http://tiny.cc/zep1tz.

20   Elaine Quijano, "Obama's Priority: Fixing the Economy," *CNN,* November 6, 2008, http://edition.cnn.com/2008/POLITICS/11/06/obama.priorities/index.html.

21   Paul Krugman, "The Lessons of Ireland," *The Guardian,* April 20, 2009, https://www.theguardian.com/commentisfree/2009/apr/21/ireland-financial-crisis.

22   Carol Baum, "U.S. Economy Overheating? We Should Be So Lucky," *Bloomberg,* January 4, 2011, https://www.bloomberg.com/news/articles/2011-01-05/economy-s-overheating-we-should-be-so-lucky-commentary-by-caroline-baum.

23   Oakescott uses the term "Rationalist" here, which is a term he develops for a specific kind of political actor of which technocrats are members. Oakescott's idea was that Rationalists eschew practical and technical knowledge in favor of abstractions, which they summarily apply without feedback from the world.

24   Paul Krugman, "The Power of Biobabble: Pseudo Economics Meets Pseudo Evolution," *Slate,* October 27, 1997, https://slate.com/business/1997/10/the-power-of-biobabble.html.

25   Talk about 'arguing with zombies.'

26   Paul Krugman, "An Institutional Economics Prize: The Conscience of a Liberal," *The New York Times*, October 12, 2009, https://krugman.blogs.nytimes.com/2009/10/12/an-institutional-economics-prize/.

27   Larry Elliot, "The Computer Model That Once Explained the British Economy," *The Guardian*, May 8, 2008, https://www.theguardian.com/business/2008/may/08/bankofenglandgovernor.economics.

28   Larry Elliot, "The Computer Model That Once Explained the British Economy".

29   Arnold Kling, "An Alternative to Hydraulic Macro," *EconLog—Library of Economics and Liberty*, August 10, 2009, .https://www.econlib.org/archives/2009/08/an_alternative_1.html.

30   Joseph Stiglitz, "Neoliberalism must be pronounced dead and buried. Where next?" *The Guardian*, May 30, 2009, https://www.theguardian.com/business/2019/may/30/neoliberalism-must-be-pronouced-dead-and-buried-where-next.

31   Friedrich August von Hayek, "Friedrich August Von Hayek—Prize Lecture," *Lecture to the Memory of Alfred Nobel* (1974).

32   "Leaked Pentagon Report Warns Climate Change May Bring Famine, War," *Institute for Agriculture and Trade Policy*, accessed November 23, 2020, https://www.iatp.org/news/leaked-pentagon-report-warns-climate-change-may-bring-famine-war.

33   Peter Schwarz and Doug Randall. "An Abrupt Climate Change Scenario and Its Implications for United States National Security," accessed November 23, 2020, https://ocov2.jpl.nasa.gov/media/publications/Abrupt_Climate_Change_Scenario.pdf.

34   Jem Bendell, *Deep Adaptation: A map for navigating climate tragedy* (2018), 1-31.

35   Paul Ehrlich, Dennis R. Parnell, and Al Silbowitz, *The Population Bomb Vol. 68* (New York: Ballantine books, 1968), xi.

36   Paul Ehrlich, Dennis R. Parnell, and Al Silbowitz, *The Population Bomb Vol. 68* (New York: Ballantine books, 1968), xi.

37   Paul Ehrlich, Dennis R. Parnell, and Al Silbowitz, *The Population Bomb Vol. 68* (New York: Ballantine books, 1968), xi.

38   Jarod Diamond, *Collapse: How societies choose to fail or succeed* (Penguin, 2011), 328.

39   Diamond, *Collapse: How societies choose to fail or succeed*, 328.

40   "Copper Prices - 45 Year Historical Chart," accessed November 4, 2020, https://www.macrotrends.net/1476/copper-prices-histori-

cal-chart-data.

41   "Copper Prices - 45 Year Historical Chart."

42   David Owen, "The World is Running Out of Sand," *The New Yorker*, May 27, 2017, https://www.newyorker.com/magazine/2017/05/29/the-world-is-running-out-of-sand.

43   Zach Mortice, "Bamboo Transcends the Tropics for Carbon Negative Construction," *Redshift*, August 7, 2019, https://www.autodesk.com/redshift/bamboo-construction/.

44   Andrew McAfee, *More from Less: The Surprising Story of How We Learned to Prosper Using Fewer Resources—and What Happens Next* (Scribner, 2019), 1.

45   United Nations, "World fertility patterns 2015," (2015)., https://www.un.org/en/development/desa/population/publications/pdf/fertility/world-fertility-patterns-2015.pdf.

46   Stanley Becker and Gary Becker, *A Treatise on the Family* (Harvard University Press, 2009).

47   Riccardo Mastini, "Degrowth: The case for a new economic paradigm," *Open Democracy*, June 8, 2017, https://www.opendemocracy.net/en/degrowth-case-for-constructing-new-economic-paradigm/.

48   Mastini, "Degrowth: The case for a new economic paradigm."

49   "The State of Food Security and Nutrition in the World 2020," *Food and Agriculture Organization of the United Nations*, accessed November 6, 2020, http://www.fao.org/state-of-forests/en/.

50   "Air Quality — National Summary," *United States Environmental Protection Agency*, accessed November 6, 2020, https://gispub.epa.gov/air/trendsreport/2020/documentation/AirTrends_Flyer.pdf.

51   Jeff Desjardins, "The end of global extreme poverty is getting closer,"*Business Insider*, November 14, 2016, https://www.businessinsider.com/end-of-global-extreme-poverty-chart-2016-11.

52   Thomas Sowell, *A Conflict of Visions: Ideological Origins of Political Struggles*, (New York: Basic Books, Revised Edition, 2007).

53   Mike Wall, "Presidential Visions for Space Exploration: From Ike to Trump," *Space.com*, February 5, 2020, https://www.space.com/11751-nasa-american-presidential-visions-space-exploration.html.

54   Thomas Sowell, *Knowledge and Decisions* (New York: Basic Books, 1996).

55   Alexa Clay, "Utopia Inc," *Aeon*, February 28, 2017, https://aeon.co/essays/like-start-ups-most-intentional-communities-fail-why.

56   Andrew Stover, "The False Promise of Moonshots," *Medium*,

March 16, 2017, https://medium.com/@AGStover/the-false-promise-of-moonshots-999bf313a1f9.

57 Chunka Mui, "Think Big, Start Small, Learn Fast," *Forbes,* January 3, 2016, https://www.forbes.com/sites/chunk-amui/2016/01/03/6-words/#3a6ab6b01a3b.

58 Thomas Sowell, *Knowledge and Decisions*, 61

59 Andrew Stover, "How "Moonshots" Destroy Wealth," *Medium*, April 4, 2017, https://medium.com/@AGStover/how-moonshots-destroy-wealth-6c7f1d6877f8.

60 Frédéric Bastiat, "That Which is Seen, and That Which is Not Seen," accessed November 6, 2020, http://bastiat.org/en/twisatwins.html.

61 Andrew Hawkins, "A hyperloop in Missouri? A new study says it's feasible, but not necessarily affordable," *The Verge*, October 7, 2018, https://www.theverge.com/2018/10/17/17989504/virgin-hyper-loop-one-missouri-feasibility-study.

62 Nic Fleming, "Plants talk to each other using an internet of fungus," *BBC Earth*, November 11, 2014, http://www.bbc.com/earth/story/20141111-plants-have-a-hidden-internet.

63 Wikipedia contributors, "Machine Age," *Wikipedia*, accessed November 7, 2020, https://en.wikipedia.org/w/index.php?title=Machine_Age&oldid=978612583.

64 Ronald Reagan, "Reagan's Farewell Speech," *PBS* (Public Broadcasting Service), accessed January 15, 2021, https://www.pbs.org/wgbh/americanexperience/features/reagan-farewell/.

65 Arnold Kling, *Patterns of Sustainable Specialization and Trade: A Re-introduction to economics* (Adam Smith Institute, 2012), 8.

66 Kling, *Specialization and Trade: A Re-introduction to economics*, 7.

67 Kling, *Specialization and Trade: A Re-introduction to economics*, 8.

68 Kling, *Specialization and Trade: A Re-introduction to economics*, 16.

69 David Sloan Wilson, "Why New Economics Needs a New Invisible Hand," Evonomics, February 8, 2019, https://evonomics.com/the-new-invisible-hand-david-sloan-wilson/.

70 David Sloan Wilson, "Why New Economics Needs a New Invisible Hand"

71 Frederic Bastiat, "How does Paris get fed?" *in Economic Sophisms* (Irvington-on-Hudson, NY: Foundation for Economic Education, Inc., 1996).

72 Daniel Dennett refers to Darwin's theory of natural selection as similar to a universal acid that eats through everything it touches.

73   David Sloan Wilson and Peter Barnes, "How to Construct a New Invisible Hand: A Conversation with Peter Barnes," *Evonomics*, March 3, 2018, https://evonomics.com/new-invisible-hand-conversation-peter-barnes-david-sloan-wilson/.

74   The Discovery Institute is a think-tank dedicated to teaching the theory of Intelligent Design in biological systems.

75   Aaron Bastani, "The World Is a Mess. We Need Fully Automated Luxury Communism," *The New York Times*, June 11, 2019, http://tiny.cc/qvt1tz.

76   Bastani, "The World Is a Mess. We Need Fully Automated Luxury Communism."

77   Nicholas Kristof, "This Has Been the Best Year Ever," *The New York Times*, December 28, 2019, http://tiny.cc/jvt1tz.

78   Paul Mason, "The end of capitalism has begun," *The Guardian*, June 17, 2015, http://tiny.cc/lvt1tz.

79   Nelson Goodman, *Ways of Worldmaking. Vol. 51* (Hackett Publishing, 1978), 19.

80   Scilla Elworthy, "Deepening Feminine Wisdom," *Dr Scilla Elworthy*, accessed January 15, 2021, https://www.scillaelworthy.com/deepening-feminine-wisdom/.

81   Dierdre N. McCloskey, "The Rhetoric of the Economy and Polity," *Prudentia*, accessed November 9, 2020, http://www.deirdremccloskey.com/articles/polity.php

82   James Pethokoukis, "5 questions for Deirdre McCloskey on the need for liberalism," *AEIdeas*, November 7, 2019, http://tiny.cc/awt1tz.

83   James Scott, *Against the Grain: a deep history of the earliest states* (Yale University Press, 2017).

84   Aylin Woodward, "With a Little Help from My Friends," *Scientific American*, May 1, 2017, http://tiny.cc/iwt1tz.

85   Paul Vallely, "Democracy: Whose idea was this?" *The Independent*, May 10, 2012, http://tiny.cc/qwt1tz.

86   Francis Fukuyama, *The End of History and the Last Man* (London: Penguin Books, 2020).

87   Yaneer Bar-Yam, *Complexity Rising: From human beings to human civilization, a complexity profile* (2000), 811.

88   Bar-Yam, *Complexity Rising: From human beings to human civilization, a complexity profile*, 812.

89   Bar-Yam, *Complexity Rising: From human beings to human civilization, a complexity profile*, 812.

90   Friedrich Hayek, "The Use of Knowledge in Society," *The Library of Economics and Liberty*, accessed November 6, 2020, https://www.econlib.org/library/Essays/hykKnw.html/.

91   Scott Shane, *Dismantling Utopia: How Information Ended the Soviet Union* (Chicago: I.R. Dee, 1995).

92   Jason Koebler, "Society Is Too Complicated to Have a President, Complex Mathematics Suggest," *Vice*, November 7, 2016," http://tiny.cc/7013tz.

93   Friedrich A. von Hayek, "The Sveriges Riksbank Prize in Economic Sciences in Memory of Alfred Nobel 1974," *NobelPrize.org*, accessed January 6, 2021, https://www.nobelprize.org/prizes/economic-sciences/1974/hayek/lecture/.

94   Matt Ridley, *The Evolution of Everything* (Harper Collins, 2015), 108.

95   Said in conversation, which I noted in 2017.

96   Deirdre Nansen McCloskey, *How Growth Happens: Liberalism, Innovism, and the Great Enrichment* (Economic History Seminar, 2018).

97   John Tierney, "Do You Suffer From Decision Fatigue?," (*The New York Times*, August 17, 2011), https://www.nytimes.com/2011/08/21/magazine/do-you-suffer-from-decision-fatigue.html.

98   John Tierney, "Do You Suffer From Decision Fatigue?"

99   Michael Huemer, "The Problem of Authority," *Cato Unbound: a Journal of Debate*, March 4, 2013, http://tiny.cc/40u1tz.

100   Ronald H. Coase, Oliver E. Williamson, and Sidney G. Winter, *The Nature of the Firm* (New York: Oxford University Press, 1993).

101   Adrian Bejan, *Design in Nature: How the Constructal Law Governs Evolution in Biology, Physcs, Technology, and Social Organization* (New York: Anchor Books, 2013).

102   Adam Ferguson, "An Essay on the History of Civil Society," 5th ed. (London: T. Cadell, 1782), accessed November 6, 2020, https://oll.libertyfund.org/titles/1428.

103   Adrian Bejan refers to this as the constructal law.

104   Jane Jacobs, *The Death and Life of Great American Cities* (Vintage, 2016).

105   Eknath Easwaran, *The Bhagavad Gita:(Classics of Indian Spirituality) Vol. 1* (Nilgiri Press, 2007), 91.

106   Easwaran, *The Bhagavad Gita:(Classics of Indian Spirituality)*, 198.

107   D. C. Lau, "Chapter 29," in *Lao Tzu ; Tao Te Ching* (New York: Penguin Books, 1963).

108	Adam Smith, *The Theory of Moral Sentiments* (Penguin, 2010).

109	"Hillel the Elder," Wikipedia (Wikimedia Foundation, December 6, 2020), https://en.wikipedia.org/wiki/Hillel_the_Elder.

110	Rolf Gates, *Meditations from the Mat: Daily reflections on the path of yoga* (Anchor, 2002).

111	Leonard P. Read, *Elements of Libertarian Leadership: Notes on the Theory, Methods, and Practice of Freedom* (Pickle Partners Publishing, 2018).

112	"Adam Smith on the 'Liberal System' of Free Trade (1776)," *Online Library of Liberty*, accessed December 10, 2020, https://oll.libertyfund.org/quotes/459.

113	D. C. Lau, "Chapter 32," in *Lao Tzu ; Tao Te Ching* (New York: Penguin Books, 1963).

114	Vincent Ostrom, *The Meaning of American Federalism: Constituting a Self-governing Society* (ICS Press, 1991), 38-39.

115	Vincent Ostrom, *The Meaning of American Federalism: Constituting a Self-governing Society* (ICS Press, 1991), 39.

116	Desh Subba, "Thomas Hobbes and his Fearolotical Philosophy," *Fearless Movement*, accessed March 31, 2020, https://fearlessnessmovement.ning.com/blog/thomas-hobbes-and-his-fearolotical-philosophy-deshsubba.

117	Scott Alexander, "Meditations On Moloc," *Slate Star Codex*, July 30, 2014, https://slatestarcodex.com/2014/07/30/meditations-on-moloch/.

118	Fred Shapiro, "Quotes Uncovered: Death and Taxes," *Freakonomics*, February 11, 2011, http://freakonomics.com/2011/02/17/quotes-uncovered-death-and-taxes/.

119	This website maps U.S. bases around the world. http://empire.is/

120	James Madison, "The Federalist Papers,#51," *Federalist* collection of essays written in favour of the new constitution of the United States of America (1788).

121	Bryan Caplan, "The Myth of the Rational Voter," *Cato Unbound*, https://www.cato-unbound.org/2006/11/05/bryan-caplan/myth-rational-voter.

122	Kevin Kelly, "The Shirky Principle," *The Technium*, accessed January 6, 2021, https://kk.org/thetechnium/the-shirky-prin/.

123	Peter T. Calcagno and Frank Hefner, "Targeted Economic Incentives: An Analysis of State Fiscal Policy and Regulatory Conditions," Mercatus Working Paper, April 2018, https://www.mercatus.org/system/files/calcagno-targeted-economic-incentives-mercatus-working-paper-v1.

pdf.

124   Cited in Conor Friedersdorf, "Enforcing the Law is Inherently Violent," *The Atlantic,* June 27, 2016, https://www.theatlantic.com/politics/archive/2016/06/enforcing-the-law-is-inherently-violent/488828/.

125   Friedersdorf, "Enforcing the Law is Inherently Violent."

126   Max Borders and Jim Rutt, "On Anarchism & Libertarianism," *Letter*, accessed November 7, 2020, https://letter.wiki/conversation/235.

127   "Edmund Burke, A Vindication of Natural Society [1756]," Online Library of Liberty, accessed November 7, 2020, https://oll.libertyfund.org/titles/burke-a-vindication-of-natural-society.

128   Michael Strong, "An Introduction to Strong's Law," *Radical Social Entrepreneurs,* November 4, 2017, http://www.radicalsocialentreps.org/2017/11/an-introduction-to-strongs-law/?fbclid=IwAR1aAyP7wDX-1BjPM6UfOqf8GApYqsBWGT6blI53lY2WSlLqxw4LRX4r_QJA.

129   Strong, "An Introduction to Strong's Law."

130   Strong, "An Introduction to Strong's Law."

131   Israel Kirzner, "Entrepreneurial Discovery and the Competitive Market Process: An Austrian approach," *Journal of Economic Literature* 35, no. 1 (1997): 60-85.

132   Kirzner, "Entrepreneurial Discovery and the Competitive Market Process," 60-85.

133   James M. Buchanan, "Public Choice: Politics Without Romance," *Policy* 19, no 3 (Spring 2003): 15, https://www.cis.org.au/app/uploads/2015/04/images/stories/policy-magazine/2003-spring/2003-19-3-james-m-buchanan.pdf

134   James M. Buchanan, "Public Choice" 15.

135   Ice-T, "Don't Hate the Playa," The Seventh Deadly Sin, (Coroner Records/Roadrunner Records/Atomic Pop, 1999).

136   Radio address "Our American Culture" broadcast during an intermission of the Metropolitan Opera. (1 March 1941).

137   Sam Haselby, "Return of the city-state," *Aeon*, September 5, 2017, https://aeon.co/essays/the-end-of-a-world-of-nation-states-may-be-upon-us.

138   "Population bottleneck," Nature Education, accessed November 7, 2020, https://www.nature.com/scitable/definition/population-bottleneck-300/.

139   Deirdre McCloskey, "Factual Free-Market Fairness," *Bleeding Heart Libertarians*, Symposium On Free Market Fairness, Economics, June 16, 2012, http://bleedingheartlibertarians.com/2012/06/factual-free-mar-

ket-fairness/.

140   McCloskey, "Factual Free-Market Fairness."

141   Frank Tang, "Chinese Pro-Market Economist Wu Jinglian Warns of 'State Capitalism' Dangers," South China Morning Post, January 21, 2009, http://tiny.cc/w3u1tz.

142   Donna Barne and Divyanshi Wadhwa, "Year in Review: 2019 in 14 Charts," The World Bank, December 20, 2019, http://tiny.cc/y3u1tz.

143   Gale L. Pooley and Marian L. Tupy, "The Simon Abundance Index 2019, Human Progress," May 30, 2019, https://humanprogress.org/article.php?p=1916.

144   Max Roser, Hannah Ritchie, and Bernadeta Dadonaite, "Child and Infant Mortality," Updated November 2019, https://ourworldindata.org/child-mortality.

145   Max Roser, Hannah Ritchie, and Bernadeta Dadonaite, "Life Expectancy," Updated November 2019, https://ourworldindata.org/life-expectancy.

146   John Gray, "Why this crisis is a turning point in history," New Statesman, April 1, 2020, http://tiny.cc/54u1tz.

147   Joseph Hogan, "The Problems of Liberalism: A Q&A With Patrick Deneen," The Nation, May 28, 2018, http://tiny.cc/b4u1tz.

148   Linda Raeder, Freedom and Political Order: Traditional American Thought and Practice (Lexington Books, 2018).

149   Linda Raeder, Freedom and Political Order.

150   Linda Raeder, Freedom and Political Order.

151   Dean Russell, "Who Is a Libertarian?" Foundation for Economic Education, May 1, 1955, https://fee.org/articles/who-is-a-libertarian/.

152   Russell, "Who Is a Libertarian?"

153   Jeffrey A. Tucker, "Against Libertarian Brutalism: Jeffrey A. Tucker," The Freeman (Foundation for Economic Education, March 12, 2014), https://fee.org/articles/against-libertarian-brutalism/.

154   James D. Vance, "End the Globalization Gravy Train," The American Mind, April 1, 2020, https://americanmind.org/essays/end-the-globalization-gravy-train/.

155   Joseph A. Schumpeter, History of Economic Analysis (New York: Oxford University Press, 1954), p. 9.

156   Elias Isquith, "Neoliberalism Poisons Everything: How free market mania threatens education -- and democracy," Salon, June 15, 2019, http://tiny.cc/v5u1tz.

157   Joseph Hogan, "The Problems of Liberalism: A Q&A With Patrick Deneen," *The Nation*, May 30, 2018, https://www.thenation.com/article/archive/the-problems-of-liberalism-a-qa-with-patrick-deneen/.

158   James Kirchick, "Op-Ed: I'm a neoliberal and I'm proud," *Los Angeles Times*, June 4, 2017, http://tiny.cc/c6u1tz.

159   Jason Brennan, "Dear Left: Corporatism Is Your Fault," *Bleeding Hearts Libertarians*, November 29, 2011, https://bleedingheartlibertarians.com/2011/11/dear-left-corporatism-is-your-fault/.

160   Shruti Rajagopalan and Alexander Tabarrok, "Premature Imitation and India's Flailing State," *The Independent Review* 24, no. 2 (2019): 165-186.

161   William Easterley, *White Man's Burden: why the West's efforts to aid the rest have done so much ill and so little good* (New York, 2006), 5-6.

162   Jeffrey Sachs, *The End of Poverty* (New York: Penguin Press, 2005).

163   Nina Munk, *The Idealist: Jeffrey Sachs and the quest to end poverty* (Signal, 2013).

164   Michael Clemens, "New Documents Reveal the Cost of 'Ending Poverty' in a Millennium Village: At Least $12,000 Per Household," Centre for Global Development, March 30, 2012, http://tiny.cc/0fb2tz.

165   Howard W. French, "Jeffrey Sachs' Failure to Eradicate Poverty in Africa," *Pacific Standard* (Pacific Standard, September 17, 2013), https://psmag.com/social-justice/smart-guy-jeffrey-sachs-nina-munk-idealist-poverty-failure-africa-65348

166   Howard W. French, "Jeffrey Sachs' Failure to Eradicate Poverty in Africa," *Pacific Standard* (Pacific Standard, September 17, 2013), https://psmag.com/social-justice/smart-guy-jeffrey-sachs-nina-munk-idealist-poverty-failure-africa-65348."

167   This index is produced by the conservative Heritage Foundation. Many readers will find this source objectionable. I encourage those readers to check the data, the methodology, and steer clear of the genetic fallacy.

168   "Key Findings of the 2019 Index," *Heritage*, accessed November 11, 2020, https://www.heritage.org/index/book/chapter-3.

169   Richard Drayton, "The wealth of the west was built on Africa's exploitation," *The Guardian*, August 20, 2005, https://www.theguardian.com/politics/2005/aug/20/past.hearafrica05.

170   Max Roser, "Economic Growth," *Our World in Data*, 2013, http://tiny.cc/wgb2tz.

171   Karl Zinsmeister, "Oseola McCarty," *Philanthropy Roundtable*, accessed January 13, 2021, https://www.philanthropyroundtable.org/almanac/people/hall-of-fame/detail/oseola-mccarty.

172   Rick Bragg, "Oseola McCarty, a Washerwoman Who Gave All She Had to Help Others, Dies at 91," *The New York Times*, September 28, 1999, http://tiny.cc/ghb2tz.

173   Karl Zinsmeister, "Oseola McCarty," *Philanthropy Roundtable*, accessed January 13, 2021, https://www.philanthropyroundtable.org/almanac/people/hall-of-fame/detail/oseola-mccarty.

174   Wikipedia contributors, "Barn raising," *Wikipedia*, accessed November 9, 2020, https://en.wikipedia.org/w/index.php?title=Barn_raising&oldid=977921232.

175   Wikipedia contributors, "Barn raising."

176   This quote from my aunt Jean Roberts came via personal email correspondence.

177   This quote from my aunt Ellen Wease came via personal email correspondence.

178   James C. Scott, *Seeing Like a State: How certain schemes to improve the human condition have failed* (New Haven, CT: Yale University Press, 2020), 88.

179   Alexis de Tocqueville, *Democracy in America*, ed. Harvey C. Mansfield and Delba Winthrop (Chicago: University of Chicago Press, 2000).

180   David Beito, "From Mutual Aid to Welfare State: How Fraternal Societies Fought Poverty and Taught Character," *The Heritage Foundation*, accessed December 10, 2020, https://www.heritage.org/political-process/report/mutual-aid-welfare-state-how-fraternal-societies-fought-poverty-and-taught.

181   David Beito, "From Mutual Aid to Welfare State."

182   Justin Arman, *New Braunfels Freemasonry: Volume 1 (1800s-1929): A Local History with Global Context (New Braunfels Freemasonry Volume 1 - 1800s to 1929)* (Independently published, 2020), 37.

183   Ron Schulz, "Adjacent Opportunities: Engaged Emergence— Part 2" *E:CO*, Vol. 11 No. 3, 2009, 85-86.

184   The Signers, "'Millionaires for Humanity' Sign On Letter," *Millionaires for Humanity*, accessed November 8, 2020, https://www.millionairesforhumanity.com/.

185   David Beito, "From Mutual Aid to Welfare State: How Fraternal Societies Fought Poverty and Taught Character," *The Heritage Foundation*, accessed December 10, 2020, https://www.heritage.org/political-process/report/mutual-aid-welfare-state-how-fraternal-societies-fought-poverty-and-taught.

186   David Beito, "From Mutual Aid to Welfare State".

187   David Brooks, "The Nuclear Family Was a Mistake," *The Atlantic*,

March 2020, http://tiny.cc/rib2tz.

188   Herbert Bronstein and Leonard Baskin, *A Passover Haggadah: the New Union Haggadah* (New York: Central Conference of American Rabbis, 1994).

189   Bronstein, *A Passover Haggadah*, 66.

190   Elizabeth Dunn, Lara Aknin, and Michael Norton, "Prosocial spending and happiness: Using money to benefit others pays off," *Current Directions in Psychological Science* 23, no. 1 (2014): 41-47.

191   Dunn, Aknin, and Norton, "Prosocial spending and happiness," 41-47.

192   Henry L. Mencken and Marion Elizabeth Rodgers, in *H.L. Mencken: Prejudices, First, Second, and Third Series* (New York: Library of America, 2010), 158.

193   Robert Greenstein, "Commentary: Universal Basic Income May Sound Attractive But, If It Occurred, Would Likelier Increase Poverty Than Reduce It," Center on Budget and Policy Priorities, June 13, 2019, https://www.cbpp.org/poverty-and-opportunity/commentary-universal-basic-income-may-sound-attractive-but-if-it-occurred.

194   Robert Greenstein, "Commentary: Universal Basic Income May Sound Attractive But, If It Occurred, Would Likelier Increase Poverty Than Reduce It".

195   Robert Greenstein, "Commentary: Universal Basic Income May Sound Attractive But, If It Occurred, Would Likelier Increase Poverty Than Reduce It".

196   "Rent trend data in Jackson, Mississippi," *Rent Jungle*, accessed November 11, 2020, https://www.rentjungle.com/average-rent-in-jackson-ms-rent-trends/.

197   "San Francisco, CA Rental Market Trends," *RentCafe*, accessed November 8, 2020, https://www.rentcafe.com/average-rent-market-trends/us/ca/san-francisco/.

198   "Rent trend data in Chattanooga, Tennessee," accessed November 8, 2020, https://www.rentjungle.com/average-rent-in-chat *Rent Jungle*, tanooga-rent-trends/.

199   "Rent trend data in New York, New York," *Rent Jungle*, accessed November 8, 2020, https://www.rentjungle.com/average-rent-in-new-york-rent-trends/.

200   Helmut Schoeck, *Envy: a Theory of Social Behaviour* (Indianapolis: Liberty Fund, 1987).

201   Henry Louis Mencken, *A Mencken Chrestomathy* (New York: Vintage Books, 1982), 162.

202   Rachel Swaby, "One Man's Nearly Impossible Quest to Make a Toaster From Scratch," *Gizmodo*, April 21, 2011, https://gizmodo.com/one-mans-nearly-impossible-quest-to-make-a-toaster-from-5794368.

203   Ivan Illich, "Questions About the Current Pandemic From the Point of View of Ivan Illich," *DavidCayley.com*, April 8, 2020, http://www.davidcayley.com/blog/2020/4/8/questions-about-the-current-pandemic-from-the-point-of-view-of-ivan-illich-1.

204   Richard Milne, "Anders Tegnell and the Swedish Covid experiment," *Financial Times*, September 10, 2020, https://www.ft.com/content/5cc92d45-fbdb-43b7-9c66-26501693a371.

205   Zeynep Tufekci, "How Hong Kong Did It," *Technology*, May 12, 2020, http://tiny.cc/bkb2tz.

206   Adrian Bejan and J. Peder Zane, „Design in nature," *Mechanical Engineering* 134, no. 06 (2012), 42-47.

207   Arthur G. Jago, "Can It Really Be True That Half of Academic Papers Are Never Read?" *The Chronicle of Higher Education*, June 1, 2018, http://tiny.cc/nkb2tz.

208   Ed Yong, "Psychology's Replication Crisis is Running Out of Excuses," The Atlantic, November 19, 2018, http://tiny.cc/rkb2tz.

209   Brian Resnick, "More social science studies just failed to replicate. Here's why this is good," *Vox*, August 27, 2018, http://tiny.cc/wkb2tz.

210   Robby Berman, "It's a movement: Amateur scientists are making huge discoveries," *Big Think*, February 3, 2018, http://tiny.cc/jmb2tz.

211   Max Black, *Models and Metaphors: Studies in language and philosophy* (Cornell University Press, 2019), 236.

212   Timur Kuran and Cass R. Sunstein, "Availability cascades and risk regulation," *Stan. L.* Rev. 51 (1998): 683.

213   Jordan Hall, "Understanding the Blue Church," Medium, Mar 30, 2017, http://tiny.cc/9nb2tz.

214   Jordan Hall, "Understanding the Blue Church," Medium, Mar 30, 2017, http://tiny.cc/9nb2tz.

215   Hall, "Understanding the Blue Church."

216   Rebecca Davis, "The Doctor Who Championed Hand-Washing And Briefly Saved Lives," *NPR*, January 12, 2015, http://tiny.cc/fnb2tz.

217   Wikipedia contributors, "Ignaz Semmelweis," *Wikipedia*, accessed November 9, 2020, http://tiny.cc/unb2tz.

218   Tugwell was a part of FDR's so-called "Brain Trust," serving as an economic advisor and social planner.

219   "How to Become a Superforecaster," *Good Judgement*, accessed

November 9, 2020, https://goodjudgment.com/how-to-become-a-super-forecaster/.

220   David J. Johnson, Trevor Tress, Nicole Burkel, Carley Taylor, Joseph Cesario. "Officer Characteristics and Racial Disparities in Fatal Officer-involved Shootings," *Proceedings of the National Academy of Sciences*, August 2019, 116 (32) 15877-15882.

221   Adam Marcus, "Authors of Study on Race and Police Killings Ask for Its Retraction, Citing 'Continued Misuse' in the Media," *Retraction Watch*, July 8, 2020, https://retractionwatch.com/2020/07/06/authors-of-study-on-race-and-police-killings-ask-for-its-retraction-citing-continued-misuse-in-the-media/.

222   Jonathan Haidt, "Universities Must Choose Between Truth or Social Justice" (October 2016), *Youtube*, https://www.youtube.com/watch?v=kaQ-ZF9S3uk.

223   Bret Stephens, "The 1619 Chronicles," (*The New York Times*, October 10, 2020), https://www.nytimes.com/2020/10/09/opinion/nyt-1619-project-criticisms.html.

224   Catherine Wynne, "The teenager who saved a man with an SS tattoo," *BBC News*, October 29, 2013, https://www.bbc.com/news/magazine-24653643.

225   Catherine Wynne, "The teenager who saved a man with an SS tattoo," *BBC News*, October 29, 2013, https://www.bbc.com/news/magazine-24653643.

226   Douglas Turner Ward's *Day of Absence* is a satirical play about an imaginary Southern town where all the black people have suddenly disappeared. The whites realize they have become utterly dependent on the blacks, which prompts the whites to beg for the blacks return.

227   Uri Harris, "How Activists Took Control of a University: The Case Study of Evergreen State," *Quillette*, December 26, 2017, https://quillette.com/2017/12/18/activists-took-control-university-case-study-evergreen-state/.

228   "The Equity Council," Evergreen, accessed November 8, 2020, http://tiny.cc/rsb2tz.

229   "Evergreen State College Racism Protests - Bret Weinstein's Letter to Rashida, Know Your Memes," accessed November, 11, 2020, http://tiny.cc/vrb2tz.

230   Daisy Grewal, "The Evolution of Prejudice," *Scientific American*, April 5, 2011, http://tiny.cc/xsb2tz.

231   Martin Luther King, "'I Have a Dream," Address Delivered at the March on Washington for Jobs and Freedom, The Martin Luther

King, Jr., Research and Education Institute, January 25, 2019, https://kinginstitute.stanford.edu/king-papers/documents/i-have-dream-address-delivered-march-washington-jobs-and-freedom.

232   Magatte Wade, Feel the Liberty, July 17, 2020, *Facebook*, https://www.facebook.com/FeelTheLiberty/posts/magatte-wade-is-a-power-house-voice-worth-listening-to/2410895842536405/.

233   Robin J. DiAngelo and Alex Tatusian, *White Fragility* (NY, NY: Public Science, 2016).

234   John McWorther, "The Dehumanizing Condescension of White Frailty," July 15, 2020, *The Atlantic,* http://tiny.cc/9pc2tz.

235   See the *Washington Post* reporting of Radley Balko, such as "The Ongoing Criminalization of Poverty".

236   "Mapping Police Violence," accessed November 9, 2020, https://mappingpoliceviolence.org/nationaltrends.

237   FBI Releases 2018 NIBRS Crime Data as Transition to NIBRS 2021 Continues, *FBI.gov*, December 19, 2019, http://tiny.cc/lpc2tz.

238   "Expanded Homicide," *FBI.org*, accessed November 8, 2020, https://ucr.fbi.gov/crime-in-the-u.s/2018/crime-in-the-u.s.-2018/topic-pages/expanded-homicide.

239   Barbara O'Brien and Kristen Parker, "African-Americans More Likely to Be Wrongfully Convicted," *Research at Michigan State University*, accessed December 10, 2020, https://research.msu.edu/innocent-african-americans-more-likely-to-be-wrongfully-convicted/.

240   Rachel Morgan and Barbara Oudekerk, "Criminal victimization, 2018 (NCJ 253043)," *Bureau of Justice Statistics Special Report*, (US Department of Justice, Washington, DC.) (2019).

241   The Game, "Love it Or Hate it," *The Documentary*, (Interscope Records, 2005).

242   Mob Deep, "Kill that Nigga," (Infamy, Sony Entertainment, 2001).

243   James Lindsay, "No, the Woke Won't Debate You. Here's Why.", *New Discourses*, July 30, 2020, https://newdiscourses.com/2020/07/woke-wont-debate-you-heres-why/.

244   James Lindsay, "No, the Woke Won't Debate You. Here's Why.", *New Discourses*, July 30, 2020, https://newdiscourses.com/2020/07/woke-wont-debate-you-heres-why/.

245   Audre Lorde, *The Master's Tools Will Never Dismantle the Master's House* (UK: Penguin, 2018).

246   Lindsay, "No, the Woke Won't Debate You. Here's Why."

247   Wendy Guzman, "Hundreds of MSU professors, GEU call to remove VP of research Stephen Hsu," *The State News*, June 15, 2020, http://tiny.cc/j2d2tz.

248   Colleen Flaherty, "Quest for 'Genius Babies'?" *Inside Higher Ed*, May 29, 2013, http://tiny.cc/l2d2tz.

249   "Rudi Dutschke," *Wikipedia* (Wikimedia Foundation, October 8, 2020), https://en.wikipedia.org/wiki/Rudi_Dutschke.

250   Antonio Gramsci and David Forgacs, *The Gramsci Reader* (NYU Press), 233.

251   Michael Strong, "Academia: The World's Leading Social Problem," *The James G. Martin Center for Academic Renewal*, June 13, 2016, https://www.jamesgmartin.center/2012/08/academia-the-worlds-leading-social-problem/.

252   Jonathan Haidt, "Where Microaggressions Really Come From: A Sociological Account," *The Righteous Mind*, April 20, 2016, https://righteousmind.com/where-microaggressions-really-come-from/.

253   Claire Lehmann, "Understanding Victimhood Culture: An Interview with Bradley Campbell and Jason Manning," *Quilette*, May 17, 2018, http://tiny.cc/i3d2tz.

254   Jonathan Haidt, "Where microaggressions really come from."

255   I suspect people who, like me, grew up in the South during the 80s and 90s might have gotten bullied. And also, like me, you might have had a mother who would suggest you shrug and a father who would suggest you bring a baseball bat to school--and be prepared to use it.

256   Conor Friedersdorf, "The New Intolerance of Student Activism," *The Atlantic*, November 9, 2015, http://tiny.cc/14d2tz.

257   Friedersdorf, "The New Intolerance of Student Activism."

258   Jonathan Haidt and Greg Lukianoff, "The coddling of the American mind," *The Atlantic* 316, no. 2 (2015): 42-52.

259   Harris, "How Activists Took Control of a University."

260   Richard Rorty. *Achieving Our Country: Leftist Thought in Twentieth-Century America* (Harvard University Press 1999).

261   NPR/PBS 2018 - Newshour/Marist Poll, http://tiny.cc/npr-pbs-poll.

262   Jordan Hall, "Understanding the Blue Church," *Medium*, Mar 30, 2017, http://tiny.cc/9nb2tz.

263   Ibram X. Kendi, "Is This the Beginning of the End of American Racism?" *The Atlantic*, September 2020, https://www.theatlantic.com/magazine/archive/2020/09/the-end-of-denial/614194/.

264   Ibram X. Kendi, Original Twitter post: https://twitter.com/dribram/status/1309916696296198146?lang=en

265   "Former Estonian Prime Minister Mart Laar Wins Friedman Prize for Liberty," *The Cato Institute*, April 20, 2005, http://tiny.cc/x4d2tz.

266   Wikipedia contributors, "List of countries by GDP (nominal) per capita," *Wikipedia*, accessed November 9, 2020, http://tiny.cc/55d2tz.

267   Antony Davies and James R. Harrigan, "Transferism, Not Socialism, Is the Drug Americans Are Hooked On," *Foundation for Economic Education*, December 6, 2019, http://tiny.cc/c5d2tz.

268   Uri Harris, "How Activists Took Control of a University: The Case Study of Evergreen State," *Quillette*, December 26, 2017, https://quillette.com/2017/12/18/activists-took-control-university-case-study-evergreen-state/.

269   Davies and Harrigan, "Transferism, Not Socialism."

270   The English translation is: "The state is that great fiction by which everyone tries to live at the expense of everyone else." I couldn't resist using the original French out of pure pretention. https://oll.libertyfund.org/quotes/145

271   Kate Davidson, "U.S. Debt Is Set to Exceed Size of the Economy Next Year, a First Since World War II," *The Wall Street Journal* (Dow Jones & Company, September 2, 2020), https://www.wsj.com/articles/u-s-debt-is-set-to-exceed-size-of-the-economy-for-year-a-first-since-world-war-ii-11599051137.

272   Rudolph Penner, "A U.S. Fiscal Crisis?" *Urban Institute*, October 17, 2018, http://tiny.cc/l5d2tz.

273   Antony Davies and James R. Harrigan, "Trillions in Debt and We're Just Scratching the Surface," *Foundation for Economic Education*, March 12, 2017, http://tiny.cc/y5d2tz.

274   Antony Davies and James R. Harrigan, "Trillions in Debt and We're Just Scratching the Surface,"

275   Kristin Tate, "The Sheer Size of Our Government Workforce is an Alarming Problem," April 14, 2019, *The Hill*, http://tiny.cc/46d2tz.

276   Kristin Tate, "The Sheer Size of Our Government Workforce is an Alarming Problem," April 14, 2019, *The Hill*, http://tiny.cc/46d2tz.

277   "Putting People Back to Work," *UShistory.org*, http://tiny.cc/FDRbacktowork.

278   "Which was Bigger: The 2009 Recovery Act or FDR's New Deal?" *Federal Reserve Bank of St. Louis*, May 30, 2017, http://tiny.cc/newdealor2008.

279   Robert D. Murphy, *The Politically Incorrect Guide to the Great Depression*, (Regnery Publishing, 2009), 103.

280   Mike Cooley's lyrics are from the song "Uncle Frank," which he wrote and performs with The Drive-By Truckers. Special thanks to Jenny Clary for drawing my attention to these lyrics.

281   Robert Higgs, "Regime uncertainty: why the Great Depression lasted so long and why prosperity resumed after the war," *The Independent Review 1*, no. 4 (1997): 561-590.

282   Steven Horwitz and Michael J. McPhillips, "The reality of the wartime economy: More historical evidence on whether world war II ended the great depression," *The Independent Review* 17, no. 3 (2013): 325-347.

283   Steven Horwitz and Michael J. McPhillips, "The reality of the wartime economy: More historical evidence on whether world war II ended the great depression," *The Independent Review* 17, no. 3 (2013): 325-347.

284   Marianne Page and Ann Huff Stevens, "Poverty in America: What a Half-Century of Progress Looks Like," *Time* (Time, January 8, 2015), https://time.com/3659383/war-on-poverty-1964/.

285   James D. Davidson and William Rees-Mogg, *The Sovereign Individual: Mastering the Transition to the Information Age* (New York: TouchStone, 1999), 313

286   "Median Household income in the United States by Race or Ethnic Group," Statistica, https://www.statista.com/statistics/233324/median-household-income-in-the-united-states-by-race-or-ethnic-group/.

287   Alexis de Tocqueville, *Democracy in America* (Hackett, 2000), 307.

288   Vincent Fitzpatrick, *H.L. Mencken* (Mercer University Press, 2004), 66.

289   Wikipedia contributors, "Thích Quảng Đức," Wikipedia, The Free Encyclopedia, accessed November 9, 2020, http://tiny.cc/jfd2tz.

290   Abby Zimet, "A Mind of Compassion," *Common Dreams*, June 11, 2013, https://www.commondreams.org/further/2013/06/11/mind-compassion.

291   Thomas Jefferson to William Smith, November 13, 1787, https://founders.archives.gov/documents/Jefferson/01-12-02-0348.

292   James Fallows, "The End of the Roman Empire Wasn't That Bad," *The Atlantic*, October 29, 2020, http://tiny.cc/xfd2tz.

293   Noelle Talmon, "How Shaolin Monks Obtain Their Superpowers," *Ripley's Believe It or Not!*, April 16, 2018, https://www.ripleys.com/weird-news/shaolin-monks/.

294   Leonard Read, *Elements of Libertarian Leadership: Notes on the Theory,*

Methods, and Practice of Freedom (Pickle Partners Publishing, 2018).

295   Satchidananda, *The Yoga Sutras of Patanjali* (Yogaville, VA: Integral Yoga, 2009).

296   Thich Nhat Hanh, *Living Buddha, Living Christ* (Penguin, 2007)

297   I owe this formulation to Chris Rufer's influence.

298   I have benefitted enormously from conversations with my friend and mentor Chris Rufer who showed me that a rule of non-harm should not be a passive political philosophy but an active practice.

299   Thich Nhat Hanh, *Living Buddha, Living Christ* (Penguin, 2007), 63.

300   Hanh, *Living Buddha, Living Christ.*

301   James Scott, *Two cheers for anarchism: Six easy pieces on autonomy, dignity, and meaningful work and play* (Princeton University Press, 2014).

302   "Civil Disobedience," *Bill of Rights Institute*, accessed November 9, 2020, http://tiny.cc/08h2tz.

303   Bruce Benson, "It takes two invisible hands to make a market: Lex Mercatoria (Law Merchant) always emerges to facilitate emerging market activity," *Studies in Emergent Order* 3 (2010): 100-128.

304   Michael C. Jensen, "Integrity: Without It Nothing Works," *SSRN*, November 22, 2009, https://papers.ssrn.com/sol3/papers.cfm?abstract_id=1511274.

305   Eknath Easwaran, *The Bhagavad Gita:(Classics of Indian Spirituality) Vol. 1* (Nilgiri Press, 2007) 7.27.

306   Robert Nozick, *Philosophical Explanations* (Cambridge, MA: Harvard University Press, 1981), 416.

307   Sally Kempton, *Awakening Shakti* (Mumbai, India: JAICO Publishing House, 2016).

308   Paul Fleischman, *Buddha Taught Nonviolence, Not Pacifism* (Pariyatti Publishing, 2002).

309   Max Borders, "The Death of Political Theory," *Social Evolution*, March 6, 2018, https://medium.com/social-evolution/the-death-of-political-theory-996f9bff369c.

310   The title of this chapter is inspired by the title of Randy Barnett's book, *Restoring the Lost Constitution.*

311   Interviews, "Coronavirus Will Change the World Permanently. Here's How," *Politico Magazine*, March 19, 2020, http://tiny.cc/bxp2tz.

312   Otto Neurath, "Anti-Spengler," *In Empiricism and sociology, pp. 158-213* (Springer, Dordrecht, 1973).

313   Michael J. Phillips, *The Lochner Court, Myth and Reality: Substantive*

Due Process from the 1890s to the 1930s (Westport, CT: Praeger, 2001). See also New State Ice Company v. Liebmann (1932).

314   Charles Murray, "What It Means to Be a Libertarian: A Personal Interpretation," *New York Times*, accessed November 9, 2020, http://tiny.cc/0qu2tz.

315   Randy E. Barnett, *Our Republican Constitution* (Broadside Books, 2016), 181.

316   Barnett, *Our Republican Constitution*, 181.

317   Barnett, *Our Republican Constitution*, 182.

318   David A. Strauss, "The Living Constitution," *The University of Chicago, The Law School*, September 29, 2010, https://www.law.uchicago.edu/news/living-constitution.

319   Strauss, "The Living Constitution."

320   Barnett, *Our Republican Constitution*, 135.

321   Strauss, "The Living Constitution."

322   Nick Szabo, "Jurisdiction as Property: The Paper," *Unenumerated*, June 3, 2006, https://unenumerated.blogspot.com/2006/06/jurisdiction-as-property-paper.html.

323   Nick Szabo, "Jurisdiction as Property: The Paper," *Unenumerated*, June 3, 2006, https://unenumerated.blogspot.com/2006/06/jurisdiction-as-property-paper.html.

324   John Hasnas, "Four Solutions to Sandefur's Problems," *Cato Unbound*, December 9, 2009, http://tiny.cc/bq03tz.

325   "To James Madison Paris, Sep. 6, 1789," accessed November 9, 2020, http://www.let.rug.nl/usa/.

326   Alexander, "Meditations On Moloc."

327   "Brutus No. 1," Khan Academy, accessed November 9, 2020, http://tiny.cc/ar03tz.

328   "Brutus No. 1".

329   "Brutus No. 1".

330   "Brutus No. 1".

331   "Brutus No. 1".

332   "Brutus No. 1".

333   "Brutus No. 1".

334   "Brutus No. 1".

335   "Brutus No. 1".

336   Trevor Burrus, "The Anti-Federalists Predicted Today's Political Morass, and Can Help Us Get Out," *Cato Institute*, November 7, 2016, http://tiny.cc/sr03tz.

337   Burrus, "The Anti-Federalists Predicted Today's Political Morass."

338   Lin-Manuel Miranda, "Non-Stop (Off-Broadway)," February 17, 2015, http://tiny.cc/3s03tz.

339   Winston S. Churchill, "The Worst Form of Government," *International Churchill Society*, March 20, 2017, https://winstonchurchill.org/resources/quotes/the-worst-form-of-government/.

340   Yaneer Bar-Yam, "Teams: A manifesto," *New England Complex Systems Institute*, July 31, 2016, https://necsi.edu/teams-a-manifesto.

341   Bar-Yam, "Teams: A manifesto."

342   From an unpublished chapter intended for the book *Holacracy*. Used with permission by Brian Robertson.

343   Eric Beinhocker, *The Origin of Wealth: Evolution, complexity, and the radical remaking of economics* (Harvard Business Press, 2006).

344   From an unpublished chapter intended for the book *Holacracy*. Used with permission by Brian Robertson.

345   Global Purpose Movement, "Tom Thomison - The For Purpose Enterprise: Templates to Move From Aspiration to a New Reality," *YouTube*, July 2, 2018, https://www.youtube.com/watch?v=1Lgxe4SYtAk.

346   Frederic Laloux, *Reinventing organizations: A guide to creating organizations inspired by the next stage in human consciousness* (Nelson Parker, 2014).

347   Frederic Laloux, "The future of management is teal," strategy+business, July 6, 2015, https://www.strategy-business.com/article/00344?gko=30876.

348   Franz Oppenheimer, *The State* (Montreal: Black Rose Books, 2007), Chapter II.

349   Deirdre N. McCloskey, *Bourgeois Equality: How Ideas, Not Capital or Institutions, Enriched the World* (Chicago: The University of Chicago Press, 2017).

350   Douglass North, "The Sveriges Riksbank Prize in Economic Sciences in Memory of Alfred Nobel 1993," *NobelPrize.org*, accessed December 11, 2020, https://www.nobelprize.org/prizes/economic-sciences/1993/north/lecture/.

351   Max Borders, *The Social Singularity: A Decentralist Manifesto,* (Social Evolution, 2018), 71.

352   Max Weber, "Max Weber," Max Weber, *On Politics* (1919),

accessed December 11, 2020, https://www.panarchy.org/weber/politics. html.

353   From an unpublished chapter intended for the book *Holacracy*. Used with permission by Brian Robertson.

354   From an unpublished chapter intended for the book *Holacracy*. Used with permission by Brian Robertson.

355   Michael Strong, "An Introduction to Strong's Law," *Radical Social Entrepreneurs*, November 4, 2017, http://www.radicalsocialentreps. org/2017/11/an-introduction-to-strongs-law/?fbclid=IwAR1aAyP7wDX-1BjPM6UfOqf8GApYqsBWGT6blI53lY2WSlLqxw4LRX4r_QJA.

356   Nick Land, "The Dark Enlightenment," www.thedarkenlighten-ment.com, accessed November 9, 2020, https://www.thedarkenlighten-ment.com/the-dark-enlightenment-by-nick-land/.

357   Nick Land, "The Dark Enlightenment."

358   Nick Land, "The Dark Enlightenment."

359   Michael P. Gibson, "The Nakamoto Consensus — How We End Bad Governance," *Medium*, April 3, 2015, http://tiny.cc/vu03tz.

360   Nick Land, "The Dark Enlightenment."

361   Anna Purna Kambhampaty, "What Is Ranked-Choice Voting? Here's How It Works," *Time* (Time, November 6, 2019), https://time. com/5718941/ranked-choice-voting/.

362   Karel Janecek, "D21 - Janeček Method," Institute H21: Seeking Consensus, accessed December 11, 2020, https://www.ih21.org/en/d21-janecekmethod.

363   Wiki Community, "Liquid Democracy," *Wikipedia* (Wikimedia Foundation, December 6, 2020), https://en.wikipedia.org/wiki/Liquid_democracy.

364   Murray Bookchin, *Social Ecology and Communalism* (Oakland, CA: AK Press, 2007).

365   Titus Gebel, *Freie Privatstädte: Mehr Wettbewerb Im Wichtigsten Markt Der Welt* (Walldorf: Aquila Urbis, 2019).

366   Titus Gebel, *Freie Privatstädte: Mehr Wettbewerb Im Wichtigsten Markt Der Welt* (Walldorf: Aquila Urbis, 2019).

367   Paul-Emile, de Puydt, "1 Panarchy," *Panarchy: Political Theories of Non-Territorial States* (2015): 21.

368   Edward O. Wilson, *On Human Nature* (Cambridge, MA: Harvard University Press, 2004), 6.

369   "Ulex: Open Source Legal System," *Institute of Competitive Governance*, accessed November 9, 2020, https://instituteforcompgov.org/ulex.

370   Robert Nozick, *Anarchy, State, and Utopia*. Vol. 5038 (New York: Basic Books, 1974).

371   Lulu Garcia-Navarro, "In Israel, Kibbutz Life Undergoes Reinvention," *NPR*, October 13, 2009, http://tiny.cc/kv03tz.

372   James M. Buchanan, "Public Choice: Politics Without Romance," *Policy* 19, no. 3 (Spring 2003): 13–18.

373   Conor Friedersdorf, "The New Intolerance of Student Activism."

374   Rudolph J. Rummel, *Death by Government: Genocide and Mass Murder Since 1900* (New York, NY: Routledge, 2018).

375   I refer to the godfather of mafia books and movies, who requires patronage.

376   James Davidson and Lord William Rees-Mogg, *The Sovereign Individual: Mastering the transition to the information age* (Simon and Schuster, 2020).

377   Deirdre McCloskey, "The Great Enrichment Was Built on Ideas, Not Capital," *Foundation for Economic Education*, November 22, 2017, http://tiny.cc/aw03tz.

378   Lihle Z. Mtshali, "Everything You Ever Wanted to Know About Those Sou-Sou Savings Clubs African and Caribbean Women Love," *Essence*, January 18, 2017, http://tiny.cc/fw03tz.

379   Wikipedia contributors, "Tanomoshiko," *Wikipedia*, accessed November 9, 2020, https://en.wikipedia.org/wiki/Tanomoshiko.

380   Wikipedia contributors, "List of regions by past GDP (PPP) per capita," Wikipedia, accessed November 9, 2020, http://tiny.cc/nw03tz.

381   Maya Adereth, "The United States Has a Long History of Mutual Aid Organizing," *Jacobin*, accessed November 9, 2020, https://jacobinmag.com/2020/06/mutual-aid-united-states-unions/.

382   The following sections are excerpted from my *Medium* article "How We Become the Social Safety Net" https://medium.com/social-evolution/how-we-become-the-social-safety-net-2994a68a53db.

383   To avoid confusion, note that we have used the acronym DISC elsewhere, referring to Eric Weinstein's Distributed Information Suppression Complex. That these share an acronym is purely coincidental.

384   Max Borders, *The Social Singularity: A Decentralist Manifesto*, (Social Evolution, 2018).

385   I credit this term to my friend, software developer Justin Goro.

386   Ephrat Livni, "Everything, including the growing income disparity, can be explained by physics," Quartz, September 23, 2017, http://tiny.cc/2x03tz.

387   Randolph Bourne, *The State* (Resistance Press, 1946).

388   Randolph Bourne, *The State.*

389   Clark Mindock, "Pentagon quietly changes 'deter war' mission statement to one that protects America's influence with 'lethal force,'" *Independent,* June 30, 2018, http://tiny.cc/gx03tz.

390   Paul Samuelson, "The Pure Theory of Public Expenditure," *Review of Economics and Statistics* 36 (1954): 387–390.

391   Christopher Coyne and Nathan Goodman, "Polycentric Defense," *Available at SSRN* 3451634 (2019).

392   Javid Ahmad and Husain Haqqani, "The Taliban still hasn't broken with al-Qaeda," *The Washington Post,* October 7, 2019, http://tiny.cc/mx03tz.

393   Richard Rorty, *Contingency, Irony, and Solidarity* (Cambridge: Cambridge University Press, 1989).

394   Leonard Read, "I, Pencil," *Foundation for Economic Education,* March 3, 2015, http://tiny.cc/1y03tz.

395   Read, "I, Pencil."

396   Tensegrity is a design principle that applies when a discontinuous set of compression elements is balanced by an opposing, continuous tensile force. The overall result is an internal prestress that stabilizes the whole structure.

397   Catherine Elgin, *Between the Absolute and the Arbitrary* (Cornell University Press, 1997).

398   Popper, Karl (1962). *Conjectures and Refutations* (NY: Basic Books).

399   Nassim Nicholas Taleb, *Skin in the Game: Hidden Asymmetries in Daily Life* (New York: Random House, 2020).

400   Robin Hanson, "Futarchy: Vote Values, But Bet Beliefs," accessed November 9, 2020, http://mason.gmu.edu/~rhanson/futarchy.html.

401   Robin Hanson, "Futarchy: Vote Values, But Bet Beliefs," accessed November 9, 2020, http://mason.gmu.edu/~rhanson/futarchy.html.

402   Andrew Moore, "The Truth Economy," *Themisia,* accessed December 11, 2020, https://themisia.org/.

403   Michael Porcelli, "Weaving Shared Reality," *Michael Porcelli* (Michael Porcelli, March 13, 2020), https://www.themichaelporcelli.com/writing/2020/3/12/weaving-shared-reality.

404   Michael Porcelli, "Weaving Shared Reality," *Michael Porcelli* (Michael Porcelli, March 13, 2020), https://www.themichaelporcelli.com/writing/2020/3/12/weaving-shared-reality.

405   Mike Elias, "Wittgenstein's Revenge," *Ribbonfarm*, September 3, 2020 https://www.ribbonfarm.com/2020/09/03/wittgensteins-revenge/.

406   *The Bhagavad-Gita*, (The University of Chicago Press, 1929) Chapter 11, Verse 13.

407   Lewis Carroll, *Alice's Adventures in Wonderland ; Alice through the Looking Glass* (London: Pushkin Children's, 2020).

408   Andrew Sullivan, "Quote For The Day," *The Atlantic* (Atlantic Media Company, July 17, 2013), https://www.theatlantic.com/daily-dish/archive/2010/05/quote-for-the-day/186997/.

409   Andrea Kaplan, "New Report Reveals Demographics of Black Lives Matter Protesters Shows Vast Majority Are White, Marched Within Their Own Cities," PR Newswire, June 18, 2020, https://www.prnewswire.com/news-releases/new-report-reveals-demographics-of-black-lives-matter-protesters-shows-vast-majority-are-white-marched-within-their-own-cities-301079234.html.

410   Meena Krishnamurthy et al., "What Martin Luther King Jr Really Thought About Riots," *Jacobin*, June 9, 2020, https://www.jacobinmag.com/2020/09/martin-luther-king-riots-looting-biden.

411   Charles Eisenstein, "The Coronation," *Charles Eisenstein*, December 9, 2020, https://charleseisenstein.org/essays/the-coronation

Lightning Source UK Ltd.
Milton Keynes UK
UKHW021832110522
402841UK00010B/2560